KB087224

적중 100
영어 기출 문제집

중2
천재 | 이재영

Best Collection

구성과 특징

교과서의 주요 학습 내용을 중심으로 학습 영역별 특성에 맞춰 단계별로 다양한 학습 기회를 제공하여 단원별 학습능력 평가는 물론 중간 및 기말고사 시험 등에 완벽하게 대비할 수 있도록 내용을 구성

Words & Expressions

Step1 Key Words 단원별 핵심 단어 설명 및 풀이
Key Expression 단원별 핵심 숙어 및 관용어 설명
Word Power 반대 또는 비슷한 뜻 단어 배우기
English Dictionary 영어로 배우는 영어 단어

Step2 실력평가 단원별 수시평가 대비 주관식, 객관식 문제풀이

Step3 서술형 대비 학업성취도 및 수행능력평가 대비 서술형 문제풀이

Conversation

Step1 핵심 의사소통 의사소통에 필요한 주요 표현 방법 요약
핵심 Check 기본적인 표현 방법 및 활용능력 확인

Step2 대화문 익히기 상황에 따른 대화문 활용 및 연습

Step3 기본평가 시험대비 기초 학습 능력 평가

Step4 실력평가 단원별 수시평가 대비 주관식, 객관식 문제풀이

Step5 서술형 대비 학업성취도 및 수행능력평가 대비 서술형 문제풀이

Grammar

Step1 주요 문법 단원별 주요 문법 사항과 예문을 알기 쉽게 설명

핵심 Check 기본 문법사항에 대한 이해 여부 확인

Step2 기본평가 시험대비 기초 학습 능력 평가

Step3 실력평가 단원별 수시평가 대비 주관식, 객관식 문제풀이

Step4 서술형 대비 학업성취도 및 수행능력평가 대비 서술형 문제풀이

Reading

Step1 구문 분석 단원별로 제시된 문장에 대한 구문별 분석과 내용 설명
확인문제 문장에 대한 기본적인 이해와 인지능력 확인

Step2 확인학습A 빈칸 채우기를 통한 문장 완성 능력 확인

Step3 확인학습B 제시된 우리말을 영어로 완성하여 작문 능력 키우기

Step4 실력평가 단원별 수시평가 대비 주관식, 객관식 문제풀이

Step5 서술형 대비 학업성취도 및 수행능력평가 대비 서술형 문제풀이
교과서 구석구석 교과서에 나오는 기타 문장까지 완벽 학습

Composition

|영역별 핵심문제|

단어 및 어휘, 대화문, 문법, 독해 등 각 영역별 기출문제의 출제 유형을 분석하여 실전에 대비하고 연습할
수 있도록 문제를 배열

|서술형 실전 및 창의사고력 문제|

학교 시험에서 점차 늘어나는 서술형 시험에 집중 대비하고 고득점을 취득하는데 만전을 기하기 위한
학습 코너

|단원별 예상문제|

기출문제를 분석한 후 새로운 시험 출제 경향을 더하여 새롭게 출제될 수 있는 문제를 포함하여 시험에 완벽
하게 대비할 수 있도록 준비

|단원별 모의고사|

영역별, 단계별 학습을 모두 마친 후 실전 연습을 위한 모의고사

INSIGHT
on the textbook

교과서 파헤치기

- **단어Test1~2** 영어 단어 우리말 쓰기와 우리말을 영어 단어로 쓰기
- **대화문Test1~2** 대화문 빈칸 완성 및 전체 대화문 쓰기
- **본문Test1~5** 빈칸 완성, 우리말 쓰기, 문장 배열연습, 영어 작문하기 복습 등 단계별 반복 학습을
  통해 교과서 지문에 대한 완벽한 습득
- **구석구석지문Test1~2** 지문 빈칸 완성 및 전문 영어로 쓰기

Lesson 5

Understanding Others

🔊 의사소통 기능

- 희망이나 바람 표현하기
  A: I have an important exam tomorrow.
  B: I hope you'll do well on the exam.

- 외모 묘사하기
  A: What does he look like?
  B: He has brown hair and brown eyes.

🔊 언어 형식

- want/ask/tell + 목적어 + to부정사
  Parents **want their children to be** honest.

- 접속사 before, after
  Before she has breakfast, Dora puts on her uniform.

교과서

Words & Expressions

Key Words

- **accuse**[əkjúːz] 동 고발하다, 비난하다
- **activity**[æktívəti] 명 활동
- **ago**[əgóu] 부 전에
- **allowance**[əláuəns] 명 용돈
- **annoucement**[ənáunsmənt] 명 발표, 공표
- **anytime**[énitàim] 부 언제든지, 언제나
- **appearance**[əpíərəns] 명 외모
- **arrest**[ərést] 동 체포하다
- **attack**[ətǽk] 동 공격하다
- **attitude**[ǽtitjùːd] 명 태도, 자세
- **avoid**[əvɔ́id] 동 피하다
- **back**[bæk] 명 등, 뒤
- **beard**[biərd] 명 턱수염
- **behind**[biháind] 전 ~ 뒤에
- **bullying**[búliiŋ] 명 약자 괴롭히기
- **carry**[kǽri] 동 휴대하다, 지니다
- **character**[kǽriktər] 명 등장인물, 캐릭터
- **choice**[tʃɔis] 명 선택
- **choose**[tʃuːz] 동 선택하다, 고르다
- **confident**[kánfədənt] 형 자신감 있는
- **curly**[kɔ́ːrli] 형 곱슬곱슬한
- **difficulty**[dífikʌlti] 명 어려움
- **enter**[éntər] 동 들어가다, 참가[출전]하다
- **face**[feis] 동 직면하다, (힘든 상황에) 처하다
- **free**[friː] 동 석방하다
- **freedom**[fríːdəm] 명 자유
- **friendly**[fréndli] 형 다정한, 친절한
- **guilty**[gílti] 형 유죄의

- **hide(-hid-hidden)**[haid] 동 숨기다
- **judge**[dʒʌdʒ] 명 판사 동 판단하다
- **lucky**[lʌ́ki] 형 운이 좋은
- **mind**[maind] 동 신경 쓰다, 꺼리다
- **missing**[mísiŋ] 형 실종된, 행방불명된
- **Mongolia**[mɑŋgóuliə] 명 몽골
- **monthly**[mʌ́nθli] 형 매월의, 한 달에 한 번의
- **neighbor**[néibər] 명 이웃
- **ordinary**[ɔ́ːrdənèri] 형 평범한
- **pass**[pæs] 동 통과하다, 지나가다
- **ponytail**[póunitèil] 명 포니테일(말꼬리 모양으로 묶은 머리)
- **popular**[pápjulər] 형 인기 있는, 대중적인
- **president**[prézədənt] 명 회장
- **prison**[prízn] 명 감옥
- **promise**[prámis] 명 공약, 약속
- **protect**[prətékt] 동 보호하다
- **receive**[risíːv] 동 받다
- **right**[rait] 명 권리
- **score**[skɔːr] 동 득점하다
- **shout**[ʃaut] 동 소리치다, 외치다
- **shy**[ʃai] 형 부끄럼을 많이 타는, 수줍어하는
- **throw(-threw-thrown)**[θrou] 동 던지다
- **truth**[truːθ] 명 진실
- **victim**[víktim] 명 희생자
- **vote**[vout] 동 투표하다
- **whisper**[hwíspər] 동 속삭이다
- **worried**[wɔ́ːrid] 형 걱정하는

Key Expressions

- **accuse A of B** B 때문에 A를 고발하다
- **agree with+사람** ~에게 동의하다
- **a little** 약간, 조금
- **be afraid of ~** ~을 두려워하다
- **be for ~** ~을 지지하다, ~을 찬성하다
- **be good at ~** ~을 잘하다
- **bulletin board** 게시판
- **calm down** 진정하다
- **care for ~** ~을 돌보다
- **cut off ~** ~을 자르다

- **do well on ~** ~을 잘하다, 잘 보다
- **fight off ~** ~을 싸워 물리치다
- **go 동사원형+ing** ~하러 가다
- **look different from ~** ~와 다르게 보이다
- **look like ~** ~처럼 보이다
- **set 목적어 free** ~을 석방하다
- **so far** 지금까지
- **thanks to ~** ~ 덕분에
- **vote for ~** ~을 뽑다, ~에게 투표하다
- **would like to+동사원형** ~하고 싶다

Word Power

※ 여러 가지 품사로 쓰이는 단어

- ☐ **cause** (명) 원인 (동) 야기하다
- ☐ **fall** (명) 가을 (동) 떨어지다
- ☐ **change** (명) 잔돈, 변화 (동) 변하다
- ☐ **train** (명) 기차 (동) 훈련하다
- ☐ **kind** (명) 종류 (형) 친절한

- ☐ **face** (명) 얼굴 (동) 직면하다, 마주하다
- ☐ **judge** (명) 판사 (동) 판단하다
- ☐ **play** (명) 연극 (동) 놀다, 경기하다
- ☐ **mean** (동) 의미하다 (형) 못된, 비열한
- ☐ **like** (동) 좋아하다 (전) ~와 같은

※ 서로 반대되는 뜻을 가진 단어

- ☐ **ordinary** (평범한) ↔ **extraordinary** (비범한)
- ☐ **friendly** (친절한) ↔ **unfriendly** (불친절한)
- ☐ **guilty** (유죄의) ↔ **innocent** (무죄의)

- ☐ **difficulty** (어려움) ↔ **ease** (쉬움)
- ☐ **avoid** (피하다) ↔ **face** (직면하다)
- ☐ **popular** (인기 있는) ↔ **unpopular** (인기 없는)

※ 다양한 접미사를 붙여 동사가 명사로 바뀌는 단어

- ☐ **allow** (주다, 지급하다) – **allowance** (용돈)
- ☐ **assist** (도와주다) – **assistance** (도움, 원조)
- ☐ **free** (자유롭게 하다) – **freedom** (자유)

- ☐ **appear** (보이다) – **appearance** (외모)
- ☐ **judge** (판단하다) – **judgement** (판단)
- ☐ **act** (행동하다) – **action** (행동)

English Dictionary

- ☐ **allowance** 용돈
  → an amount of money that parents give to a child each week
  부모가 매주 아이에게 주는 돈

- ☐ **arrest** 체포하다
  → to take the person away to ask them about a crime that they might have committed
  저질렀을지도 모르는 범죄에 대해 심문하기 위해 사람을 데려가다

- ☐ **attack** 공격하다
  → to use violence to hurt or damage someone
  폭력을 사용하여 사람을 다치게 하거나 피해를 주다

- ☐ **attitude** 태도
  → how you think or feel about something
  어떤 것에 대해 생각하고 느끼는 방식

- ☐ **avoid** 피하다
  → to stay away from a person or place
  사람이나 장소로부터 멀리하다

- ☐ **bullying** 괴롭히기
  → an action to try to frighten someone who is smaller or weaker
  더 작거나 약한 사람을 겁주려고 하는 행위

- ☐ **cause** 야기하다
  → to make something happen
  어떤 일이 일어나도록 만들다

- ☐ **change** 잔돈
  → the money you get back when you pay more money than something costs
  어떤 것의 비용보다 더 많은 돈을 지불했을 때 돌려받는 돈

- ☐ **choose** 선택하다, 고르다
  → to decide which thing you want
  어느 것을 원하는지 결정하다

- ☐ **confidence** 자신감
  → the belief that you are able to do things well or be successful
  일을 잘하거나 성공할 수 있다는 믿음

- ☐ **neighbor** 이웃
  → someone who lives near you
  당신 근처에 사는 사람

- ☐ **protect** 보호하다
  → to keep someone or something safe from something dangerous or bad
  위험하거나 나쁜 것으로부터 어떤 사람이나 사물을 지키다

- ☐ **victim** 피해자, 희생자
  → someone who has been hurt or killed
  다치거나 살해된 사람

- ☐ **whisper** 속삭이다
  → to speak very quietly so that other people cannot hear
  다른 사람들이 들을 수 없도록 매우 조용히 말하다

서답형

01 다음 짝지어진 두 단어의 관계가 같도록 주어진 철자로 시작하는 단어를 쓰시오.

> friendly : unfriendly
> – extraordinary : o_____

[내신]

02 다음 글의 빈칸에 영영 풀이에 맞는 알맞은 형태의 단어를 쓰시오.

> • We'll go out and look for him. Also, we'll make an _____ about a missing child.
> <영영 풀이> something that someone says officially, giving new information about something

➡ _____

03 다음 중 밑줄 친 단어의 우리말 뜻이 잘못된 것은?

① All my classmates are very friendly. 다정한
② I'll vote for Jang Jimin. ~에게 투표하다
③ Bullying is a big problem in many schools. 괴롭히기
④ When you face difficulties, just call me. 직면하다
⑤ They whispered behind his back, "What is he trying to hide?" 외쳤다

[04~05] **중요** 다음 영영 풀이에 해당하는 단어를 고르시오.

04

> to keep someone or something safe from something dangerous or bad

① avoid   ② protect
③ choose   ④ change
⑤ cause

05

> an amount of money that parents give to a child each week

① victim   ② attitude
③ choice   ④ judge
⑤ allowance

서답형

06 다음 우리말에 맞게 주어진 철자로 시작하는 단어를 쓰시오.

> 그들은 그에게 턱수염을 그만 기르라고 말했다. Joseph은 신경 쓰지 않았다.
> ➡ They told him to stop growing a beard. Joseph did not m_____.

➡ _____

07 다음 빈칸에 들어갈 말로 알맞은 것은?

> People did not like a long beard very much. So they _____ the man with a beard.

① whispered   ② believed
③ avoided   ④ cared
⑤ freed

중요

08 다음 빈칸에 들어갈 단어가 알맞게 짝지어진 것은?

> Joseph was a big man, and he was able to fight them _____. But the men called the police and _____ him of attacking them. Poor Joseph was arrested.

① on – caused
② of – set
③ off – caused
④ off – accused
⑤ of – accused

01 다음 문장의 밑줄 친 단어를 알맞은 형태로 바꾸어 쓰시오.

(1) We should not judge people by their <u>appear</u>.

(2) He just wanted the <u>free</u> to have his beard.

➡ (1) _____ (2) _____

02 다음 영영 풀이에 해당하는 단어를 쓰시오.

(1) • to make something different
   • the money you get back when you pay more money than something costs

(2) • to teach a person or an animal how to do something
   • a number of cars connected together on a railway

➡ (1) _____ (2) _____

03 다음 문장에 공통으로 들어갈 단어를 쓰시오.

(1) • He said to the _____, "I'm the victim here."
   • We should not _____ people by the way they look.

(2) • You _____ the girl from Mongolia?
   • The police officer was not kind. He was _____ to her.

➡ (1) _____ (2) _____

04 다음 빈칸에 들어갈 말을 〈보기〉에서 찾아 쓰시오. (필요하면 변형하여 쓰시오.)

┌─ 보기 ┤
thanks to, care for, do well on, calm down
└──────

(1) I hope you'll _____ the exam.

(2) 42-year-old Joseph Palmer was an ordinary person. He had a job and _____ his family.

(3) He was freed _____ his son's letters.

05 다음 우리말과 같은 표현이 되도록 괄호 안의 지시대로 문장의 빈칸을 채우시오.

(1) 매사추세츠에 있는 작은 도시로 이사한 후에 그는 어려움에 직면하기 시작했다.
   ➡ After he moved to a small town in Massachusetts, he began to _____ _____. (복수형을 쓸 것.)

(2) Joseph은 다른 사람들과 달라 보였다.
   ➡ Joseph _____ _____ _____ other people. (look을 이용할 것.)

(3) 사람들은 Joseph이 단지 자신과 자신의 턱수염을 지키려다 감옥에 갇혔다는 것을 알게 되었다. (동명사를 이용할 것)
   ➡ People learned that Joseph was _____ _____ just for _____ himself and his beard.

Conversation

1 희망이나 바람 표현하기

A I have an important exam tomorrow. 나는 내일 중요한 시험이 있어.

B I hope you'll do well on the exam. 네가 시험을 잘 보길 바라.

- 'I hope ~.'는 '나는 ~을 희망한다.'라는 뜻으로 자신의 소망을 나타낼 때 쓰는 표현이며 뒤에는 to부정사, 'that+주어+동사'가 온다. 경우에 따라 hope 대신 want 또는 wish를 사용할 수 있다.

희망이나 바람을 표현하기

- I hope to be a famous singer. 나는 유명한 가수가 되길 희망해.
  = I want to be a famous singer.
  = I'd like to be a famous singer.
- I hope to be a basketball player. 나는 농구선수가 되기를 희망한다.
- I want to be a famous writer. 나는 유명한 작가가 되고 싶다.

핵심 Check

1. 다음 대화의 빈칸에 알맞은 말을 고르시오.

A: Are you going to watch a movie?

B: Yes, _____

① I hope you'll find him soon.
② I hope to watch an action movie.
③ you will watch a movie tonight.
④ I go to the movies once a month.
⑤ I hope to be a famous actor.

2. 다음 대화의 밑줄 친 부분의 의도로 알맞은 것은?

- I have an important exam tomorrow! I hope I will pass it.

① 바람 표현하기　　　② 의도 묻기
③ 충고하기　　　　　④ 안부 묻기
⑤ 칭찬하기

② 외모 묘사하기

A What does he look like? 그는 어떻게 생겼나요?

B He has brown hair and brown eyes. 그는 갈색 머리카락과 갈색 눈을 지녔어요.

■ 인물의 외모나 모습을 묘사할 경우, 체형을 설명할 때는 주로 be동사를 사용하며, 이목구비나 머리 모양을 묘사할 때는 have동사를 사용한다. 또한 모자, 안경, 옷 등의 착용 상태를 묘사할 때는 '주어 + be동사+wearing ~.'으로 표현한다.

■ 현재 진행 중인 동작을 생생하게 묘사할 때에는 'be동사의 현재형+동사원형-ing'의 현재진행형을 사용한다.

외모를 묘사하는 표현들

• **A:** What does he look like? 그는 어떻게 생겼니?

  B: He's tall and he has curly hair. 그는 키가 크고, 머리가 곱슬이야.

• **A:** Sujin, where is your sister, Somin? 수진아, 너의 여동생 소민이 어디에 있니?

  B: She's over there. She's wearing glasses. 그녀는 저기에 있어. 그녀는 안경을 쓰고 있어.

• **A:** What does he look like? 그는 어떻게 생겼나요?

  B: He has brown hair and brown eyes. 그는 갈색 머리이고 갈색 눈을 지녔어요.

  A: What is he wearing? 그는 무엇을 입고 있나요?

  B: He is wearing a green shirt. 그는 초록색 셔츠를 입고 있어요.

핵심 Check

3. 다음 대화의 빈칸에 들어갈 말로 알맞은 것을 모두 고르시오.

  A: What does she look like?

  B: _____

  ① She is playing the guitar.
  ② She always wears black pants.
  ③ She has brown hair and is wearing glasses.
  ④ She is boring.
  ⑤ She's tall and has long straight hair.

4. 다음 우리말에 맞도록 빈칸에 알맞은 것을 쓰시오.

  • 그녀의 개는 어떻게 생겼니?

  ➡ What does her dog _____ _____?

Communicate: Listen-Listen and Answer. Talk

G: Hi, I'm Gacha. I'm from Mongolia. ❶When I first came to Songji Middle School two months ago, I was so worried. I was a little shy, and ❷I wasn't good at Korean. However, I'm a lucky girl. All my classmates are nice and friendly. ❸I enjoy playing handball with them in P.E. class. I'm a good player ❹They call me "Golden Hand." ❺There will be a sports day next week. ❻I hope my class will win in the handball event.

여: 안녕, 나는 Gacha라고 해. 나는 몽골에서 왔어. 두 달 전에 내가 처음 송지 중학교에 왔을 때, 나는 무척 걱정이 되었어. 나는 좀 수줍음을 탔고 한국어를 잘 못했어. 하지만 난 운이 좋은 아이야. 내 학급 친구들은 모두 멋지고 다정해. 나는 체육 시간에 신구를과 핸드볼 하는 것을 즐겨. 난 실력이 좋은 선수야. 친구들은 나를 '황금 손'이라고 불러. 다음 주에 운동회가 있을 거야. 난 우리 반이 핸드볼 대회에서 이기길 바라.

❶ When은 '~할 때'의 의미로 부사절을 이끄는 접속사이다. two months ago라는 과거 시점이 있어서 과거시제 came을 사용한다.
❷ be good at ~은 '~을 잘하다'라는 의미다.
❸ enjoy는 동명사를 목적어로 취하는 동사로 playing을 사용했다.
❹ 'call+목적어+목적보어'의 형태로 '~을 …라고 부르다'로 해석한다.
❺ next week이라는 미래 시점과 사용되어서 미래시제 will be를 사용했다.
❻ 'I hope (that)+주어+동사 ~'는 희망이나 바람을 나타내는 표현이다.

Check(√) True or False

(1) Gacha was worried and a little shy at first.　　　　T ☐ F ☐

(2) Though Gacha likes playing handball, she isn't good at playing handball.　　T ☐ F ☐

 Communicate: Listen-Listen and Answer. Dialog

B: Hi, Minsol. Is your class winning?

G: Of course. We have a great handball player.

B: ❶You mean the girl from Mongolia?

G: Yes, her name is Gacha.

B: I've heard a lot about her. But ❷what does she look like?

G: She's very tall and has a ponytail.

B: Oh, is she the girl ❸who scored the goal just now?

G: Yes, that's her seventh goal.

B: Wow, she's really great.

남: 안녕, 민솔아. 너희 반이 이기고 있니?
여: 물론이지. 우리는 훌륭한 핸드볼 선수가 있거든.
남: 몽골에서 온 여자아이 말하는 거니?
여: 응, 그녀의 이름은 Gacha야.
남: 그녀에 대해 많이 들었어. 그런데 그녀는 어떻게 생겼어?
여: 그녀는 키가 크고 말총머리를 하고 있어.
남: 아, 지금 막 골을 넣은 여자아이가 그녀니?
여: 맞아, 저건 그녀의 일곱 번째 골이야.
남: 와, 그녀는 정말 잘하는구나.

❶ 일반동사 의문문 'Do you mean ~?'에서 Do가 생략된 형태로 '~을 말하는 거니?'라는 의미다.
❷ 사람의 외모를 묻는 표현이다.
❸ 선행사(사람)를 수식할 때 관계대명사절을 이끄는 who를 사용한다.

Check(√) True or False

(3) Minsol's class is winning the handball game.　　　T ☐ F ☐

(4) Gacha is very tall and has a ponytail.　　　　　　T ☐ F ☐

Communicate: Listen-Listen More

M: ❶What can I do for you?
G: I lost my younger brother.
M: Okay, ❷calm down. What's your brother's name?
G: His name is Wally Brown. He's five years old.
M: ❸What does he look like?
G: He has brown hair and brown eyes.
M: What is he wearing?
G: He is wearing a green shirt and black pants.
M: Can you tell me more?
G: Oh, he is carrying a red backpack.
M: All right. We'll go out and look for him. Also, we'll make an announcement about ❹a missing child.
G: Thank you so much. ❺I hope I'll find him soon.

❶ 상대방에게 도움을 주고자 할 때 사용하는 표현으로, '무엇을 도와줄까요?'라는 뜻이다.
❷ '진정해'라는 뜻이다.
❸ 사람의 외모를 묻는 표현이다.
❹ missing은 형용사로 '실종된, 행방불명된'의 뜻이다.
❺ 'I hope (that)+주어+동사 ~'는 희망이나 바람을 나타내는 표현이다.

 Communicate: Speak 2-Talk in pairs

A: I have an important exam tomorrow!
B: ❶I hope you'll do well on the exam.
A: ❷I hope so, too. Thanks.

❶ 희망이나 바람을 나타내는 표현으로, do well on은 '~을 잘하다'라는 뜻이다.
❷ '나도 그러길 바라'라는 의미다.

 Communicate: Speak 2-Talk in groups

A: What is your character's name?
B: His name is Buster.
A: ❶What does he look like?
B: ❷He has no hair.
A: Does he have big eyes?
B: Yes, he does.

❶ 사람의 외모를 묻는 표현이다.
❷ 사람의 이목구비나 머리 모양을 묘사할 때는 동사 have를 사용한다.

 Communicate: Speak-Rap Time

A: I hope you'll do your best in the final game.
B: Thanks. ❶I wish you the same.

A: ❷What does your sister look like, Claire?
B: She's tall and has long straight hair.

❶ '나도 네가 그러길 바라.'라는 뜻이다.
❷ 사람의 외모를 묻는 표현이다.

 My Speaking Portfolio

G: Look at the bulletin board. ❶There are posters for the next school president.
B: Yeah, I've already made my choice. ❷I'll vote for Jang Jimin.
G: You mean the boy with glasses? He looks smart, but I don't like his promises.
B: Then who will you choose?
G: Well, I am for number 1, Han Siwon. She wants to make our school a safe place.
B: She always has a ponytail, right?
G: Yes, and Hong Jiho seems okay.
B: ❸She looks friendly, but I don't like talent shows.

❶ 'There are+복수 명사' 형태로 '~가 있다'는 뜻이다.
❷ vote for ~는 '~에게 투표하다'라는 뜻이다.
❸ 'look+형용사' 형태로 '~처럼 보이다'라는 뜻이다.

 Wrap Up

1.
B: I hear there is a new student in your class.
G: Yes. She's from Jejudo. Oh, she's over there!
B: ❶ Which one? What does she look like?
G: ❷She has curly hair and is wearing glasses.

2.
G: You look sad. What's wrong, Jongmin?
B: My sister broke her arm this morning.
G: What happened?
B: She fell off her bike.
G: That's too bad. ❸I hope she'll get better soon.

❶ '어느 아이니?'의 뜻이다.
❷ 사람의 외모를 표현하는 말로 머리 모양을 묘사할 때는 동사 have를 사용한다.
❸ 희망이나 바람을 나타내는 표현이다.

● 다음 우리말과 일치하도록 빈칸에 알맞은 말을 쓰시오.

Communicate: Listen-Listen and Answer. Talk

G: Hi, I'm Gacha. I'm _____ Mongolia. When I first came to Songji Middle School two months _____, I was so _____. I was a little _____, and I wasn't _____ at Korean. However, I'm a _____ girl. All my classmates are nice and _____, I enjoy handball with them in P.E. class. I'm a good player. They _____ me "Golden Hand." There will be a sports day next week. _____ _____ my class will win in the handball event.

Communicate: Listen-Listen and Answer. Dialog

B: Hi, Minsol. Is your class _____?
G: Of course. We have a _____ handball player.
B: You _____ the girl from Mongolia?
G: Yes, her name is Gacha.
B: I've heard a lot about her. But _____ does she _____ _____?
G: She's very tall and _____ a _____.
B: Oh, is she the girl _____ _____ the goal just now?
G: Yes, that's her _____ goal.
B: Wow, she's really great.

Communicate: Listen-Listen More

M: _____ can I do for you?
G: I _____ my younger brother.
M: Okay, _____ _____. What's your brother's name?
G: His name is Wally Brown. He's five years old.
M: _____ does he _____ _____?
G: He _____ brown hair and brown eyes.
M: What is he _____?
G: He is _____ a green shirt and black pants.
M: Can you tell me more?
G: Oh, he is _____ a red backpack.
M: All right. We'll go out and _____ _____ him. Also, we'll make an _____ about a _____ child.
G: Thank you so much. _____ _____ I'll find him soon.

Communicate: Speak 2-Talk in pairs

A: I _____ an _____ exam tomorrow!
B: I hope you'll _____ _____ _____ the exam.
A: I hope _____, too. Thanks.

Communicate: Speak 2-Talk in groups

A: _____ is your character's name?

B: His name is Buster.

A: _____ _____ he look _____ ?

B: He has _____ hair.

A: Does he _____ big eyes?

B: Yes, he does.

Communicate: Speak-Rap Time

(1) A: I lost my puppy this afternoon.

   B: _____ _____ you'll _____ him soon.

(2) A: I hope you'll _____ your _____ in the final game.

   B: Thanks. I wish you _____ _____ .

(3) A: What does your sister _____ _____ , Claire?

   B: She's tall and has long _____ hair.

(4) A: Is your father _____ a blue cap?

   B: Yeah. Now, he's _____ a map.

My Speaking Portfolio

G: Look at the _____ _____ . There _____ posters for the next school president.

B: Yeah, I've already _____ my _____ . I'll _____ _____ Jang Jimin.

G: You _____ the boy with glasses? He looks smart, but I don't like his _____ .

B: Then who will you _____ ?

G: Well, I am for number 1, Han Siwon. She wants to make our school a safe place.

B: She always has a ponytail, right?

G: Yes, and Hong Jiho _____ _____ .

B: She looks _____ , but I don't like _____ _____ .

Wrap Up

1. B: I hear there is a new student in your class.

   G: Yes. She's from Jejudo. Oh, she's _____ _____ !

   B: _____ one? _____ she _____ like?

   G: She has _____ hair and is _____ glasses.

2. G: You look _____ . What's _____ , Jongmin?

   B: My sister broke her arm this morning.

   G: What _____ ?

   B: She _____ _____ her bike.

   G: _____ _____ _____ _____ . _____ _____ she'll _____
   _____ soon.

해석

A: 네 캐릭터의 이름은 뭐니?

B: 그의 이름은 Buster야.

A: 그는 어떻게 생겼니?

B: 그는 머리카락이 없어.

A: 그는 눈이 크니?

B: 응, 맞아.

(1) A: 나는 오늘 오후에 내 강아지를 잃어버렸어.
    B: 네가 그를 곧 찾기를 바랄게.
(2) A: 나는 네가 결선에서 최선을 다하길 바라.
    B: 고마워. 나도 네가 그러길 바라.
(3) A: 네 언니는 어떻게 생겼니, Claire?
    B: 그녀는 키가 크고 긴 생머리야.
(4) A: 네 아버지는 파란 모자를 쓰고 계시니?
    B: 응. 지금 지도를 보고 계셔.

여: 이 게시판을 봐. 다음 학생회장의 포스터가 있어.

남: 응, 나는 이미 결정을 내렸어. 나는 장지민에게 투표할 거야.

여: 안경을 쓴 남자아이 얘기하는 거야? 그는 똑똑해 보이지만 나는 그의 공약이 마음에 들지 않아.

남: 그럼 넌 누굴 선택할 거야?

여: 음, 나는 1 번 한시원을 지지해. 그녀는 우리 학교를 안전한 장소로 만들고 싶어 해.

남: 그녀는 항상 말총머리를 해, 그렇지?

여: 맞아, 그리고 홍지호도 괜찮아 보여.

남: 그녀는 친절해 보이지만, 나는 장기자랑이 싫어.

1. 남: 너희 반에 새로 온 학생이 있다고 들었어.
   여: 응. 그녀는 제주도에서 왔어. 어, 그녀가 저기에 있어!
   남: 어느 아이? 어떻게 생겼어?
   여: 그녀는 곱슬머리이고 안경을 끼고 있어.
2. 여: 너 슬퍼 보여. 무슨 일이니, 종민아?
   남: 여동생이 오늘 아침에 팔이 부러졌어.
   여: 무슨 일이 있었는데?
   남: 자전거에서 떨어졌어.
   여: 안됐구나. 그녀가 곧 회복되기를 바라.

01 다음 우리말에 맞도록 빈칸에 알맞은 말을 쓰시오.

> **A:** 네 언니는 어떻게 생겼니, Claire?
> **B:** She's tall and has long straight hair.

➡ _____ does your sister _____ _____

02 다음 대화의 빈칸에 들어갈 말로 알맞은 것은?

> **A:** I lost my puppy this afternoon.
> **B:** _____

① She's tall and has long straight hair.
② I hope she'll get better soon.
③ I hope you'll find him soon.
④ He has brown hair and brown eyes.
⑤ He has no hair.

03 다음 대화의 빈칸에 들어갈 말로 가장 적절한 것은?

> **A:** I have an important exam tomorrow!
> **B:** I hope you'll _____ the exam.
> **A:** I hope so, too. Thanks.

① look like   ② do well on
③ care for   ④ look different from
⑤ get better

04 다음 대화의 밑줄 친 우리말에 맞게 주어진 단어를 알맞은 순서로 배열하시오.

> **A:** I hope you'll do your best in the final game.
> **B:** Thanks. <u>나도 네가 그러길 바라.</u>

(wish, you, I, the, same)

➡ _____

[01~03] 다음 대화를 읽고 물음에 답하시오.

Ben: Hi, Minsol. Is your class winning?

Minsol: Of course. We have a great handball player.

Ben: ___(A)___ the girl from Mongolia?

Minsol: Yes, her name is Gacha.

Ben: I've heard a lot about her. But what does she look like?

Minsol: She's very tall and has a ponytail.

Ben: Oh, is she the girl (B)지금 막 골을 넣은?

Minsol: Yes, that's her seventh goal.

Ben: Wow, she's really great.

01 위 대화의 빈칸 (A)에 들어갈 말로 알맞은 것은?

① I mean   ② She is

③ You mean   ④ You know

⑤ Guess what

서답형

02 위 대화의 밑줄 친 (B)의 우리말에 맞게 주어진 단어를 알맞은 순서로 배열하시오.

> the, scored, who, goal, just, now

➡ _____

03 위 대화의 내용과 일치하지 <u>않는</u> 것은?

① Minsol and Ben are watching a handball game.

② Gacha is from Mongolia.

③ Minsol and Gacha are in the same class.

④ Gacha is very tall and has a ponytail.

⑤ Ben doesn't know about Gacha.

[04~05] 다음 대화를 읽고 물음에 답하시오.

G: Look at the bulletin board. There are posters for ___(A)___.

B: Yeah, I've already made my choice. I'll vote for Jang Jimin.

G: You mean the boy with glasses? He looks smart, but I don't like his promises.

B: Then who will you choose?

G: Well, I am for number 1, Han Siwon. She wants to make our school a safe place.

B: (B)She always has a ponytail, right?

G: Yes, and Hong Jiho seems okay.

B: She looks friendly, but I don't like talent shows.

04 위 대화의 빈칸 (A)에 들어갈 말로 알맞은 것은?

① talent shows

② a safe school

③ the next school president

④ a beauty contest

⑤ class president election

05 밑줄 친 (B)의 답을 얻을 수 있는 질문으로 알맞은 것은?

① What do you think of her?

② What does she look like?

③ How does she feel?

④ What is she looking for?

⑤ What does she like?

[06~07] 다음 대화를 읽고 물음에 답하시오.

B: My sister broke her arm this morning.

G: What happened?

B: She fell off her bike.

G: ___(A)___. (B) 그녀가 곧 회복되기를 바라.

서답형

06 위 대화의 빈칸 (A)에 알맞은 말을 주어진 단어를 이용하여 쓰시오.

> that, bad

서답형 ➡ _____

07 위 대화의 밑줄 친 (B)의 우리말에 맞게 주어진 단어를 알맞은 순서로 배열하시오.

> she'll, hope, better, I, get, soon

➡ _____

[08~09] 다음 대화를 읽고 물음에 답하시오.

M: What can I do for you?

G: I lost my younger brother.

M: Okay, calm down. What's your brother's name?

G: His name is Wally Brown. He's five years old.

M: _____(A)

G: He has brown hair and brown eyes.

M: What is he wearing?

G: He is wearing a green shirt and black pants.

M: _____(B)

G: Oh, he is carrying a red backpack.

M: All right. We'll go out and look for him. Also, we'll make an announcement about a missing child.

G: Thank you so much. I hope I'll find him soon.

서답형

08 위 대화의 빈칸 (A), (B)에 들어갈 말을 <보기>에서 찾아 쓰시오.

> ┌ 보기 ┐
> • You mean the boy with glasses?
> • What does he look like?
> • Can you tell me more?

➡ (A) _____

(B) _____

09 위 대화를 읽고 질문에 답할 수 <u>없는</u> 것을 고르시오.

① What's the girl's brother's name?

② How old is the girl's brother?

③ What does the girl's brother look like?

④ Where's the girl's brother?

⑤ What will the man do after the dialog?

10 다음 중 짝지어진 대화가 <u>어색한</u> 것을 고르시오.

① A: You look sad. What's wrong, Jongmin?

B: My sister broke her arm this morning.

② A: I fell off my bike.

B: I'm glad to hear that. I hope you'll get better soon.

③ A: Is your father wearing a blue cap?

B: Yeah. Now, he's reading a map.

④ A: What does he look like?

B: He has no hair.

⑤ A: What does she look like?

B: She's very tall and has a ponytail.

서답형

11 다음 대화를 읽고, 주어진 문장을 완성하시오.

> B: I hear there is a new student in your class.
>
> G: Yes. She's from Jejudo. Oh, she's over there!
>
> B: Which one? What does she look like?
>
> G: She has curly hair and is wearing glasses.

➡ The new student has _____ _____ and is wearing _____.

[01~02] 다음 대화를 읽고 물음에 답하시오.

B: Hi, Minsol. Is your class winning?

G: Of course. We have a great handball player.

B: You mean the girl from Mongolia?

G: Yes, her name is Gacha.

B: I've heard a lot about her. But ____(A)____?

G: She's very tall and has a ponytail.

B: Oh, is she the girl who scored the goal just now?

G: Yes, that's her seventh goal.

B: Wow, she's really great.

01 다음은 Minsol이 Gacha에 관해 언급한 글이다. 빈칸을 완성하시오.

➡ Gacha _____ _____ Mongolia. Gacha and I are in the _____ class. She has scored _____ goals so far.

02 위 대화의 빈칸 (A)에 알맞은 말을 쓰시오.

➡ _____

[03~04] 다음 대화를 읽고 물음에 답하시오.

G: Look at the bulletin board. There are posters for the next school president.

B: Yeah, I've already made my choice. I'll ____(A)____ Jang Jimin.

G: You mean the boy with ____(B)____? He looks smart, but I don't like his promises.

B: Then who will you choose?

G: Well, I am for number 1, Han Siwon. She wants to make our school a ____(C)____.

B: She always has a ____(D)____, right?

G: Yes, and Hong Jiho seems okay.

B: She looks friendly, but I don't like talent shows.

03 위 대화의 빈칸 (A)에 들어갈 표현을 주어진 영영 풀이를 참고하여 두 단어로 쓰시오.

> to choose someone in an election by making a mark on an official piece of paper

➡ _____

04 아래 그림을 참고하여 위 대화의 빈칸 (B)와 (D)에는 외모에 관한 단어를, (C)에는 공약에 관한 글을 쓰시오.

➡ (B) _____ (C) _____ (D) _____

05 다음 대화의 밑줄 친 우리말에 맞게 주어진 어휘를 알맞게 배열하시오.

M: What can I do for you?

G: I lost my younger brother.

M: Okay, calm down. What's your brother's name?

G: His name is Wally Brown. He's five years old.

M: What does he look like?

G: He has brown hair and brown eyes.

M: All right. We'll go out and look for him. Also, we'll 미아 방송을 할 겁니다. (about, announcement, make, missing, a, an, child)

G: Thank you so much. I hope I'll find him soon.

➡ _____

Grammar

① want/ask/tell + 목적어 + to부정사

- Parents **want** their children **to be** honest. 부모들은 그들의 아이들이 정직하기를 원한다.
- They **told** him **to stop** growing a beard. 그들은 그에게 턱수염을 그만 기르라고 말했다.

■ 형태: want/ask/tell + 목적어 + to부정사

■ 의미: ~가 …하기를 바라다, ~에게 …하기를 요청하다, ~에게 …하라고 말하다

■ 동사 want, ask, tell 뒤에 목적어와 'to+동사원형'이 이어지면 '(목적어)가 ~하도록 원하다/요청하다/말하다'라는 의미를 나타낸다.

  • I **want** you **to finish** your homework first. 나는 네가 숙제를 먼저 끝내길 원한다.

  • Mom **told** me **to put** out the trash. 엄마는 나에게 쓰레기를 내놓으라고 말씀하셨다.

■ to부정사를 목적격보어로 취하는 동사에는 want, ask, tell 외에도 advise, allow, beg, cause, enable, encourage, expect, force, get, help, need, order, persuade, require, teach, would like 등이 있다.

  • They **advised** him **to leave** the place as soon as possible.
    그들은 그에게 가능한 한 빨리 그 장소를 떠나라고 조언했다.

  • Will you please **help** him **to clear[clear]** the table? 그가 식탁 치우는 거 거들어 줄래?

■ to부정사의 부정형은 'not[never]+to 동사원형'이다.

  • She **asked** me **not to say** anything. 그녀는 나에게 아무 말도 하지 말라고 요청했다.

  • The doctor **ordered** me **not to drink** alcohol. 의사는 나에게 술을 마시지 말라고 명령했다.

핵심 Check

1. 다음 우리말과 일치하도록 빈칸에 알맞은 말을 쓰시오. (철자가 주어진 것도 있음.)

(1) 우리는 그녀가 늦을 것이라고 예상했다.

➡ We _____ her _____ _____ late.

(2) 갑작스런 꿍음 때문에 나는 펄쩍 뛰었다.

➡ A sudden noise c_____ me _____ j_____.

(3) 그들은 그에게 서류에 서명하도록 강요했다.

➡ They f_____ him _____ _____ the paper.

② 접속사 before, after

- **Before** she has breakfast, Dora puts on her uniform.
  아침을 먹기 전에 Dora는 교복을 입는다.

- **After** he was freed, Joseph traveled and told his story to lots of people.
  Joseph은 석방된 뒤에 순회를 하며 많은 사람들에게 자신의 이야기를 전했다.

■ 형태: Before/After + 주어 + 동사 ~, 주어 + 동사 …

   주어 + 동사 … before/after + 주어 + 동사 ~.

■ 의미: before: ~하기 전에 / after: ~한 후에

■ before와 after는 두 개의 절을 연결해 주는 접속사로 어떤 일이 일어나기 전이나 후의 시간 관계를 나타낸다.

- Please swing to the door **after** you entered. 들어오고 나서. 문 좀 닫아주세요.

- Did she leave a message **before** she went? 그녀가 가기 전에 전갈을 남겼어요?

■ 시간이나 조건의 부사절에서는 현재시제를 사용하여 미래를 나타낸다.

- It will be long **before** we meet again. 한참 지나야 다시 만나게 되겠군요.

- I'll start **after** he comes. 그가 온 후에 출발하겠다.

- **If** it is warm tomorrow, we will drive in the country. 내일 날씨가 포근하면 시골로 드라이브 가자.

핵심 Check

2. 다음 괄호 안에서 알맞은 말을 고르시오.

   (1) (Before / After) you leave the room, turn out the light.

   (2) After she (comes / will come), we will go on a picnic.

   (3) The road became wet (before / after) it rained.

   ➡ (1) _____ (2) _____ (3) _____

[01~02] 다음 문장의 빈칸에 들어갈 알맞은 말을 고르시오.

01

> I asked him _____ off the TV.

① turn　　　　② turns　　　　③ turned
④ turning　　　⑤ to turn

02

> _____ Jacob went to bed, he washed his hands.

① Before　　　② After　　　③ While
④ During　　　⑤ If

03 다음 중 가장 자연스러운 것은?

① Before I woke up, I ate a cup of coffee.
② Before I went to the library, I borrowed books at the library.
③ Do it after you forget.
④ Wendy understood the situation after she heard it from Sue.
⑤ After she went to bed, she took a shower.

04 다음 문장에서 어법상 어색한 것을 바르게 고쳐 다시 쓰시오.

(1) I want you clean the windows.
　　➡ _____

(2) Before I will have dinner, I will clean my room.
　　➡ _____

(3) He took my hand and asked me marrying him.
　　➡ _____

(4) Tell her buys a comfortable pair of shoes!
　　➡ _____

05 주어진 어휘를 이용하여 다음 우리말을 영작하시오.

> Justin은 축구를 한 후에 과일을 먹었다. (had, soccer, some fruit)
> (Justin으로 시작할 것)

➡ _____

01 다음 빈칸에 알맞은 것은?

> My parents want me _____ healthy food.

① eat   ② eats

③ ate   ④ eating

⑤ to eat

02 다음 빈칸에 들어갈 가장 알맞은 것은?

> • I turn off my phone. And then I pass the school gate.
> = _____ I pass the school gate, I turn off my phone.

① As   ② Before   ③ After

④ But   ⑤ When

03 다음 중 어법상 바르지 <u>않은</u> 것은?

> My homeroom teacher ①told ②me ③be ④on time ⑤for class.

①   ②   ③   ④   ⑤

04 다음 우리말을 영어로 바르게 옮긴 것은?

> 진수는 아침을 먹기 전에 양치질을 한다.

① Jinsu brushes his teeth when he has breakfast.

② Jinsu brushes his teeth while he has breakfast.

③ Jinsu brushes his teeth after he has breakfast.

④ Jinsu brushes his teeth before he has breakfast.

⑤ Jinsu brushes his teeth if he has breakfast.

---

05 다음 괄호 안에서 알맞은 말을 고르시오.

(1) He told me (came / to come) home before 9 o'clock.

(2) Harry wanted me (doing / to do) it at once.

(3) My mom (expects / hopes) me to be a teacher.

(4) She allowed her daughter (go / to go) to the K-pop concert.

(5) The class started (after / before) the teacher arrived.

(6) I wash my hands (before / after) I go to bed.

➡ (1) _____ (2) _____ (3) _____

(4) _____ (5) _____ (6) _____

06 다음 빈칸에 적절하지 <u>않은</u> 것은?

> I _____ her to take part in the party.

① watched   ② wanted   ③ told

④ persuaded   ⑤ expected

07 다음 중 어법상 바르지 <u>않은</u> 것은?

① He knew the truth already before we told him about it.

② After she will come tomorrow, we will go camping.

③ He arrived at the station after the train left.

④ Before he meets her, he is already in love with her.

⑤ He will go see a movie with Kelly after he meets her.

08 다음 중 두 문장의 의미가 <u>다른</u> 것은?

① Sean expected that his son would exercise to be healthy.
➡ Sean expected his son to exercise to be healthy.

② I got up before the sun rises.
➡ After the sun rose, I got up.

③ Anna told me that I must wear a long sleeve shirt at the campsite.
➡ Anna told me to wear a long sleeve shirt at the campsite.

④ Take a bath before you go to bed.
➡ Take a bath before going to bed.

⑤ The restaurant was crowded, but we found a table.
➡ Though the restaurant was crowded, we found a table.

09 다음 두 문장이 뜻이 같도록 빈칸에 들어갈 알맞은 말은?

• Before you get into the swimming pool, do some exercises to warm up.
= _____ you do some exercises to warm up, get into the swimming pool.

① Before   ② After   ③ As
④ When   ⑤ While

서답형

10 괄호 안의 동사를 어법에 맞게 고쳐 쓰시오.

(1) The police asked him (tell) them the truth.
(2) Her parents encouraged her (study) hard.
(3) Please help me (push) the boat.
➡ (1) _____ (2) _____ (3) _____

11 두 문장의 의미가 같도록 빈칸에 알맞은 말을 쓰시오.

Ms. Rose drank coffee after she finished cleaning the living room.
= Ms. Rose finished cleaning the living room _____ she drank coffee.

➡ _____

12 다음 중 어법상 <u>어색한</u> 부분을 찾아 바르게 고친 것은?

Yejun asked his mom play badminton with him that afternoon.

① asked → has asked
② his → him
③ play → to play
④ with → to
⑤ that → this

서답형

13 주어진 어휘를 바르게 배열하여 다음 우리말을 영어로 쓰시오.

(1) 그들은 테니스를 친 후에 쇼핑을 갔다. (they, they, went, played, shopping, tennis, after)
➡ _____
(2) 은지는 영화를 보기 전에 모자를 샀다. (Eunji, she, a hat, the movie, bought, watched, before)
➡ _____
(3) 선생님은 우리에게 체육관에 모이라고 말씀하셨다. (the teacher, the gym, us, gather, told, at, to)
➡ _____
(4) 지호는 도훈이에게 창문을 닦아 달라고 부탁했다. (Jiho, Dohun, the window, clean, asked, to)
➡ _____

14 다음 빈칸에 들어갈 동사 do의 형태가 다른 하나는?

① Jim wanted me _____ the dishes.

② She planned _____ some exercise regularly.

③ Our teacher asked us _____ our homework.

④ Did you expect him _____ his best?

⑤ Mom made us _____ it.

17 다음 빈칸에 적절하지 않은 것은?

> _____ he visits my office, I will call you immediately.

① When   ② After   ③ If

④ Even if   ⑤ As soon as

[15~16] 다음 중 어법상 옳은 것을 고르시오.

15 ① I read a book after I fell asleep last night.

② I brushed my teeth after I went to bed.

③ Before he eats food, he always washes his hands.

④ Before he bought the book, he read it.

⑤ Eric will go swimming when Sue will arrive.

18 다음 빈칸에 알맞은 말이 바르게 짝지어진 것은?

> When Yewon asked her dad _____ her bike, he told her _____ it.

① to fix – bringing

② to fix – to bring

③ fixing – to bring

④ fixing – bringing

⑤ fix – bring

16 ① The typhoon caused the old bridge to fall.

② They expect her participates in the ceremony.

③ Judy asked him make sandwiches.

④ Do you want me waking you up tomorrow morning?

⑤ The math teacher told us solving 10 problems every day.

서답형

19 다음 문장에서 어법상 어색한 부분을 바르게 고쳐 다시 쓰시오.

(1) She asked her brother helping her with her homework.

➡ _____

(2) Jim wanted her go shopping with him.

➡ _____

(3) They advised him left the place as soon as possible.

➡ _____

(4) After he rode his bike, Jason put on his helmet.

➡ _____

(5) She will be a good wife when she will get married.

➡ _____

01 다음 문장에서 어법상 어색한 부분을 바르게 고쳐 다시 쓰시오.

(1) Lucy's dad wants her is a police officer.

➡ _____

_____

(2) My mother asked me buy milk on my way home.

➡ _____

_____

(3) The teacher told the students bringing some water.

➡ _____

_____

(4) She got her two sons divided a cake exactly in half.

➡ _____

_____

(5) Her family environment forced her to not continue her studies.

➡ _____

_____

02 주어진 단어를 바르게 배열하여 다음 우리말을 영어로 쓰시오.

(1) 내가 결정을 내리자마자 너에게 내 마음을 알릴 것이다. (I로 시작할 것)

(I, my, will, let, you, know, mind, I, make, a, decision, as soon as)

➡ _____

_____

(2) Nancy는 오빠가 자기에게 라면을 끓여 주기를 원했다.

(Nancy, brother, ramyeon, her, her, cook, wanted, for, to)

➡ _____

_____

03 주어진 동사를 어법에 맞게 빈칸에 쓰시오.

(1) My best friend Jiho often asks me _____ him. (help)

(2) My dad doesn't allow me _____ out at night. (go)

(3) Marianne ordered him _____ with her. (stay)

(4) The manager warned him _____ any pictures there. (take, not)

(5) When Jenny _____, we will leave for Seoul. (come)

(6) The boys will go hiking after they _____ lunch. (have)

04 다음 우리말에 맞도록 빈칸에 알맞은 말을 쓰시오.

(1) Audrey는 숙제를 끝낸 후에 TV를 본다.

= Audrey _____ TV _____ she finishes her homework.

(2) 그는 수영하기 전에 준비 운동을 했다.

= _____ he swam, he _____ some warm-up exercises.

(3) 그가 돌아오면 저한테 전화해 달라고 부탁해 주시겠어요?

= Will you ask him _____ me when he _____ back?

(4) 그녀는 자기 딸에게 개에게 먹이를 주라고 말했다.

= She told her daughter _____ the dog.

05 적절한 접속사를 이용하여 〈보기〉에 주어진 문장과 연결하여 자연스러운 하나의 문장을 만드시오.

---- 보기 ----

• The students took a bus for one hour.
• They arrived at the museum.
• They went to the beach.

(1) They took their swimming suit.

➡ _____

_____

(2) They arrived at their destination.

➡ _____

_____

(3) They appreciated the works in the museum.

➡ _____

_____

06 다음은 Angelina의 일요일 일정표이다. 빈칸에 알맞은 말을 시간의 전후 관계가 표현된 완전한 영어 문장으로 쓰시오.

time	what to do
10:00	go to church
13:00	have lunch with her family
15:00	study math in her room
18:00	go to the movie with James

(1) Angelina will have lunch with her family

_____ .

(2) Angelina will study math in her room

_____

_____ .

(3) Angelina will go to the movie with James _____ .

07 다음 문장을 읽고 빈칸에 알맞은 말을 쓰시오.

> Laura: I'm worried about my history grade.
>
> Teacher: Study history a little harder. You can do it.

➡ The teacher encourages _____

_____ a little harder.

08 다음 문장에서 어법상 어색한 부분을 바르게 고쳐 쓰시오.

(1) Before the sun sets, they can see many stars.

_____ ➡ _____

(2) Turn off the light after you leave the room.

_____ ➡ _____

(3) The migrating birds will come back when spring will come next year.

_____ ➡ _____

(4) I would like you meeting a friend of mine.

_____ ➡ _____

09 주어진 단어를 활용하여 다음 우리말을 영어로 쓰시오.

(1) 나의 부모님은 항상 내게 학교에서 최선을 다하라고 말씀하신다. (always, best, in school)

➡ _____

(2) 건강했기 때문에 그는 그 계획을 수행할 수 있었다. (good health, carry out, enable)

➡ _____

(3) Yuri는 내일 아침을 먹은 후에 교복을 입을 것이다. (put, her uniform) (Yuri로 시작할 것)

➡ _____

Reading

The Right To Be Different

In many ways, 42-year-old Joseph Palmer was an ordinary
> 42-years-old(×)

person. He had a job and cared for his family. But in 1830, after he
> 접속사 after 뒤에 오는 절이 먼저 일어난 일. 주절은 after가 이끄는 절보다 나중에 일어난 일

moved to a small town in Massachusetts, he began to face difficulties.
> ~으로 이사했다   = facing

Joseph looked different from other people: he had a long beard. People
> 감각동사 look+형용사 보어: ~하게 보이다

did not like it very much.
> a long beard

The town's people avoided the man with a beard. They did not want
> 피했다   = Joseph Palmer

to sit next to him. They even whispered behind his back, "What is he
> want는 목적어로 to부정사를 취한다.   behind somebody's back: ~의 등 뒤에서

trying to hide?"
> try+to부정사: ~을 하려고 노력하다

Some neighbors broke his windows. Others threw stones at him when
> some .... others ...: 어떤 것[사람]들은 …, 다른 것[사람]들은

he walked down the street. They told him to stop growing a beard.
> tell+목적어+to부정사: (목적어)에게 ~라고 말하다. stop은 동명사를 목적어로 취하는 동사

Joseph did not mind. He just wanted the freedom to have his beard.
> the freedom을 꾸며 주는 형용사적 용법의 to부정사

---

right 권리
ordinary 평범한, 보통의
care for ~을 돌보다
face 직면하다, 대면하다
beard 수염, 턱수염
avoid 피하다
whisper 속삭이다, 속닥거리다
hide 숨기다
mind 신경 쓰다, 언짢아하다
freedom 자유

확인문제

● 다음 문장이 본문의 내용과 일치하면 T, 일치하지 않으면 F를 쓰시오.

1 Joseph Palmer had a job and cared for his family. ☐

2 Before he moved to a small town in Massachusetts, Joseph began to face difficulties. ☐

3 Joseph looked different from other people. ☐

4 People liked Joseph's long beard very much. ☐

5 Some neighbors broke Joseph's windows. ☐

6 Joseph just wanted the freedom to live alone. ☐

One day, four men <u>attacked</u> Joseph and <u>threw</u> <u>him</u> on the ground.

V1   V2   = Joseph

"We're going to <u>cut off</u> your beard!" they shouted. Joseph was a big

자르다

man, and he was able to <u>fight them off</u>. But the men called the police

목적어가 인칭대명사이므로 fight off them이 아니라 fight them off가 적절하다.

and <u>accused him of attacking</u> them. Poor Joseph <u>was arrested</u>. He said

accuse A of B: A를 B 때문에 고발하다   수동태

to the judge, "I'm the victim here." <u>Sadly</u>, no one believed a man <u>with</u>

문장 전체를 수식하는 부사   ~을 가진

a beard, and he went to prison <u>for over a year</u>. 일 년이 넘는 기간 동안

감옥에 갔다. / the가 없는 경우에는 건물의 본래 목적을 나타낸다. go to school(학교에 다니다)과 비슷한 맥락으로 이해할 수 있다.

Joseph's son, Thomas, <u>wanted people to know</u> the truth. He sent

want + 목적어 + to부정사: (목적어)가 ~하기를 원하다

<u>letters</u> to newspapers across the country. People learned <u>that</u> Joseph

send는 to를 사용하여 3형식으로 고친다.   명사절을 이끄는 접속사

was in prison just for protecting <u>himself</u> and his beard. Many people

him(×)

became angry about <u>this</u>, so the judge finally decided <u>to set</u> Joseph

= Joseph was in prison just for protecting himself and his beard.   decide는 목적어로 to부정사를 취한다.

free.

After he <u>was freed</u>, Joseph traveled and told his story to <u>lots of</u>

석방되다   = many

people. Slowly, people's attitudes toward beards changed. <u>Before</u>

접속사 before는 '~ 전에'라는 뜻. 주절은 before가 이끄는 절에 앞서 일어난 일을 나타낸다.

Joseph died, <u>a man with a beard</u> became the President of the United

턱수염을 가진 남자

States. His name was Abraham Lincoln. <u>He</u> made beards popular, but

= Abraham Lincoln

Joseph Palmer fought for the right <u>to have</u> <u>them</u>.

the right를 수식하는 형용사적 용법의 to부정사   = beards

---

attack 공격하다

fight off ~을 싸워 물리치다

accuse 고발하다, 기소하다

arrest 체포하다

judge 판사

victim 희생자

prison 감옥

truth 진실

set free 석방하다

attitude 태도

toward ~을 향한

president 대통령

확인문제

• 다음 문장이 본문의 내용과 일치하면 T, 일치하지 <u>않으면</u> F를 쓰시오.

1 Joseph said to the judge, "I'm the victim here." ☐

2 The judge believed Joseph and set him free. ☐

3 Joseph's son sent letters to newspapers across the country. ☐

4 People learned that Joseph was in prison just for protecting his family. ☐

5 After he was freed, Joseph traveled and told his story to lots of people. ☐

6 Joseph died before Abraham Lincoln became the President of America. ☐

● 우리말을 참고하여 빈칸에 알맞은 말을 쓰시오.

1 The Right To _____ _____

2 In many ways, 42-year-old Joseph Palmer was _____ _____ _____.

3 He had a job and _____ _____ his family.

4 But in 1830, after he moved to a small town in Massachusetts, he began _____ _____ _____.

5 Joseph _____ _____ from other people: he had a long beard.

6 People _____ _____ _____ _____ very much.

7 The town's people avoided _____ _____ _____ _____ _____.

8 They did not want to _____ _____ _____ _____.

9 They even whispered _____ _____ _____, "What is he trying to hide?"

10 Some neighbors _____ _____ _____.

11 Others _____ _____ _____ him when he walked down the street.

12 They told him to _____ _____ a beard.

13 Joseph did not _____.

14 He just wanted the freedom _____ _____ his beard.

15 One day, four men _____ Joseph and _____ him on the ground.

---

1 다를 권리

2 여러 면에서 42살의 Joseph Palmer는 평범한 사람이었다.

3 그는 직업이 있었고 가족을 돌보았다.

4 하지만 1830년에 매사추세츠에 있는 작은 도시로 이사를 한 후에 그는 어려움에 직면하기 시작했다.

5 Joseph은 다른 사람들과 달라 보였다. 그는 기다란 턱수염을 기르고 있었다.

6 사람들은 그것을 별로 좋아하지 않았다.

7 마을 사람들은 턱수염을 가진 그 남자를 피했다.

8 그들은 그의 곁에 앉고 싶어 하지 않았다.

9 그들은 심지어 그의 등 뒤에서 "그가 무엇을 숨기려는 거지?"라고 속삭였다.

10 어떤 이웃들은 그의 창문을 깼다.

11 다른 사람들은 그가 길을 걸어 내려갈 때 그에게 돌을 던졌다.

12 그들은 그에게 턱수염을 그만 기르라고 말했다.

13 Joseph은 신경 쓰지 않았다.

14 그는 그저 자신의 턱수염을 기를 자유를 원했다.

15 어느 날, 네 명의 남자가 Joseph을 공격했고 그를 바닥에 던졌다.

16 "We're going to _____ _____ your beard!" they shouted.

17 Joseph was a big man, and he was able to _____ _____ _____.

18 But the men called the police and _____ _____ _____ attacking them.

19 Poor Joseph _____ _____.

20 He said to the judge, "I'm _____ _____ here."

21 Sadly, no one believed _____ _____ _____ _____ _____, and he _____ _____ _____ for over a year.

22 Joseph's son, Thomas, _____ people _____ _____ the truth.

23 He _____ letters _____ newspapers across the country.

24 People learned that Joseph _____ _____ _____ just for _____ _____ and his beard.

25 Many people _____ _____ about this, so the judge finally decided _____ _____ Joseph _____.

26 After he _____ _____, Joseph traveled and told his story to lots of people.

27 Slowly, people's _____ _____ _____ changed.

28 Before Joseph died, a man _____ _____ _____ became the President of the United States.

29 _____ _____ was Abraham Lincoln.

30 He made beards _____, but Joseph Palmer _____ _____ the right to have them.

16 "우리가 당신의 턱수염을 잘라 버리겠어!"라고 그들은 소리쳤다.

17 Joseph은 덩치가 큰 사람이었고, 그는 그들을 싸워 물리칠 수 있었다.

18 하지만 그 남자들은 경찰을 불렀고, 자신들을 공격한 것으로 그를 고발했다.

19 불쌍한 Joseph은 체포되었다.

20 그는 "저는 여기서 희생자입니다."라고 판사에게 말했다.

21 슬프게도, 아무도 턱수염을 가진 남자를 믿지 않았고, 그는 일 년이 넘는 기간 동안 감옥에 갔다.

22 Joseph의 아들인 Thomas는 사람들이 진실을 알기를 원했다.

23 그는 전국에 있는 신문사에 편지를 보냈다.

24 사람들은 Joseph이 단지 자신과 자신의 턱수염을 지키려다 감옥에 갇혔다는 것을 알게 되었다.

25 많은 사람들은 이에 대해 분개했고, 그래서 판사는 결국 Joseph을 석방하기로 결정했다.

26 Joseph은 석방된 뒤에 순회를 하며 많은 사람들에게 자신의 이야기를 전했다.

27 사람들의 턱수염에 대한 태도는 서서히 변해갔다.

28 Joseph이 죽기 전에, 턱수염을 가진 남자가 미국의 대통령이 되었다.

29 그의 이름은 Abraham Lincoln (에이브러햄 링컨)이었다.

30 그는 턱수염을 대중적으로 만들었지만, Joseph Palmer는 그것을 기를 권리를 위하여 싸웠다.

● 우리말을 참고하여 본문을 영작하시오.

1 다를 권리

➡ _____

2 여러 면에서 42살의 Joseph Palmer는 평범한 사람이었다.

➡ _____

3 그는 직업이 있었고 가족을 돌보았다.

➡ _____

4 하지만 1830년에 매사추세츠에 있는 작은 도시로 이사를 한 후에 그는 어려움에 직면하기 시작했다.

➡ _____

5 Joseph은 다른 사람들과 달라 보였다. 그는 기다란 턱수염을 기르고 있었다.

➡ _____

6 사람들은 그것을 별로 좋아하지 않았다.

➡ _____

7 마을 사람들은 턱수염을 가진 그 남자를 피했다.

➡ _____

8 그들은 그의 곁에 앉고 싶어 하지 않았다.

➡ _____

9 그들은 심지어 그의 등 뒤에서 "그가 무엇을 숨기려는 거지?"라고 속삭였다.

➡ _____

10 어떤 이웃들은 그의 창문을 깼다.

➡ _____

11 다른 사람들은 그가 길을 걸어 내려갈 때 그에게 돌을 던졌다.

➡ _____

12 그들은 그에게 턱수염을 그만 기르라고 말했다.

➡ _____

13 Joseph은 신경 쓰지 않았다.

➡ _____

14 그는 그저 자신의 턱수염을 기를 자유를 원했다.

➡ _____

15 어느 날, 네 명의 남자가 Joseph을 공격했고 그를 바닥에 던졌다.

➡ _____

16 "우리가 당신의 턱수염을 잘라 버리겠어!"라고 그들은 소리쳤다.

➡ _____

17 Joseph은 덩치가 큰 사람이었고, 그는 그들을 싸워 물리칠 수 있었다.

➡ _____

18 하지만 그 남자들은 경찰을 불렀고, 자신들을 공격한 것으로 그를 고발했다.

➡ _____

19 불쌍한 Joseph은 체포되었다.

➡ _____

20 그는 "저는 여기서 희생자입니다."라고 판사에게 말했다.

➡ _____

21 슬프게도, 아무도 턱수염을 가진 남자를 믿지 않았고, 그는 일 년이 넘는 기간 동안 감옥에 갔다.

➡ _____

22 Joseph의 아들인 Thomas는 사람들이 진실을 알기를 원했다.

➡ _____

23 그는 전국에 있는 신문사에 편지를 보냈다.

➡ _____

24 사람들은 Joseph이 단지 자신과 자신의 턱수염을 지키려다 감옥에 갇혔다는 것을 알게 되었다.

➡ _____

25 많은 사람들은 이에 대해 분개했고, 그래서 판사는 결국 Joseph을 석방하기로 결정했다.

➡ _____

26 Joseph은 석방된 뒤에 순회를 하며 많은 사람들에게 자신의 이야기를 전했다.

➡ _____

27 사람들의 턱수염에 대한 태도는 서서히 변해갔다.

➡ _____

28 Joseph이 죽기 전에, 턱수염을 가진 남자가 미국의 대통령이 되었다.

➡ _____

29 그의 이름은 Abraham Lincoln(에이브러햄 링컨)이었다.

➡ _____

30 그는 턱수염을 대중적으로 만들었지만, Joseph Palmer는 그것을 기를 권리를 위하여 싸웠다.

➡ _____

[01~03] 다음 글을 읽고 물음에 답하시오.

In many ways, 42-year-old Joseph Palmer was an ordinary person. He had a job and ⓐ cared for his family. But in 1830, after he moved to a small town in Massachusetts, he began to face difficulties. Joseph looked different ___ⓑ___ other people: he had a long beard. People did not like it very much.

The town's people avoided the man ___ⓒ___ a beard. They did not want to sit next to him. They even whispered behind his back, "What is he trying to hide?"

01 위 글의 밑줄 친 ⓐcared for와 바꿔 쓸 수 있는 말을 모두 고르시오.

① cared about ② looked after
③ looked for ④ took off
⑤ took care of

02 위 글의 빈칸 ⓑ와 ⓒ에 들어갈 전치사가 바르게 짝지어진 것은?

① in – from ② from – on
③ from – with ④ for – on
⑤ for – with

03 Joseph Palmer에 대한 설명으로 옳지 <u>않은</u> 것을 고르시오.

① 그는 직업이 있었고 가족을 돌보았다.
② 매사추세츠주의 작은 도시로 이사를 한 후에 어려움에 직면하기 시작했다.
③ 그는 기다란 턱수염을 기르고 있었다.
④ 마을 사람들은 그를 피했고 그의 곁에 앉고 싶어 하지 않았다.
⑤ 그는 등 뒤에 무엇을 숨기고 있었다.

[04~06] 다음 글을 읽고 물음에 답하시오.

Some neighbors broke his windows. Others threw stones at him when he walked down the street. They told him ___ⓐ___ growing a beard. Joseph did not mind. He just wanted the freedom to have his beard.

One day, four men attacked Joseph and threw him on the ground. "We're going to cut off your beard!" they shouted. Joseph was a big man, and he was able to fight (A)[it / them] off. But the men called the police and accused him of attacking them. Poor Joseph was arrested. He said to the judge, ⓑ"I'm the victim here." (B)[Luckily / Sadly], no one believed a man with a beard, and he went to prison (C)[during / for] over a year.

서답형
04 위 글의 빈칸 ⓐ에 stop을 이용하여 알맞은 어구를 쓰시오.

➡ _____

서답형
05 위 글의 괄호 (A)~(C)에서 문맥이나 어법상 알맞은 낱말을 골라 쓰시오.

➡ (A) _____ (B) _____ (C) _____

중요
06 밑줄 친 ⓑ를 통해 자신이 체포된 것에 대해 Joseph이 표현하고자 한 심경으로 가장 알맞은 것을 고르시오.

① bored ② scared
③ unfair ④ excited
⑤ ashamed

[07~10] 다음 글을 읽고 물음에 답하시오.

Joseph's son, Thomas, wanted people to know the truth. ⓐHe sent letters to newspapers across the country. People learned that Joseph was in prison just for protecting ⓑhimself and his beard. Many people became angry about this, so the judge Ⓐfinally decided to set Joseph free.

After he was freed, Joseph traveled and told ⓒhis story to lots of people. Slowly, people's attitudes toward beards changed. Before Joseph died, ⓓa man with a beard became the President of the United States. His name was Abraham Lincoln. ⓔHe made beards popular, but Joseph Palmer fought for the right Ⓑto have them.

07 위 글의 제목으로 알맞은 것을 고르시오.

① Inform People of the Truth
② Hard-Won Right to Have a Beard
③ The Pressure of Public Opinion
④ Notice the Attitudes toward Beards
⑤ Abraham Lincoln vs Joseph Palmer

08 위 글의 밑줄 친 ⓐ~ⓔ 중 가리키는 대상이 같은 것끼리 짝 지어진 것은?

① ⓐ – ⓑ   ② ⓐ – ⓒ
③ ⓑ – ⓒ   ④ ⓒ – ⓓ
⑤ ⓒ – ⓔ

09 위 글의 밑줄 친 Ⓐfinally와 의미가 다른 말을 모두 고르시오.

① immediately   ② at last
③ after all   ④ exactly
⑤ in the end

10 위 글의 밑줄 친 Ⓑto have와 to부정사의 용법이 다른 것을 모두 고르시오.

① Are there any questions for me to answer?
② It is important to do your homework.
③ She was surprised to see the sight.
④ I want a book to read during my vacation.
⑤ It's time to leave for New York.

[11~13] 다음 독서 기록장을 읽고 물음에 답하시오.

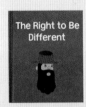

A Story About Joseph Palmer

I read the story about Joseph Palmer last week. I really enjoyed it. I learned from the story that we should not judge people by their _____ⓐ_____. Students who talk about other people's _____ⓐ_____ must read the story. However, I have a question about it. Why did Joseph Palmer want to have a beard?

서답형

11 위 독서 기록장의 빈칸 ⓐ에 appear를 알맞은 형태로 쓰시오.

➡ _____

서답형

12 다음 질문에 대한 알맞은 대답을 주어진 말로 시작하여 쓰시오. (7 단어)

> **Q:** To whom does the writer want to recommend this story?
> **A:** The writer wants to recommend this story to _____.

➡ _____

13 위 독서 기록장에서 알 수 <u>없는</u> 것을 고르시오.

① 제목　　　　　　② 주인공

③ 교훈　　　　　　④ 구입 장소

⑤ 궁금한 점

[14~16] 다음 글을 읽고 물음에 답하시오.

ⓐIn many ways, 42-year-old Joseph Palmer was an extraordinary person. He had a job and cared for his family. But in 1830, after he moved to a small town in Massachusetts, he began to face difficulties. Joseph looked different from other people: he had a long beard. People did not like it very much.

The town's people avoided the man with a beard. They did not want to sit next to him. They even whispered ⓑ그의 등 뒤에서, "What is he trying ⓒto hide?"

서답형

14 위 글의 밑줄 친 ⓐ에서 흐름상 어색한 부분을 찾아 고치시오.

➡ ＿＿＿＿＿＿＿＿＿＿＿＿＿

서답형

15 위 글의 밑줄 친 ⓑ의 우리말에 맞게 3 단어로 영작하시오.

➡ ＿＿＿＿＿＿＿＿＿＿＿＿＿

16 위 글의 밑줄 친 ⓒto hide와 to부정사의 용법이 <u>다른</u> 것을 모두 고르시오.

① Who is the best man to do the work?

② Her first mistake was to tell the information carelessly.

③ Tom decided to wash the dishes for his mom.

④ He got up early to go on a picnic.

⑤ It's not easy to lose weight in a short period of time.

[17~19] 다음 글을 읽고 물음에 답하시오.

＿＿ⓐ＿＿ neighbors broke his windows. ＿＿ⓑ＿＿ threw stones at him when he walked down the street. They told him to stop growing a beard. Joseph did not mind. He just wanted the freedom to have his beard.

One day, four men attacked Joseph and threw him on the ground. "We're going to cut off your beard!" they shouted. Joseph was a big man, and he was able to fight them off. But the men called the police and accused him of attacking them. Poor Joseph was arrested. He said to the judge, "I'm the victim here." Sadly, no one believed a man with a beard, and he went to prison for over a year.

17 위 글의 빈칸 ⓐ와 ⓑ에 들어갈 알맞은 말을 고르시오.

① Some – The other

② Others – The others

③ Some – Others

④ Some – Another

⑤ Others – Some

18 위 글에서 Joseph에 대한 이웃들의 태도에 어울리는 속담을 고르시오.

① It never rains but it pours.

② Every dog has his day.

③ A stitch in time saves nine.

④ Don't count your chickens before they are hatched.

⑤ A tall tree catches much wind.

19 위 글의 내용과 일치하지 <u>않는</u> 것은?

① 어떤 이웃들은 Joseph의 집 창문을 깼다.
② Joseph은 그저 자신의 턱수염을 기를 자유를 원했다.
③ 어느 날, 네 명의 남자가 Joseph을 공격했고 그를 바닥에 던졌다.
④ Joseph은 덩치가 큰 사람이었지만 네 명의 남자들을 싸워 물리칠 수 없었다.
⑤ Joseph은 일 년이 넘는 기간 동안 감옥에 갔다.

[20~22] 다음 글을 읽고 물음에 답하시오.

> **A Story About Steve Jobs**
>
> I read a story about Steve Jobs. I really enjoyed ___ⓐ___ his story. I learned from the story that we should think (A)[different / differently]. Young people who study for the future must read the story. However, I have a question about the story. How was his middle school life? I still remember his saying, "Stay (B)[hungry / hungrily]. Stay (C)[foolish / foolishly]."

서답형

20 위 글의 빈칸 ⓐ에 read를 알맞은 형태로 쓰시오.

➡ _____

서답형

21 위 글의 괄호 (A)~(C)에서 어법상 알맞은 낱말을 골라 쓰시오.

➡ (A) _____ (B) _____ (C) _____

중요

22 위 글의 종류로 알맞은 것을 고르시오.

① article   ② book report
③ diary   ④ essay
⑤ biography

[23~25] 다음 글을 읽고 물음에 답하시오.

> Joseph's son, Thomas, wanted people to know the truth. (①) He sent letters to newspapers across the country. (②) Many people became angry about this, so the judge finally decided to set Joseph free. (③)
> After he was freed, Joseph traveled and told his story to lots of people. (④) Slowly, people's attitudes toward beards changed. (⑤) Before Joseph died, a man with a beard became the President of the United States. His name was Abraham Lincoln. He made beards popular, but Joseph Palmer fought for the ⓐright to have them.

23 위 글의 흐름으로 보아, 주어진 문장이 들어가기에 가장 적절한 곳은?

> People learned that Joseph was in prison just for protecting himself and his beard.

①   ②   ③   ④   ⑤

중요

24 위 글에서 알 수 있는 Joseph Palmer의 성격으로 알맞은 것을 고르시오.

① funny   ② curious
③ generous   ④ creative
⑤ strong-willed

25 위 글의 밑줄 친 ⓐright과 같은 의미로 쓰인 것을 고르시오.

① She had every right to be angry.
② Is this the right way to the beach?
③ Lee was standing right behind her.
④ Keep on the right side of the road.
⑤ Nothing goes right with me.

[01~03] 다음 글을 읽고 물음에 답하시오.

In many ways, (A)[42-year-old / 42-years-old] Joseph Palmer was an ordinary person. He had a job and cared for his family. But in 1830, after he moved to a small town in Massachusetts, he began to face difficulties. Joseph looked (B)[different / differently] from other people: he had a long beard. People did not like ⓐit very much.

The town's people avoided the man with a beard. They did not want (C)[sitting / to sit] next to him. They even whispered behind his back, "What is he trying to hide?"

⭐ 중요
01 위 글의 괄호 (A)~(C)에서 어법상 알맞은 낱말을 골라 쓰시오.

➡ (A) _____ (B) _____ (C) _____

02 위 글의 밑줄 친 ⓐit이 가리키는 것을 본문에서 찾아 쓰시오.

➡ _____

🏠 고난이도
03 Joseph Palmer가 매사추세츠주의 작은 도시로 이사를 한 후에 직면했던 어려움 네 가지를 우리말로 쓰시오.

➡ (1) _____
   (2) _____
   (3) _____
   (4) _____

[04~05] 다음 글을 읽고 물음에 답하시오.

Some neighbors broke his windows. Others threw stones at him when he walked down the street. They told him to stop growing a beard. Joseph did not mind. He just wanted the freedom to have his beard.

One day, four men attacked Joseph and threw him on the ground. "We're going to cut off your beard!" they shouted. Joseph was a big man, and he was able to fight them off. But the men called the police and accused him of attacking them. Poor Joseph was arrested. He said to the judge, "I'm the victim here." Sadly, no one believed a man with a beard, and he went to prison for over a year.

⭐ 중요
04 다음 문장에서 위 글의 내용과 <u>다른</u> 부분을 고쳐 문장을 다시 쓰시오.

Joseph called the police and accused the four men of attacking him.

➡ _____
   _____

05 have를 알맞은 형태로 변형하여, 다음 질문에 대한 대답을 쓰시오. (4 단어)

Q: When Joseph said to the judge, "I'm the victim here," why did no one believe him?
A: Because _____ .

➡ _____

[06~08] 다음 글을 읽고 물음에 답하시오.

ⓐ<u>Joseph의 아들인 Thomas는 사람들이 진실을 알기를 원했다.</u> He sent letters to newspapers across the country. People learned that Joseph was ①<u>in</u> prison just ②<u>for</u> protecting himself and his beard. Many people became angry ③<u>about</u> this, so the judge finally decided to set Joseph free.

After he was freed, Joseph traveled and told his story to lots of people. Slowly, people's attitudes ④toward beards changed. Before Joseph died, a man with a beard became the President of the United States. His name was Abraham Lincoln. ⓑHe made beards popular, but Joseph Palmer fought ⑤against the right to have them.

중요

06 위 글의 밑줄 친 ⓐ의 우리말에 맞게 주어진 어휘를 이용하여 9 단어로 영작하시오.

> people, truth

➡ _____

_____

07 위 글의 밑줄 친 ①~⑤에서 전치사의 쓰임이 **틀린** 것을 찾아 고치시오.

_____ 번, ➡ _____

08 위 글의 밑줄 친 ⓑHe가 가리키는 것을 본문에서 찾아 쓰시오.

➡ _____

[09~13] 다음 글을 읽고 물음에 답하시오.

Some neighbors broke his windows. ⓐThe others threw stones at him when he walked down the street. They told him to stop ⓑgrow a beard. Joseph did not mind. He just wanted the freedom to have his beard.

One day, four men attacked Joseph and threw him on the ground. "We're going to cut off your beard!" they shouted. Joseph

was a big man, and he was able to fight them off. But the men called the police and ⓒ자신들을 공격한 것으로 그를 고발했다. Poor Joseph was arrested. He said to the judge, "I'm the _____ⓓ_____ here." Sadly, no one believed a man with a beard, and he went to prison for over a year.

09 위 글의 밑줄 친 ⓐ에서 어법상 틀린 것을 고치시오.

_____ ➡ _____

10 위 글의 밑줄 친 ⓑ를 알맞은 어형으로 고치시오.

➡ _____

11 위 글의 밑줄 친 ⓒ의 우리말에 맞게 한 단어를 보충하여, 주어진 어휘를 알맞게 배열하시오.

> attacking / them / him / accused

➡ _____

12 주어진 영영풀이를 참고하여 빈칸 ⓓ에 철자 v로 시작하는 단어를 쓰시오.

> someone who has been hurt or killed

➡ _____

13 다음 빈칸 (A)와 (B)에 알맞은 단어를 넣어 Joseph에 대한 소개를 완성하시오.

> Joseph just wanted the freedom to have his beard, but he went to prison for (A)_____ _____ _____ because of the prejudice of the neighbors about a man with (B)_____ _____.
>
> *prejudice: 편견

My Speaking Portfolio

I will vote for Han Siwon. She looks confident and smart. She thinks school
look+형용사 보어: ~하게 보이다

should be a safe place. I agree with her. I like her promises such as no more
~이어야 한다   ~와 같은

bullying. I hope Han Siwon becomes the next school president. I really want
hope와 Han 사이에 접속사 that 생략   = will become

my school to be a safer place.
want의 목적격보어로 쓰인 to부정사

구문해설
· vote for: ~을 뽑다, ~에게 투표하다   · agree with: ~에 동의하다
· bully: (약자를) 괴롭히다[왕따시키다], 협박하다

해석

나는 한시원을 뽑을 겁니다. 그녀는 자신감 있고 똑똑해 보입니다. 그녀는 학교가 안전한 장소가 되어야 한다고 생각합니다. 저는 그녀에게 동의합니다. 나는 집난 괴롭힘 없애기 같은 공약들이 좋습니다. 나는 한시원이 다음 학생회장이 되길 바랍니다. 나는 우리 학교가 더 안전한 장소가 되길 정말 바랍니다.

My Writing Portfolio: My Book Report

The Right to Be Different
형용사적 용법

A Story About Joseph Palmer

I read the story about Joseph Palmer last week. I really enjoyed it. I learned
the story about Joseph Palmer

from the story that we should not judge people by their appearance. Students
접속사   그들의 외모로

who talk about other people's appearance must read the story. However, I have
주격 관계대명사   ~해야 한다   그러나

a question about it. Why did Joseph Palmer want to have a beard?
want는 목적어로 to부정사를 취한다.

구문해설
· right 권리   · judge: (~로 미루어) 판단하다[여기다]   · appearance: 외모
· however: 그러나   · beard: 턱수염

다를 권리

Joseph Palmer에 관한 이야기

나는 지난주에 Joseph Palmer에 관한 이야기를 읽었다. 나는 그게 정말 재미있었다. 나는 그 이야기로부터 우리는 사람들을 외모로 판단해서는 안 된다는 것을 배웠다. 다른 사람들의 외모에 관해 이야기하는 학생들은 이 이야기를 꼭 읽어야 한다. 하지만, 나는 그것에 관한 질문이 하나 있다. Joseph Palmer는 왜 턱수염을 기르고 싶었을까?

Words in Action

Welcome to the travel fair. Admission is free. What countries do you have in
~을 마음에 두다

mind? If you want to visit South America, you can look around the booths on
부사절을 이끄는 접속사로 '만약 ~ 한다면'의 의미   형용사구

the left. If you get hungry, you can have drinks and a light snack.
get+형용사: ~해지다

구문해설
· fair 박람회   · admission 입장료   · free 무료의   · look around 둘러보다
· light 가벼운

여행 박람회에 오신 것을 환영합니다. 입장료는 무료입니다. 여러분은 어떤 나라들을 마음에 두고 있나요? 여러분이 남아메리카를 방문하고 싶다면, 왼쪽에 있는 부스들을 살펴볼 수 있습니다. 배가 고파진다면, 음료와 간단한 간식을 드실 수 있습니다.

01 다음 주어진 두 단어의 관계가 같도록 빈칸에 알맞은 단어를 쓰시오.

> act : action – appear : _____

02 다음 글의 빈칸 ⓐ와 ⓑ에 들어갈 단어가 바르게 짝지어진 것은?

> One day, four men ____ⓐ____ed Joseph and threw him on the ground. "We're going to ____ⓑ____ your beard!" they shouted.

① avoid – protect　　② avoid – cut off
③ wait – protect　　④ attack – fight off
⑤ attack – cut off

03 다음 밑줄 친 부분의 뜻이 잘못된 것은?

① After he was freed, Joseph traveled. 석방되었다
② Joseph Palmer fought for the right to have beards. 권리
③ Joseph Palmer was an ordinary person. 평범한
④ He said to the judge, "I'm the victim here." 판단하다
⑤ Joseph looked different from other people. 다르게 보였다

04 다음 영영 풀이에 해당하는 것을 고르시오.

> • to make something happen
> • the reason that something happens

① cut　　② cause　　③ fall
④ change　　⑤ mean

05 다음 문장의 빈칸에 공통으로 들어갈 말을 쓰시오.

> • I do well in subjects _____ social studies and history.
> • He looks smart, but I don't _____ his promises.

06 빈칸에 주어진 단어를 알맞은 형태로 고쳐 쓰시오.

> • The men called the police and accused him of attacking them. Poor Joseph _____ (arrest).

➡ _____

07 주어진 문장이 들어갈 위치로 알맞은 것은?

> But what does she look like?

B: Hi, Minsol. Is your class winning?
G: Of course. We have a great handball player. (①)
B: You mean the girl from Mongolia?
G: Yes, her name is Gacha. (②)
B: I've heard a lot about her. (③)
G: She's very tall and has a ponytail. (④)
B: Oh, is she the girl who scored the goal just now?
G: Yes, that's her seventh goal. (⑤)
B: Wow, she's really great.

①　　②　　③　　④　　⑤

08 다음 질문에 대한 답으로 적절하지 <u>않은</u> 것은?

> A: What does he look like?

① He has long straight hair.
② He has a big head.
③ He is very tall.
④ He's reading a map.
⑤ He has no hair.

[09~10] 다음 대화를 읽고 물음에 답하시오.

M: What can I do for you?
G: I lost my younger brother.
M: Okay, calm down. What's your brother's name?
G: His name is Wally Brown. He's five years old.
M: What does he look like?
G: He has brown hair and brown eyes.
M: What is he wearing?
G: He is wearing a green shirt and black pants.
M: Can you tell me more?
G: Oh, he is carrying a red backpack.
M: All right. We'll go out and look for him. Also, we'll make an announcement about a missing child.
G: Thank you so much. _____ (A) _____

09 위 대화의 빈칸 (A)에 들어갈 말로 적절한 것은?

① I hope you'll do well on the exam.
② I hope I'll find him soon.
③ I hope he'll enjoy an announcement about a missing child.
④ I hope so, too.
⑤ My cat is missing.

10 위 대화의 소녀의 남동생에 관한 정보로 일치하지 <u>않은</u> 것은?

① His name is Wally Brown.
② He's five years old.
③ He has brown hair and brown eyes.
④ He's wearing a green shirt and black pants.
⑤ He'll go out and look for a child.

11 다음 대화의 빈칸 (A)에 들어갈 말로 알맞은 것은?

> B: I hear there is a new student in your class.
> G: Yes. She's from Jejudo. Oh, she's over there!
> B: Which one? _____ (A) _____
> G: She has curly hair and is wearing glasses.

① What does she look like?
② What is she looking for?
③ Where is she?
④ How do you know her?
⑤ Where is she going?

12 주어진 말에 이어질 대화의 순서로 알맞은 것은?

> You look sad. What's wrong, Jongmin?

> (A) What happened?
> (B) She fell off her bike.
> (C) My sister broke her arm this morning.
> (D) That's too bad. I hope she'll get better soon.

① (A) – (B) – (C) – (D)
② (B) – (A) – (C) – (D)
③ (C) – (A) – (B) – (D)
④ (C) – (B) – (A) – (D)
⑤ (D) – (A) – (B) – (C)

Grammar

13 다음 빈칸에 들어갈 말로 어법상 적절한 것을 <u>모두</u> 고르시오.

> _____ John gets a haircut, he will wash his hair.

① Before   ② Although   ③ If
④ After   ⑤ Because

14 지난 토요일에 Emily가 다음 그림 속의 1~3 순서대로 동물들을 보고 왔다. 내용에 맞게 빈칸을 알맞게 채우시오.

(1) Emily saw an elephant before _____ _____.

(2) Emily saw a giraffe _____ she saw a lion.

(3) Emily saw a lion _____.

15 다음 빈칸에 공통으로 들어갈 수 있는 것을 고르시오.

> • Wayne _____ her to take part in the party.
> • Harold _____ to know what was inside the box.

① asked   ② wanted
③ invited   ④ told
⑤ advised

16 다음 중 어법상 바르지 <u>않은</u> 것은?

① After they finished their homework, Miso and Mijin went out for dinner.
② He persuaded her coming to his party.
③ Before I get an allowance, I do a lot of house chores.
④ Did you made him paint the gate?
⑤ She forced him to give up smoking and drinking.

17 다음 문장을 주어진 단어로 시작하는 문장으로 바꾸어 쓰시오.

(1) Before we watched the movie, we ate ice cream.
   ➡ A f t e r _____

_____.

(2) After I pass the school gate, I untie my hair.
   ➡ Before _____

_____.

18 다음 문장에서 어법상 잘못된 부분을 바르게 고쳐 문장을 다시 쓰시오.

(1) I will take a photo of myself after I will get a haircut tomorrow.
   ➡ _____

_____

(2) Fiona wants Andrew doesn't come to the party.
   ➡ _____

(3) The situation required me have strong belief.
   ➡ _____

_____

19 다음 빈칸에 들어갈 말로 알맞게 짝지어진 것은?

> • Vida warned her son _____ fast food.
> • Jerome asked me _____ the TV volume.

① not to eat – to turn down
② not eating – to turn down
③ not to eat – turning down
④ not eating – turning down
⑤ not eat – turn down

20 주어진 어휘를 이용하여 영작하시오. (8단어)

> 잠자리에 들기 전에 양치질을 해라. (brush, bed)

➡ _____

Reading

[21~22] 다음 글을 읽고 물음에 답하시오.

> In many ways, 42-year-old Joseph Palmer was an ordinary person. He had a job and cared for his family. But in 1830, after he moved to a small town in Massachusetts, he began to ⓐface difficulties. Joseph looked different from other people: he had a long ___ⓑ___. People did not like it very much.
> The town's people avoided the man with a ___ⓑ___. They did not want to sit next to him. They even whispered behind his back, "What is he trying to hide?"

21 위 글의 밑줄 친 ⓐface와 같은 의미로 쓰인 것을 고르시오.

① He buried his face in his hands.
② Look at the north face of the mountain.
③ He didn't face a financial crisis.
④ The face of the clock is covered with a simple glass cover.
⑤ Don't lose your face.

22 주어진 영영풀이를 참고하여 빈칸 ⓑ에 철자 b로 시작하는 단어를 쓰시오.

> the hair that grows on one's chin and cheeks

➡ _____

[23~25] 다음 글을 읽고 물음에 답하시오.

> Some neighbors broke his windows. Others threw stones at him when he walked down the street. They told him to stop growing a beard. Joseph did not mind. He just wanted the freedom ⓐto have his beard.
> One day, four men attacked Joseph and threw him on the ground. "We're going to cut off your beard!" they shouted. Joseph was a big man, and he was able to fight them off. But the men called the police and accused him of attacking them. Poor Joseph was arrested. He said to the judge, "I'm the victim here." Sadly, no one believed a man with a beard, and he went to prison for over a year.

23 위 글의 밑줄 친 ⓐto have와 to부정사의 용법이 같은 것을 모두 고르시오.

① Did you want to go there then?
② I have no house to live in.
③ She wants something cold to drink.
④ I'm happy to get the birthday present.
⑤ Jane had the kindness to help me.

24 위 글의 주제로 알맞은 것을 고르시오.

① various cases of bullying in our society
② the judge who sent the victim to prison
③ the importance of the good neighbors
④ unfair behavior towards a man with a beard
⑤ the way to grow a wonderful beard

25 위 글을 읽고 대답할 수 없는 질문은?

① When did some neighbors break Joseph's windows?

② Who told Joseph to stop growing a beard?

③ What did Joseph want?

④ What did Joseph say to the judge?

⑤ How long did Joseph go to prison?

[26~28] 다음 글을 읽고 물음에 답하시오.

Joseph's son, Thomas, wanted people to know the truth. He sent letters to newspapers across the country. People learned that Joseph was in prison just for protecting himself and his beard. Many people became angry about ⓐthis, so the judge finally decided to set Joseph free.

After he was freed, Joseph traveled and told his story to lots of people. Slowly, people's attitudes toward beards changed. Before Joseph died, a man with a beard became the President of the United States. His name was Abraham Lincoln. ⓑHe made beards popular, but Joseph Palmer fought for the right to have it.

26 위 글의 밑줄 친 ⓐthis가 가리키는 것을 본문에서 찾아 쓰시오.

➡ _____

27 위 글의 밑줄 친 ⓑ에서 어법상 틀린 부분을 찾아 고치시오.

➡ _____

28 위 글의 내용과 일치하지 <u>않는</u> 것은?

① Joseph's son sent letters to newspapers across the country.

② Before Joseph traveled and told his story to lots of people, he was freed.

③ Joseph died after Abraham Lincoln became the President of the United States.

④ Joseph Palmer made beards popular.

⑤ Joseph fought for the right to have beards.

[29~30] 다음 독서 기록장을 읽고 물음에 답하시오.

A Story About Joseph Palmer

I read the story about Joseph Palmer last week. I really enjoyed it. I learned from the story that we should not judge people by their appearance. Students who talk about other people's appearance must read the story. ____ⓐ____, I have a question about it. Why did Joseph Palmer want to have a beard?

29 위 독서 기록장의 빈칸 ⓐ에 들어갈 알맞은 말을 고르시오.

① In addition　② Therefore

③ However　④ For example

⑤ Moreover

30 위 독서 기록장의 교훈으로 어울리는 속담을 고르시오.

① Too many cooks spoil the broth.

② Make hay while the sun shines.

③ Don't cry over spilt milk.

④ The grass is greener on the other side of the fence.

⑤ Don't judge a book by its cover.

01 출제율 90%

다음 짝지어진 단어의 관계가 같도록 빈칸에 알맞은 말을 쓰시오.

> guilty : innocent = friendly : _____

02 출제율 95%

〈보기〉에서 알맞은 단어를 선택하여 문장을 완성하시오.

> ┌─ 보기 ┤
>
> attack   attitude   avoid   whisper

- When a dog tried to (A)_____ me, my cat meowed loudly.
- I like your good (B)_____ : you always look on the bright side.

[03~04] 다음 대화를 읽고 물음에 답하시오.

M: What can I do for you?

G: I lost my younger brother.

M: Okay, ⓐcalm down. What's your brother's name?

G: His name is Wally Brown. He's five years old.

M: ⓑWhat does he look for?

G: He has brown hair and brown eyes.

M: What is he wearing?

G: ⓒHe is wearing a green shirt and black pants.

M: ⓓCan you tell me more?

G: Oh, he is carrying a red backpack.

M: All right. We'll go out and look for him. Also, we'll make an announcement about a missing child.

G: Thank you so much. ⓔI hope I'll find him soon.

03 출제율 85%

How does the girl feel and why? Complete the sentence.

➡ She is _____ because she _____ her younger brother.

04 출제율 95%

위 대화의 밑줄 친 어구의 쓰임이 적절하지 <u>않은</u> 것은?

① ⓐ   ② ⓑ   ③ ⓒ   ④ ⓓ   ⑤ ⓔ

05 출제율 100%

다음 중 짝지어진 대화가 <u>어색한</u> 것을 고르시오.

① A: I lost my puppy this afternoon.
  B: I hope you'll find him soon.

② A: What does your sister look like?
  B: She's a little fat and has long straight hair.

③ A: I plan to go fishing with my uncle on the weekend.
  B: I hope you'll find it soon.

④ A: I'll enter the school dance contest next week. I hope I won't make mistakes.
  B: Don't worry!

⑤ A: What does she look like?
  B: She has an oval face and big black eyes.

[06~07] 다음 대화를 읽고 물음에 답하시오.

Somin: Look at the bulletin board. There are posters for the next school president.

Dain: Yeah, I've already made my choice. I'll vote for Jang Jimin.

Somin: You mean the boy with glasses? He looks smart, but I don't like his promises.

Dain: Then who will you choose?

Somin: Well, I am for number 3, Hong Jiho. She wants to make our school fun and exciting.

Dain: She always has short hair, right?

Somin: Yes, and she looks friendly.

06 위 대화와 포스터를 참고하여 Somin이가 지지하는 후보자에 관한 글을 완성하시오.

monthly talent shows
more club activity hours
Let's Make a Fun and Exciting School
3
Hong Jiho

I will _____ _____ Hong Jiho. She has _____ _____. She looks _____. She thinks school should be _____ _____ _____. I agree with her. I like her _____ such as monthly talent shows. I hope Hong Jiho becomes the next school president.

출제율 95%

07 위 대화의 내용과 일치하지 <u>않는</u> 것은?

① There will be an election for the next school president.
② Dain supports Jang Jimin.
③ Jimin wears glasses.
④ Somin doesn't like Jimin's promises.
⑤ Hong Jiho is Somin's friend.

[08~09] 다음 글을 읽고 물음에 답하시오.

Hi, I'm Gacha. I'm from Mongolia. When I first came to Songji Middle School two months ago, I was so (A)[happy / worried]. I was a little shy, and I wasn't good at Korean. (B)[However / Moreover], I'm a lucky girl. All my classmates are nice and friendly. I enjoy playing handball with them in P.E. class. I'm a (C)[good / bad] player. They call me "Golden Hand." There will be a sports day next week. I hope my class will win in the handball event.

출제율 90%

08 위 글을 읽고 다음 질문의 답을 완성하시오.

What is Gacha's hope for the sports day?

➡ She _____ her _____ _____ _____ in the _____ event.

출제율 100%

09 위 글의 괄호 (A)~(C)에서 알맞은 것을 고르시오.

	(A)	(B)	(C)
①	happy	However	bad
②	happy	Moreover	good
③	worried	Moreover	bad
④	worried	However	good
⑤	worried	However	bad

출제율 95%

10 다음 대화의 빈칸 (A)와 (B)에 들어갈 말로 알맞은 것은?

A: What is your character's name?
B: Her name is Prettian.
C: _____ (A) _____
B: She's short and has a big head. She has an oval face and big black eyes.
D: _____ (B) _____
B: She's wearing a blue dress and big earrings.

① (A) What does she look like?
　 (B) What is she wearing?
② (A) How does she look like?
　 (B) What is she wearing?
③ (A) What does she look like?
　 (B) Is she wearing sunglasses?
④ (A) How does she look like?
　 (B) Can you tell me more?
⑤ (A) What is she looking at?
　 (B) Where is she?

11 다음 중 어법상 바르지 <u>않은</u> 것은? (2개)

> I am sure ①that he ②will beg me ③ buy ④him a toy when we ⑤will arrive at the shop.

12 다음 중 어법상 <u>어색한</u> 문장의 개수는?

> ⓐ Sora dropped by her aunt's before she went to school.
> ⓑ Would you like me bringing any food to the party?
> ⓒ Her parents expected her won the contest.
> ⓓ After he had a long trip, he was very tired.
> ⓔ She told him was on time.

① 1개　② 2개　③ 3개　④ 4개　⑤ 5개

13 주어진 어휘를 이용하여 다음 우리말을 영작하시오.

(1) 선생님은 내게 문을 닫아달라고 부탁하셨다.
(the teacher, ask, the door)
➡ _____

(2) Dr. Smith는 그녀에게 일찍 잠자리에 들라고 충고했다. (advise, early, go to bed)
➡ _____

(3) 축구 경기가 끝난 후에 선수들은 잔디 위에 누웠다. (the soccer match, the players, on the grass, lie, over)
➡ _____
_____

14 다음 문장에서 어법상 어색한 부분을 바르게 고쳐 다시 쓰시오.

(1) Judy asked him made sandwiches.
➡ _____

(2) Tom expected Jane be thin.
➡ _____

(3) My advice caused him stop smoking.
➡ _____

[15~16] 다음 글을 읽고 물음에 답하시오.

> In many ways, 42-year-old Joseph Palmer was an ordinary person. He had a job and cared for his family. But in 1830, after he moved to a small town in Massachusetts, he began to face difficulties. ⓐJoseph looked like different from other people: he had a long beard. People did not like it very much.
>
> The town's people avoided ⓑthe man with a beard. They did not want to sit next to him. They even whispered behind his back, "What is he trying to hide?"

15 위 글의 밑줄 친 ⓐ에서 어법상 틀린 부분을 고치시오.

_____ ➡ _____

16 위 글의 밑줄 친 ⓑthe man with a beard가 가리키는 것을 본문에서 찾아 쓰시오.

➡ _____

[17~19] 다음 글을 읽고 물음에 답하시오.

> Some neighbors broke his windows. Others threw stones at him when he walked down the street. They told him to stop (A)[growing / to grow] a beard. Joseph did not ⓐmind. He just wanted the freedom (B)[having / to have] his beard.

One day, four men attacked Joseph and threw him on the ground. "We're going to cut off your beard!" they shouted. Joseph was a big man, and he was able to fight them off. But the men called the police and accused him of attacking them. Poor Joseph (C)[arrested / was arrested]. He said to the judge, "I'm the ⓑ_____ here." Sadly, no one believed a man with a beard, and he went to prison for over a year.

17 위 글의 괄호 (A)~(C)에서 어법상 알맞은 낱말을 골라 쓰시오.

➡ (A) _____ (B) _____ (C) _____

18 위 글의 밑줄 친 ⓐmind와 같은 의미로 쓰인 것을 고르시오.

① Out of sight, out of mind.
② Never mind! She didn't mean what she said.
③ Keep your mind on your work!
④ I want to meet the greatest mind of the time.
⑤ A sound mind in a sound body.

19 위 글의 빈칸 ⓑ에 들어갈 알맞은 말을 고르시오.

① attacker   ② lawyer   ③ prisoner
④ bully   ⑤ victim

[20~22] 다음 글을 읽고 물음에 답하시오.

Joseph's son, Thomas, wanted people to know the truth. He sent letters to newspapers across the country. People learned that Joseph was in prison just for protecting himself and his beard. Many people became angry about this, so the judge finally decided to set Joseph free.

After he was freed, Joseph traveled and told his story to lots of people. Slowly, people's attitudes toward beards changed. Before Joseph died, a man with a beard became the President of the United States. His name was Abraham Lincoln. He made beards popular, but Joseph Palmer fought for the right to have them.

20 본문의 내용과 일치하도록 다음 빈칸 (A)와 (B)에 알맞은 단어를 쓰시오.

(A)_____ _____ finally decided to set Joseph free because many people became angry about the truth that Joseph was in prison just for protecting himself and (B)_____ _____.

21 위 글의 내용에 어울리는 속담을 고르시오.

① No news is good news.
② The grass is greener on the other side of the fence.
③ Where there is a will, there is a way.
④ Look before you leap.
⑤ Practice makes perfect.

22 위 글을 읽고 답할 수 없는 것을 고르시오.

① Why did Joseph's son send letters to newspapers across the country?
② What did people learn through the letters?
③ After Joseph was freed, what did he do?
④ How many people changed their attitudes toward beards?
⑤ Who made beards popular?

서술형 실전문제

01 다음 대화의 빈칸 (A)에 Gacha의 외모를 묻는 말을 쓰시오. (대명사를 이용할 것)

> B: Hi, Minsol. Is your class winning?
> G: Of course. We have a great handball player.
> B: You mean the girl from Mongolia?
> G: Yes, her name is Gacha.
> B: I've heard a lot about her. But ___(A)___
> G: She's very tall and has a ponytail.
> B: Oh, is she the girl who scored the goal just now?
> G: Yes, that's her seventh goal.
> B: Wow, she's really great.

➡ _____

02 다음 글은 학생회장 후보를 지지하는 글이다. 글을 보고 아래의 대화를 완성하시오.

> "I will vote for Han Siwon. She looks confident and smart. She thinks school should be a safe place. I agree with her. I like her promises such as no more bullying. I hope Han Siwon becomes the next school president. I really want my school to be a safer place."

⬇

> G: Look at the bulletin board. There are posters for the next _____ _____.
> B: Yeah, I've already made my choice. I'll _____ for Han Siwon.
> G: She always has a ponytail, right?
> B: Yes. She looks _____ and smart. And she wants to make _____ _____ _____ _____.

03 다음 대화의 밑줄 친 우리말에 맞게 주어진 어휘를 이용하여 문장을 완성하시오.

> A: I have an important exam tomorrow!
> B: (A)나는 네가 시험을 잘 보길 바라. (hope, will, do well)
> A: (B)나도 그러길 바라. (hope, so) Thanks.

➡ (A) _____
　 (B) _____

04 다음 문장에서 어법상 어색한 부분을 바르게 고쳐 다시 쓰시오.

(1) My history teacher told us handed in the project by tomorrow.

➡ _____
_____

(2) The teacher warned the students be quiet in class.

➡ _____
_____

(3) Amy's best friend wants her listens to his songs.

➡ _____
_____

(4) Her manager always forces Melanie throwing away the trash.

➡ _____
_____

(5) The doctor encouraged Jack to not give up doing exercise.

➡ _____
_____

05 주어진 어휘를 이용하여 다음 우리말을 영작하시오.

(1) 엄마는 내게 그 개를 산책시키라고 말씀하셨다.
(mom, walk the dog)

➡ _____

(2) Mark는 Maria가 복귀할 때까지 그녀의 고객들을 관리할 것이다. (control, customers, return)

➡ _____

06 다음 문장을 주어진 단어로 시작하는 문장으로 바꾸어 쓰시오.

> I set my alarm clock before I went to bed.

➡ After _____.

[07~09] 다음 글을 읽고 물음에 답하시오.

Some neighbors broke his windows. Others threw stones at him when he walked down the street. They told him to stop growing a beard. Joseph did not mind. He just wanted the ___ⓐ___ to have his beard.

One day, four men attacked Joseph and threw him on the ground. "We're going to cut off your beard!" they shouted. ⓑJoseph은 덩치가 큰 사람이었고, 그는 그들을 싸워 물리칠 수 있었다. But the men called the police and accused him of attacking them. Poor Joseph was arrested. He said to the judge, "I'm the victim here." Sadly, no one believed a man with a beard, and he went to prison for over a year.

07 위 글의 빈칸 ⓐ에 free를 알맞은 형태로 쓰시오.

➡ _____

08 위 글의 밑줄 친 ⓑ의 우리말에 맞게 주어진 어휘를 이용하여 13 단어로 영작하시오.

> big, able, fight, off

➡ _____
_____

09 위 글의 내용과 일치하도록 다음 빈칸 (A)와 (B)에 알맞은 단어를 쓰시오.

> Though Joseph was a (A)_____ of bullying, he went to prison for over a year because no one believed a man with a (B)_____.

[10~11] 다음 글을 읽고 물음에 답하시오.

Joseph's son, Thomas, wanted people to know the truth. He sent letters to newspapers across the country. People learned that Joseph was in prison just for (A)[preventing / protecting] himself and his beard. Many people became (B)[angry / angrily] about this, so the judge finally decided to set Joseph (C)[free / freely].

10 위 글의 괄호 (A)~(C)에서 문맥이나 어법상 알맞은 낱말을 골라 쓰시오.

➡ (A) _____ (B) _____ (C) _____

11 다음 질문에 대한 알맞은 대답을 주어진 단어로 시작하여 쓰시오. (10 단어)

> Q: How did people learn that Joseph was in prison just for protecting himself and his beard?
>
> A: They learned it because _____
> _____
> _____.

01 (A)에 제시된 어구를 보고 사람의 외모를 묻는 질문과 그에 대한 대답을 쓰고, (B)는 주어진 상황에서 가질 수 있는 적절한 바람을 찾아 쓰시오.

> (A) Minsu – short hair, wearing jeans / Sumi – tall, a ponytail, wearing glasses
>
> (B) [상황] I lost my puppy this afternoon. / I have an important exam tomorrow!
>   I'm going to my favorite singer's concert tonight.
>
>   [바람] I hope you'll do well on the exam. / I hope you'll find it soon. /
>   I hope you have a good time.

02 다음 〈보기〉의 동사와 to부정사를 이용하여 여러 가지 문장을 쓰시오.

> ┌─ 보기 ─────────────────────────────────────┐
>
>   want   ask   tell   allow   advise   force
>
> └───┘

(1) _____

(2) _____

(3) _____

(4) _____

(5) _____

(6) _____

03 다음 내용을 바탕으로 인물에 관한 책이나 이야기 중 감명 깊게 읽은 것을 정리하는 글을 쓰시오.

> • 주인공: Steve Jobs   • 교훈: We should think differently.
> • 추천 독자층: young people who study for the future
> • 궁금한 점: How was his middle school life?   • 기억에 남는 문구: Stay hungry. Stay foolish.

> A Story about Steve Jobs
>
> I read a story about Steve Jobs. I really enjoyed (A)_____ his story. I learned from the story that we should think (B)_____. Young people (C)_____ study for the future must read the story. However, I have a question about the story. (D)_____ was his middle school life? I still remember his saying, "(E)_____ Stay foolish."

단원별 모의고사

01 다음 단어에 대한 영어 설명이 <u>어색한</u> 것은?

① victim: someone who has been hurt or killed

② choose: to decide which thing you want

③ attack: an action to try to frighten someone who is smaller or weaker

④ attitude: how you think or feel about something

⑤ arrest: to take the person away to ask them about a crime that they might have committed

02 다음 짝지어진 단어의 관계가 같도록 빈칸에 알맞은 말을 쓰시오.

guilty : innocent = ease : _____

03 다음 영영풀이에 해당하는 단어를 고르시오.

v. drop down to the floor
n. the season between summer and winter

① fall   ② continue   ③ spring
④ autumn   ⑤ face

04 대화의 빈칸에 들어갈 말로 <u>어색한</u> 것은?

A: What is your character's name?
B: His name is Buster.
A: What does he look like?
B: _____
A: Does he have big eyes?
B: Yes, he does.

① He has no hair.

② He's tall and has curly hair.

③ He has brown hair and is wearing glasses.

④ He is very kind and attractive.

⑤ He has a round face and short straight hair.

05 대화의 빈칸에 들어갈 알맞은 말은?

G: You look sad. What's wrong, Jongmin?
B: My sister broke her arm this morning.
G: What happened?
B: She ___(A)___ her bike.
G: That's too bad. I hope she'll ___(B)___ soon.

　　(A)　　　(B)
① broke – get better
② broke – fix it
③ felled – care for herself
④ got off – find him soon
⑤ fell off – get better

06 대화를 알맞은 순서로 배열한 것은?

(A) She has curly hair and is wearing glasses.
(B) I hear there is a new student in your class.
(C) Which one? What does she look like?
(D) Yes. She's from Jejudo. Oh, she's over there!

① (B) – (C) – (A) – (D)
② (B) – (D) – (C) – (A)
③ (C) – (A) – (B) – (D)
④ (C) – (B) – (D) – (A)
⑤ (D) – (C) – (B) – (A)

07 다음 대화의 빈칸에 들어갈 말로 가장 적절한 것은?

> A: I hope you'll do your best in the final game.
>
> B: Thanks. _____

① I'm a good player.
② I don't like your promises.
③ I wish you the same.
④ I don't like talent shows.
⑤ I hope you'll do well on the exam.

[08~10] 다음 대화를 읽고 물음에 답하시오.

> Man: What can I do for you?
> Girl: I lost my younger brother.
> Man: Okay, calm down. What's your brother's name? (①)
> Girl: His name is Wally Brown. He's five years old.
> Man: What does he look like? (②)
> Girl: He has brown hair and brown eyes.
> Man: What is he wearing? (③)
> Girl: He is wearing a green shirt and black pants.
> Man: _____(A)_____
> Girl: Oh, he is carrying a red backpack. (④)
> Man: All right. We'll go out and look for him. (⑤)
> Girl: Thank you so much. I hope I'll find him soon.

08 위 대화의 빈칸 (A)에 들어갈 말로 가장 자연스러운 것은?

① What does he like?
② Can you tell me more?
③ What does he look like?
④ Do you know where he is?
⑤ Is your brother wearing a blue cap?

09 위 대화의 (①)~(⑤) 중 주어진 문장이 들어갈 위치로 알맞은 것은?

> Also, we'll make an announcement about a missing child.

①   ②   ③   ④   ⑤

10 위 대화를 읽고 추론할 수 없거나 답을 할 수 없는 질문은?

① How does the girl feel?
② Where did the girl lose her brother?
③ Does the girl's brother have black hair?
④ What kind of color is her brother's backpack?
⑤ What will the man do after the dialog?

[11~12] 다음 대화를 읽고 물음에 답하시오.

> B: Hi, Minsol. Is your class winning?
> G: Of course. We have a great handball player.
> B: _____(A)_____
> G: Yes, her name is Gacha.
> B: I've heard a lot about her. But what does she look like?
> G: She's very tall and has a ponytail.
> B: Oh, (B)지금 막 골을 넣은 여자아이가 그녀니?
> G: Yes, that's her seventh goal.
> B: Wow, she's really great.

11 위 대화의 빈칸 (A)에 들어갈 말로 알맞은 것은?

① Who is she?
② What is her name?
③ Do you know where she is from?
④ What will you do for her?
⑤ You mean the girl from Mongolia?

12 위 대화의 밑줄 친 (B)의 우리말에 맞게 주어진 어구를 알맞게 배열하시오.

> she, is, who, the goal, the girl, scored, just now

➡ _____

13 다음 중 어법상 올바른 것은?

① Do you want me clean your house for you?
② He told Perry putting on a penguin shirt.
③ I would like you to explain the accident in more detail.
④ The doctor advised Kathy stopped smoking.
⑤ Ms. Green asked him carries the boxes.

14 다음 중 어법상 <u>어색한</u> 것은?

① I will go straight to the gym after I pass the school gate.
② I will wait for her until she will come back to me.
③ Before she passes the school gate, she ties her hair with a hairband.
④ After he did his homework, he watched TV.
⑤ She will buy a new coat as soon as she receives the money.

15 다음 빈칸에 들어갈 말로 알맞게 짝지어진 것은?

> • Do you expect me _____ up my dreams?
> • The students will ride bikes before they _____ lunch.

① to give – have   ② to give – will have
③ giving – have   ④ giving – will have
⑤ give – had

16 다음 상황에 알맞은 말을 어법에 맞게 빈칸에 쓰시오.

(1) The driver drove his car very fast. He said to the driver, "Don't drive so fast."
➡ He told the driver _____ _____ _____ _____ _____ .

(2) Paul is good at playing the guitar. So Bella said to Paul, "Will you play the piano for us?"
➡ Bella asked Paul _____ _____ _____ _____ _____ _____ .

17 그림을 참고하여 빈칸을 알맞게 채우시오.

18:00   20:00

➡ Bomi studied history _____ .
➡ Bomi had dinner _____ .

[18~19] 다음 글을 읽고 물음에 답하시오.

In many ways, 42-year-old Joseph Palmer was an ordinary person. He had a job and cared for his family. But in 1830, after he moved to a small town in Massachusetts, he began to face difficulties. Joseph looked different from other people: he had a long beard. People did not like it very much.

The town's people avoided the man with a beard. They did not want to sit next to him. They even whispered behind his ⓐ , "What is he trying to hide?"

18 다음 질문에 대한 알맞은 대답을 주어진 단어로 시작하여 쓰시오. (5 단어)

> Q: Why did Joseph Palmer look different from other people?
> A: Because _____ .

➡ _____

19 위 글의 빈칸 ⓐ에 들어갈 알맞은 말을 고르시오.

① legs   ② head   ③ hands
④ back   ⑤ shoulders

[20~22] 다음 글을 읽고 물음에 답하시오.

Some neighbors broke his windows. Others threw stones ___ⓐ___ him when he walked down the street. They told him to stop growing a beard. Joseph did not mind. He just wanted the freedom to have his beard.

One day, four men attacked Joseph and threw him on the ground. "We're going to cut off your beard!" they shouted. Joseph was a big man, and he was able to fight ⓑthem off. But the men called the police and accused him ___ⓒ___ attacking them. Poor Joseph was arrested. He said to the ⓓjudge, "I'm the victim here." Sadly, no one believed a man with a beard, and he went to prison for over a year.

20 위 글의 빈칸 ⓐ와 ⓒ에 들어갈 전치사가 바르게 짝지어진 것은?

① at – of   ② in – of   ③ in – from
④ to – in   ⑤ at – by

21 위 글의 밑줄 친 ⓑthem이 가리키는 것을 본문에서 찾아 쓰시오.

➡ _____

22 위 글의 밑줄 친 ⓓjudge와 같은 의미로 쓰인 것을 고르시오.

① Did the court judge him guilty?
② The judge sentenced him to five years in prison.
③ God will judge all men.
④ He is a good judge of wine.
⑤ You must not judge a man by his income.

[23~24] 다음 글을 읽고 물음에 답하시오.

Joseph's son, Thomas, wanted people to know the truth. He sent letters to newspapers across the country. ⓐ사람들은 Joseph이 단지 자신과 자신의 턱수염을 지키려다 감옥에 갔다는 것을 알게 되었다. Many people became angry about this, so the judge finally decided to set Joseph free.

After he was freed, Joseph traveled and told his story to lots of people. Slowly, people's attitudes toward beards changed. Before Joseph died, a man with a beard became the President of the United States. His name was Abraham Lincoln. He made beards popular, but Joseph Palmer fought for the right to have them.

23 위 글의 밑줄 친 ⓐ의 우리말에 맞게 한 단어를 보충하여, 주어진 어휘를 알맞게 배열하시오.

> that / people / his beard / Joseph / learned / himself / in prison / and / protecting / just / was

➡ _____
_____

24 Who made beards popular? Answer in English. (three words)

➡ _____

Lesson 6

Near and Dear

🔊 의사소통 기능

- 불만 나타내기
  A: I'm not happy with this restaurant.
  B: What's the problem?
  A: The food is too salty.

- 상기시키기
  A: I'm going to go hiking.
  B: Don't forget to take water.

🔊 언어 형식

- 사역동사
  I will **let** Robby **have** a pet.

- too+형용사/부사+to부정사
  The child is **too** short **to** ride the roller coaster.

Words & Expressions

Key Words

- **bowl** [boul] 몡 사발, 그릇
- **catch** [kætʃ] 동 잡다
- **common** [kámən] 혱 흔한, 보통의
- **customer service** 고객 지원 (센터)
- **discussion** [diskʌ́ʃən] 몡 토론
- **either** [íːðər] (부정문에서) ~도 역시
- **exchange** [ikstʃéindʒ] 몡 교환 동 교환하다
- **experience** [ikspíəriəns] 몡 경험
- **feed** [fiːd] 동 먹이다
- **forget** [fərɡét] 동 잊다, 망각하다
- **guest** [ɡest] 몡 손님
- **hairdryer** [héərdràiər] 몡 헤어드라이어
- **lie** [lai] 몡 거짓말
- **listener** [lísnər] 몡 청취자
- **message** [mésidʒ] 몡 전갈, 메시지
- **parent** [pέərənt] 몡 어버이(아버지 또는 어머니)
- **pour** [pɔːr] 동 쏟다, 붓다
- **promise** [prámis] 동 약속하다
- **puppy** [pʌ́pi] 몡 강아지
- **receipt** [risíːt] 몡 영수증
- **refund** [rifʌ́nd] 몡 환불, 환불금

- **repair** [ripέər] 동 고치다
- **sadness** [sǽdnis] 몡 슬픔
- **salty** [sɔ́ːlti] 혱 짠
- **scared** [skɛərd] 혱 겁먹은
- **secret** [síːkrit] 몡 비밀
- **share** [ʃɛər] 동 공유하다
- **stuff** [stʌf] 몡 물건
- **suggestion** [səɡdʒéstʃən] 몡 제안, 의견
- **tear** [tiər] 동 찢다
- **teenage** [tíneidʒ] 혱 십 대의
- **text** [tekst] 동 문자 메시지를 보내다
- **traditional** [trədíʃənl] 혱 전통적인
- **training** [tréiniŋ] 몡 훈련, 훈육
- **trash** [træʃ] 몡 쓰레기
- **truth** [truːθ] 몡 진실, 사실
- **understand** [ʌndərstǽnd] 동 이해하다
- **upset** [ʌ́pset] 혱 화난
- **wall** [wɔːl] 몡 벽
- **without** [wiðáut] 전 ~ 없이
- **work** [wəːrk] 동 (기계가) 작동하다, 일하다
- **wrong** [rɔːŋ] 혱 잘못된

Key Expressions

- **be in trouble** 곤경에 처하다
- **be sure to** ~ 반드시 ~하다
- **break down** 부수다
- **drop by** ~에 들르다
- **find out** 발견하다, 알아내다
- **give it a try** 한번 해 보다

- **near and dear** (관계가) 매우 친절한, 소중한
- **not ~ anymore** 더 이상 ~ 아니다
- **on one's own** 혼자 힘으로
- **start off with** ~으로 시작하다
- **take care of** ~을 돌보다, ~을 처리하다
- **tell a lie** 거짓말하다

Word Power

※ 서로 반대되는 뜻을 가진 어휘

□ **speaker** (화자) ↔ **listener** (청취자)

□ **happy** (행복한) ↔ **unhappy** (불행한)

□ **true** (사실의) ↔ **false** (거짓의)

□ **tell a lie** (거짓말하다) ↔ **tell the truth** (사실대로 말하다)

□ **guest** (손님) ↔ **host** (주인)

□ **kind** (친절한) ↔ **unkind** (불친절한)

□ **forget** (잊다) ↔ **remember** (기억하다)

□ **ancient** (고대의) ↔ **modern** (현대의)

□ **wrong** (잘못된) ↔ **right** (올바른)

□ **leave** (떠나다) ↔ **arrive** (도착하다)

English Dictionary

□ **exchange** 교환하다
→ to give something to somebody and at the same time receive the same type of thing from them
누군가에게 무언가를 주고 동시에 그들로부터 같은 유형의 것을 받다

□ **feed** 먹이다
→ to give food to a person or an animal
사람이나 동물에게 음식을 주다

□ **guest** 손님
→ a person that you have invited to your house or to a particular event that you are paying for
당신의 집이나 당신이 지불하는 특정 행사에 초대된 사람

□ **hairdryer** 헤어드라이어
→ a small machine used for drying your hair by blowing hot air over it
뜨거운 공기를 머리 위로 불어서 당신의 머리를 건조시키기 위해 사용되는 작은 기계

□ **listener** 청취자
→ a person who listens
듣는 사람

□ **promise** 약속하다
→ to tell somebody that you will definitely do or not do something, or that something will definitely happen
누군가에게 당신이 반드시 무언가를 하거나 하지 않을 것이라고, 또는 무언가가 반드시 일어날 것이라고 이야기하다

□ **puppy** 강아지
→ a young dog
어린 개

□ **receipt** 영수증
→ a piece of paper that shows that goods or services have been paid for
상품이나 서비스가 지불되었다는 것을 보여주는 종이 조각

□ **refund** 환불
→ a sum of money that is paid back to you, especially because you paid too much or because you returned goods to a shop/store
당신이 너무 많이 지불했거나 또는 당신이 상품을 가게에 돌려주었기 때문에 당신에게 다시 지불되어야 하는 돈의 합계

□ **repair** 고치다
→ to restore something that is broken, damaged or torn to good condition
부서지거나, 손상되거나 또는 찢어진 무언가를 좋은 상태로 회복시키다

□ **secret** 비밀
→ something that is known about by only a few people and not told to others
오직 몇몇 사람에 의해서만 알려지거나 다른 사람들에게 말하지 않은 것

□ **suggestion** 제안
→ an idea or a plan that you mention for somebody else to think about
당신이 다른 누군가에게 생각해 보도록 언급하는 생각이나 계획

□ **text** 문자 메시지를 보내다
→ to send somebody a written message using a mobile/cell phone
휴대폰을 사용하여 쓴 메시지를 누군가에게 보내다

□ **wall** 벽
→ a long vertical solid structure, made of stone, brick or concrete, that surrounds, divides or protects an area of land
한 지역의 땅을 감싸거나, 나누거나 또는 보호하는 돌, 벽돌, 또는 콘크리트로 만들어진 길고 수직의 견고한 구조물

서답형

01 다음 짝지어진 단어의 관계가 같도록 빈칸에 알맞은 말을 쓰시오.

> wrong : right = speaker : _____

02 다음 영영풀이가 가리키는 것을 고르시오.

> a sum of money that is paid back to you, especially because you paid too much or because you returned goods to a shop/store

① repair   ② refund
③ promise   ④ share
⑤ tear

중요

03 다음 중 밑줄 친 부분의 뜻풀이가 바르지 <u>않은</u> 것은?

① Don't <u>forget</u> to bring your helmet. 잊다
② Would you like my old TV in <u>exchange</u> for this camera? 환불
③ There were 20 <u>guests</u> at the party. 손님들
④ My <u>hairdryer</u> was broken, so I needed a new one. 헤어드라이어
⑤ The radio program has lots of young <u>listeners</u>. 청취자들

서답형

04 다음 문장의 빈칸에 들어갈 말을 〈보기〉에서 골라 쓰시오.

> ┤ 보기 ├
> take care of / drop by / break down / find out / start off with

(1) I will _____ your office tomorrow morning.

(2) Can you _____ those problems?
(3) Some day he will _____ the truth.
(4) You can _____ some movie clips.
(5) The fire fighters _____ the door to get into the house.

05 다음 주어진 문장의 밑줄 친 text와 같은 의미로 쓰인 것은?

> <u>Text</u> me when you get there.

① My job is to find out the errors on the <u>text</u>.
② I'll <u>text</u> you the final score.
③ The newspaper printed the full <u>text</u> of the President's speech.
④ Read the <u>text</u> carefully and answer the questions.
⑤ Have you ever read the medical <u>text</u>?

서답형

06 다음 문장의 빈칸에 들어갈 말을 〈보기〉에서 골라 쓰시오.

> ┤ 보기 ├
> suggestions / without / either / stuff / leave

(1) We cannot live _____ computers now.
(2) Can you remove all the _____ on your desk?
(3) Can I _____ a message for Mr. Winter?
(4) Yuri can't go to the party, and I can't _____.
(5) I have some _____ for you.

60 Lesson 6. Near and Dear

01 다음 짝지어진 단어의 관계가 같도록 빈칸에 알맞은 말을 쓰시오.

> leave : arrive = forget : _____

02 다음 우리말에 맞게 빈칸에 알맞은 말을 쓰시오.

(1) 경찰들은 규칙적으로 훈련을 받아야 한다.
➡ Police officers should receive _____ regularly.

(2) 아이들을 먼저 먹이고 나중에 우리의 저녁을 먹자.
➡ Let's _____ the kids first and have our dinner later.

(3) 그 회사는 좋은 고객 지원 센터로 유명하다.
➡ The company is famous for its good _____.

03 다음 문장의 빈칸에 들어갈 말을 〈보기〉에서 골라 쓰시오.

> ┤ 보기 ├
> text / wall / secret / sharing / experience

(1) When I was young, I didn't like _____ a room with my sister.

(2) The war was a terrible _____ for everyone.

(3) There was a high _____ around the house.

(4) I won't tell anyone your _____.

(5) Can you _____ me the information now?

04 다음 우리말에 맞게 주어진 단어를 사용하여 영작하시오.

(1) 당신의 주문 영수증을 보여 주시겠어요? (order, can)
➡ _____

(2) 그들은 내가 구매한 물건 값을 전액 환불해 주었다. (full, purchase)
➡ _____

(3) Jessie는 그 소식을 비밀로 하겠다고 약속했다. (a secret, keep)
➡ _____

05 다음 우리말과 일치하도록 주어진 단어를 모두 배열하여 영작하시오.

(1) 당신은 새로운 언어를 공부하기 시작할 때, 약간의 어휘부터 시작해야 한다.
(should / when / with / you / you / a / language / off / new / start / some / study / vocabulary)
➡ _____
_____

(2) 만약 네가 친구들에게 거짓말을 하면, 너는 그들을 잃을 수도 있다.
(friends / can / you / them / if / lose / a / lie / your / tell / to / you)
➡ _____
_____

(3) 벽을 부수기 위해 내가 무엇을 해야 하나요?
(the / do / to / what / I / down / wall / should / break)
➡ _____
_____

Conversation

① 불만 나타내기

A **I'm not happy with this restaurant.** 나는 이 식당이 마음에 들지 않아.

B **What's the problem?** 문제가 무엇이야?

A **The food is too salty.** 음식이 너무 짜.

■ 불만을 나타낼 때 'I'm not happy with ~' 표현을 사용하여 나타낼 수 있다. 불만을 나타내는 말에 'What's the problem?', 'What's the matter?' 또는 'What's wrong with you?' 등을 사용하여 불만의 구체적인 이유를 물을 수 있다.

불만 나타내기

• I'm not happy with this computer. 나는 이 컴퓨터가 마음에 들지 않아.

• I want to complain about the noise from upstairs. 나는 윗층에서 나는 소음에 대해 불평하고 싶어요.

• I'm sorry to say this, but the waiters in this restaurant aren't very polite.
  이런 말해서 미안하지만, 이 식당의 웨이터들이 별로 공손하지 않네요.

• I've got a complaint about this restaurant. 이 식당에 대해 불만이 있어요.

핵심 Check

1. 다음 우리말과 일치하도록 빈칸에 알맞은 말을 쓰시오.

(1) **A:** I'm not _____ with this hair salon. (이 미용실이 마음에 들지 않네요.)

B: What's _____? (문제가 무엇이에요?)

A: I waited too long. (나는 너무 오래 기다렸어요.)

(2) **A:** I want to _____ about the plate in this restaurant.
   (나는 이 식당의 접시에 대해 불평하고 싶어요.)

B: What's the _____? (문제가 무엇이죠?)

A: The plate isn't clean. (접시가 깨끗하지 않아요.)

② 상기시키기

A I'm going to go hiking. 나는 하이킹을 갈 거야.

B Don't forget to take water. 물을 가져가는 것을 잊지 마.

■ 'Don't forget to ~'는 상대방에게 어떤 일을 해야 한다고 알려주거나 해야 할 일을 상기시켜 주기 위해 사용하는 표현으로 'Remember to + 동사원형' 또는 'Make sure that 주어 + 동사' 또는 'Be sure to + 동사원형' 등으로 바꾸어 쓸 수 있다.

상기시키기

- Don't forget to finish your report. 네 보고서를 끝마치는 것을 잊지 마.
- Remember to bring your homework tomorrow. 내일 네 숙제를 가져와야 하는 것을 기억해라.
- Be sure to drive slowly. 반드시 천천히 운전해야 해.

■ forget이나 remember 뒤에 -ing를 쓰면 '(과거에) ~했던 것을 잊다 또는 기억하다'라는 의미가 되고, 'to+동사원형'을 쓰면 '(미래에) ~해야 할 것을 잊다, 또는 기억하다'라는 의미를 나타낸다.

- forget + -ing: (과거에) ~했던 것을 잊다
- forget + to 동사원형: (미래에) ~해야 할 것을 잊다
- remember + -ing: (과거에) ~했던 것을 기억하다
- remember + to 동사원형: (미래에) ~해야 할 것을 기억하다

핵심 Check

2. 다음 우리말과 일치하도록 빈칸에 알맞은 말을 쓰시오.

(1) **A:** _____ _____ _____ take your umbrella. (너의 우산을 가져갈 것을 잊지 마라.)

B: Okay, I see. (응. 알겠어.)

(2) **A:** It looks like it's going to rain soon. _____ _____ close the windows.

(곧 비가 올 것 같아. 창문을 닫아야 한다는 것을 기억해라.)

B: Okay, I will. (응. 그렇게.)

(3) **A:** I'm going skating. (나는 스케이트를 타러 갈 거야.)

B: Be _____ _____ put gloves on. (반드시 장갑을 껴야 해.)

Communication Listen – Dialog 1

> Minsol: ❶I'm not happy with Buster.
> Dad: What's wrong?
> Minsol: He ❷tore my homework into pieces again.
> Dad: Puppies often do ❸that.
> Minsol: This is not the first time. Sometimes I find my socks in the dog house.
> Dad: Please be kind to ❹him. ❹He's just five months old.
> Minsol: You're too nice to ❹him! ❹He needs some training.
> Dad: Okay. Let's start ❺training in a few weeks.

> Minsol: 저는 Buster가 마음에 들지 않아요.
> Dad: 무엇이 문제니?
> Minsol: Buster가 또다시 제 숙제를 찢어 놓았어요.
> Dad: 강아지들은 종종 그런 일을 저지르지.
> Minsol: 이번이 처음이 아니에요. 가끔 저는 제 양말을 개집에서 찾기도 해요.
> Dad: Buster에게 잘해 주렴. 태어난 지 다섯 달 밖에 안 되었잖니.
> Minsol: 아빠는 그를 너무 다정하게 대해 주세요! 그에게는 훈련이 좀 필요해요.
> Dad: 좋아. 몇 주 뒤에 훈련을 시작해 보자꾸나.

❶ I'm not happy with ~: '나는 ~가 마음에 들지 않다'라는 의미로 불만족을 나타내는 표현이다.
❷ tear 찢다 – tore (과거형) – torn (과거분사형)
❸ that은 숙제를 찢어 놓은 것을 가리킨다.
❹ him과 He 모두 Buster를 가리킨다.
❺ start는 동명사와 to부정사를 모두 목적어로 취할 수 있다.

Check(√) True or False

(1) Minsol feels bad because of Buster.   T ☐ F ☐

(2) Dad is angry because Buster tore his socks.   T ☐ F ☐

Communication: Listen – Listen More

> *(The phone rings.)*
> Mike: Customer Service. ❶How can I help you?
> Sora: I bought a hairdryer at your store last week. I'm not happy with ❷it.
> Mike: What is the problem?
> Sora: It doesn't work well. I mean the air isn't hot enough.
> Mike: I'm sorry. Do you want to ❸exchange it?
> Sora: Well, can I get a ❹refund?
> Mike: Sure. Will you please visit our store with the dryer?
> Sora: Yes, I'll ❺drop by tomorrow afternoon.
> Mike: Don't forget to bring the ❻receipt.
> Sora: Okay. Thanks.

> *(전화벨이 울린다.)*
> Mike: 고객 센터입니다. 어떻게 도와드릴까요?
> Sora: 제가 지난주에 가게에서 헤어드라이어를 샀는데요. 마음에 들지 않네요.
> Mike: 무엇이 문제인가요?
> Sora: 작동이 잘되지 않아요. 제 말은 충분히 뜨거운 바람이 나오질 않는다는 거예요.
> Mike: 죄송합니다. 교환을 원하시나요?
> Sora: 음. 환불받을 수 있을까요?
> Mike: 물론이죠. 드라이어를 가지고 저희 가게를 방문해 주시겠어요?
> Sora: 네. 내일 오후에 들를게요.
> Mike: 영수증 가지고 오시는 걸 잊지 마세요.
> Sora: 네. 고맙습니다.

❶ 도움을 제공할 때 쓰는 표현으로 'What can I do for you?' 등으로 바꾸어 쓸 수 있다.
❷ it은 지난주에 산 헤어드라이어를 가리킨다.
❸ exchange: 교환하다   ❹ refund: 환불
❺ drop by: ~에 들르다   ❻ receipt: 영수증

Check(√) True or False

(3) Sora is not satisfied with the hairdryer that she bought last week.   T ☐ F ☐

(4) Sora doesn't need to bring the receipt to get a refund.   T ☐ F ☐

Communication: Listen – Dialog 2

Mom: Minsu, I'm ❶going out with your dad for a movie.

Minsu: When will you ❷be back, Mom?

Mom: ❸Around 8 o'clock. Don't forget to ❹feed Buster.

Minsu: Okay.

Mom: ❺Be sure to give him some water, too.

Minsu: No problem.

Mom: One more thing. Can you help Minsol with her science homework? Buster tore her homework into pieces.

Minsu: Hmm .... Okay. I'll do ❻that.

❶ go out: 외출하다, 나가다
❷ be back: 돌아오다
❸ around: 약, ~쯤
❹ feed: 먹이다
❺ be sure to: 반드시 ~하다
❻ that은 민솔이의 과학 숙제를 도와주는 것을 가리킨다.

❶ 같은 뜻의 표현으로 What's wrong?을 쓸 수 있다.
❷ for too long: 너무 오랫동안
❸ 상대방의 기분에 공감할 때 쓰는 표현으로 'I understand how you feel.'로 바꾸어 쓸 수 있다.
❹ get up과 병렬 구조를 나타낸다.
❺ give it a try: 한번 해 보다, 시도하다

Wrap Up – Listening ❺

G: You ❶look upset, Tommy.

B: I'm not happy with Sojin.

G: ❷What's wrong with her?

B: She isn't doing her ❸part of the group project.

G: ❹I think you should talk to her.

❶ look+형용사: ~처럼 보이다
❷ 문제가 무엇인지 묻는 질문으로 'What's the matter with her?' 또는 'What's the problem?' 등으로 바꾸어 쓸 수 있다.
❸ part: 역할
❹ 조언을 하는 표현으로 'In my opinion, you need to talk to her.' 또는 'I advise you to talk to her.' 등으로 바꾸어 쓸 수 있다.

My Speaking Portfolio – Step 3

A: I'm not very happy with my brother.

B: ❶What's the problem?

A: He uses the bathroom ❷for too long in the morning.

B: ❸I know how you feel.

A: What can I do?

B: Well, you can get up earlier and ❹use the bathroom first.

A: Okay, I'll ❺give it a try.

Wrap Up – Listening ❻

M: ❶Are you ready for your trip, Suji?

G: Yes, I am, Dad. ❷I'm ready to leave.

M: Do you have your ticket with you?

G: Yeah, I have ❸it on my phone.

M: Good. Don't forget to call me when you ❹ get to the train station.

G: Sure.

❶ be ready for: ~의 준비가 되다
❷ be ready to ~: ~할 준비가 되다
❸ it은 'the ticket'을 가리킨다.
❹ get to: ~에 도착하다

● 다음 우리말과 일치하도록 빈칸에 알맞은 말을 쓰시오.

Communication: Listen – Dialog 1

Minsol: I'm not _____ with Buster.

Dad: What's _____?

Minsol: He _____ my homework into _____ again.

Dad: Puppies often do _____.

Minsol: This is not the first time. Sometimes I find my _____ in the dog house.

Dad: Please be _____ to him. He's just _____ _____ old.

Minsol: You're _____ nice _____ him! He needs some _____.

Dad: Okay. Let's _____ _____ in a few weeks.

Communication: Listen – Dialog 2

Mom: Minsu, I'm _____ _____ with your dad for a movie.

Minsu: When will you be _____, Mom?

Mom: Around 8 o'clock. Don't forget _____ _____ Buster.

Minsu: Okay.

Mom: Be _____ to give him some water, too.

Minsu: No _____.

Mom: One _____ _____. Can you _____ Minsol _____ her science homework? Buster _____ her homework into pieces.

Minsu: Hmm .... Okay. I'll do that.

Communication: Listen – Listen More

(The phone rings.)

Mike: Customer Service. _____ can I _____ _____?

Sora: I bought a _____ at your _____ last week. I'm not _____ with it.

Mike: What is _____ _____?

Sora: It doesn't _____ well. I mean the air isn't hot _____.

Mike: I'm sorry. Do you want to _____ it?

Sora: Well, can I get a _____?

Mike: Sure. Will you please _____ our _____ with the dryer?

Sora: Yes, I'll _____ _____ tomorrow afternoon.

Mike: Don't forget to bring the _____.

Sora: Okay. Thanks.

해석

Minsol: 저는 Buster가 마음에 들지 않아요.

Dad: 무엇이 문제니?

Minsol: Buster가 또 제 숙제를 찢어 놓았어요.

Dad: 강아지들은 종종 그런 일을 저지르지.

Minsol: 이번이 처음이 아니에요. 가끔 저는 제 양말을 개집에서 찾기도 해요.

Dad: Buster에게 잘해 주렴. 태어난 지 다섯 달 밖에 안 되었잖니.

Minsol: 아빠는 그를 너무 다정하게 대해 주세요! 그에게는 훈련이 좀 필요해요.

Dad: 좋아. 몇 주 뒤에 훈련을 시작해 보자꾸나.

Mom: 민수야, 엄마는 아빠랑 영화 보러 나간다.

Minsu: 언제 돌아오실 거예요, 엄마?

Mom: 8시쯤. Buster에게 밥 주는 것 잊지 말렴.

Minsu: 네.

Mom: 물도 꼭 주려무나.

Minsu: 그럴게요.

Mom: 한 가지 더. 민솔이 과학 숙제를 도와줄 수 있겠니? Buster가 민솔이의 숙제를 찢어 놓았거든.

Minsu: 음 …. 알겠어요. 그렇게 할게요.

(전화벨이 울린다.)

Mike: 고객 센터입니다. 어떻게 도와드릴까요?

Sora: 제가 지난주에 가게에서 헤어드라이어를 샀는데요. 마음에 들지 않네요.

Mike: 무엇이 문제인가요?

Sora: 작동이 잘되지 않아요. 제 말은 충분히 뜨거운 바람이 나오질 않는다는 거예요.

Mike: 죄송합니다. 교환을 원하시나요?

Sora: 음. 환불받을 수 있을까요?

Mike: 물론이죠. 드라이어를 가지고 저희 가게를 방문해 주시겠어요?

Sora: 네. 내일 오후에 들를게요.

Mike: 영수증 가지고 오시는 걸 잊지 마세요.

Sora: 네. 고맙습니다.

My Speaking Portfolio – Step 3

A: I'm _____ _____ _____ with my brother.

B: What's _____ _____?

A: He uses the _____ for too long in the morning.

B: I know _____ you _____.

A: What _____ I do?

B: Well, you can _____ _____ earlier and use the bathroom first.

A: Okay, I'll _____ it _____ _____.

해석

A: 나는 내 남동생이 별로 마음에 들지 않아.
B: 뭐가 문제니?
A: 그는 아침에 너무 오랫동안 욕실을 사용해.
B: 네 기분이 어떤지 알아.
A: 내가 무엇을 할 수 있을까?
B: 음, 너는 더 일찍 일어나서 욕실을 먼저 사용할 수 있어.
A: 알겠어, 내가 한번 해 볼게.

Wrap Up – Listening ❺

G: You look _____, Tommy.

B: I'm not _____ _____ Sojin.

G: What's _____ with her?

B: She isn't doing her _____ of the group project.

G: I think you _____ talk _____ her.

여: Tommy야, 기분이 안 좋아 보이는구나.
남: 나는 소진이 때문에 속상해.
여: 그 애에게 무슨 문제가 있니?
남: 그 애가 모둠 과제에서 맡은 일을 안 해.
여: 내 생각에 너는 그 애랑 이야기를 해 봐야 할 것 같아.

Wrap Up – Listening ❻

M: Are you ready for your _____, Suji?

G: Yes, I am, Dad. I'm _____ to leave.

M: Do you have your _____ with you?

G: Yeah, I have it _____ _____ _____.

M: Good. _____ _____ _____ _____ me when you _____ _____ the train station.

G: _____.

남: 여행 갈 준비 되었니, 수지야?
여: 네, 아빠. 저는 떠날 준비가 되었어요.
남: 표는 네가 가지고 있고?
여: 네, 제 전화기에 저장해 놓았어요.
남: 잘했구나. 기차역에 도착하면 내게 전화하는 걸 잊지 말렴.
여: 물론이죠.

[01~02] 다음 대화를 읽고 물음에 답하시오.

Mike: Customer Service. How can I help you?

Sora: I bought a hairdryer at your store last week. I'm not happy with it.

Mike: What is the problem? (A)

Sora: It doesn't work well. (B)

Mike: I'm sorry. Do you want to exchange it? (C)

Sora: Well, can I get a refund? (D)

Mike: Sure. Will you please visit our store with the dryer? (E)

Sora: Yes, I'll drop by tomorrow afternoon.

Mike: Don't forget to bring the receipt.

Sora: Okay. Thanks.

01 위 대화의 (A)~(E) 중 주어진 문장이 들어가기에 적절한 곳은?

> I mean the air isn't hot enough.

① (A) ② (B) ③ (C) ④ (D) ⑤ (E)

02 위 대화를 읽고 대답할 수 <u>없는</u> 것은?

① What did Sora buy at Mike's store last week?

② What was the matter with Sora's hairdryer?

③ What does Sora want Mike to do?

④ What should Sora bring to get a refund?

⑤ What is Sora going to exchange with her hairdryer?

03 다음 대화가 자연스럽게 이어지도록 순서대로 배열하시오.

> I'm not very happy with my brother.

(A) What can I do?

(B) What's the problem?

(C) I know how you feel.

(D) He uses the bathroom for too long in the morning.

(E) Well, you can get up earlier and use the bathroom first.

➡ _____

[01~03] 다음 대화를 읽고 물음에 답하시오.

Minsol: I'm not happy with Buster.

Dad: What's wrong?

Minsol: He tore my homework into pieces again.

Dad: Puppies often do that.

Minsol: This is not the first time. Sometimes I find my socks in the dog house.

Dad: Please be kind to him. He's just five months old.

Minsol: _____(A)_____ He needs some training.

Dad: Okay. Let's start training in a few weeks.

01 위 대화의 빈칸 (A)에 들어갈 말로 알맞은 것은?

① How kind you are!

② You're too nice to him!

③ He is too young to train a lot.

④ He is growing up so fast.

⑤ You need to keep your socks in your closet.

02 위 대화에서 나타난 Minsol의 기분으로 적절한 것은?

① excited　　　② happy

③ nervous　　　④ unpleased

⑤ satisfied

03 위 대화의 내용과 일치하지 <u>않는</u> 것은?

① Minsol은 Buster 때문에 기분이 좋지 않다.

② Buster는 Minsol의 숙제를 또 다시 찢어 놓았다.

③ Minsol은 가끔 양말을 개집에서 찾기도 한다.

④ Buster는 5살 되었다.

⑤ Minsol은 Buster가 훈련이 필요하다고 생각한다.

[04~06] 다음 대화를 읽고 물음에 답하시오.

Mom: Minsu, I'm going out with your dad for a movie.

Minsu: When will you be back, Mom?

Mom: Around 8 o'clock. Don't forget to feed Buster.

Minsu: Okay.

Mom: (a)Be sure to give him some water, too.

Minsu: No problem.

Mom: _____(A)_____ Can you help Minsol with her science homework? Buster tore her homework into pieces.

Minsu: Hmm .... Okay. I'll do that.

04 위 대화의 빈칸 (A)에 들어갈 말로 적절한 것은?

① One more thing　　② Conversely

③ However　　　　　④ Therefore

⑤ On the other hand

05 위 대화의 밑줄 친 (a)와 바꾸어 쓸 수 있는 것을 <u>모두</u> 고르시오.

① Don't forget to give him some water, too.

② I'm doubtful if you can give him some water, too.

③ I'm curious if you can give him some water, too.

④ Remember to give him some water, too.

⑤ Do you want to give him some water, too?

서답형
06 위 대화에서 엄마가 부탁한 일의 목록을 완성하시오.

< To Do List>		
1	(A)_____	Buster
2	Give (B)_____	to Buster
3	Help Minsol with (C)_____	

[07~08] 다음 대화를 읽고 물음에 답하시오.

Amy: I'm not very happy with my brother.

Brian: What's the problem?

Amy: He uses the bathroom for too long in the morning.

Brian: I know ___(A)___ you feel.

Amy: What can I do?

Brian: Well, (B)you can get up earlier and use the bathroom first.

Amy: Okay, I'll give it a try.

07 위 대화의 빈칸 (A)에 알맞은 말을 쓰시오.

➡ _____

08 위 대화의 밑줄 친 (B)와 바꾸어 쓸 수 <u>없는</u> 것은?

① how about getting up earlier and using the bathroom first?

② why don't you get up earlier and use the bathroom first?

③ I advise you to get up earlier and use the bathroom first.

④ I think you should get up earlier and use the bathroom first.

⑤ I'm wondering why you should get up earlier and use the bathroom first.

09 다음 대화가 자연스럽게 이어지도록 순서대로 배열하시오.

(A) What's wrong with her?

(B) I'm not happy with Sojin.

(C) I think you should talk to her.

(D) You look upset, Tommy.

(E) She isn't doing her part of the group project.

➡ _____

[10~11] 다음 대화를 읽고 물음에 답하시오.

Dad: Are you ready for your trip, Suji?

Suji: Yes, I am, Dad. (A) <u>저는 떠날 준비가 되었어요</u>. (leave)

Dad: Do you have your ticket with you?

Suji: Yeah, I have it on my phone.

Dad: Good. Don't forget to call me when you get to the train station.

Suji: Sure.

서답형

10 위 대화의 밑줄 친 (A)의 우리말을 주어진 말을 써서 영작하시오.

➡ _____

11 위 대화의 내용과 일치하지 <u>않는</u> 것은?

① 수지는 떠날 준비가 되었다.

② 수지는 표를 전화기에 저장해 놓았다.

③ 수지는 기차를 탈 것이다.

④ 수지는 도착하면 아빠에게 전화를 할 것이다.

⑤ 수지는 기차역에서 표를 구매할 것이다.

12 다음 중 짝지어진 대화가 <u>어색한</u> 것은?

① A: I'm not happy with the science class. It's too boring.

B: Same here. I hope it gets more exciting.

② A: I don't like this shirt. It's too small.

B: Too small? You can exchange it at the mall.

③ A: Don't forget to finish your report.

B: Okay. I won't forget.

④ A: It's raining heavily.

B: Yes. Don't forget to drive slowly.

⑤ A: I'm going to walk my dog.

B: Don't forget to bring your homework.

[01~02] 다음 대화를 읽고 물음에 답하시오.

> Dad: Are you ready for your trip, Suji?
> Suji: Yes, I am, Dad. I'm ready to leave.
> Dad: Do you have your ticket with you?
> Suji: Yeah, I have it on my phone.
> Dad: Good. Don't forget to call me when you get to the train station.
> Suji: Sure.

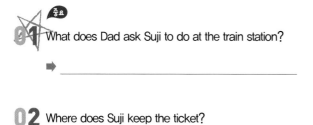
01 What does Dad ask Suji to do at the train station?

➡ _____

02 Where does Suji keep the ticket?

➡ _____

[03~05] 다음 대화를 읽고 물음에 답하시오.

> Mom: Minsu, I'm going out with your dad for a movie.
> Minsu: When will you be back, Mom?
> Mom: Around 8 o'clock. Don't forget to feed Buster.
> Minsu: Okay.
> Mom: Be sure to give him some water, too.
> Minsu: No problem.
> Mom: One more thing. Can you help Minsol with her science homework? Buster tore her homework into pieces.
> Minsu: Hmm .... Okay. I'll do that.

03 When will Minsu's mom come back?

➡ _____

04 What should Minsu do for Buster?

➡ _____

05 Why does Minsu's mom ask him to help Minsol with her homework?

➡ _____

06 다음 대화의 내용과 일치하도록 고객 상담 카드를 완성하시오.

> Mike: Customer Service. How can I help you?
> Sora: I bought a hairdryer at your store last week. I'm not happy with it.
> Mike: What is the problem?
> Sora: It doesn't work well. I mean the air isn't hot enough.
> Mike: I'm sorry. Do you want to exchange it?
> Sora: Well, can I get a refund?
> Mike: Sure. Will you please visit our store with the dryer?
> Sora: Yes, I'll drop by tomorrow afternoon.
> Mike: Don't forget to bring the receipt.
> Sora: Okay. Thanks.

<Customer Service>	
Customer Information	Name: Han Sora
Item	(A) _____
Problem	(B) _____
Request	(C) _____

07 다음 대화의 밑줄 친 우리말을 주어진 단어를 써서 영작하시오.

> A: 나는 학교 점심 메뉴가 마음에 들지 않아요. (happy) I like the meat, but there isn't enough meat for me.
> B: How about taking your own lunch box?

➡ _____

교과서
Grammar

1 사역동사

> • He **made** his sister **do** the dishes. 그는 여동생이 설거지를 하게 했다.
> • Alicia **had** me **find** her car key. Alicia는 내가 그녀의 자동차 열쇠를 찾게 했다.

■ 사역동사는 문장의 주어가 목적어에게 어떠한 행동을 하도록 시키는 동사로 make, have, let 등이 이에
  속한다.
  • Gloria **had** us **sing** together. Gloria는 우리가 함께 노래를 하게 했다.
  • Paul **made** his wife **think** carefully. Paul은 그의 아내가 주의 깊게 생각하게 했다.
  • I **let** him **use** my smartphone. 나는 그가 내 스마트폰을 사용하게 했다.

■ 사역동사는 5형식에 속하여 목적격 보어를 갖는데, 사역동사의 목적격 보어는 동사원형의 형태를 취하
  며, '～에게 …을 하게 하다'라고 해석한다.
  • The teacher **made** us **help** each other. 선생님은 우리가 서로를 돕게 하셨다.
  • Mom **made** me **cook** ramyeon for Dad. 엄마는 내가 아빠를 위해 라면을 끓이게 하셨다.
  • Mr. Park **had** me **finish** the project by five. 박 선생님은 내가 그 프로젝트를 다섯 시까지 끝내게 하셨다.
  • We **let** them **play** on the garden. 우리는 그들이 정원에서 놀게 했다.

■ 준사역동사인 help는 목적격 보어로 to부정사나 동사원형 형태를 취한다.
  • David **helped** the woman **(to) cross** the road. David는 그 여성이 길을 건너는 것을 도와주었다.

■ 목적어와 목적격 보어의 관계가 수동인 경우 have와 get은 목적격 보어로 과거분사를 쓰며, let은 목적
  격 보어로 'be+p.p.' 형태를 쓴다.
  • I **had** my car **fixed**. 나는 내 차가 수리되게 했다.
  • **Let** it **be done** as they ask. 그들이 요청하는 대로 되게 하여라.

핵심 Check

1. 다음 우리말과 일치하도록 빈칸에 알맞은 말을 쓰시오.
   (1) 그들은 우리가 최선을 다하게 만든다.
      ➡ They make us ＿＿＿＿ ＿＿＿＿ ＿＿＿＿.
   (2) 그 남자는 우리가 그의 개를 찾게 했다.
      ➡ The man made ＿＿＿＿ ＿＿＿＿ ＿＿＿＿ ＿＿＿＿.
   (3) 우리는 그 남자가 혼자 힘으로 설 수 있도록 도왔다.
      ➡ We ＿＿＿＿ the man ＿＿＿＿ on his own.

② too+형용사/부사+to부정사

> • I am **too** tired **to** work more. 나는 너무 피곤해서 더 이상 일을 할 수 없다.
>
> • This table is **too** heavy **to** move. 이 탁자는 옮기기에 너무 무겁다.

■ 'too ~ to V'는 '너무 ~해서 V할 수 없는'이라는 의미이다.

• He is **too** young **to** ride the bike. 그는 너무 어려서 자전거를 탈 수 없어.

• You spent money **too** much **to** save it. 너는 돈을 너무 많이 써서 돈을 저축할 수 없어.

■ 'too ~ to V'는 'so ~ that 주어 can't 동사원형'으로 바꾸어 쓸 수 있다.

• This soup is **too** salty **to** eat.
= This soup is **so** salty **that** I can't eat it. 이 수프는 너무 짜서 먹을 수 없다.

• Molly is **too** lazy **to** take the job.
= Molly is **so** lazy **that** she can't take the job. Molly는 너무 게을러서 그 일자리를 잡을 수 없다.

■ 반면, '충분히 ~해서 …할 수 있다'는 의미를 나타낼 때에는 '형용사/부사+enough+to부정사'를 쓰고, 이는 'so+형용사/부사+that+주어+can+동사원형'과 같다.

• The man is diligent **enough to** do the work.
= The man is **so** diligent **that** he can do the work. 그 남자는 그 일을 할 만큼 충분히 부지런하다.

• This house is warm **enough to** live in.
= This house is **so** warm **that** we can live in it. 그 집은 살기에 충분히 따뜻해.

• These roses are beautiful **enough to** attract many people.
= These roses are **so** beautiful **that** they can attract many people.
이 장미들은 많은 사람들을 끌어 모으기에 충분히 아름답다.

핵심 Check

2. 다음 우리말과 일치하도록 빈칸에 알맞은 말을 쓰시오.

(1) 그는 너무 피곤해서 나와 대화할 수 없어.

➡ He is _____ _____ _____ _____ with me.

➡ He is _____ _____ _____ _____ _____ _____ with me.

(2) 나는 너를 데리러 가기에 충분할 만큼 운전을 잘해.

➡ I drive _____ _____ _____ _____ you up.

➡ I drive _____ _____ _____ _____ _____ _____ you up.

01 다음 문장에서 어법상 <u>어색한</u> 부분을 바르게 고쳐 쓰시오.

(1) The sisters made me to buy the car.

_____ ➡ _____

(2) I had my sister fixed dinner.

_____ ➡ _____

(3) This chance is too good to missing.

_____ ➡ _____

(4) She is too sleepy that drive.

_____ ➡ _____

02 괄호 안에 주어진 단어를 어법에 맞게 바르게 배열하시오.

(1) Mom didn't let _____. (play / me / go out / and)

(2) Dad _____ my room every day. (clean / me / made)

(3) He didn't _____ home early. (go / me / let)

(4) Mr. Han is _____. (drive / tired / to / too)

(5) She was _____ she couldn't go to the party. (that / busy / so)

03 주어진 어구를 바르게 배열하여 다음 우리말을 영어로 쓰시오. 필요하다면 어형을 바꾸시오.   (1) instead of: ~ 대신에

(1) 그녀는 그녀를 대신하여 내가 그 일을 하도록 시킨다. (have / do / instead of / she / her / the job / me)

➡ _____

(2) Ms. Jones는 Mike가 그녀의 차를 운전하게 했다. (let / Ms. Jones / Mike / her / drive / car)

➡ _____

(3) 밖으로 나가기에는 너무 어둡다. (be / go / too / it / dark / to / outside)

➡ _____

(4) 그는 너무 아파서 학교에 갈 수 없었다. (to school / he / he / so sick / was / couldn't / that / go)

➡ _____

01 다음 빈칸에 들어갈 말로 가장 적절한 것은?

> Katherine had the man _____ the roof.

① fixed　② to fixing　③ fix
④ fixing　⑤ to fix

02 다음 중 빈칸에 들어갈 말로 가장 적절한 것은?

> A: Did you do well on the test?
> B: No. I was _____ on the test.

① so nervous to do well
② too nervous that I couldn't do well
③ so nervous that I can't do well
④ too nervous to do well
⑤ too nervous doing well

03 다음 중 빈칸에 들어갈 동사의 형태가 다른 하나는?

① Please let me _____ to his concert.
② Juliet had us _____ to school early in the morning.
③ Jack helped us _____ to the zoo by train.
④ Amelia made me _____ fishing with my brother.
⑤ They wanted me _____ there alone.

서답형
04 주어진 단어를 활용하여 다음 우리말을 영어로 쓰시오.

> 너는 너무 어려서 자동차를 운전할 수 없어. (to / a car)

➡ _____

05 다음 중 빈칸에 들어갈 수 <u>없는</u> 것은?

> She _____ her brother take care of the cat during the holidays.

① let　② made
③ had　④ helped
⑤ encouraged

06 다음 우리말을 영어로 바르게 옮긴 것을 <u>모두</u> 고르시오.

> Jimmy는 너무 약해서 그것을 들 수 없어.

① Jimmy is too weak to lifting it.
② Jimmy is so weak that he can't lift it.
③ Jimmy is weak enough to lift it.
④ Jimmy is too weak to lift it.
⑤ Jimmy is very weak that he couldn't lift it.

07 다음 중 빈칸에 들어갈 말이 바르게 짝지어진 것은?

> • Jamie made me _____ out loud.
> • They slept _____ there in time.

① laughing – too much going
② laughing – so much that they could go
③ laugh – too much to go
④ laugh – much enough to going
⑤ to laugh – too much to go

서답형

08 to부정사를 이용하여 다음 문장과 같은 의미의 문장을 쓰시오.

> This coffee is so hot that I can't drink it.

➡ _____

중요

09 다음 중 어법상 <u>어색한</u> 것은?

① This bag is too heavy to carry.
② They walked so fast that I couldn't catch up with them.
③ Jessica made us doing the laundry.
④ Paul helped me to do my homework.
⑤ Did she let you play with your friends last night?

10 다음 중 주어진 문장과 같은 의미의 문장은?

> Brian was too busy to answer the phone.

① Brian was too busy that he can't answer the phone.
② Brian was very busy that he couldn't answer the phone.
③ Brian was busy enough to answer the phone.
④ Brian was so busy that he couldn't answer the phone.
⑤ Brian was so busy that he can't answer the phone.

중요

11 빈칸에 들어갈 알맞은 말을 고르시오.

> Mike had me _____ his bag while he was doing his job.

① to watch   ② watched
③ watch   ④ watching
⑤ to watching

서답형

12 to부정사를 이용하여 다음 두 문장을 하나의 문장으로 쓰시오.

> Ron got up so late. So, he couldn't catch the train.

➡ _____

중요

13 다음 중 어법상 <u>어색한</u> 것은?

> It was ①<u>too late</u> ②<u>to go</u> out alone. Did your parents ③<u>let</u> you ④<u>going out</u> ⑤ with your friends?

①   ②   ③   ④   ⑤

14 to부정사를 이용하여 다음 우리말을 영어로 옮길 때 여섯 번째로 오는 단어는?

> 나는 숙제를 끝마치기에는 너무 졸렸다.

① too   ② sleepy   ③ to
④ finish   ⑤ my

중요

15 다음 중 우리말을 영어로 바르게 옮기지 <u>않은</u> 것은?

① 그녀는 내가 그녀의 가방을 옮기게 했다.
  → She made me carry her bag.
② 나는 여동생이 내 방을 청소하게 했다.
  → I had my room clean by my sister.
③ Tom은 그의 여동생이 자신을 위해 파티를 열게 했다.
  → Tom had his sister throw a party for him.
④ Jenny는 너무 아파서 교회에 갈 수 없었다.
  → Jenny was too sick to go to church.
⑤ 그들은 내가 계속 무언가를 말하게 만들었다.
  → They made me keep talking something.

서답형

16 주어진 단어를 활용하여 다음 우리말을 that절을 이용하여 영어로 쓰시오.

> Judy는 너무 빨라서 결승선에서 멈출 수 없었다. (the finish line)

➡ _____

_____

17 다음 문장과 같은 의미의 문장은?

> I am too busy to spend much time with my family.

① My family is so busy that I can't spend time with them.
② I am so busy that I can spend much time with my family.
③ I am busy enough to spend much time with my family.
④ I am so busy that I can't spend much time with my family.
⑤ I can't spend much time with my family because they are too busy.

18 다음 빈칸에 들어갈 말로 가장 적절한 것은?

> Ms. Austin _____ her son eat the vegetables.

① wants　　② has　　③ forces
④ allows　　⑤ tells

19 다음 빈칸에 들어갈 말로 가장 적절한 것은?

> The traveler was _____ walk anymore. He needed something to drink.

① too thirsty to　　② to thirsty too
③ thirsty enough to　　④ to sleep too
⑤ too tired to

서답형

20 주어진 문장과 같은 의미의 문장을 쓰시오.

> The boy is so young that he can't solve the puzzle.

➡ _____

21 다음 빈칸에 들어갈 말로 적절한 것을 모두 고르시오.

> Amelia is _____ give us advice. Let's ask her.

① too wise to
② wise enough to
③ so wise that she couldn't
④ so wise that she can
⑤ so wise that she can't

22 다음 빈칸에 들어갈 말이 바르게 짝지어진 것은?

> • Please let me _____ the answer.
> • Miss White was too afraid _____ anything.

① seeing – to saying　　② see – say
③ see – to say　　④ to see – to say
⑤ to see – saying

23 다음 중 어법상 어색한 것은?

① Exercising regularly helps me to stay healthy.
② The teacher made us study hard.
③ Kelly was too shy to talk in front of many people.
④ Amelia let me take her umbrella.
⑤ Victor is so slow to walk with us.

01 다음 문장과 같은 의미의 문장을 지시에 맞게 쓰시오.

> Kevin is really tired. So, he can't go out.

(1) to부정사를 이용하여 한 문장으로

➡ _____

(2) that절을 이용하여 한 문장으로

➡ _____

02 다음 그림에 맞게 빈칸에 알맞은 말을 쓰시오.

> Today is Lion's birthday. Fox had Elephant _____. He also had the table _____. Hippo let Squirrel _____. Owl let Monkey _____ on the stage.

03 주어진 어구를 바르게 배열하여 다음 우리말을 영어로 쓰시오.

> 몇몇 학생들은 버스를 잡기에는 너무 늦었다.
> (the bus / some students / to / too / late / catch / were)

➡ _____

04 주어진 어구를 바르게 배열하여 다음 우리말을 영어로 쓰시오. 필요하다면 어형을 바꾸시오.

> 그 의사는 내가 여섯 시간마다 그 약을 먹게 했다. (every six hours / the doctor / take / have / the medicine / me)

➡ _____

_____

05 다음 대화의 빈칸에 들어갈 알맞은 말을 쓰시오.

> A: Mom, I want to live alone.
> B: Cindy, I can't let you _____.
> You are too young _____.

06 다음 우리말을 지시에 맞게 영어로 쓰시오.

> Patrick은 충분히 키가 커서 농구를 잘할 수 있어.

(1) to부정사를 활용하여

➡ _____

_____

(2) that절을 활용하여

➡ _____

_____

07 다음 대화의 빈칸에 알맞은 말을 쓰시오.

> A: Why were you crying then?
> B: I saw a sad movie. It made me _____.

08 주어진 단어를 이용하여 다음 우리말을 영어로 쓰시오. 필요한 경우 단어 형태를 바꾸시오.

(1) 무엇이 네가 그렇게 생각하게 만들었니? (think / make)

➡ _____

(2) 어머니는 내가 자전거 사는 것을 허락하셨다. (let / buy)

➡ _____

(3) 너는 잠을 너무 많이 자서 그곳에 정시에 도착할 수 없었어. (sleep / to / get / on time)

➡ _____

09 다음 대화를 읽고 빈칸에 알맞은 말을 쓰시오.

A: What's wrong, Papa Smurf? You look sad.
B: I can't ride a roller coaster. I'm too old.
A: Oh, that's too bad.

➡ Papa Smurf is too _____ a roller coaster, so he looks sad.

10 다음 주어진 문장과 같은 의미의 문장을 지시에 맞게 쓰시오.

I was very shy, so I couldn't make friends easily.

(1) to부정사를 이용하여

➡ _____

(2) that절을 이용하여

➡ _____

11 다음 문장에서 어색한 부분을 찾아 바르게 고쳐 쓰시오.

(1) Frank usually lets his children to watch TV on weekends.

_____ ➡ _____

(2) My homeroom teacher had us left early today.

_____ ➡ _____

12 주어진 단어를 활용하여 다음 우리말을 영어로 쓰시오.

나의 삼촌은 내가 케이크 한 조각을 먹게 허락하셨다. (let / have)

➡ _____

13 주어진 단어를 활용하여 다음 대화를 영어로 쓰시오.

A: 그가 너에게 이 문제를 풀게 했니? (make)
B: 응. 하지만 이 문제는 너무 어려워서 풀 수 없어. (difficult / to)

➡ A: _____
   B: _____

14 to부정사를 이용하여 다음 문장과 같은 의미의 문장을 쓰시오.

She is so kind that she can accept your apology.

➡ _____

Reading

교과서

Do You Hear Me?

Breeze: Good evening, listeners. This is your DJ, Breeze. Today
we have a special guest, Andy Kim. He's a hip-hop artist.
Welcome, Andy.

Andy: Nice to meet you and thank you for having me.

Breeze: Okay. What do our listeners want to tell their family? This
evening we will find out by reading some letters from them.
Andy, will you start off with the letter from a teenage girl?

Andy: Sure.

Andy: Hello. I'm a 15-year-old girl from Wonju. I want to tell you
about my mom. My mom tries to do everything for me. She
cleans my room without asking me, so it's sometimes hard to
find my stuff. She also buys books and makes me study them.
I want to say to my mom, "I know you love me, but I'm not a
baby anymore. Please let me take care of things myself."

guest: 손님
find out: 알아내다
start off with: ~으로 시작하다
teenage: 십 대의
without: ~ 없이
stuff: 물건
not anymore: 더 이상 ~가 아니다
take care of: ~을 처리하다, 돌보다

확인문제

● 다음 문장이 본문의 내용과 일치하면 T, 일치하지 않으면 F를 쓰시오.

1 Breeze is a radio show host. ☐

2 Andy wants to tell something to his family. ☐

3 The girl wants to thank her mom for organizing her things instead of her. ☐

4 The girl doesn't want to be treated like a baby. ☐

5 The girl wants her mom to allow her to take care of things herself. ☐

Breeze: I felt the same way when I was in middle school.
똑같이

Andy: Many moms think their kids are too young to do things on their
너무 ~해서 V할 수 없는   by themselves: 스스로

own. I hope the girl's mom will get the message.

Breeze: So do I. Andy, will you please read the next letter?
I hope so, too.

Andy: Hi. I'm a father of two children. One is a high school girl, and

the other is a middle school boy. They're too busy to talk with
나머지 다른 하나를 가리키는 대명사   They are so busy that they can't talk with me

me. When I get home from work, they just say hi and go back
단지   인사를 하다

to their rooms. Sometimes I ask them about their school life,

but they only give short answers. We don't talk much at the
식탁에서

table, either. I want to say to my kids, "I love you so much, and
부정에 대한 동의 (~도 역시)

I want to spend more time with you."

Breeze: Andy, did you talk with your parents often when you were
부사절 접속사

younger?

Andy: Not really. I loved them very much, but I thought they were too
they were so old that they couldn't understand me.

old to understand me.

Breeze: I see. Does anyone have suggestions for the "sad" dad? Text
understand

your idea to us.
=us your idea

📎 **확인문제**

● 다음 문장이 본문의 내용과 일치하면 T, 일치하지 않으면 F를 쓰시오.

1 A number of moms thinks that their kids are old enough to do things by themselves. ☐

2 Breeze wants the girl's mom to get the message. ☐

3 Breeze doesn't understand the girl's feelings well. ☐

4 The father wants their children to study harder. ☐

5 Andy had a lot of conversation with his parents when he was younger. ☐

6 Listeners can text their suggestions for the sad father to the radio program. ☐

---

on one's own: 혼자 힘으로

message: 전갈, 메시지

either: (부정문에서) ~도 역시

suggestion: 제안, 의견

text: 문자 메시지를 보내다

● 우리말을 참고하여 빈칸에 알맞은 말을 쓰시오.

1 Breeze: _____ _____, listeners. _____ _____ your DJ, Breeze.

2 Today we have _____ _____ _____, Andy Kim.

3 He's a hip-hop artist. _____, Andy.

4 Andy: Nice _____ _____ _____ and thank you _____ _____ _____.

5 Breeze: Okay. What do our listeners _____ _____ _____ their family?

6 This evening we will find out _____ _____ _____ _____ from them.

7 Andy, will you _____ _____ _____ the letter _____ a teenage girl?

8 Andy: _____.

9 Andy: Hello. I'm a 15-year-old girl _____ Wonju.

10 I want _____ _____ _____ about my mom.

11 My mom _____ _____ _____ everything for me.

12 She cleans my room _____ _____ me, so it's sometimes _____ _____ _____ my stuff.

13 She also _____ books and makes _____ _____ _____.

14 I want _____ _____ to my mom, "I know you love me, but I'm not a baby _____. Please _____ _____ _____ _____ _____ things myself."

---

1 Breeze: 안녕하세요, 청취자 여러분. 저는 여러분의 디제이, Breeze입니다.

2 오늘은 특별한 손님, Andy Kim 씨를 모셨습니다.

3 그는 힙합 아티스트이시죠. 환영합니다, Andy.

4 Andy: 반갑습니다, 그리고 초대해 주셔서 고맙습니다.

5 Breeze: 네. 우리 청취자분들은 가족에게 무슨 말을 하고 싶어 하실까요?

6 오늘 저녁에 우리는 청취자분들로부터 온 몇몇 편지들을 읽으며 알아보려 합니다.

7 Andy, 십 대 소녀에게서 온 편지로 시작해 주시겠어요?

8 Andy: 알겠습니다.

9 Andy: 안녕하세요. 저는 원주에 사는 15세 소녀입니다.

10 저는 저의 엄마에 관해 이야기하고 싶습니다.

11 엄마는 저를 위해 모든 것을 해 주려고 하십니다.

12 엄마는 제게 물어보지도 않고 방을 청소해 주시고, 그래서 가끔은 제 물건을 찾기가 힘들 때도 있습니다.

13 또 엄마는 책을 사 와서는 저에게 그것들을 공부하라고 시키세요.

14 저는 엄마께 "엄마가 저를 사랑하는 것은 알지만 전 더 이상 아기가 아니에요. 제 일을 스스로 할 수 있게 해 주세요."라고 말씀드리고 싶습니다.

15 Breeze: I felt _____ _____ _____ when I was in middle school.

16 Andy: Many moms think their kids are _____ _____ _____ _____ things on their own.

17 I hope the girl's mom will _____ _____ _____.

18 Breeze: So _____ _____. Andy, will you please read the next letter?

19 Andy: Hi. I'm a father _____ _____ _____.

20 _____ is a high school girl, and _____ _____ is a middle school boy.

21 They're _____ _____ _____ _____ with me.

22 When I _____ home from work, they just say hi and _____ _____ _____ their rooms.

23 Sometimes I ask _____ about their school life, but they only _____ _____ _____.

24 We _____ _____ _____ at the table, _____.

25 I want to say to my kids, "I love you so much, and I want _____ _____ _____ _____ with you."

26 Breeze: Andy, did you talk with your parents _____ when you were _____?

27 Andy: Not really. I loved _____ very much, but I thought they were _____ _____ _____ _____ me.

28 Breeze: I see. Does anyone have _____ for the "sad" dad? _____ _____ _____ to us.

15 Breeze: 저도 중학교 때 똑같은 기분을 느꼈습니다.

16 Andy: 많은 어머님들이 자녀들이 혼자 힘으로 무언가를 하기에는 너무 어리다고 생각합니다.

17 소녀의 어머님께서 메시지를 들으시길 바랍니다.

18 Breeze: 동감입니다. Andy, 다음 편지를 읽어 주시겠어요?

19 Andy: 안녕하세요. 저는 두 아이의 아버지입니다.

20 한 명은 고등학생인 여자아이이고, 나머지 한 명은 중학생인 남자아이입니다.

21 아이들은 저와 대화를 하기에는 너무 바쁩니다.

22 제가 일을 하고 집에 돌아오면, 아이들은 그저 인사만 하고 자신의 방으로 돌아갑니다.

23 가끔씩 저는 아이들에게 학교생활에 관해 묻기도 하지만, 아이들은 그냥 짧막한 대답만 합니다.

24 우리는 식사 자리에서조차 대화를 많이 하지 않습니다.

25 저는 아이들에게 "너희들을 무척 사랑한단다, 그리고 너희들과 더 많은 시간을 보내고 싶단다."라고 말하고 싶습니다.

26 Breeze: Andy, 어렸을 때 부모님과 자주 대화를 했나요?

27 Andy: 사실 그렇지는 않습니다. 저는 부모님을 무척 사랑하지만, 부모님이 저를 이해해 주시기에는 너무 나이가 들었다고 생각했습니다.

28 Breeze: 그렇군요. '슬픈' 아빠에게 해 드릴 제안이 있으신 분 계신가요? 여러분의 생각을 저희에게 문자로 보내 주세요.

● 우리말을 참고하여 본문을 영작하시오.

1 Breeze: 안녕하세요, 청취자 여러분. 저는 여러분의 디제이, Breeze입니다.

➡ _____

2 오늘은 특별한 손님, Andy Kim 씨를 모셨습니다.

➡ _____

3 그는 힙합 아티스트이시죠. 환영합니다, Andy.

➡ _____

4 Andy: 반갑습니다, 그리고 초대해 주셔서 고맙습니다.

➡ _____

5 Breeze: 네. 우리 청취자분들은 가족에게 무슨 말을 하고 싶어 하실까요?

➡ _____

6 오늘 저녁에 우리는 청취자분들로부터 온 몇몇 편지들을 읽으며 알아보려 합니다.

➡ _____

7 Andy, 십 대 소녀에게서 온 편지로 시작해 주시겠어요?

➡ _____

8 Andy: 알겠습니다.

➡ _____

9 Andy: 안녕하세요. 저는 원주에 사는 15세 소녀입니다.

➡ _____

10 저는 저의 엄마에 관해 이야기하고 싶습니다.

➡ _____

11 엄마는 저를 위해 모든 것을 해 주려고 하십니다.

➡ _____

12 엄마는 제게 물어보지도 않고 방을 청소해 주시고, 그래서 가끔은 제 물건을 찾기가 힘들 때도 있습니다.

➡ _____

13 또 엄마는 책을 사 와서는 저에게 그것들을 공부하라고 시키세요.

➡ _____

14 저는 엄마께 "엄마가 저를 사랑하는 것은 알지만 전 더 이상 아기가 아니에요. 제 일을 스스로 할 수 있게 해 주세요."라고 말씀드리고 싶습니다.

➡ _____

_____

15 Breeze: 저도 중학교 때 똑같은 기분을 느꼈습니다.

➡ _____

16 Andy: 많은 어머님들이 자녀들이 혼자 힘으로 무언가를 하기 에는 너무 어리다고 생각합니다.

➡ _____

17 소녀의 어머님께서 메시지를 들으시길 바랍니다.

➡ _____

18 Breeze: 동감입니다. Andy, 다음 편지를 읽어 주시겠어요?

➡ _____

19 Andy: 안녕하세요. 저는 두 아이의 아버지입니다.

➡ _____

20 한 명은 고등학생인 여자아이이고, 나머지 한 명은 중학생인 남자아이입니다.

➡ _____

21 아이들은 저와 대화를 하기에는 너무 바쁩니다.

➡ _____

22 제가 일을 하고 집에 돌아오면, 아이들은 그저 인사만 하고 자신의 방으로 돌아갑니다.

➡ _____

23 가끔씩 저는 아이들에게 학교생활에 관해 묻기도 하지만, 아이들은 그냥 짤막한 대답만 합니다.

➡ _____

24 우리는 식사 자리에서조차 대화를 많이 하지 않습니다.

➡ _____

25 저는 아이들에게 "너희들을 무척 사랑한단다, 그리고 너희들과 더 많은 시간을 보내고 싶단다." 라고 말하고 싶습니다.

➡ _____

26 Breeze: Andy, 어렸을 때 부모님과 자주 대화를 했나요?

➡ _____

27 Andy: 사실 그렇지는 않습니다. 저는 부모님을 무척 사랑하지만, 부모님이 저를 이해해 주시기에는 너무 나이가 들었다고 생각했습니다.

➡ _____

28 Breeze: 그렇군요. '슬픈' 아빠에게 해 드릴 제안이 있으신 분 계신가요? 여러분의 생각을 저희에게 문자로 보내 주세요.

➡ _____

[01~03] 다음 글을 읽고 물음에 답하시오.

Breeze: Good evening, listeners. This is your DJ, Breeze. Today we have a special guest, Andy Kim. He's a hip-hop artist. Welcome, Andy.

Andy: Nice to meet you and thank you for having me.

Breeze: Okay. What do our listeners want to tell their family? This evening we will find out by reading some letters from them. Andy, will you start off with the letter from a teenage girl?

Andy: Sure.

01 다음 중 위 글의 내용과 일치하지 <u>않는</u> 것은?

① 이 방송은 저녁 방송이다.
② 청취자들과 함께하는 방송이다.
③ Andy는 특별 손님이다.
④ DJ가 직접 사연을 읽어 준다.
⑤ 청취자들은 이 프로그램을 통해 가족에게 하고 싶은 말을 한다.

02 다음 중 위 글에 이어질 내용으로 가장 적절한 것은?

① Talking about family problems with Breeze
② Reading a letter from a listener
③ Singing one of his songs
④ Calling one of the listeners
⑤ Writing a letter to their listeners to make them happy

서답형

03 다음과 같이 풀이되는 말을 위 글에서 찾아 쓰시오.

someone who is invited to an event

➡ _____

[04~07] 다음 글을 읽고 물음에 답하시오.

Andy: Hello. ⓐI'm a 15-year-old girl from Wonju. I want to tell you about my mom. My mom tries to do everything for me. She cleans my room without asking me, so it's sometimes hard to find my stuff. She also buys books and makes me study them. I want to say to my mom, "I know you love me, but I'm not a baby anymore. Please let me take care of things myself."

Breeze: I felt ⓑthe same way when I was in middle school.

Andy: Many moms think their kids are too young to do things ⓒon their own. I hope the girl's mom will get the message.

04 다음 중 밑줄 친 ⓐ에 관하여 답할 수 <u>없는</u> 것은?

① Where does she live?
② Who does the girl want to talk about?
③ How often does her mother clean her room?
④ Why is it hard for her to find her stuff?
⑤ What does her mom buy for her?

05 밑줄 친 ⓑ의 의미로 가장 적절한 것은?

① 엄마에 대한 사랑
② 엄마가 방 청소를 해 주는 것
③ 엄마와 사이가 좋지 않은 것
④ 엄마가 자신을 아기 취급을 하는 것
⑤ 엄마와 대화가 없는 것

서답형

06 What does the girl's mom try to do for her? Answer in English with a full sentence.

➡ _____

07 다음 중 밑줄 친 ⓒ를 대신하여 쓸 수 있는 것은?

① on their minds
② by themselves
③ with some help
④ at their surprise
⑤ in that way

[08~12] 다음 글을 읽고 물음에 답하시오.

> **Breeze:** So do I. Andy, will you please read the next letter?
>
> **Andy:** Hi. I'm a father of two children. One is a high school girl, and __(A)__ is a middle school boy. They're too busy to talk with me. When I get home __(B)__ work, they just say hi and go back to their rooms. Sometimes I ask them about their school life, but they only give short answers. We don't talk much at the table, either. I want to say to my kids, "I love you so much, and I want to spend more time with you."
>
> **Breeze:** Andy, did you talk with your parents often when you were younger?
>
> **Andy:** Not really. I loved them very much, but I thought they were too old to understand me.
>
> **Breeze:** I (C)see. Does anyone have suggestions for the "sad" dad? Text your idea to us.

08 다음 중 빈칸 (A)에 들어갈 말로 가장 적절한 것은?

① the others
② another
③ other
④ the other
⑤ others

중요

09 다음 중 빈칸 (B)에 들어갈 말과 같은 말이 들어가는 것은?

① Who took care _____ your plants while you were away?
② My father graduated _____ Harvard University.
③ I want to get out _____ this room.
④ The box was full _____ interesting things.
⑤ We are really looking forward _____ meeting you again.

서답형

10 Why don't the children talk with their father much? Answer in English with a full sentence. Use the word 'Because.'

➡ _____

11 다음 중 밑줄 친 (C)를 대신하여 쓸 수 있는 것은?

① am sorry
② don't know
③ understand
④ watch
⑤ imagine

중요

12 다음 중 위 글의 내용과 일치하지 않는 것은?

① Andy reads the next letter.
② Listeners can text their ideas about the sad dad.
③ Andy used to talk with his parents a lot.
④ The man who wrote the letter has two children.
⑤ The father wants to spend more time with his children.

[13~18] 다음 글을 읽고 물음에 답하시오.

Breeze: Good evening, listeners. This is your DJ, Breeze. Today we have a special guest, Andy Kim. He's a hip-hop artist. Welcome, Andy.

Andy: Nice to meet you and thank you _____(A)_____.

Breeze: Okay. What do our listeners want to tell their family? This evening we will find out by reading some letters from (B)them. Andy, will you start off with the letter from a teenage girl?

Andy: Sure.

Andy: Hello. I'm a 15-year-old girl from Wonju. I want to tell you about my mom. My mom tries to do everything for me. She cleans my room without asking me, so it's sometimes hard to find my stuff. She also buys books and makes me study them. I want to say to my mom, "I know you love me, but I'm not a baby anymore. Please let me take care of things (C)myself."

13 문맥상 빈칸 (A)에 들어갈 말로 가장 적절한 것은?

① to let me read this letter
② to seeing me coming here
③ for having me
④ for watching me read it
⑤ for reading it to me

서답형
14 밑줄 친 (B)가 가리키는 것을 위 글에서 찾아 쓰시오.

➡ _____

서답형
15 What does the girl try to talk about in the letter? Answer in English with a full sentence.

➡ _____

16 다음 중 위 글을 읽고 알 수 없는 것은?

① the name of the radio DJ
② the subject of the broadcast
③ what the guest does for a living
④ the name of the guest
⑤ the name of the person who sent a letter

17 다음 중 밑줄 친 (C)와 쓰임이 같은 것은?

① I couldn't make myself understood.
② Did you enjoy yourself?
③ Stella looked at herself through the mirror.
④ Did you really make the cookies yourself?
⑤ Tom kept talking about himself.

18 다음 중 위 글의 내용과 일치하는 것은?

① The radio host is Andy.
② There are a couple of guests.
③ Andy wants the DJ to read a letter.
④ Listeners send letters to the program.
⑤ The girl says in the letter that she doesn't want to study.

[19~23] 다음 글을 읽고 물음에 답하시오.

Breeze: I felt the same way when I was in middle school.

Andy: Many moms think their kids are too young to do things ①on their own. I hope the girl's mom will get the message.

Breeze: (A)So do I. Andy, will you please read the next letter?

Andy: Hi. I'm a father of two children. One is a high school girl, and the other is a middle school boy. They're ②<u>too busy</u> to talk with me. When I get home from work, they just say hi and go back to their rooms. Sometimes I ③<u>ask</u> them about their school life, but they only give short answers. We ④<u>talk</u> much at the table, either. I want to say to my kids, "I love you so much, and I want to spend more time with you."

Breeze: Andy, did you talk with your parents often when you were younger?

Andy: ⑤<u>Not really.</u> I loved them very much, but I thought they were too old to understand me.

Breeze: I see. Does anyone have suggestions for the "sad" dad? Text your idea to us.

19 밑줄 친 (A)의 의미로 가장 적절한 것은?

① I want you to understand that, too.

② I hope to get the message, too.

③ I am too young to do anything alone, either.

④ I felt the same way when I was young, too.

⑤ I hope that she gets the message, too.

서답형

20 How many children does the father have? Answer in English with a full sentence.

➡ _____

21 다음 중 사연 신청자가 집에서 느끼는 감정으로 가장 적절한 것은?

① happy   ② satisfied

③ lonely   ④ excited

⑤ nervous

22 다음 중 위 글을 읽고 답할 수 있는 것은?

① Who sent the first letter?

② How many family members does the father have?

③ Why are the father's children busy?

④ What does the father want to say to their children?

⑤ How many listeners will text their idea?

 ①~⑤ 중 글의 흐름상 어색한 것은?

①   ②   ③   ④   ⑤

[24~25] 다음 글을 읽고 물음에 답하시오.

This is a letter from a father who wants to share his experience with the "sad" father.

My kids and I did not talk much. There was a wall between us. I wanted to break it ___(A)___ . I tried to spend more time with my children on weekends. We played computer games, rode bikes, and went shopping together. In this way, I had more chances to talk with them. I came to know more about them.

24 다음 중 빈칸 (A)에 들어갈 말로 가장 적절한 것은?

① into   ② down   ③ up

④ away   ⑤ off

서답형

25 What did the father do to have more chances to talk with his children? Answer in English and use the words below.

| (and / with / on weekends) |

➡ _____

_____

[01~03] 다음 글을 읽고 물음에 답하시오.

> Breeze: Good evening, listeners. This is your DJ, Breeze. Today we have a special guest, Andy Kim. He's a hip-hop artist. Welcome, Andy.
>
> Andy: Nice to meet you and thank you for having me.
>
> Breeze: Okay. What do our listeners want to tell their family? This evening we will find out by reading some letters from them. Andy, will you start off with the letter from a teenage girl?
>
> Andy: Sure.

01 What does Andy Kim do? Answer in English with a full sentence.

➡ _____

02 How will Breeze find out what listeners want to tell their family? Answer in English with a full sentence.

➡ _____

03 위 글의 내용에 맞게 빈칸에 알맞은 말을 쓰시오.

> On the radio show, Breeze introduces a
> _____ _____, _____ _____.
> She wants him _____ _____ a
> letter from one of the listeners. He will
> _____ _____ with the letter sent by
> a _____ _____.

[04~06] 다음 글을 읽고 물음에 답하시오.

> Andy: Hello. I'm a 15-year-old girl from Wonju. I want to tell you about my mom. My mom tries to do everything for me. She cleans my room without asking me, so it's sometimes hard to find my stuff. She also buys books and makes me study them. I want to say to my mom, "I know you love me, but I'm not a baby anymore. (A)제 일을 스스로 할 수 있게 해 주세요."
>
> Breeze: I felt the same way when I was in middle school.

04 주어진 단어를 바르게 배열하여 밑줄 친 우리말 (A)를 영어로 쓰시오. (please로 시작할 것)

> (things / me / myself / let / of / take / please / care)

➡ _____

05 What problem does the girl have when her mother cleans her room? Answer in English with a full sentence.

➡ _____

06 According to the letter, what does the girl's mom try to do? Answer in English with a full sentence. Use the word 'daughter.'

➡ _____

[07~10] 다음 글을 읽고 물음에 답하시오.

> Andy: Many moms think their kids are too young to do things on their own. I hope the girl's mom will get the message.

Breeze: So do I. Andy, will you please read the next letter?

Andy: Hi. I'm a father of two children. One is a high school girl, and the other is a middle school boy. (A)They're too busy to talk with me. When I get home from work, they just say hi and go back to their rooms. Sometimes I ask them about their school life, but they only give short answers. We don't talk much at the table, either. I want to say to my kids, "I love you so much, and I want to spend more time with you."

Breeze: Andy, did you talk with your parents often when you were younger?

Andy: Not really. I loved them very much, but I thought they were too old to understand me.

Breeze: I see. Does anyone have suggestions for the "sad" dad? Text your idea to us.

07 주어진 단어를 이용하여 밑줄 친 (A)를 대신하여 쓸 수 있는 문장을 쓰시오.

(that)

➡ _____

08 위 글의 내용에 맞게 빈칸에 알맞은 말을 쓰시오.

The person who wrote the letter is a dad of _____ _____. The problem he has is that his kids don't have time to _____ _____ _____. He wishes to _____ _____ _____ with his kids.

09 According to the conversation, what do many moms think about their kids? Use the phrase below.

(many of them)

➡ _____
_____

10 Write the reason why Andy didn't talk with his parents often when he was young. Use the phrase 'It's because.'

➡ _____
_____

[11~12] 다음 글을 읽고 물음에 답하시오.

This is a letter from a father who wants to share his experience with the "sad" father.

My kids and I did not talk much. There was a wall between us. I wanted to break (A)it down. I tried to spend more time with my children on weekends. We played computer games, rode bikes, and went shopping together. In this way, (B)저는 아이들과 이야기할 기회를 더 많이 가졌습니다. I came to know more about them.

11 밑줄 친 (A)가 가리키는 것을 위 글에서 찾아 쓰시오.

➡ _____

12 주어진 단어를 활용하여 밑줄 친 우리말 (B)를 8 단어로 이루어진 한 문장의 영어로 쓰시오.

(chance)

➡ _____

구석구석

My Writing Portfolio

Hello, I am a 15-year-old girl from Busan. I want to say to my brother Jaeho,
to부정사를 목적어로 취하는 동사

"Sorry." I told Mom his secret last Friday. Mom got so angry, so he was in
4형식 동사(tell+간접목적어+직접목적어)   *= became*

trouble. I was too scared to say sorry to him at that time. I promise I will never
I was so scared that I couldn't say sorry to him at that time.

tell his secrets again.

구문해설 • be in trouble: 곤경에 처하다 • scared: 무서운 • promise: ~을 약속하다

안녕하세요. 저는 부산에 살고 있는 15살 소녀예요. 저는 저의 오빠 재호에게 "미안해."라고 말하고 싶어요. 저는 지난주에 오빠의 비밀을 엄마께 말씀드렸어요. 엄마는 정말 화가 나셨고, 오빠는 곤경에 처했죠. 그 당시에 저는 오빠에게 미안하다고 말하기엔 너무 무서웠어요. 오빠의 비밀을 다시는 이야기하지 않겠다고 약속할게요.

Have Fun Together

• I have nothing to do. I have no friends.
to부정사의 형용사적 용법

• Everything is too small. I don't like this place very much.

• Heungbu is richer than me now. I'm not happy with it.
비교급+than   *~이 마음에 들지 않는다*

• Mom made us leave home. We're not happy with it.
사역동사+목적어+동사원형: (목적어)가 ~하게 하다

• This soup smells good, but I can't eat it.
감각동사+형용사

구문해설 • place: 곳, 장소 • leave: 떠나다 • smell: 냄새가 나다

• 나는 할 일이 없어. 나는 친구가 없어.

• 모든 것이 너무 작아. 나는 이곳이 별로 마음에 안 들어.

• 이제 흥부가 나보다 더 부자야. 나는 그것이 마음에 안 들어.

• 엄마는 우리가 집을 떠나게 하셨어. 우리는 그것이 마음이 안 들어.

• 이 수프는 냄새가 좋은데, 나는 그것을 먹을 수 없어.

Wrap Up – Reading Read and answer 3

This is a letter from a father who wants to share his experience with the "sad"
주격 관계대명사

father.

My kids and I did not talk much. There was a wall between us. I wanted to

break it down. I tried to spend more time with my children on weekends. We
= the wall   *= ~하려고 노력했다*

played computer games, rode bikes, and went shopping together. In this way, I

had more chances to talk with them. I came to know more about them.
= opportunities   *= my children*   *come to+동사원형: ~하게 되다*   *= my children*

구문해설 • wall: 벽 • share: 공유하다, 나누다 • break down: 허물다, 부수다

이것은 '슬픈' 아버지와 경험을 공유하고 싶은 한 아버지로부터 온 편지입니다.

제 아이들과 저는 대화를 많이 하지 않았습니다. 우리 사이에는 벽이 있었어요. 저는 그것을 허물고 싶었습니다. 저는 주말마다 아이들과 더 많은 시간을 보내려고 노력했어요. 우리는 함께 컴퓨터 게임을 했고, 자전거를 탔고, 쇼핑을 갔습니다. 이 방법으로 저는 아이들과 이야기할 기회를 더 많이 가졌습니다. 저는 그들을 더 잘 알게 되었죠.

Words & Expressions

01 다음 짝지어진 단어의 관계가 같도록 빈칸에 알맞은 말을 쓰시오.

> happy : unhappy = true : _____

02 다음 중 밑줄 친 부분의 뜻풀이가 바르지 <u>않은</u> 것은?

① I'm <u>scared</u> of spiders. 무서워하는

② Do you have any <u>suggestions</u>? 제안들

③ My sister was so upset because the dog <u>tore</u> up her new shoes. 찢었다

④ This magazine is for <u>teenage</u> boys and girls. 십대의

⑤ I think I can't live <u>without</u> a car. ~와 함께

03 다음 우리말에 맞게 빈칸에 알맞은 말을 쓰시오.

(1) 네 도시락을 반드시 가져와라.
➡ Be _____ to bring your lunch box.

(2) 상점은 내게 다른 가방으로 교환해 주었다.
➡ The store gave me an _____ for another bag.

(3) 영수증을 안전한 장소에 보관해라.
➡ Keep the _____ in a safe place.

(4) Emma는 내게 매우 소중하다.
➡ Emma is _____ _____ _____ to me.

(5) 당신의 세 개의 정답이 잘못되었다.
➡ Three of your answers were _____.

(6) 그의 옷은 낡고 찢기었다.
➡ His clothes were old and _____.

04 다음 영영풀이가 가리키는 것을 고르시오.

> to give something to somebody and at the same time receive the same type of thing from them

① catch
② tear
③ vote
④ promise
⑤ exchange

05 다음 문장에 공통으로 들어갈 말을 고르시오.

> • Jane suffered from her family _____s.
> • When I was in _____, I usually talk to my parents.
> • I have _____ sleeping at night.

① wall
② bowl
③ trouble
④ stuff
⑤ training

06 다음 우리말을 주어진 단어를 이용하여 영작하시오.

(1) 그녀는 절대 거짓말을 하지 않는다. (tell)
➡ _____

(2) Tom은 규칙을 위반했기 때문에 곤경에 처했다. (trouble, because)
➡ _____

(3) Jimmy는 더 이상 그 팀의 일원이 아니었다. (anymore)
➡ _____

Conversation

[07~09] 다음 대화를 읽고 물음에 답하시오.

Minsol: I'm not happy ⓐwith Buster.

Dad: _____ (A)

Minsol: He ⓑteared my homework into pieces again

Dad: Puppies often ⓒdo that.

Minsol: This is not the first time. Sometimes I find my socks in the dog house.

Dad: Please be kind to him. He's just five months ⓓold.

Minsol: You're too nice to him! He needs some training.

Dad: Okay. Let's start ⓔtraining in a few weeks.

07 위 대화의 빈칸 (A)에 들어갈 말로 어색한 것은?

① What's the matter?

② What's wrong?

③ What's the problem?

④ Is anything wrong?

⑤ What do you do?

08 위 대화에서 밑줄 친 ⓐ~ⓔ 중 어법상 어색한 것을 찾아 바르게 고치시오.

➡ _____ ➡ _____

09 위 대화를 읽고 대답할 수 없는 것은?

① How does Minsol feel about Buster?

② Why isn't Minsol happy with Buster?

③ How many times has Buster torn Minsol's homework?

④ What are Dad and Minsol going to do with Buster?

⑤ Who brought Minsol's socks to the dog house?

10 다음 대화가 자연스럽게 이어지도록 순서대로 배열하시오.

Mike: Customer Service. How can I help you?

Sora: I bought a hairdryer at your store last week. I'm not happy with it.

Mike: What is the problem?

(A) Well, can I get a refund?

(B) Yes, I'll drop by tomorrow afternoon.

(C) I'm sorry. Do you want to exchange it?

(D) Sure. Will you please visit our store with the dryer?

(E) It doesn't work well. I mean the air isn't hot enough.

➡ _____

[11~13] 다음 대화를 읽고 물음에 답하시오.

Mom: Minsu, I'm ⓐgoing out with your dad for a movie.

Minsu: When will you be back, Mom?

Mom: ⓑAround 8 o'clock. Don't forget ⓒfeeding Buster.

Minsu: Okay.

Mom: Be sure ⓓto give him some water, too.

Minsu: No problem.

Mom: One more thing. Can you help Minsol with her science homework? Buster tore her homework ⓔinto pieces.

Minsu: Hmm .... Okay. I'll do that.

11 위 대화의 밑줄 친 ⓐ~ⓔ 중 어색한 것을 찾아 바르게 고치시오.

_____ ➡ _____

12 위 대화에서 다음 영영풀이가 가리키는 말을 찾아 쓰시오.

to give food to a person or an animal

➡ _____

13 위 대화의 내용과 일치하지 <u>않는</u> 것은?

① 엄마와 아빠는 영화 보러 나갈 것이다.

② 엄마와 아빠는 8시에 영화를 볼 것이다.

③ 엄마는 민수에게 Buster에게 밥을 줄 것을 부탁하였다.

④ 엄마는 민수에게 민솔의 과학 숙제를 도와줄 것을 요청하였다.

⑤ Buster가 민솔의 과학 숙제를 찢었다.

[14~15] 다음 대화를 읽고 물음에 답하시오.

Amy: I'm not very happy with my brother.

Brian: What's the problem?

Amy: He uses the bathroom for too long in the morning.

Brian: I know how you feel.

Amy: What can I do?

Brian: Well, you can get up earlier and use the bathroom first.

Amy: Okay, I'll give it a try.

14 What's the matter with Amy?

➡ _____

_____

15 What is Brian's suggestion?

➡ _____

_____

Grammar

16 다음 중 어법상 <u>어색한</u> 것은?

① They felt so happy that they could help everyone.

② Does he let you play with your friends?

③ Mrs. James has us read a book carefully.

④ We are too hungry to waiting in line.

⑤ Don't make me sing in front of many people.

17 다음 중 빈칸에 들어갈 말로 가장 적절한 것은?

My uncle made me _____ the dog.

① walking ② to walk ③ walk

④ to walking ⑤ walked

18 다음 주어진 문장과 같은 의미의 문장은?

I allowed my younger sister to use my computer.

① I wanted my younger sister to use my computer.

② I told my younger sister to use my computer.

③ I made my younger sister to use my computer.

④ I let my younger sister use my computer.

⑤ I didn't know my younger sister used my computer.

19 다음 빈칸에 들어갈 말로 가장 적절한 것은?

• You always make me _____ good.

• I am too busy _____ care of plants.

① to feel – taking ② to feel – to take

③ feel – take ④ feel – to take

⑤ feeling – to take

20 다음 우리말을 영어로 바르게 옮긴 것은?

그 선생님은 우리가 일기를 쓰게 하셨다.

① The teacher wanted us keep a diary.

② The teacher promised us to keep a diary.

③ The teacher had us keep a diary.

④ The teacher thought we kept a diary.

⑤ The teacher told us to keep a diary.

21 that절을 이용하여 다음 우리말을 영어로 옮길 때 네 번째와 일곱 번째로 오는 단어는?

> 그 개는 공원까지 달려가기에는 너무 약했다.

① dog – weak ② so – that
③ so – he ④ weak – couldn't
⑤ weak – run

22 다음 중 빈칸에 들어갈 말로 적절하지 <u>않은</u> 것은?

> The woman _____ Kathy to wear a dress.

① wanted ② told ③ helped
④ asked ⑤ made

23 다음 중 어법상 바르지 <u>않은</u> 것은?

> Mr. Kim ①had me ②answer the question. But I was ③too upset ④that I ⑤couldn't answer the question.

①　　②　　③　　④　　⑤

24 다음 그림에 맞게 빈칸에 알맞은 말을 쓰시오.

Catch the smurfs.

Gargamel

I'm too tired.

Azrael

> Gargamel tells Azrael to catch the smurfs, but Azrael is _____ _____ _____ them.

25 주어진 어구를 바르게 배열하여 다음 우리말을 영어로 쓰시오. 필요하다면 단어의 형태를 바꾸시오.

> 그 버스 운전사는 내가 버스에서 내리게 하였다.
> (make / the bus driver / me / the bus / get off)

➡ _____

26 주어진 어구를 바르게 배열하여 다음 우리말을 영어로 쓰시오.

> 보건 선생님은 내가 양호실에서 쉬도록 허락하셨다.
> (the nurse's office / the nurse teacher / in / me / rest / let)

➡ _____

Reading

[27~29] 다음 글을 읽고 물음에 답하시오.

> **Breeze:** Good evening, listeners. This is your DJ, Breeze. Today we have a special guest, Andy Kim. He's a hip-hop artist. Welcome, Andy.
>
> **Andy:** Nice to meet you and thank you for (A) <u>having me</u>.
>
> **Breeze:** Okay. What do our listeners want to tell their family? This evening we will find out ____ⓐ____ reading some letters from them. Andy, will you start off with the letter from a teenage girl?
>
> **Andy:** Sure.

27 다음 중 빈칸 ⓐ에 들어갈 말로 가장 적절한 것은?

① on ② in ③ by ④ at ⑤ to

28 다음 중 밑줄 친 (A)를 대신할 수 있는 말로 가장 적절한 것은?

① eating lunch with me
② inviting me
③ having a good time with me
④ bringing some letters to me
⑤ talking about me

29 다음 중 위 글의 내용과 일치하는 것은?

① Andy Kim is the program host.
② You can hear the show in the morning.
③ Andy Kim is an artist who draws paintings.
④ Andy wrote some letters for the show.
⑤ There are two people at the show.

[30~33] 다음 글을 읽고 물음에 답하시오.

Andy: Hello. I'm a 15-year-old girl from Wonju. I want to tell you about my mom. My mom tries to do ①everything for me. She cleans my room ②with asking me, so it's sometimes hard (A)to find my stuff. She also buys books and makes me ⓐ＿＿ them. I want to say to my mom, "I know you ③love me, but I'm not a baby anymore. Please let ④me take care of things ⑤myself."
Breeze: I felt the same way when I was in middle school.
Andy: Many moms think their kids are too young to do things on their own. I hope the girl's mom will get the message.

30 빈칸 ⓐ에 study를 어법에 맞게 쓰시오.

➡ ＿＿＿＿＿＿＿＿＿＿＿＿＿＿＿

31 ①～⑤ 중 글의 흐름상 어색한 것은?

① ② ③ ④ ⑤

32 다음 중 밑줄 친 (A)와 그 쓰임이 같은 것은?

① To achieve the goal, I really tried hard.
② I went to the market to buy some fruit.
③ She has something to tell you.
④ It was not easy to forgive you.
⑤ I was happy to meet them again.

33 다음 빈칸에 들어갈 말이 위 글의 내용에 맞게 바르게 짝지어진 것은?

The girl is ＿＿＿＿ with her mother who treats her like a ＿＿＿＿.

① satisfied – grown-up
② happy – teenager
③ sad – stranger
④ unhappy – baby
⑤ thankful – lady

34 자연스러운 글이 되도록 [A]~[C]를 바르게 배열하시오.

My kids and I did not talk much. There was a wall between us.
[A] We played computer games, rode bikes, and went shopping together.
[B] I wanted to break it down. I tried to spend more time with my children on weekends.
[C] In this way, I had more chances to talk with them. I came to know more about them.

➡ ＿＿＿＿＿＿＿＿＿＿＿＿＿＿＿

출제율 85%

01 다음 영영풀이가 가리키는 것을 고르시오.

> a small machine used for drying your hair by blowing hot air over it

① trash　　　　② wall
③ receipt　　　④ hairdryer
⑤ secret

출제율 95%

02 다음 대화가 자연스럽게 이어지도록 순서대로 배열하시오.

> Minsol: I'm not happy with Buster.
> Dad: What's wrong?
> Minsol: He tore my homework into pieces again.

(A) This is not the first time. Sometimes I find my socks in the dog house.
(B) Okay. Let's start training in a few weeks.
(C) Puppies often do that.
(D) You're too nice to him! He needs some training.
(E) Please be kind to him. He's just five months old.

➡ _____

[03~04] 다음 대화를 읽고 물음에 답하시오.

> Mom: Minsu, I'm going out with your dad for a movie.
> Minsu: When will you be back, Mom?
> Mom: Around 8 o'clock. Don't (A)[remember / forget] to feed Buster.
> Minsu: Okay.
> Mom: Be (B)[sure / unsure] to give him some water, too.

> Minsu: No problem.
> Mom: One more thing. Can you help Minsol with her science homework? Buster tore her homework into (C)[pieces / peace].
> Minsu: Hmm .... Okay. I'll do that.

출제율 90%

03 위 대화의 괄호 (A)~(C)에 들어갈 말로 바르게 짝지어진 것은?

	(A)	(B)	(C)
①	remember	sure	pieces
②	remember	unsure	peace
③	forget	unsure	pieces
④	forget	unsure	peace
⑤	forget	sure	pieces

출제율 100%

04 위 대화의 내용과 일치하지 <u>않는</u> 것은?

① Minsu's mom asks him to feed Buster.
② Minsu is going to give water to Buster.
③ Minsu is going to help Minsol with her science homework.
④ Minsol's homework was torn by Buster.
⑤ Minsu is going to be back at home around 8 o'clock.

[05~07] 다음 대화를 읽고 물음에 답하시오.

> Mike: Customer Service. How can I help you?
> Sora: I bought a hairdryer at your store last week. I'm not happy with it.
> Mike: What is the problem?
> Sora: It doesn't work well. I mean the air isn't hot enough.
> Mike: I'm sorry. Do you want to exchange it?
> Sora: Well, can I get a refund?

Mike: Sure. Will you please visit our store with the dryer?

Sora: Yes, I'll drop by tomorrow afternoon.

Mike: Don't forget to bring the receipt.

Sora: Okay. Thanks.

05 What's the problem of Sora's hairdryer?

➡ _____

06 What should Sora bring to the store to get a refund?

➡ _____

07 When is Sora going to visit the store with the dryer?

➡ _____

[08~09] 다음 대화를 읽고 물음에 답하시오.

Emma: You look upset, Tommy.

Tommy: I'm not happy with Sojin.

Emma: What's wrong with her?

Tommy: She isn't doing her part of the group project.

Emma: _____(A)_____

08 위 대화의 빈칸 (A)에 들어갈 말을 〈보기〉에 주어진 단어들을 모두 배열하여 완성하시오.

┌─ 보기 ─────────────────────────┐
│ think / talk / her / I / you / to / should │
└──────────────────────────────┘

➡ _____

09 위 대화에서 나타난 Tommy의 기분으로 적절한 것은?

① annoyed   ② lonely

③ excited   ④ satisfied

⑤ nervous

10 다음 우리말을 주어진 단어를 이용하여 영작하시오.

(1) Kelly는 이번 주말 삼촌 댁에 들를 것이다. (drop)

➡ _____

_____

(2) 그녀는 혼자 힘으로 그 수학 문제를 풀었다. (own)

➡ _____

(3) Mike는 Steve가 거둔 성공의 비밀을 알아내고 싶어 했다. (out)

➡ _____

_____

11 다음 우리말을 영어로 바르게 옮긴 것을 <u>모두</u> 고르시오.

┌──────────────────────────────┐
│ 나는 너무 실망해서 잠을 잘 수 없었어. │
└──────────────────────────────┘

① I was very disappointed because I couldn't fall asleep.

② I was too disappointed to fall asleep.

③ I fell asleep because I was very disappointed.

④ I was disappointed enough to fall asleep.

⑤ I was so disappointed that I couldn't fall asleep.

12 다음 중 빈칸에 들어갈 수 <u>없는</u> 것은? 출제율 90%

> My parents _____ me visit my grandparents more often.

① made   ② had

③ let   ④ helped

⑤ advised

13 빈칸에 들어갈 말이 바르게 짝지어진 것은? 출제율 95%

> • He didn't let my brother _____ with his robot.
> • You are _____ to work for a living.

① to play – too young

② to play – so young

③ play – so young

④ play – too young

⑤ play – very young

14 다음 중 어법상 바르지 <u>않은</u> 것은? 출제율 95%

① Did you make her go home alone?

② Everyone is too busy to play with me.

③ Mr. Park had me finished my job by five.

④ Let me go to my favorite singer's concert.

⑤ The truck is too tall to go through the tunnel.

15 다음 대화의 빈칸에 알맞은 말을 쓰시오. 출제율 85%

> A: Jason, why didn't you play soccer yesterday?
> B: I was so sick _____.

➡ _____

16 주어진 단어를 활용하여 다음 우리말을 영어로 쓰시오. 출제율 95%

> 그 화가는 너무 화가 나서 그의 그림에 집중할 수 없었다. (painter / angry / too / focus on)

➡ _____

17 적절한 사역동사를 사용하여 다음 빈칸에 알맞은 말을 쓰시오. 출제율 90%

> A: Who allowed you to use the science room?
> B: Mr. White _____.

➡ _____

[18~22] 다음 글을 읽고 물음에 답하시오.

> Breeze: ①So do I. Andy, will you please read the next letter?
>
> Andy: Hi. I'm a father of two children. One is a high school girl, and the other is a middle school boy. They're too busy ②to talk with me. When I get home ____ⓐ____ work, they just say hi and go back ____ⓑ____ their rooms. Sometimes I ask ③them about their school life, but they only give short answers. We don't talk much at the table, ④too. I want to say to my kids, "I love you so ⑤much, and I want to spend more time with you."
>
> Breeze: Andy, did you talk with your parents often when you were younger?
>
> Andy: Not really. I loved them very much, but I thought (A)they were too old to understand me.
>
> Breeze: I see. Does anyone have suggestions for the "sad" dad? Text your idea to us.

18 빈칸 ⓐ와 ⓑ에 들어갈 말이 바르게 짝지어진 것은?

출제율 90%

① to – into   ② to – to
③ from – from   ④ from – to
⑤ into – from

19 ①~⑤ 중 어법상 바르지 <u>않은</u> 것은?

출제율 95%

①   ②   ③   ④   ⑤

20 다음 중 위 글의 내용과 일치하지 <u>않는</u> 것은?

출제율 90%

① Andy is reading a letter from a father of two children.
② The father's daughter is a high school student.
③ He has more conversation with his children at the table.
④ The father wants to have more time with his kids.
⑤ The father wants to tell his kids that he loves them.

21 빈칸에 알맞은 말을 써서 밑줄 친 (A)를 대신할 수 있는 문장을 완성하시오.

출제율 90%

they were _____ _____ _____
_____ _____ understand me.

22 What do the children do when their father asks them about their school life? Answer in English with six words.

출제율 90%

➡ _____

[23~25] 다음 글을 읽고 물음에 답하시오.

Breeze: Do you want to say ___(A)___ to your family or a friend? Please leave your story. We will share your story with our listeners.

Jiwon: Hello, I am a 15-year-old girl from Busan. I want to say to my brother Jaeho, "Sorry." I told Mom his secret last Friday. Mom got so angry, so he was in trouble. I was too scared to say sorry to him at that time. I promise I will never tell his secrets again.

23 글의 흐름상 빈칸 (A)에 들어갈 말로 가장 적절한 것은?

출제율 95%

① your secret   ② thanks
③ sorry   ④ everything
⑤ how lovely they are

24 다음 중 위 글을 읽고 답할 수 <u>없는</u> 것은?

출제율 100%

① How old is Jiwon?
② Where does Jiwon live?
③ When did Jiwon tell his brother's secret to her mom?
④ What was her brother's secret?
⑤ Why didn't Jiwon say sorry to her brother at that time?

25 What does Jiwon promise? Answer in English with a full sentence.

출제율 90%

➡ _____
_____

서술형 실전문제

[01~03] 다음 대화를 읽고 물음에 답하시오.

> Minsol: (A)저는 Buster가 마음에 들지 않아요.
> (happy)
>
> Dad: What's wrong?
>
> Minsol: He tore my homework into pieces again.
>
> Dad: Puppies often do that.
>
> Minsol: This is not the first time. Sometimes I find my socks in the dog house.
>
> Dad: Please be kind to him. He's just five months old.
>
> Minsol: You're too nice to him! He needs some training.
>
> Dad: Okay. Let's start training in a few weeks.

01 위 대화의 밑줄 친 (A)의 우리말을 주어진 단어를 사용하여 영작하시오.

➡ _____

02 How old is Buster?

➡ _____

03 What does Minsol suggest to her father?

➡ _____

04 to부정사를 활용하여 다음 주어진 문장과 같은 의미의 문장을 쓰시오.

> Yesterday they were very busy, so they couldn't start their meeting on time.

➡ _____
_____

05 다음 그림을 보고 빈칸에 알맞은 말을 쓰시오.

> Greedy is picking a lot of apples. However, Lazy is too _____ them.

06 주어진 문장과 같은 의미의 문장을 쓰시오.

> My dog is too big to go into the dog house.

➡ _____

07 주어진 단어를 활용하여 다음 우리말을 영어로 쓰시오.

> 그 남자는 내가 그의 차를 밀게 했다.
> (make / push)

➡ _____

08 다음 대화의 빈칸에 알맞은 말을 쓰시오. 한 칸에 하나의 단어만 쓰시오.

> A: The hall looks very small. I think it can't hold all the students.
> B: I agree. The hall is _____ _____ _____ _____ all the students.

09 주어진 단어를 활용하여 다음 우리말을 영어로 쓰시오.

(1) 그녀는 내가 그녀의 피아노를 연주하게 했다.
(have)

➡ _____

(2) 나는 그들이 산책을 하게 허락했다. (let, take)

➡ _____

(3) 그는 네가 그 산을 오르게 했니? (make)

➡ _____

[10~12] 다음 글을 읽고 물음에 답하시오.

Breeze: Good evening, listeners. This is your DJ, Breeze. Today we have a special guest, Andy Kim. He's a hip-hop artist. Welcome, Andy.

Andy: Nice to meet you and thank you for having me.

Breeze: Okay. What do our listeners want to tell their family? This evening we will find out by reading some letters from them. Andy, will you start off with the letter from a teenage girl?

Andy: Sure.

Andy: Hello. I'm a 15-year-old girl from Wonju. I want to tell you about my mom. My mom tries to do everything for me. She cleans my room without asking me, so it's sometimes hard to find my stuff. She also buys books and makes me study them. I want to say to my mom, "I know you love me, but I'm not a baby anymore. Please let me take care of things myself."

10 Whose letter will Andy read first? Answer in English with a full sentence.

➡ _____

11 Write the reason why the girl sometimes has hard time finding her stuff. Use the phrase 'It's because.'

➡ _____
_____

12 위 글의 내용에 맞게 빈칸에 알맞은 말을 쓰시오.

The girl's mom treats her like a baby. She cleans her room and even makes her _____ _____ that she buys for her.

[13~14] 다음 글을 읽고 물음에 답하시오.

This is a letter from a father who wants to share his experience with the "sad" father.

My kids and I did not ①talk much. There was a wall between us. I wanted to ②break it down. I tried to spend more time with my children on weekends. We played computer games, rode bikes, and went shopping ③together. In this way, I had ④less chances to ⑤talk with them. I came to know more about them.

13 ①~⑤ 중 글의 흐름상 어색한 것을 찾아 바르게 고쳐 쓰시오.

_____ ➡ _____

14 By sending a letter, what does the father want to do? Answer in English with a full sentence.

➡ _____
_____

01 다음 대화의 내용과 일치하도록 Sora의 일기를 완성하시오.

Mike: Customer Service. How can I help you?

Sora: I bought a hairdryer at your store last week. I'm not happy with it.

Mike: What is the problem?

Sora: It doesn't work well. I mean the air isn't hot enough.

Mike: I'm sorry. Do you want to exchange it?

Sora: Well, can I get a refund?

Mike: Sure. Will you please visit our store with the dryer?

Sora: Yes, I'll drop by tomorrow afternoon.

Mike: Don't forget to bring the receipt.

Sora: Okay. Thanks.

Mon, Sep 23th, 2019

I bought a new hairdryer at the store last week but I was not satisfied with it. It had a problem that (A)_____. I called the customer service and explained this matter. I wanted to (B)_____ rather than exchanging the hairdryer. To get the refund, I need to visit the store (C)_____. So, I'll drop by the store tomorrow afternoon.

---

02 다음 라디오 신청자의 사연을 완성하시오.

• 사과하고 싶은 사람: my mother

• 내가 한 일: I talked back to her in a very rude way.

• 한 일의 결과: We haven't talked to each other for several days.

• 하고 싶은 말: I will never talk back to you in such a rude way again.

Hello. I'm a 15-year-old boy from Seoul. I want to say sorry to _____. The other day, I had an argument with my mother. She complained about my tight school uniform, and _____. Since then, _____.
"Mom, I promise _____. Please accept my apology."

단원별 모의고사

01 다음 주어진 문장의 밑줄 친 work와 같은 의미로 쓰인 것은?

> The switch doesn't <u>work</u>, so I need to call the repair man.

① Doctors often <u>work</u> very long hours.
② This machine <u>works</u> by electricity.
③ Tony <u>works</u> for an engineering company.
④ My daughter is <u>working</u> as a police officer.
⑤ Jane <u>works</u> too hard.

02 다음 문장에 공통으로 들어갈 말을 고르시오.

> • I believe my son won't tell a _____.
> • Please _____ on the bed.
> • Why did you _____ to me?

① lie   ② understand
③ feed   ④ pour
⑤ exchange

03 다음 우리말과 일치하도록 주어진 단어를 모두 배열하여 영작하시오.

(1) 모든 학생들을 먹일 충분한 음식이 없다.
   (is / all / food / to / there / not / students / enough / feed)
   ➡ _____

(2) 우유를 이 그릇에 부어주시겠어요?
   (you / this / would / milk / bowl / pour / into)
   ➡ _____

(3) 짠 음식은 네 건강에 좋지 않다.
   (not / food / your / is / health / for / salty / good)
   ➡ _____

[04~05] 다음 대화를 읽고 물음에 답하시오.

> Emma: You look upset, Tommy.
> Tommy: _____ (A)
> Emma: What's wrong with her?
> Tommy: She isn't doing her part of the group project.
> Emma: I think you should talk to her.

04 위 대화의 빈칸 (A)에 들어갈 말로 적절한 것을 <u>모두</u> 고르시오.

① I was fascinated with Sojin.
② I'm not happy with Sojin.
③ I'm satisfied with Sojin.
④ I don't feel good with Sojin.
⑤ I really appreciate Sojin.

05 Why is Tommy upset?

➡ _____
_____

[06~07] 다음 대화를 읽고 물음에 답하시오.

> Amy: I'm not very happy with my brother.
> Brian: What's the problem?
> Amy: He uses the bathroom for too long in the morning.
> Brian: I know how you feel.
> Amy: What can I do?
> Brian: Well, (A)<u>너는 더 일찍 일어나서 욕실을 먼저 사용할 수 있을 거야.</u>
> Amy: Okay, I'll give it a try.

06 위 대화의 밑줄 친 (A)의 우리말을 <보기>에 주어진 어구를 모두 배열하여 영작하시오.

> ┤ 보기 ├
> get up / and / earlier / you / the bathroom / first / use / can

➡ _____

07 위 대화의 내용과 일치하지 <u>않는</u> 것은?

① Amy는 남동생 때문에 기분이 좋지 않다.

② Amy의 남동생은 아침에 너무 오랫동안 욕실을 사용한다.

③ Brian은 Amy의 기분에 공감하였다.

④ Brian은 아침에 일찍 일어나 욕실을 먼저 사용할 것을 조언하였다.

⑤ Amy는 남동생과 욕실 사용 문제에 대해 이야기할 것이다.

[08~10] 다음 대화를 읽고 물음에 답하시오.

Mike: Customer Service. How can I help you?

Sora: I bought a hairdryer at your store last week. _____ (A)

Mike: What is the problem?

Sora: It doesn't work well. I mean the air isn't hot enough.

Mike: I'm sorry. Do you want to exchange it?

Sora: Well, can I get a refund?

Mike: Sure. Will you please visit our store with the dryer?

Sora: Yes, I'll drop by tomorrow afternoon.

Mike: Don't forget to bring the receipt.

Sora: Okay. Thanks.

08 위 대화의 빈칸 (A)에 들어갈 말로 <u>어색한</u> 것은?

① I'm sorry to say this, but I don't like it.

② I'm not happy with it.

③ I want to complain about it.

④ I'm not satisfied with it.

⑤ I'm so glad to have it.

09 위 대화에서 다음의 영영풀이가 나타내는 말을 찾아 쓰시오.

> a piece of paper that shows that goods or services have been paid for

➡ _____

10 위 대화의 내용과 일치하지 <u>않는</u> 것은?

① 소라는 지난주에 헤어드라이어를 샀다.

② 헤어드라이어가 잘 작동하지 않는다.

③ 헤어드라이어가 충분히 뜨거운 바람이 나오지 않는다.

④ 소라는 헤어드라이어를 교환하기를 원한다.

⑤ 소라는 영수증을 갖고 내일 오후에 가게에 들릴 것이다.

[11~12] 다음 대화를 읽고 물음에 답하시오.

Minsol: I'm not (A)[sad / happy] with Buster.

Dad: What's wrong?

Minsol: _____ ⓐ _____

Dad: Puppies often do that.

Minsol: This is not the first time. Sometimes I find my socks in the dog house.

Dad: Please be kind to him. He's just five months old.

Minsol: You're too (B)[strict / nice] to him! He needs some training.

Dad: Okay. Let's start training in (C)[a few / few] weeks.

11 빈칸 ⓐ에 들어갈 말을 〈보기〉에 주어진 단어들을 모두 배열하여 영작하시오.

> ┤ 보기 ├
> tore / again / he / into / my / pieces / homework

➡ _____

12 위 대화의 (A)~(C)에 들어갈 말로 바르게 짝지어진 것은?

	(A)	(B)	(C)
①	sad	strict	a few
②	sad	nice	few
③	happy	nice	a few
④	happy	nice	few
⑤	happy	strict	a few

13 다음 중 빈칸에 들어갈 말로 적절하지 <u>않은</u> 것은?

> Mom _____ us clean the windows.

① made ② helped
③ had ④ taught
⑤ let

14 다음 중 어법상 바르지 <u>않은</u> 것을 <u>모두</u> 고르면?

① Sora let us use her smartphone anytime we wanted.
② Julia is brave enough to say what she wants.
③ Wendy woke up so late to hear the news.
④ What made you call me at night?
⑤ Do you have her goes to school on foot?

15 다음 중 주어진 문장과 같은 의미의 문장은?

> My room is too dirty to invite my friends.

① My room is dirty enough to invite my friends.
② My room is so dirty that I can't invite my friends.
③ My room is so dirty that I can invite my friends.
④ My room is very dirty because I invite my friends.
⑤ My room is so dirty that I couldn't invite my friends.

16 주어진 단어를 활용하여 다음 우리말을 영어로 쓰시오.

> 나는 Jamie가 창문을 열게 했다. (make)

➡ _____

17 빈칸에 알맞은 말을 써서 다음 문장과 같은 의미의 문장을 완성하시오.

> I couldn't hear what you were saying because I was too far away from you.

➡ I was too _____
what you were saying.

[18~22] 다음 글을 읽고 물음에 답하시오.

Breeze: Good evening, listeners. This is your DJ, Breeze. Today we have a special guest, Andy Kim. He's a hip-hop artist. Welcome, Andy.

Andy: Nice to meet you and thank you for having me.

Breeze: Okay. What do our listeners want to tell their family? This evening we will find out by reading some letters from them. Andy, will you start off with the letter from a teenage girl?

Andy: Sure.

Andy: Hello. I'm a 15-year-old girl from Wonju. I want to tell you about my mom. My mom tries to do everything for me. She cleans my room without asking me, so it's sometimes hard to find my stuff. She also buys books and makes me study them. I want to say to my mom, "I know you love me, but I'm not a baby anymore. Please let me take care of things myself."

Breeze: I felt the same way when I was in middle school.

Andy: Many moms think their kids are too young to do things ___(A)___ their own. I hope the girl's mom will get the message.

18 다음 중 빈칸 (A)에 들어갈 말로 가장 적절한 것은?

① by   ② at   ③ on   ④ for   ⑤ in

19 다음 물음에 대한 대답을 글의 내용에 맞게 완성하시오.

> Q: How did Breeze feel about her mother when she was in middle school?
>
> A: She felt that _____ _____
>
> _____ _____ _____ _____
>
> _____ .

20 다음 중 위 글의 사연을 잘못 이해한 사람은?

① Sally: Breeze understands the girl's feelings.
② David: She is satisfied with her mom because she cleans her room instead of her.
③ Peter: The girl doesn't want her mom to do everything for her.
④ Julia: I hope that someday I can be a special guest of a show like Andy.
⑤ Kathy: If I have something to tell my family, I will send a letter to the show.

21 What does the girl want her mother to do?

➡ _____

_____

22 다음 빈칸에 들어갈 말로 가장 적절한 것은?

> Andy thinks the girl's problem is very _____ .

① unique   ② special
③ boring   ④ common
⑤ difficult

[23~24] 다음 글을 읽고 물음에 답하시오.

Andy: Hi. I'm a father of two children. One is a high school girl, and the other is a middle school boy. They're too busy to talk with me. When I get home from work, they just say hi and go back to their rooms. Sometimes I ask them about their school life, but they only give short answers. We don't talk much at the table, either. I want to say to my kids, "I love you so much, and I want to spend more time with you."

Breeze: Andy, did you talk with your parents often when you were younger?

Andy: Not really. I loved them very much, but I thought they were too old to understand me.

Breeze: I see. Does anyone have suggestions for the "sad" dad? Text your idea to us.

23 다음 중 위 글의 내용과 일치하지 않는 것은?

① The father has a son who is a middle school student.
② The father thinks there is not enough talking in his house.
③ Andy hardly talked with his parents when he was younger.
④ The kids are so busy that they can't talk with his father.
⑤ Andy didn't talk with his parents because he didn't love them.

24 What does Breeze ask the listeners to do? Use the words below.

> (by texting them)

➡ _____

_____

Reading for Fun 3

Diary

A Diary from Athens

Words & Expressions

Key Words

- **about** [əbáut] 부 약, 대략
- **Agora** [ǽgərə] 명 아고라 (고대 그리스) 시민의 정치 집회, 집회장, 시장, 광장
- **almost** [ɔ́:lmoust] 부 거의
- **assembly** [əsémbli] 명 집회, 국회, 민회
- **Athenian** [əθí:niən] 명 아테네 사람
- **Athens** [ǽθinz] 명 아테네
- **character** [kǽriktər] 명 등장인물
- **citizen** [sítəzən] 명 시민
- **count** [kaunt] 동 수를 세다
- **develop** [divéləp] 동 개발하다, 발달시키다
- **diary** [dáiəri] 명 일기
- **discussion** [diskʌ́ʃən] 명 토론
- **final** [fáinl] 형 마지막의, 최종의
- **hold** [hould] 동 담다, 수용하다
- **gather** [gǽðər] 동 모으다, 모이다, 집결하다
- **impossible** [impásəbl] 형 불가능한
- **male** [meil] 형 남자의, 수컷의
- **matter** [mǽtər] 명 일, 문제, 안건
- **meaning** [mí:niŋ] 명 의미
- **outdoor** [áutdɔr] 형 야외의, 실외의
- **person** [pə́:rsn] 명 사람, 인간, 인물
- **question** [kwéstʃən] 동 질문하다
- **sadness** [sǽdnis] 명 슬픔
- **state** [steit] 명 국가
- **stay** [stei] 명 체류, 방문
- **talent** [tǽlənt] 명 재능
- **traditional** [trədíʃənl] 형 전통적인
- **vote** [vout] 동 투표하다
- **way** [wei] 명 방식

Key Expressions

- **a lot of** 많은
- **be busy -ing** ~하느라 바쁘다
- **between A and B** A와 B 사이에
- **by -ing** ~함으로써
- **gathering place** 모이는 장소
- **in addition to** ~에 더하여, ~일뿐 아니라
- **over the age of 20** 20살 이상의
- **so far** 지금까지
- **take part in** ~에 참여하다
- **thousands of** 수천의
- **too ~ to ...** 너무 ~해서 …하다

Word Power

※ 서로 반대되는 뜻을 가진 어휘

- □ **final** (마지막의, 최종의) ↔ **initial** (처음의, 최초의)
- □ **male** (남자의, 수컷의) ↔ **female** (여자의, 암컷의)
- □ **ask** (질문하다) ↔ **answer** (답하다)

- □ **possible** (가능한) ↔ **impossible** (불가능한)
- □ **outdoor** (실외의) ↔ **indoor** (실내의)
- □ **sad** (슬픈) ↔ **glad** (기쁜)

※ 서로 비슷한 뜻을 가진 어휘

- □ **almost** (거의) : **nearly** (거의)
- □ **gather** (모으다, 모이다, 집결하다) : **assemble** (모으다, 모이다)
- □ **talent** (재능) : **gift** (재능)
- □ **vote** (투표하다) : **elect, choose** (선거하다, 뽑다)

- □ **develop** (개발하다) : **cultivate** (계발[연마]하다)
- □ **stay** (체류, 방문) : **visit** (방문)
- □ **traditional** (전통적인) : **conventional** (전통적인)
- □ **way** (방식) : **method** (방법, 방식)

English Dictionary

- □ **assembly** 집회, 국회, 민회
  → a meeting of a large group of people, especially one that happens regularly for a particular purpose
  특히 특정한 목적을 위해 정기적으로 일어나는 많은 사람들의 모임

- □ **citizen** 시민
  → someone who lives in a particular town or city
  특정한 마을이나 도시에 사는 사람

- □ **count** 수를 세다
  → to say numbers
  수를 말하다

- □ **hold** 담다, 수용하다
  → to contain something
  무언가를 포함하다

- □ **impossible** 불가능한
  → not able to happen
  일어날 수 없는

- □ **male** 남자의, 수컷의
  → typical of or relating to men or boys
  남자들이나 소년들에게 전형적인 또는 관련된

- □ **outdoor** 야외의, 실외의
  → happening or used outside; not in a building
  밖에서 일어나거나 사용되는; 건물 안에서가 아닌

- □ **question** 질문하다
  → to ask someone questions
  누군가에게 질문을 묻다

- □ **state** 국가
  → the government of a country
  한 국가의 정부

- □ **stay** 체류, 방문
  → a period of time that you spend in a place
  한 장소에서 보내는 기간

- □ **talent** 재능
  → a natural ability to do something
  어떤 것을 하는 타고난 능력

- □ **vote** 투표하다
  → to choose someone in an election
  투표에서 누군가를 선택하다

A Diary from Athens

1st Day _ I am visiting my aunt and uncle in Athens. Today I went to the Agora in the center of the city. It is a gathering place for Athenians.
<small>형용사구　　　　= The Agora　　　　　아테네 시민들</small>

There were a lot of stores, and people were busy talking and shopping.
<small>There were+복수 명사　= many　　　　be busy -ing: ~하느라 바쁘다, talking과 shopping은 병렬 관계</small>

2nd Day _ My uncle went to the Assembly. Any male citizens over
<small>민회, 집회　　　　주어</small>
the age of 20 can take part in the Assembly and vote on important
<small>형용사구　　~에 참여하다　　　　　　　take와 병렬 관계 ~에 관한</small>
matters. After they each speak freely about the matters, they vote
<small>시간 부사절 접속사 '~한 후에'　부사로 동사 'speak'수식</small>
by showing their hands. My uncle said, "Counting thousands of hands
<small>by -ing: ~함으로써　　　　　동명사 주어　　수천 의</small>
is almost impossible."
<small>단수 동사　거의(부사)</small>

3rd Day _ I went to the Agora again. I heard a very interesting
discussion between a teacher named Socrates and his students. Socrates
<small>between A and B: A와 B 사이의　　과거분사로 a teacher 수식</small>
questioned his students on the meaning of life. I was too young to
<small>질문했다　　　　　~에 관해　　　　　　　</small>
understand it, but I liked their way of discussing matters.
<small>too 형용사 to부정사: 너무 ~해서 ~할 수 없다　　discuss는 타동사이므로 전치사 'about'을 사용하지 않는다.
(= so young that I couldn't understand it)</small>

확인문제

● 다음 문장이 본문의 내용과 일치하면 T, 일치하지 않으면 F를 쓰시오.

1 Agora is a place where Athenians gather. ☐

2 Agora had many stores in the past. ☐

3 All the male citizens had to participate in the Assembly. ☐

4 Socrates and his students discussed the meaning of life. ☐

---

**Side glossary:**

assembly 집회, 국회, 민회
male 남자의, 수컷의
citizen 시민
take part in ~에 참여하다
vote 투표하다
count 수를 세다
impossible 불가능한
question 질문하다
meaning 의미
discuss ~에 관해 토론하다

4th Day _ Today was the best day so far. I went to the Theater of
지금까지

Dionysus. At the outdoor theater which can hold about 17,000 people,
선행사   주격 관계대명사   대략(부사)

we watched *Antigone*, a play by Sophocles. In addition to traditional
'Antigone'을 설명하는 동격구   ~에 더하여

songs and dances, the play had an interesting story. I sat far from the
연극(= *Antigone*)   ~로부터 멀리

stage, but I could feel the characters' sadness.

5th Day _ Today is the final day of my stay in Athens. My aunt and

uncle said to me, "You must develop your talent. You can help make
간접화법: My aunt and uncle told me to develop my talent.   help+동사원형/to부정사

Athens a great state." Now I want to go to school and become a better
want는 to부정사를 목적어로 취한다.   go와 병렬 관계. to go and (to) become

person.

so far 지금까지	
outdoor 야외의, 실외의	
hold 담다, 수용하다	
traditional 전통적인	
stay 체류, 방문	
talent 재능	
state 국가	
character 등장인물	
sadness 슬픔	

확인문제

● 다음 문장이 본문의 내용과 일치하면 T, 일치하지 <u>않으면</u> F를 쓰시오.

1 The writer thought today was the best day because he went to the Theater of
Dionysus. ☐

2 *Antigone* was the play which had an interesting story as well as traditional songs
and dances. ☐

3 The writer watched *Antigone*, a play by Sophocles, at the indoor theater. ☐

4 The writer stayed in Athens for five days. ☐

5 The writer wants to go to school and to learn from Socrates. ☐

● 우리말을 참고하여 빈칸에 알맞은 말을 쓰시오.

1 A _____ from _____.

2 **1st Day** _ I am _____ my _____ and _____ in _____.

3 Today I went to the Agora in the _____ of the city.

4 It is a _____ place for Athenians.

5 There _____ _____ _____ _____ stores, and people were _____ _____ and _____.

6 **2nd Day** _ My uncle went to the _____.

7 _____ _____ _____ over the age of 20 can _____ _____ _____ the Assembly and _____ on important _____.

8 After they _____ speak _____ about the _____, they _____ _____ _____ their hands.

9 My uncle said, "_____ _____ _____ hands is _____ impossible."

10 **3rd Day** _ I went to the Agora _____.

11 I _____ a very _____ _____ a teacher _____ Socrates _____ his students.

---

1 아테네에서 쓴 일기

2 첫째 날: 나는 아테네에 있는 숙부와 숙모 댁을 방문 중이다.

3 오늘은 도시 중심에 있는 아고라에 갔다.

4 아고라는 아테네 사람들이 모이는 장소이다.

5 많은 상점들이 있었고, 사람들은 이야기하고 쇼핑하느라 분주했다.

6 둘째 날: 숙부는 민회로 가셨다.

7 20살 이상의 모든 남자 시민은 민회에 참여하여 중요한 안건에 관해 투표할 수 있다.

8 그들은 각자 안건에 관해 자유롭게 의견을 말한 후, 손을 들어 투표한다.

9 숙부는 "수천 명의 손을 세는 것은 거의 불가능해."라고 말씀하셨다.

10 셋째 날: 나는 또 아고라에 갔다.

11 소크라테스라고 불리는 선생님과 그의 제자들이 나누고 있는 매우 재미있는 토론을 경청했다.

12 Socrates _____ his students _____ the _____ of life.

12 소크라테스는 제자들에게 인생의 의미에 관해 질문하였다.

13 I was _____ young _____ understand it, but I liked their _____ of _____ matters.

13 나는 그것을 이해하기에 너무 어렸지만, 나는 그들의 토론 방식이 마음에 들었다.

14 **4th Day** _ Today was the _____ day _____ _____ .

14 넷째 날: 오늘은 지금까지의 날 중 최고의 날이었다.

15 I _____ to the Theater of Dionysus.

15 나는 디오니소스 극장에 갔다.

16 At the _____ theater _____ can _____ _____ 17,000 people, we _____ *Antigone*, a _____ by Sophocles.

16 약 17,000 명을 수용할 수 있는 야외 극장에서 소포클레스의 연극 '안티고네'를 관람하였다.

17 _____ _____ _____ _____ songs and dances, the _____ had an _____ story.

17 전통적으로 있던 노래와 춤에 더하여, '안티고네'에는 흥미로운 이야기가 있었다.

18 I sat _____ from the _____ , but I could feel the _____ _____ .

18 나는 무대에서 먼 곳에 앉아 있었지만, 등장인물들의 슬픔을 느낄 수 있었다.

19 **5th Day** _ Today is the _____ day of my _____ in Athens.

19 다섯째 날: 오늘은 아테네에서 머무는 마지막 날이다.

20 My aunt and uncle said to me, "You _____ _____ your _____ . You can _____ _____ Athens a great _____ ."

20 숙부와 숙모는 "네 재능을 개발해야 된다. 너는 아테네를 위대한 국가로 만드는 데에 기여할 수 있어."라고 말씀하셨다.

21 Now I _____ _____ _____ to school and become _____ _____ person.

21 이제 나는 학교에 다니며 더 나은 사람이 되고 싶다.

● 우리말을 참고하여 본문을 영작하시오.

1 아테네에서 쓴 일기

➡ _____

2 첫째 날: 나는 아테네에 있는 숙부와 숙모 댁을 방문 중이다.

➡ _____

3 오늘은 도시 중심에 있는 아고라에 갔다.

➡ _____

4 아고라는 아테네 사람들이 모이는 장소이다.

➡ _____

5 많은 상점들이 있었고, 사람들은 이야기하고 쇼핑하느라 분주했다.

➡ _____

6 둘째 날: 숙부는 민회로 가셨다.

➡ _____

7 20살 이상의 모든 남자 시민은 민회에 참여하여 중요한 안건에 관해 투표할 수 있다.

➡ _____

8 그들은 각자 안건에 관해 자유롭게 의견을 말한 후, 손을 들어 투표한다.

➡ _____

9 숙부는 "수천 명의 손을 세는 것은 거의 불가능해."라고 말씀하셨다.

➡ _____

10 셋째 날: 나는 또 아고라에 갔다.

➡ _____

11 소크라테스라고 불리는 선생님과 그의 제자들이 나누고 있는 매우 재미있는 토론을 경청했다.

➡ _____

12 ▶ 소크라테스는 제자들에게 인생의 의미에 관해 질문하였다.

➡ _____

13 ▶ 나는 그것을 이해하기에 너무 어렸지만, 나는 그들의 토론 방식이 마음에 들었다.

➡ _____

14 ▶ 넷째 날: 오늘은 지금까지의 날 중 최고의 날이었다.

➡ _____

15 ▶ 나는 디오니소스 극장에 갔다.

➡ _____

16 ▶ 약 17,000명을 수용할 수 있는 야외 극장에서 소포클레스의 연극 '안티고네'를 관람하였다.

➡ _____

17 ▶ 전통적으로 있던 노래와 춤에 더하여, '안티고네'에는 흥미로운 이야기가 있었다.

➡ _____

18 ▶ 나는 무대에서 먼 곳에 앉아 있었지만, 등장인물들의 슬픔을 느낄 수 있었다.

➡ _____

19 ▶ 다섯째 날: 오늘은 아테네에서 머무는 마지막 날이다.

➡ _____

20 ▶ 숙부와 숙모는 "네 재능을 개발해야 된다. 너는 아테네를 위대한 국가로 만드는 데에 기여할 수 있어."

라고 말씀하셨다.

➡ _____

_____

21 ▶ 이제 나는 학교에 다니며 더 나은 사람이 되고 싶다.

➡ _____

01 다음 빈칸에 알맞은 말을 〈보기〉에서 골라 쓰시오.

┌─ 보기 ─┐
assembly, hold, so far, discussion, take part in, talent, question
└────┘

(1) He didn't _____ the weekly meeting.

(2) She showed an early _____ for drawing.

(3) Our school has _____ on Fridays.

(4) _____ everything about their plan went well.

(5) The elevator _____s about 10 people.

(6) The English teacher will _____ her students about grammar.

(7) We had a _____ about solving the problem.

02 다음 영영풀이에 해당하는 단어를 〈보기〉에서 찾아 쓰시오.

┌─ 보기 ─┐
vote, stay, citizen, hold, impossible
└────┘

(1) someone who lives in a particular town or city
➡ _____

(2) to contain something
➡ _____

(3) a period of time that you spend in a place
➡ _____

(4) to choose someone in an election
➡ _____

(5) not able to happen
➡ _____

03 주어진 우리말에 맞게 빈칸에 알맞은 말을 쓰시오.

(1) 현대적인 도시 이외에도 멕시코에는 많은 고대 유적들이 있다.
• _____ _____ _____ modern cities, Mexico has many ancient ruins.

(2) Kathy는 한국 무용 대회에 참가했었어.
• Kathy _____ _____ _____ the Korean dance contest.

(3) 내 친구들이랑 겨울 스포츠를 즐기느라 바빴어.
• I _____ _____ _____ winter sports with my friends.

(4) 이 선수들은 나이가 23세가 넘을 수 있다.
• These players can be _____ _____ _____ 23.

(5) 그렇게 해서 그는 부자가 되었다.
• He became rich _____ _____ that.

(6) 남녀 간에 다를 게 없잖아요.
• There's no difference _____ men _____ women.

04 다음 문장을 어법에 맞게 고쳐 쓰시오.

(1) They were busy to prepare for class.
➡ _____

(2) A lot of preparation were needed.
➡ _____

(3) I liked their way of discussion matters.
➡ _____

05 다음 문장을 같은 뜻을 갖는 문장으로 바꿔 쓰시오.

(1) Charlotte is too sick to go to school today.
➡ _____
_____

(2) The box is too heavy for me to carry.

➡ _____

_____

(3) The math problems were easy enough for us to solve.

➡ _____

_____

(4) The ribbon was too short to tie with.

➡ _____

_____

중요

06 다음 우리말을 괄호 안에 주어진 어휘를 이용하여 영작하시오.

(1) 그가 너무 빨리 말해서 나는 이해할 수가 없었다. (speak, to, fast, 8 단어)

➡ _____

(2) 그는 너무 어려서 운전할 수 없다. (young, that, drive a car, 10 단어)

➡ _____

(3) 사람들을 기억하는 것은 중요하다.
(remember, important, 4 단어)

➡ _____

[07~09] 다음 글을 읽고 물음에 답하시오.

1st Day _ I am visiting my aunt and uncle in Athens. Today I went to the Agora in the center of the city. It is a gathering place for Athenians. There were a lot of stores, and (A) 사람들은 이야기하고 쇼핑하느라 분주했다.

2nd Day _ My uncle went to the Assembly. Any male citizens over the age of 20 can take part in the Assembly and vote on important matters. After they each speak freely about the matters, they vote by showing their hands. My uncle said, "Counting thousands of hands is almost impossible."

중요

07 위 글의 밑줄 친 (A)의 우리말 해석에 맞게 주어진 단어를 활용하여 영어로 쓰시오.

be / busy

➡ _____

08 위 글에서 다음 영영풀이에 해당하는 단어를 찾아 쓰시오.

a meeting of a large group of people, especially one that happens regularly for a particular purpose

➡ _____

09 What did male citizens do in the Assembly? (Fill in the blanks.)

➡ They _____ on _____ _____ _____ _____ their hands.

[10~12] 다음 글을 읽고 물음에 답하시오.

3rd Day _ I went to the Agora again. I heard a very interesting discussion between a teacher named Socrates and his students. Socrates questioned his students on the meaning of life. (A)I was too young to understand it, but I liked their way of discussing matters.

4th Day _ Today was the best day so far. I went to the Theater of Dionysus. (B) 약 17,000명을 수용할 수 있는 야외 극장에서, we watched *Antigone*, a play by Sophocles. In addition to traditional songs and dances, the play had an interesting story. I sat far from the stage, but I could feel the characters' sadness.

10 위 글의 밑줄 친 (A)와 같은 의미가 되도록 'so'를 이용하여 쓰시오.

➡ _____

11 위 글 (B)의 우리말 해석에 맞게 주어진 단어를 알맞은 순서로 배열하시오.

> the / which / can / at / about / outdoor / theater / hold / 17,000 people

➡ _____
_____

12 Where did the writer go on the fourth day of the stay?

➡ _____

[13~14] 다음 글을 읽고 물음에 답하시오.

5th Day _ Today is the final day of my stay in Athens. (A)My aunt and uncle said to me, "You must develop your talent. You can help make Athens a great state." Now I want to go to school and become a better person.

13 위 글의 밑줄 친 (A)를 같은 표현으로 바꿀 때, 'tell'과 'to부정사'를 이용하여 쓰시오.

➡ _____

14 위 글은 아테네 방문 5일차의 일기다. 일기의 내용에 어울리는 제목을 주어진 철자로 시작하는 단어로 완성하시오.

> A New G_____ for My Life

15 다음 글을 읽고, 글의 내용과 일치하지 않는 문장을 찾아 바르게 고쳐 쓰시오. (본문에 있는 문장을 적을 것)

2nd Day _ My uncle went to the Assembly. Any male citizens over the age of 20 can take part in the Assembly and vote on important matters. After they each speak freely about the matters, they vote by showing their hands. My uncle said, "Counting thousands of hands is almost impossible."

3rd Day _ I went to the Agora again. I heard a very interesting discussion between a teacher named Socrates and his students. Socrates questioned his students on the meaning of life. I was too young to understand the meaning of life, but I liked their way of discussing matters.

① On the second day, the writer learned about the Assembly.
② Every citizen can take part in the Assembly to vote on important matters.
③ The writer heard Socrates and his students discussing the meaning of life.
④ Socrates' students were too young to understand the meaning of life.

➡ 틀린 문장 번호: _____

➡ 바르게 고친 문장:
(1) _____
_____
(2) _____
_____

출제율 90%

01 다음 중 짝지어진 단어의 관계가 나머지와 <u>다른</u> 하나는?

① wide : narrow
② male : female
③ sad : glad
④ stay : visit
⑤ impossible : possible

출제율 90%

02 다음 영영풀이에 해당하는 단어로 알맞은 것은?

> happening or used outside; not in a building

① assembly
② question
③ nearly
④ almost
⑤ outdoor

출제율 100%

03 다음 빈칸에 공통으로 들어갈 말을 고르시오.

> • He speaks Japanese well in addition _____ English.
> • The soup is too hot _____ eat.

① at
② to
③ for
④ of
⑤ from

출제율 90%

04 다음 빈칸에 알맞은 말이 바르게 짝지어진 것은?

> • How many countries have you been to so _____?
> • Most people think he is an adult _____ the age of 18.

① far – over
② far – under
③ now – over
④ now – under
⑤ near – below

출제율 90%

05 다음 영영풀이에 해당하는 단어를 주어진 철자로 시작하여 쓰시오.

> typical of or relating to men or boys

① count
② final
③ male
④ meaning
⑤ traditional

출제율 95%

06 다음 우리말에 맞게 빈칸에 알맞은 말을 쓰시오.

(1) 그는 종종 바보 같은 질문을 해서 나를 놀린다.
  • He often makes fun of me _____ asking silly questions.

(2) 나는 '지구 살리기' 캠페인에 참가해야만 해.
  • I must _____ _____ in the 'Save the Earth' campaign.

(3) 지금까지 전 이 옷에 만족해요.
  • So _____, I am satisfied with this dress.

(4) Boston과 New York 사이의 거리는 400킬로미터이다.
  • The distance _____ Boston and New York is 400 km.

출제율 100%

07 다음 중 어법상 <u>어색한</u> 것은?

① She is too weak to go there.
② There is a lot of guys selling things.
③ They were busy reading many fun books.
④ Having good friends is very important.
⑤ The writer of the diary stayed in Athens for five days.

출제율 95%

08 다음 중 어법상 적절한 것은?

① She is tired enough to walk.

② My aunt said me that I must develop my talent.

③ They vote by showing their hands.

④ The writer decided going to school.

⑤ I heard a very interesting discussion between a teacher naming Socrates and his students.

출제율 100%

09 다음 문장을 같은 뜻을 갖는 문장으로 바꿔 쓰시오.

(1) The soup is too hot for us to eat.

➡ _____

(2) I was too tired to visit you.

➡ _____

(3) Anne is wise enough to lead them.

➡ _____

출제율 90%

10 다음 문장을 어법에 맞게 고쳐 쓰시오.

(1) I saw something calling a walking bus.

➡ _____

(2) I was busy to take notes and to listen to the teacher.

➡ _____

(3) Consumers are smart enough knowing that.

➡ _____

(4) His family was very poor to educate him further.

➡ _____

(5) The bag was big enough that it could hold almost 1,000 presents.

➡ _____

(6) But he became too heavy that he couldn't move at all.

➡ _____

(7) This problem is so hard that I can't solve.

➡ _____

(8) This computer is small enough to me to carry.

➡ _____

[11~13] 다음 글을 읽고 물음에 답하시오.

1st Day _ I ⓐam visiting my aunt and uncle in Athens. Today I went to the Agora in the center of the city. It is a gathering place for Athenians. There ⓑwere a lot of stores, and people were busy talking and shopping.

2nd Day _ My uncle went to the Assembly. Any male citizens over the age of 20 can take part in the Assembly and ⓒvote on important matters. After they each speak ⓓfreely about the matters, _____(A)_____. My uncle said, "Counting thousands of hands ⓔare almost impossible."

11 위 글의 밑줄 친 ⓐ~ⓔ 중 어법상 어색한 것은?

① ⓐ   ② ⓑ   ③ ⓒ   ④ ⓓ   ⑤ ⓔ

출제율 90%

12 위 글의 빈칸 (A)에 알맞은 말을 다음 주어진 단어를 이용하여 쓰시오. (한 단어를 추가하고 필요하면 어형을 바꿀 것.)

> show / by / their / they / hands

➡ _____

출제율 100%

13 위 글의 내용과 일치하지 않는 것은?

① The writer is visiting his aunt and uncle in Athens.
② On the first day, the writer visited the Agora.
③ The Assembly seems to function as a place for democracy.
④ The writer took part in the Assembly and voted on the important matters.
⑤ We can guess that thousands of people voted on the important matters in the Assembly.

[14~15] 다음 글을 읽고 물음에 답하시오.

> Today is the final day of my stay in Athens. My aunt and uncle said to me, "You must develop your talent. 너는 아테네를 위대한 국가로 만드는 데에 기여할 수 있어." Now I want to go to school and become a better person.

출제율 100%

14 위 글의 마지막 부분에서 필자가 느끼는 심경으로 가장 알맞은 것을 고르시오.

① embarrassed   ② excited
③ ashamed   ④ bored
⑤ determined

출제율 90%

15 위 글의 밑줄 친 우리말에 맞게 주어진 어구를 이용하여 영어로 쓰시오.

> help / Athens / a great state

➡ _____

[16~18] 다음 글을 읽고 물음에 답하시오.

> I went to the Agora again. I heard a very ____(A)____ (interest) discussion between a teacher ____(B)____ (name) Socrates and his students. Socrates ____(C)____ (question) his students on the meaning of life. I was too young to understand ⓐit, but 나는 그들의 토론 방식이 마음에 들었다.

출제율 95%

16 위 글의 빈칸 (A)~(C)에 괄호 안에 주어진 단어를 알맞은 형태로 변형해서 쓰시오.

➡ (A) _____ (B) _____ (C) _____

출제율 85%

17 위 글의 밑줄 친 우리말에 맞게 주어진 단어를 활용하여 영어로 쓰시오.

> like / way / of / discuss / matters

➡ _____

출제율 90%

18 위 글의 밑줄 친 ⓐ가 가리키는 내용을 본문에서 찾아 쓰시오.

➡ _____

[19~20] 다음 글을 읽고 물음에 답하시오.

4th Day _ Today was the best day so ___ⓐ___ . I went to the Theater of Dionysus. At the outdoor theater which can hold about 17,000 people, we watched *Antigone*, a play by Sophocles. ___(A)___ traditional songs and dances, the play had an interesting story. I sat ___ⓑ___ from the stage, but I could feel the characters' sadness.

🖉 출제율 95%

19 위 글의 빈칸 (A)에 들어갈 알맞은 말을 고르시오.

① Because of   ② In spite of

③ Thanks to   ④ In addition to

⑤ According to

🖉 출제율 95%

20 위 글의 ⓐ와 ⓑ에 공통으로 들어갈 말로 알맞은 것은?

① on   ② far   ③ away

④ near   ⑤ under

[21~23] 다음 글을 읽고 물음에 답하시오.

1st Day _ I am visiting my aunt and uncle in Athens. Today I went to the Agora in the center of the city. It is a gathering place for Athenians. There were a lot of stores, and people were busy talking and shopping.

2nd Day _ My uncle went to the Assembly. Any male citizens over the age of 20 can take part in the Assembly and vote on important matters. After they each speak freely about the matters, they vote by showing their hands. My uncle said, "(A)수천 명의 손을 세는 것은 거의 불가능해."

3rd Day _ I went to the Agora again. I heard a very interesting discussion between a teacher named Socrates and his students. Socrates questioned his students on the meaning of life. I was too young to understand it, but I liked their way of discussing matters.

4th Day _ Today was the best day so far. I went to the Theater of Dionysus. At the outdoor theater which can hold about 17,000 people, we watched *Antigone*, a play by Sophocles. In addition to traditional songs and dances, the play had an interesting story. I sat far from the stage, but I could feel the characters' sadness.

5th Day _ Today is the final day of my stay in Athens. My aunt and uncle said to me, "You must develop your talent. You can help make Athens a great state." Now I want to go to school and become a better person.

🖉 출제율 95%

21 위 글의 제목으로 알맞은 것을 고르시오.

① Athens: A New City

② Socrates and His Way of Discussion

③ History Travels to Athens

④ A Diary from Athens

⑤ What a Wonderful Play!

🖉 출제율 100%

22 다음은 위 글에서 언급된 'Agora'의 기능을 요약한 글이다. 첫째 날과 셋째 날을 참고하여 빈칸에 알맞은 말을 쓰시오.

➡ Agora is the place for gathering, _____, _____ and _____.

🖉 출제율 90%

23 위 글의 밑줄 친 (A)의 우리말 해석에 맞게 주어진 단어를 활용하여 영어로 쓰시오. (동명사 주어로 시작할 것)

thousand / almost / impossible

➡ _____

Lesson 7

A Life Full of Fun

🎤 의사소통 기능

- 경험 묻고 답하기
  A: Have you ever touched a snake?
  B: No, I haven't.

- 절차 묻고 답하기
  A: Do you know how to make fried rice?
  B: Sure. It's easy. First, cut the vegetables into small pieces. Next, ...

🎤 언어 형식

- 현재완료
  Ms. Green **has studied** Spanish for three years.

- 명사를 수식하는 현재분사와 과거분사
  Look at the **falling** leaves.

Words & Expressions

Key Words

- **alive**[əláiv] 형 살아 있는
- **among**[əmʌ́ŋ] 전 ~ 중에
- **amusing**[əmjúːziŋ] 형 재미있는, 즐거운
- **animated movie** 만화영화
- **appear**[əpíər] 동 나타나다, 등장하다
- **boil**[bɔil] 동 끓이다, 끓다
- **box office** 극장 매표소
- **caricature**[kǽrikətʃər] 명 캐리커쳐, (풍자) 만화
- **cartoon**[kɑːrtúːn] 명 만화
- **cartoonist**[kɑːrtúːnist] 명 만화가
- **chef**[ʃef] 명 요리사
- **choose**[tʃuːz] 동 고르다, 선택하다
- **comic strip** 신문 연재만화
- **common**[kɑ́mən] 형 공통의
- **creative**[kriéitiv] 형 창의적인, 독창적인
- **develop**[divéləp] 동 개발하다, 만들다
- **dirty**[də́ːrti] 형 더러운
- **drawing**[drɔ́ːiŋ] 명 그림
- **education**[èdʒukéiʃən] 명 교육
- **fascinating**[fǽsənèitiŋ] 형 매력적인
- **fry**[frai] 동 볶다, 튀기다
- **lastly**[lǽstli] 부 마지막으로
- **machine**[məʃíːn] 명 기계
- **movement**[múːvmənt] 명 움직임
- **pepper**[pépər] 명 고추
- **plate**[pleit] 명 접시
- **pollute**[pəlúːt] 동 오염시키다
- **pour**[pɔːr] 동 붓다
- **probably**[prɑ́bəbli] 부 아마도
- **publish**[pʌ́bliʃ] 동 출판하다
- **recipe**[résəpi] 명 조리법, 비법
- **remain**[riméin] 동 계속 ~이다
- **sauce**[sɔːs] 명 소스
- **select**[silékt] 동 선택하다, 고르다
- **showtime**[ʃóutaim] 명 상영 시간
- **silly**[síli] 형 어리석은
- **simple**[símpl] 형 간단한, 단순한
- **sneaker**[sníkər] 명 운동화
- **spread**[spred] 동 펴 바르다
- **sunscreen**[sʌ́nskriːn] 명 자외선 차단제
- **taste**[teist] 동 맛보다, 먹다
- **translate**[trænsléit] 동 번역하다
- **type**[taip] 명 형태
- **usual**[júːʒuəl] 형 평소의, 보통의
- **washing powder** (세탁용) 세제, 가루비누
- **well-known** 형 유명한, 잘 알려진

Key Expressions

- **be made into** ~로 만들어지다
- **can't wait to** ~가 기대되다
- **catch one's interest** ~의 관심을 끌다
- **come together** 합쳐지다
- **cut A into pieces** A를 조각으로 자르다
- **jump out at** ~에게 금방 눈에 띄다, ~에게 분명히 보이다
- **make fun of** ~을 놀리다
- **of all ages** 모든 연령의
- **pay for** ~에 대한 돈을 내다
- **play a role** 역할을 하다
- **take a look** 살펴보다
- **ups and downs** 기복
- **watch out** 조심하다

Word Power

※ 서로 반대되는 뜻을 가진 어휘

□ **appear** (나타나다) ↔ **disappear** (사라지다)

□ **dirty** (더러운) ↔ **clean** (깨끗한)

□ **silly** (어리석은) ↔ **clever, bright** (영리한)

□ **kind** (친절한) ↔ **unkind** (불친절한)

□ **alive** (살아 있는) ↔ **dead** (죽은)

□ **usual** (평소의, 보통의) ↔ **unusual** (특이한)

□ **first** (처음(으로), 맨 먼저) ↔ **lastly** (마지막으로)

□ **high** (높은) ↔ **low** (낮은)

※ 요리와 관련된 어휘

□ **cut** (자르다)　　□ **put** (놓다)　　□ **pour** (붓다)　　□ **add** (더하다)

□ **boil** (끓이다)　　□ **fry** (볶다, 튀기다)　　□ **spread** (바르다)　　□ **bake** (굽다)

English Dictionary

□ **amusing** 재미있는, 즐거운
→ causing laughter
웃음을 유발하는

□ **appear** 나타나다
→ to start to be seen
보이기 시작하다

□ **caricature** 풍자만화
→ a funny drawing of somebody that exaggerates some of their features
누군가의 어떤 특징들을 과장하는 재미있는 그림

□ **develop** 개발하다, 만들다
→ to invent something new
새로운 무언가를 고안하다

□ **education** 교육
→ a process of teaching and learning
가르치고 배우는 과정

□ **fascinating** 매력적인
→ extremely interesting
매우 흥미로운

□ **fry** 볶다, 튀기다
→ to cook something in hot fat or oil
뜨거운 지방 또는 기름으로 무언가를 요리하다

□ **movement** 움직임
→ the act of moving
움직이는 행동

□ **publish** 출판하다
→ to make information available to people in a book, magazine, or newspaper
책, 잡지, 또는 신문으로 사람들에게 이용 가능한 정보를 만들다

□ **remain** 계속 ~하다
→ to stay in the same place or in the same condition
같은 장소 또는 같은 상태에 머무르다

□ **silly** 어리석은
→ showing little thought; foolish
생각이 거의 없음을 보여주는; 바보 같은

□ **sunscreen** 자외선 차단제
→ a type of lotion that you put on your skin to protect it from being damaged by the sun
태양에 의해 손상되는 것으로부터 피부를 보호하기 위해 피부에 바르는 로션의 한 유형

□ **translate** 번역하다
→ to be changed from one language to another
하나의 언어에서 다른 언어로 바뀌다

□ **usual** 평소의, 보통의
→ normal; happening most often
보통의; 가장 자주 일어나는

01 다음 단어들 중 요리와 관련이 없는 것은?

① pour　　　　② bake
③ fry　　　　　④ cook
⑤ publish

02 다음 중 단어의 명사형이 틀린 것은?

① educate – education
② pollute – pollution
③ suggest – suggestion
④ translate – translation
⑤ agree – agreetion

03 다음 영영풀이가 가리키는 것을 고르시오.

> to be changed from one language to another

① translate　　　② publish
③ remain　　　　④ pour
⑤ taste

04 다음 중 밑줄 친 부분의 뜻풀이가 바르지 않은 것은?

① Cindy is a <u>creative</u> storybook writer. 창의적인
② Korean people think <u>education</u> for children is important for the future. 교육
③ Do you know how to use this washing <u>machine</u>? 기계
④ It's <u>fascinating</u> to see how babies grow into children. 당황스러운
⑤ <u>Cartoonists</u> often work with writers who create ideas. 만화가

서답형
05 다음 우리말에 맞게 빈칸에 알맞은 말을 쓰시오.

(1) 마지막으로, 뜨거운 물을 붓고 기다리세요.
　➡ _____, pour hot water and wait.
(2) 나는 빵에 버터와 잼을 발랐다.
　➡ I _____ butter and jam on the bread.
(3) 접시 위에 어떤 음식도 남기지 마라.
　➡ Don't leave any food on your _____.
(4) 콩으로 간장을 담근다.
　➡ Soybean _____ _____ _____ soy sauce.
(5) 이 그림은 나의 관심을 끌었다.
　➡ This picture _____ _____ _____.
(6) 지도 좀 함께 보자.
　➡ Let's _____ _____ _____ at the map together.

06 다음 주어진 문장의 밑줄 친 spread와 같은 의미로 쓰인 것은?

> I need a knife to <u>spread</u> butter on bread.

① I'll <u>spread</u> strawberry jam on the toast for you.
② I saw the bird <u>spread</u> its wings.
③ Before the party, we need to <u>spread</u> a cloth on the table.
④ Virus <u>spread</u> rapidly during the holidays.
⑤ The fire <u>spread</u> to the building before the fire fighters arrived.

01 다음 짝지어진 단어의 관계가 같도록 빈칸에 알맞은 말을 쓰시오.

clean : dirty = _____ : alive

02 다음 문장의 빈칸에 들어갈 말을 〈보기〉에서 골라 쓰시오.

── 보기 ──
usual / well-known / creative / silly / cartoonist

(1) She came up with a _____ solution to the problem.
(2) The _____ is good at drawing cute animals.
(3) I hope I didn't make any _____ mistakes.
(4) There was more rainfall than _____ this summer.
(5) Stephen Hawking is one of the most _____ scientists.

03 다음 우리말에 맞게 빈칸에 알맞은 말을 쓰시오.

(1) 극장의 극장 매표소 옆에 매점이 있다.
➡ There is a snack bar next to the _____ _____ in the theater.
(2) 다른 상영 시간을 골라줄 수 있나요?
➡ Can you pick another _____?
(3) 책에 얼마의 돈을 냈나요?
➡ How much did you _____ _____ the book?

04 다음 우리말과 일치하도록 주어진 어구를 모두 배열하여 완성하시오.

(1) 너는 네 친구들을 놀려서는 안 된다.
(make / friends / your / you / should / of / fun / not)
➡ _____

(2) Lucy는 삶의 기복에서 항상 침착하다.
(Lucy / downs / life's / calm / always / is / through / and / ups)
➡ _____

(3) 나는 매일 그날의 웹툰을 살펴본다.
(take / at / a look / the webtoons / I / the day / of)
➡ _____

05 다음 〈보기〉에 주어진 단어를 사용하여 빈칸을 완성하시오.

── 보기 ──
agreement / suggestion / amusement / education / pollution

<The Best Animated Movie for Children's _____>
Animals welcome to the city's plan to build an _____ park in the forest. However, they soon suffer from serious _____. An old elephant makes a _____. The animals and the city reach an _____ to create a better world for everyone.

Conderversation

교과서

① 경험 묻고 답하기

> **A** Have you ever touched a snake? 뱀을 만져 본 적 있니?
> **B** No, I haven't. 아니, 없어.

- 'Have you ever + 과거분사 ~?'는 경험을 묻는 표현으로 'Have you ever been to ~?'는 '~에 가 본 적이 있니?'라는 의미이다. 이에 대한 대답으로 긍정일 때는 'Yes, I have.', 부정일 때는 'No, I haven't.'로 대답한다. Have you?는 상대방에게서 받은 질문을 다시 상대방에게 묻는 표현으로 반복된 부분은 생략한다.

- **경험 묻고 답하기**
  - 현재까지의 경험을 물을 때 현재완료 시제를 사용하므로 'Have you ever + 과거분사 ~?' 형태에 유의한다.
  - 경험하지 못한 것으로 '전혀 ~해 본 적이 없다.'라고 강조하기 위해 'No, I've never ~'로 대답할 수 있다.
  - 과거의 경험은 과거 시제를 이용한다.

  ex) Did you touch the snake? – 과거에 뱀을 만졌는지 묻는 표현

  　　Have you ever touched the snake? – 과거부터 현재까지 뱀을 만져 본 적이 있는지 묻는 표현

핵심 Check

1. 다음 우리말과 일치하도록 빈칸에 알맞은 말을 쓰시오.

(1) **A:** Have you ever _____ a sport star? (스포츠 스타를 만나 본 적 있어?)

　　B: No, I _____. _____ you? (아니, 없어. 너는?)

　　A: Yes, I _____. (나는 만나 본 적이 있어.)

(2) **A:** _____ _____ _____ _____ to Dokdo? (독도에 가 본 적 있니?)

　　B: Yes, I _____ _____ there. (응. 거기에 가 보았어.)

　　A: Wow, when _____ you go there? (와, 언제 그곳에 갔었니?)

2 절차 묻고 답하기

A Do you know how to make fried rice? 어떻게 볶음밥을 만드는지 아니?

B Sure. It's easy. First, cut the vegetables into small pieces. Next, ...
물론이죠. 쉬워요. 첫째, 채소를 작은 조각으로 자르세요. 다음 ....

■ 서수를 사용하여 어떤 절차의 순서를 열거할 수 있다. 이때, 'Second, Third' 대신에 'Next, Then'을 쓸 수 있다.

- first / first of all: 먼저, 우선
- then / next: 다음에는
- lastly / finally: 마지막으로

■ **절차 묻고 답하기**

- How can I buy a subway ticket from a machine? 기계로부터 지하철 표를 어떻게 살 수 있나요?

  1. First, select "Language." 첫째, 언어를 선택하세요.
  2. Second, choose where to go. 둘째, 어디로 갈지 선택하세요.
  3. Lastly, pay the fare, and get the ticket. 마지막으로, 요금을 지불하고, 표를 받으세요.

핵심 Check

2. 다음 우리말과 일치하도록 빈칸에 알맞은 말을 쓰시오.

(1) **A:** Do you know _____ _____ make *ramyeon*? (어떻게 라면을 만드는지 아니?)

B: Sure. It's easy to make. _____, boil water in a pot. _____, put noodles in the pot. (물론이지. 만들기 쉬워. 첫째, 냄비에 물을 끓여. 둘째, 면을 냄비에 넣어.)

A: Okay. What should I do _____? (알겠어. 그 다음에는 무엇을 해야 하니?)

B: _____ them for 3-4 minutes. (그것을 3–4분 동안 끓여.)

(2) **A:** Do you know how to _____ _____ _____?

(너는 어떻게 쉽게 잠이 드는지 알고 있니?)

B: _____ _____ _____, take a warm bath and drink a glass of milk. _____, stretch and relax your body. _____, read a boring book. (우선, 따뜻한 목욕을 하고 우유 한 잔을 마셔. 다음, 몸을 스트레칭하고 휴식을 취해. 마지막으로, 지루한 책을 읽어.)

A: I see. Thank you for your advice. (알겠어. 조언해 주어 고마워.)

Conversation 교과서 대화문 익히기

 A. Communication: Listen –Dialog 1

Jane: Kevin, you look ❶down.

Kevin: Nothing ❷serious. Sometimes my feelings change a lot.

Jane: I understand. Many teens have ❸ups and downs in their feelings.

Kevin: Oh, really?

Jane: ❹Have you watched the ❺animated movie "Shining Days"?

Kevin: ❻No, I haven't. Why do you ask?

Jane: ❼It is about a teenager's feelings. ❼It will help you ❽understand your feelings better.

Kevin: That sounds good! I'll watch ❼it.

Jane: Kevin, 너 기분이 안 좋아 보이는구나.

Kevin: 별거 아니에요. 때때로 제 감정이 많이 바뀌어요.

Jane: 이해한단다. 많은 십 대가 감정의 기복이 있지.

Kevin: 아, 정말요?

Jane: 'Shining Days'라는 만화 영화를 본 적이 있니?

Kevin: 아니요, 본 적이 없어요. 왜 물으세요?

Jane: 그건 십 대의 감정에 관한 거야. 그건 네가 네 감정을 더 잘 이해하도록 도와줄 거야.

Kevin: 괜찮은 거 같네요! 그걸 볼게요.

❶ down: 우울한 = depressed = blue   ❷ serious: 심각한
❸ ups and downs: 기복
❹ Have you ever p.p. ~?: '~해 본 적이 있니?'라고 경험을 묻는 표현이다.
❺ animated movie: 만화영화
❻ 경험 유무를 묻는 질문에 'Yes, I have.' 또는 'No, I haven't.'로 대답한다.
❼ It은 모두 "Shining Days"를 가리킨다.
❽ help의 목적격 보어로 원형부정사 understand가 쓰였다.

Check(√) True or False

(1) Kevin looks down because of serious problems.   T ☐ F ☐

(2) Kevin hasn't watched the animated movie "Shining Days".   T ☐ F ☐

 B. Wrap Up – Listening ❺

Judy: ❶Have you ever been to Sokcho?

Minsu: Yes, I have. ❷Actually my uncle lives ❸there, so I visit ❹him every year.

Judy: Really? Then, you've climbed Mt. Seorak, ❺haven't you?

Minsu: Yes, I've climbed to the top of the mountain ❻twice.

Judy: 너는 속초에 가 본 적이 있니?

Minsu: 응. 가 본 적이 있어. 사실은 내 삼촌이 거기 살아서, 나는 매년 그를 방문해.

Judy: 정말? 그러면, 너는 설악산을 올라 본 적이 있지, 그렇지 않니?

Minsu: 응. 그 산의 정상에 올라간 적이 두 번 있어.

❶ Have you ever been to ~?: ~에 가 본 적이 있니?   ❷ actually: 사실은, 실제로
❸ there는 Sokcho를 가리킨다.   ❹ him은 Minsu's uncle을 가리킨다.
❺ 부가의문문으로 '그렇지 않니?'라며 다시 한 번 확인하는 표현이다.
❻ twice: 두 번

Check(√) True or False

(3) Minsu's uncle lives in Sokcho.   T ☐ F ☐

(4) Minsu climbs to the top of Mt. Seorak every year.   T ☐ F ☐

Communication: Listen – Dialog 2

Emily: Oh, look at the long line at the ❶box office.

Tony: Yeah, there's a ticket machine over there. Let's buy the tickets from the machine.

Emily: All right. Do you know how to use the machine?

Tony: Sure. It's easy. ❷First, select a movie and a showtime.

Emily: Okay. We can watch the seven o'clock show. Then what?

Tony: Well, ❸select ❹the number of tickets and choose our seats.

Emily: Okay. Two tickets, and I want to sit in the back.

Tony: No problem. ❺Lastly, ❻pay for the tickets.

Emily: It's very simple.

❶ box office: 극장 매표소
❷ 절차를 답하는 표현으로 first(첫째), second(둘째), next(다음) 등을 사용한다.
❸ 명령문이므로 동사원형으로 시작한다.
❹ the number of: ~의 수, cf. a number of: 많은
❺ lastly: 마지막으로
❻ pay for: ~에 대한 돈을 내다

Communication – Listen more

Suji: Good morning, ❶Chef Garcia!

Garcia: Hello, Suji. ❷Have you ever made nacho pizza?

Suji: Nacho pizza? ❸No, I haven't.

Garcia: Kids will love ❹it, and I'll tell you how to make ❹it.

Suji: Sounds good!

Garcia: It's easy to make. First, ❺put nacho chips on a plate and ❻spread pizza sauce on ❼them.

Suji: Okay. Let me help you with the pizza sauce.

Garcia: Thanks. Next, put some ham, onions, and ❽peppers on top.

Suji: Okay. Then?

Garcia: Add cheese and bake for about 12 minutes in the oven.

Suji: I ❾can't wait to taste it!

❶ chef: 요리사
❷ Have you ever ~?: '~해 본 적이 있니?'라며 경험을 묻는 질문이다.
❸ 경험이 없을 때는 No, I haven't., 경험이 있을 때는 'Yes, I have.'라고 대답한다.
❹ it은 모두 'nacho pizza'를 가리킨다.
❺ put A on B: A를 B 위에 놓다
❻ spread: 바르다
❼ them은 nacho chips를 가리킨다.
❽ pepper: 고추
❾ can't wait to ~: ~가 기대되다

Communicate: Speak

Anna: Do you know how to make ❶fried rice?

Jinsu: Sure. It's easy. First, ❷cut the vegetables into small ❸pieces.

Anna: Okay. What do you do next?

Jinsu: Put some oil in the pan. ❹Then, fry the vegetables with rice.

Anna: Wow, it's really simple.

❶ fried rice: 볶음밥
❷ cut A into B: A를 B로 자르다
❸ piece: 조각
❹ Next 또는 After that 등으로 바꾸어 쓸 수 있다.

Wrap Up – Listen ❻

Mike: Today, I'll tell you how to ❶draw a bear's face. First, draw a big circle for the face. ❷Next, make two circles on top of the face. ❸After that, draw two circles for its eyes and ❹color ❺them black. Then, draw a small circle for the nose. Lastly, make a mouth.

❶ draw: 그리다
❷ Next는 Second로 바꾸어 쓸 수 있다.
❸ After that은 Third 또는 Next로 바꾸어 쓸 수 있다.
❹ color는 동사로 '색칠하다'를 뜻한다.
❺ them은 two circles를 가리킨다.

● 다음 우리말과 일치하도록 빈칸에 알맞은 말을 쓰시오.

Communication: Listen – Dialog 1

Jane: Kevin, you look _____.

Kevin: Nothing _____. Sometimes my feelings change _____ _____.

Jane: I understand. Many teens have _____ _____ _____ in their feelings.

Kevin: Oh, really?

Jane: _____ _____ _____ the animated movie "Shining Days"?

Kevin: No, _____ _____. _____ do you ask?

Jane: It is about a teenager's _____. It will help you _____ your feelings _____.

Kevin: That _____ good! I'll _____ it.

해석

Jane: Kevin, 너 기분이 안 좋아 보이는 구나.
Kevin: 별거 아니에요. 때때로 제 감정 이 많이 바뀌어요.
Jane: 이해한단다. 많은 십 대가 감정의 기복이 있지
Kevin: 아, 정말요?
Jane: 'Shining Days'라는 만화영화를 본 적이 있니?
Kevin: 아니요, 본 적이 없어요. 왜 물으 세요?
Jane: 그건 십 대의 감정에 관한 거야. 그건 네가 네 감정을 더 잘 이해 하도록 도와줄 거야.
Kevin: 괜찮은 거 같네요! 그걸 볼게요.

Communication: Listen – Dialog 2

Emily: Oh, look at the long _____ at the box office.

Tony: Yeah, there's a _____ _____ over there. Let's buy the tickets _____ the _____.

Emily: All right. Do you know _____ _____ _____ _____ _____?

Tony: Sure. It's easy. First, _____ a movie and a showtime.

Emily: Okay. We can _____ the seven o'clock show. Then _____?

Tony: Well, _____ the number of tickets and choose our _____.

Emily: Okay. Two tickets, and I want to sit in the _____.

Tony: No problem. _____, _____ _____ the tickets.

Emily: It's very _____.

Emily: 아, 극장 매표소에 길게 늘어선 줄을 좀 봐.
Tony: 네, 저쪽에 발매기가 하나 있어요. 저 기계에서 표를 사요.
Emily: 좋아. 그 기계를 어떻게 쓰는지 아니?
Tony: 그럼요. 쉬워요. 먼저, 영화와 상 영 시간을 골라요.
Emily: 알았어. 우리는 7시 영화를 볼 수 있겠네. 그리고 뭘 하니?
Tony: 음, 표 매수를 선택하고 우리의 좌석을 골라요.
Emily: 좋아. 표 두 장, 그리고 나는 뒤 에 앉고 싶어.
Tony: 좋아요. 마지막으로 표 값을 내요.
Emily: 정말 간단하구나.

Communication: Listen More

Suji: Good morning, Chef Garcia!

Garcia: Hello, Suji. _____ _____ _____ _____ nacho pizza?

Suji: Nacho pizza? _____, _____ _____.

Garcia: Kids will love it, and I'll tell you _____ _____ _____ it.

Suji: Sounds good!

Garcia: It's easy to make. _____, _____ nacho chips _____ a plate and _____ pizza sauce on them.

Suji: Okay. Let me _____ you _____ the pizza sauce.

Garcia: Thanks. _____, put some ham, onions, and _____ on top.

Suji: Okay. Then?

Garcia: _____ cheese and _____ for about 12 minutes in the _____.

Suji: I can't _____ to _____ it!

Communicate: Speak

Anna: Do you know how to make _____ _____?

Jinsu: Sure. It's easy. First, _____ the vegetables _____ small pieces.

Anna: Okay. What do you do _____?

Jinsu: _____ some oil in the pan. Then, _____ the vegetables with rice.

Anna: Wow, it's really _____.

Wrap Up – Listening ❺

Judy: _____ you ever _____ to Sokcho?

Minsu: Yes, I _____. _____ my uncle lives there, so I visit him every year.

Judy: Really? Then, _____ _____ Mt. Seorak, _____ _____?

Minsu: Yes, I've climbed to the top of the mountain _____.

Wrap Up – Listening ❻

Mike: Today, I'll tell you _____ _____ _____ a bear's face. _____, draw a big _____ for the face. _____, make two circles on top of the face. After that, _____ two circles for its eyes and _____ them black. Then, draw a small _____ for the nose. _____, make a mouth.

해석

Suji: 안녕하세요, Garcia 셰프님!
Garcia: 안녕하세요, 수지 씨. 나초 피자를 만들어 본 적 있나요?
Suji: 나초 피자요? 아뇨, 만들어 본 적 없어요.
Garcia: 아이들이 그걸 매우 좋아할 거예요. 그럼 제가 어떻게 만드는지 알려 드리죠.
Suji: 좋아요!
Garcia: 만들기 쉬워요. 첫째로 접시 위에 나초 칩을 올려놓고 그것들 위에 피자 소스를 바르세요.
Suji: 네, 피자 소스를 제가 도와드릴게요.
Garcia: 고맙습니다. 다음으로 햄, 양파, 피망을 위에 올리세요.
Suji: 네. 그다음에는요?
Garcia: 치즈를 올리고 오븐에서 약 12분 동안 구우세요.
Suji: 빨리 맛보고 싶군요!

Anna: 너는 볶음밥을 만드는 법을 아니?
Jinsu: 물론이야. 그건 쉬워. 먼저 채소를 작은 조각으로 잘라.
Anna: 알았어. 다음엔 뭘 하니?
Jinsu: 팬에 기름을 둘러. 그리고는 채소를 밥과 함께 볶아.
Anna: 와, 정말 간단하구나.

Judy: 너는 속초에 가 본 적이 있니?
Minsu: 응, 가 본 적이 있어. 사실은 내 삼촌이 거기 살아서, 나는 매년 그를 방문해.
Judy: 정말? 그러면, 너는 설악산을 올라 본 적이 있지, 그렇지 않니?
Judy: 응, 그 산의 정상에 올라간 적이 두 번 있어.

Mike: 오늘 나는 곰의 얼굴을 그리는 방법을 네게 말해 줄게. 첫 번째로, 얼굴에 해당하는 큰 원을 그려. 다음에, 얼굴 위에 두 개의 원을 그려. 그 후에 눈에 해당하는 두 개의 원을 그리고 그것들을 검게 색칠해. 그리고 코에 해당하는 작은 원을 그려. 마지막으로 입을 만들어.

Conversation 시험대비 기본평가

[01~02] 다음 설명을 읽고 물음에 답하시오.

> Mike: Today, I'll tell you how to draw a bear's face. First, draw a big circle for the face. Next, make two circles on top of the face. After that, draw two circles for its eyes and color them black. Then, draw a small circle for the nose. Lastly, make a mouth.

01 How many circles do Mike need to draw a bear's face?

➡ _____

02 위 설명의 내용과 일치하지 <u>않는</u> 것은?

① Mike는 곰의 얼굴을 그리는 법을 설명하고 있다.
② 첫 번째로, 얼굴에 해당하는 큰 원을 그린다.
③ 두 번째로, 얼굴 위에 두 개의 원을 그린다.
④ 세 번째로, 눈에 해당하는 두 개의 원을 그리고 검게 색칠한다.
⑤ 마지막으로, 코에 해당하는 작은 원을 그린다.

[03~04] 다음 대화를 읽고 물음에 답하시오.

> Anna: <u>너는 볶음밥을 만드는 법을 아니?</u> (fried, how)
> Jinsu: Sure. It's easy. First, cut the vegetables into small pieces.
> Anna: Okay. What do you do next?
> Jinsu: Put some oil in the pan. Then, fry the vegetables with rice.
> Anna: Wow, it's really simple.

03 위 대화의 밑줄 친 우리말을 주어진 단어를 사용하여 영작하시오.

➡ _____

04 위 대화에서 언급한 볶음밥을 만드는 법을 간략히 우리말로 설명하시오.

➡ _____

05 다음 우리말을 주어진 단어를 모두 배열하여 영작하시오.

(1) 나는 전에 Baltimore에 가 본 적이 없다. (been / I've / before / Baltimore / never / to)
➡ _____

(2) 너는 중국에 가 보았니? (ever / China / you / to / have / been)
➡ _____

[01~03] 다음 대화를 읽고 물음에 답하시오.

Jane: Kevin, you look (A)down.

Kevin: Nothing serious. Sometimes my feelings change a lot.

Jane: I understand. Many teens have ups and downs in their feelings.

Kevin: Oh, really?

Jane: (B)"Shining Days"라는 만화영화를 본 적이 있니?

Kevin: _____(a)_____ Why do you ask?

Jane: It is about a teenager's feelings. It will help you understand your feelings better.

Kevin: That sounds good! I'll watch it.

01 위 대화의 빈칸 (a)에 들어갈 말로 적절한 것은?

① No, I'm not.　② No, I haven't.
③ No, I don't.　④ No, I have.
⑤ No, I didn't.

02 위 대화의 밑줄 친 (A)와 바꾸어 쓸 수 있는 것은?

① depressed　② happy
③ satisfied　④ excited
⑤ pleased

서답형

03 위 대화의 밑줄 친 (B)의 우리말을 다음 〈보기〉의 주어진 어구를 모두 배열하여 영작하시오.

┌─ 보기 ├─
watched / the / have / animated / you / movie "Shining Days"

➡ _____

_____

[04~05] 다음 대화를 읽고 물음에 답하시오.

Emily: Oh, look at the long line at the box office.

Tony: Yeah, there's a ticket machine over there. Let's buy the tickets from the machine.

Emily: All right. Do you know (A)[how / what] to use the machine?

Tony: Sure. It's easy. First, select a movie and a showtime.

Emily: Okay. We can watch the seven o'clock show. Then what?

Tony: Well, select the number of tickets and (B)[to choose / choose] our seats.

Emily: Okay. Two tickets, and I want to sit in the back.

Tony: No problem. (C)[Lately / Lastly], pay for the tickets.

Emily: It's very simple.

04 위 대화의 빈칸 (A)~(C)에 들어갈 말로 적절한 것끼리 짝지어진 것은?

	(A)	(B)	(C)
①	how	to choose	Lately
②	how	choose	Lately
③	how	choose	Lastly
④	what	choose	Lastly
⑤	what	to choose	Lately

05 위 대화의 내용과 일치하지 <u>않는</u> 것은?

① 극장 매표소에 줄이 길게 늘어서 있다.
② Emily와 Tony는 발매기에서 표를 샀다.
③ 발매기에서 표를 사기 위해 먼저 영화와 상영 시간을 골라야 한다.
④ 표 값을 지불 한 후 표 매수와 좌석을 고를 수 있다.
⑤ Emily는 뒷좌석에 앉고 싶어 한다.

[06~07] 다음 대화를 읽고 물음에 답하시오.

> Suji: Good morning, Chef Garcia!
> Garcia: Hello, Suji. Have you ever made nacho pizza?
> Suji: Nacho pizza? No, I haven't.
> Garcia: Kids will love it, and I'll tell you how to make it.
> Suji: Sounds good!
> Garcia: It's easy to make. First, ___ⓐ___ nacho chips on a plate and spread pizza sauce on them.
> Suji: Okay. Let me ___ⓑ___ you with the pizza sauce.
> Garcia: Thanks. Next, put some ham, onions, and peppers on top.
> Suji: Okay. Then?
> Garcia: Add cheese and ___ⓒ___ for about 12 minutes in the oven.
> Suji: I can't ___ⓓ___ to taste it!

서답형

06 다음 〈보기〉에 주어진 단어를 위 대화의 빈칸에 알맞게 쓰시오.

> ┌── 보기 ──┐
> put / bake / wait / help

➡ ⓐ _____ ⓑ _____
　 ⓒ _____ ⓓ _____

중요

07 위 대화를 읽고 대답할 수 <u>없는</u> 것은?

① What is Garcia talking about?
② What do Garcia and Suji need to make the nacho pizza?
③ How long should Garcia and Suji bake the pizza in the oven?
④ What should Garcia and Suji do after spreading pizza source on the nacho chips?
⑤ What ingredient should Garcia and Suji prepare to make pizza source?

서답형

08 다음 대화가 자연스럽게 이어지도록 순서대로 배열하시오.

> (A) Okay. What do you do next?
> (B) Wow, it's really simple.
> (C) Sure. It's easy. First, cut the vegetables into small pieces.
> (D) Put some oil in the pan. Then, fry the vegetables with rice.
> (E) Do you know how to make fried rice?

➡ _____

서답형

[09~10] 다음 대화를 읽고 물음에 답하시오.

> Judy: (a)속초에 가 본 적이 있니?
> Minsu: Yes, I have. Actually my uncle lives there, so I visit him every year.
> Judy: Really? Then, you've climbed Mt. Seorak, ___(A)___?
> Minsu: Yes, I've climbed to the top of the mountain twice.

09 위 대화의 빈칸 (A)에 들어갈 부가의문문을 완성하시오.

➡ _____

10 밑줄 친 (a)의 우리말을 영작하시오.

➡ _____

서답형

11 다음 주어진 우리말과 일치하도록 주어진 단어를 모두 배열하여 완성하시오.

(1) 독도에 가 본 적이 있니?
　　(ever / to / you / have / Dokdo / been)
　　➡ _____

(2) 나는 해리포터 시리즈를 읽어 본 적이 있다.
　　(have / the / I / read / series / Harry Potter)
　　➡ _____

[01~04] 다음 대화를 읽고 물음에 답하시오.

Suji: Good morning, Chef Garcia!

Garcia: Hello, Suji. Have you ever made nacho pizza?

Suji: Nacho pizza? No, I haven't.

Garcia: Kids will love it, and I'll tell you how to make it.

Suji: Sounds good!

Garcia: It's easy to make. First, put nacho chips on a plate and spread pizza sauce on them.

Suji: Okay. Let me help you with the pizza sauce.

Garcia: Thanks. Next, put some ham, onions, and peppers on top.

Suji: Okay. Then?

Garcia: Add cheese and bake for about 12 minutes in the oven.

Suji: I can't wait to taste it!

01 대화에 맞게 조리 순서를 빈칸에 쓰시오.

➡ _____

02 What will the cook make?

➡ _____

03 What did the cook do first to make the dish?

➡ _____

04 What ingredients did the cook put on the chips?

➡ _____

05 다음 대화에서 (A)~(E)가 자연스럽게 이어지도록 순서대로 배열하시오.

Emily: Oh, look at the long line at the box office.

Tony: Yeah, there's a ticket machine over there. Let's buy the tickets from the machine.

Emily: All right. Do you know how to use the machine?

(A) Okay. Two tickets, and I want to sit in the back.

(B) No problem. Lastly, pay for the tickets.

(C) Second, select the number of tickets and choose our seats.

(D) Sure. It's easy. First, select a movie and a showtime.

(E) Okay. We can watch the seven o'clock show. Then what?

➡ _____

[06~07] 다음 대화를 읽고 물음에 답하시오.

Judy: Have you ever been to Sokcho?

Minsu: Yes, I have. Actually my uncle lives there, so I visit him every year.

Judy: Really? Then, you've climbed Mt. Seorak, haven't you?

Minsu: Yes, I've climbed to the top of the mountain twice.

06 Has Minsu climbed Mt. Seorak?

➡ _____

07 Why does Minsu visit Sokcho every year?

➡ _____

Grammar

1 현재완료

- They **have known** each other for five years. 그들은 5년째 서로를 알고 있다.
- **Have** you **been** to Japan? 일본에 가 본 적이 있니?

■ 현재완료는 과거의 사건이 현재까지 영향을 미칠 때 사용한다. 'have[has]+p.p.'의 형태로, 부정형은 'have[has] not+p.p.'이며, 의문형은 'Have[Has]+주어+p.p. ~?'로 나타낸다.

- She **has talked** with him for an hour. 그녀는 그와 한 시간 동안 대화를 나누었어.
- I **have seen** the play once. 나는 그 연극을 한 번 본 적이 있어.

■ 현재완료는 '완료, 경험, 계속, 결과'의 네 가지 용법으로 쓰인다. 완료 용법은 'just, already, yet'과 같은 부사와 주로 함께 쓰이며, 경험은 'ever, never, once, before' 등과 같은 부사와 함께 쓰인다. 'How long ~?'으로 묻는 질문이나 'for+기간', 'since+특정 시점'은 현재완료의 계속 용법에 속한다. 결과 용법은 특별한 부사와 어울리지 않고 과거에 발생한 사건으로 인하여 현재까지 영향을 미치고 있는 상태를 나타내는 용법이다.

- Diana **has finished** her laundry. Diana는 그녀의 빨래를 끝냈다. 〈완료〉
- Paul **has made** bread since 2 o'clock. Paul은 두 시부터 빵을 만들어 왔다. 〈계속〉
- They **have** never **been to** China. 그들은 중국에 가 본 적이 없어. 〈경험〉
- The boys **have gone to** their home. 그 소년들은 집에 가고 없어. 〈결과〉

* have been to와 have gone to의 사용에 유의한다. '~에 가 본 적이 있다'는 경험은 have been to로 표현하고, '~에 가고 없다'는 결과는 have gone to로 표현한다.

■ 현재완료는 과거의 일이 현재까지 영향을 미칠 때 쓰는 시제이므로 과거를 나타내는 어구인 yesterday, last year, ~ ago 등과 함께 쓸 수 없다.

- When have you eaten the food? (×)
- When **did** you **eat** the food?　　(○)

핵심 Check

1. 다음 우리말과 일치하도록 빈칸에 알맞은 말을 쓰시오.

(1) Jason은 세 시간 동안 깨어 있다.

➡ Jason ＿＿＿＿＿ ＿＿＿＿＿ awake for three hours.

(2) 그 기차는 막 떠났다.

➡ The train ＿＿＿＿＿ just ＿＿＿＿＿.

(3) 나는 지금까지 너에게 여러 번 전화했어.

➡ I ＿＿＿＿＿ ＿＿＿＿＿ you so many times until now.

140 Lesson 7. A Life Full of Fun

② 명사를 수식하는 현재분사와 과거분사

> • Be quiet. There is a **sleeping** baby. 조용히 해. 자고 있는 아기가 있어.
>
> • Pick up a **fallen** leaf. 떨어진 잎 하나를 주워라.

■ 분사는 Ving 형태를 취하는 현재분사와, p.p. 형태를 취하는 과거분사로 나뉘며, 모두 명사를 수식하거나 설명하는 형용사 역할을 한다. 현재분사는 '~하는'이라는 의미로 주로 해석되어 능동이나 진행의 의미를 나타내고, 과거분사는 '~된'이라는 의미로 주로 해석되어 수동이나 완료의 의미를 나타낸다.

  • I saw **singing** girls. 나는 노래하는 소녀들을 봤어.

  • The **disappointing** behavior made my mom upset. 그 실망스러운 행동은 우리 엄마를 화나게 했다.

■ 분사가 단독으로 명사를 수식할 때에는 일반적으로 명사 앞에서 수식하지만, 분사가 다른 어구와 함께 명사를 수식할 때에는 명사 뒤에서 수식한다.

  • Do you see the boys **playing** basketball? 농구하는 소년들이 보이나요?

  • Kevin found a vase **broken** by Sally. Kevin은 Sally에 의해 깨진 꽃병을 발견했다.

  • People **living** in the town felt happy. 그 마을에 사는 사람들은 행복했다.

■ '사역동사(have, make)+목적어+과거분사', '지각동사+목적어+과거분사', 'get+목적어+과거분사'는 목적어와 목적보어의 관계가 수동인 경우 쓰인다.

  • Jason **had** the woman **ask** some questions. Jason은 그 여자가 몇 가지 질문을 하게 했다.
    = Jason **had** some questions **asked** by the woman.

■ 'Ving'로 형태가 같은 현재분사와 동명사의 차이를 구별해야 한다. 현재분사는 '~하는', '~하는 중인'이라고 해석되고, 동명사는 '~하는 것'이라고 해석되거나 'V를 용도로 하는 명사'로 해석된다.

  • There is a woman **waiting** for someone. 누군가를 기다리는 여자가 있습니다. – **현재분사**

  • I can't find the **waiting** room. 나는 대기실을 찾을 수 없어요. – **동명사 (기다리는 용도로 쓰이는 방 – 대기실)**

핵심 Check

2. 다음 주어진 동사를 어법에 맞게 빈칸에 쓰시오.

(1) 무언가를 타이핑하는 그 소녀를 아니?

➡ Do you know the girl _____ something? (type)

(2) Adam은 우리에게 지루한 이야기를 해줬어.

➡ Adam told us a _____ story. (bore)

(3) 그것은 BTS에 의해 불러진 노래야.

➡ It is a song _____ by BTS. (sing)

Grammar 시험대비 기본평가

01 다음 문장에서 어법상 <u>어색한</u> 부분을 바르게 고쳐 쓰시오.

(1) My father hasn't gone to the museum until now.

_____ ➡ _____

(2) We saw the program several times until now.

_____ ➡ _____

(3) I did nothing since yesterday.

_____ ➡ _____

(4) We have work for this company for five years.

_____ ➡ _____

02 다음 주어진 단어를 어법에 맞게 빈칸에 쓰시오.

(1) People _____ in the town felt happy. (live)

(2) Do you know a baby _____ over there? (cry)

(3) I read the book _____ by a famous author. (write)

(4) Nick was holding a spoon _____ of gold. (make)

(5) Watch out for the _____ dog. (bark)

03 주어진 단어를 바르게 배열하여 다음 우리말을 영어로 쓰시오. 필요하다면 어형을 바꾸시오.

(1) 여섯 살 이후로 나는 책을 500권 읽었다. (read / since / was / I / have / 500 books / six / I)

➡ _____

(2) 그 소년은 벌써 우유를 마셨어. (the milk / the boy / drink / has / already)

➡ _____

(3) 이것은 구워진 감자인가요? (this / is / bake / a / potato)

➡ _____

(4) 너의 침낭을 찾았니? (bag / sleep / find / did / you / your)

➡ _____

> (4) sleeping bag: 침낭

01 다음 빈칸에 들어갈 말로 가장 적절한 것은?

> The man has worked for the company _____ 2010.

① at   ② in   ③ for
④ since   ⑤ during

중요
02 다음 빈칸에 들어갈 말로 적절하지 않은 것은?

> Have you ever _____ Jenny before?

① called   ② met
③ saw   ④ played with
⑤ talked with

03 다음 빈칸에 들어갈 말이 바르게 짝지어진 것은?

> • I saw something _____ in the kitchen.
> • A girl _____ Jessica came to see you.

① burned – name
② burned – named
③ burning – named
④ burning – naming
⑤ burning – to name

중요
04 다음 중 어법상 바르지 않은 것은?

① Have you ever taken first prize before?
② When did he go out last night?
③ People have stoped buying our products recently.
④ They made her go there alone.
⑤ We have never seen the boys and girls before.

05 다음 중 밑줄 친 부분과 쓰임이 같은 것은?

> I <u>have been</u> to Mexico several times.

① Colin <u>has gone</u> to the theater without an umbrella.
② We <u>have</u> just <u>made</u> some cookies.
③ Terry <u>hasn't called</u> her friends yet.
④ He <u>has played</u> the guitar since he was an elementary school student.
⑤ They <u>have visited</u> the museum four times.

06 다음 빈칸에 들어갈 말로 가장 적절한 것은?

> He _____ her for three years until now.

① met   ② is meeting
③ meets   ④ has met
⑤ is met

중요
07 다음 중 빈칸에 들어갈 말로 적절하지 않은 것은? (2개)

> My parents _____ the fence fixed.

① had   ② saw
③ got   ④ helped
⑤ seemed

서답형
08 적절한 시제를 활용하여 다음 두 문장을 하나의 문장으로 표현하시오.

> Eunji started to live in Busan when she was five years old. She still lives in Busan.

➡ _____

_____

09 다음 문장의 밑줄 친 부분과 쓰임이 같은 것은?

> The boring movie made students fall asleep.

① Writing a letter is easy.
② Did you enjoy baking bread?
③ I am not interested in playing computer games.
④ She kept yelling at me.
⑤ Who is the girl raising her hand?

10 다음 중 어법상 틀린 것은?

> A: ①Has your brother ②climbed Mt. Seorak?
> B: Yes, he ③does. He ④has climbed Mt. Seorak two times ⑤before.

① ② ③ ④ ⑤

11 다음 우리말을 영어로 바르게 옮긴 것은?

① 웃고 있는 저 소녀를 아니?
➡ Do you know that smile girl?
② 그 부상당한 남자는 어디에 있니?
➡ Where is the injuring man?
③ 언제 그녀를 처음 만났니?
➡ When have you met her first?
④ 그 책을 몇 번이나 읽었니?
➡ How many times have you read the book?
⑤ 나는 이곳에서 3년 동안 살고 있어요.
➡ I have lived here since three years.

서답형

12 현재완료 시제와 주어진 단어를 활용하여 다음 우리말을 영어로 쓰시오.

> 나는 지금 막 냉동피자 한 조각을 먹었어.
> (freeze / just / have / piece)

➡ _____

13 (A)~(C)에 들어갈 말이 바르게 짝지어진 것은?

> • The (A)[exciting / excited] game made us pleased.
> • I (B)[played / have played] the guitar since I was five years old.
> • (C)[Have you found / Did you find] your wallet yesterday?

① excited – have played – Have you found
② excited – played – Did you find
③ exciting – have played – Have you found
④ exciting – played – Have you found
⑤ exciting – have played – Did you find

14 다음 대화의 빈칸에 들어갈 말로 가장 적절한 것은?

> A: _____ this movie?
> B: Yes. I have seen it once.

① Have you made
② Have you heard about
③ Have you seen
④ Did you see
⑤ Did you want to see

15 빈칸에 들어갈 말을 바르게 짝지은 것은?

> Tom is Paul's English teacher. Tom _____ Paul since he was ten years old. Tom _____ Paul very well.

① teaches – has known
② will teach – knew
③ is teaching – is knowing
④ has taught – knows
⑤ has taught – has known

서답형

16 주어진 단어를 활용하여 다음 우리말을 영어로 쓰시오.

> 나는 중고차 한 대를 샀어.

➡ _____

중요

17 다음 중 빈칸에 들어갈 말이 다른 하나는?

① I haven't seen her _____ yesterday.

② Jina has danced ballet _____ she was very young.

③ He has talked with someone _____ an hour.

④ Julie has knitted a hat _____ last month.

⑤ My sisters have ridden their bikes _____ this morning.

18 다음 밑줄 친 두 문장을 하나의 문장으로 바르게 바꾼 것은?

> A: Where is your brother?
> B: He went out to a mall. He is not here.

① He used to be in a mall.

② He has been here.

③ He wanted to go to a mall.

④ He has been in a mall.

⑤ He has gone to a mall.

중요

19 빈칸에 들어갈 말이 바르게 짝지어진 것은?

> He _____ all day under the _____ sun since this morning. He is very tired.

① is working – burned

② works – burning

③ worked – burned

④ has worked – burning

⑤ has worked – burned

중요

20 다음 중 어법상 바르지 않은 것은?

> A: How long ①have you played the drums?
> B: I ②have played the drums ③for 5 years.
> A: Do you like playing them?
> B: Yes. Playing the drums ④makes me ⑤ amusing.

①　　　②　　　③　　　④　　　⑤

서답형

21 주어진 단어를 활용하여 다음 우리말을 영어로 쓰시오.

> 그 놀라운 소식은 사실이 아니야.
> (surprise / true)

➡ _____

22 다음 우리말을 영어로 옮길 때 세 번째와 일곱 번째 오는 단어를 바르게 짝지은 것은?

> 나는 전에 내 남동생과 싸운 적이 있어요.

① have – with

② have – brother

③ with – before

④ fought – brother

⑤ fought – before

서답형

23 주어진 단어를 바르게 배열하여 다음 우리말을 영어로 쓰시오. 두 개의 단어는 어법에 맞게 변형하시오.

> 부서진 창문을 통해 집 안으로 찬바람이 불어 왔다. (the / house / the / break / into / through / window / cold / blow / winds)

➡ _____

_____

서답형

24 excite를 어법에 맞게 빈칸에 쓰시오.

> A: The concert was _____!
> B: I agree. The _____ fans rushed into the stadium.

01 다음 우리말 의미에 맞게 주어진 단어를 빈칸에 쓰시오.

> bake / slice / sleep / cheer / rise / dance

(1) 우리는 아침 일찍 해변에서 일출을 봤습니다.

➡ Early in the morning, we saw the _____ sun at the beach.

(2) 잠자는 고양이 앞에 있는 구운 감자가 보이니?

➡ Do you see the _____ potatoes in front of the _____ cat?

(3) 나의 친구들은 무대에서 춤추는 소녀들이야.

➡ My friends are the girls _____ on the stage.

(4) 나는 환호하는 군중들 중 한 명이었어.

➡ I was one of the _____ crowds.

(5) 이 자른 치즈를 어디에 두어야 하나요?

➡ Where should I put this _____ cheese?

02 적절한 시제를 활용하여 다음 두 문장을 하나의 문장으로 표현하시오.

> • Jenny made friends with Christina in 2010.
> • They are still friends.

➡ _____

03 주어진 단어를 활용하여 다음 대화를 영어로 쓰시오.

> A: 볶음밥을 요리해 본 적이 있니?
> (cook / ever / fry)
> B: 응, 나는 그것을 여러 번 요리해 봤어.
> (many times)

➡ A: _____
   B: _____

04 주어진 단어를 활용하여 다음 우리말을 영어로 쓰시오.

> 전에 다른 나라에 가 본 적이 있니?
> (before / other)

➡ _____

05 주어진 동사를 내용과 어법에 맞게 빈칸에 쓰시오.

> be / rain / lose / drive / read

(1) My uncle _____ the car in 2009.
(2) The weather _____ warm recently. It's still warm.
(3) It _____ since last night.
(4) Clara _____ her key the other day.
(5) Zach _____ the book several times until now.

06 주어진 어구를 바르게 배열하여 다음 우리말을 영어로 쓰시오. 필요하다면 어형을 바꾸시오.

> 빨간 모자를 쓰고 있는 소년을 보아라.
> (a red cap / the boy / at / wear / look)

➡ _____

07 주어진 단어를 활용하여 다음 우리말을 영어로 쓰시오.

> 나의 남동생은 어젯밤부터 아파요. (sick)

➡ _____

08 다음 밑줄 친 부분이 현재분사인지 동명사인지 구별하고, 그렇게 구별한 이유를 서술하시오.

> (1) Look! There is a <u>swimming</u> baby.
> (2) Where can we find a <u>swimming</u> pool?

➡ (1) _____ 이유: _____

_____

(2) _____ 이유: _____

_____

09 주어진 어구를 활용하여 다음 우리말을 영어로 쓰시오.

(1) 나는 지금까지 제주도에 두 번 가봤어요.
(Jejudo / twice / until now)

➡ _____

(2) 나는 어제 그 유리창을 깼어요. (break)

➡ _____

(3) 우리는 아직 그 영화를 보지 못했습니다.
(have)

➡ _____

10 다음 상황을 읽고 빈칸에 알맞은 말을 쓰시오.

> Jason was born in Canada in 2001. He moved to Seoul in 2011. He started to learn *taekwondo* as soon as he arrived in Seoul. He is eighteen years old now. He still learns *taekwondo*. He likes *taekwondo*.

> Jason _____ (live) in Seoul since _____. He took his first *taekwondo* lesson in _____. He _____ (learn) *taekwondo* _____ eight years.

11 다음 상황을 설명하는 문장을 한 문장으로 바꿔 쓰시오.

> My grandmother broke her right arm last month. She can't use it now.

➡ _____

12 주어진 단어를 바르게 배열하여 다음 우리말을 영어로 쓰시오. 필요하다면 어형을 변형하시오.

> 그녀는 내게 삶은 달걀 하나와 다진 당근을 가져오게 하였다.
> (carrot / she / make / boil / chop / a / and / egg / bring / me)

➡ _____

13 다음 대화의 빈칸에 알맞은 말을 쓰시오.

> A: Does James work for this company?
> B: Yes, he does. Actually he _____ for this company for five years.

➡ _____

14 다음 문장에서 어법상 <u>어색한</u> 부분을 찾아 바르게 고쳐 쓰시오.

(1) I am boring with his lecture.
_____ ➡ _____

(2) This is a bag making in China.
_____ ➡ _____

(3) It is an excited adventure movie.
_____ ➡ _____

(4) He approached the barked dog.
_____ ➡ _____

The World of Cartoons

Boat! Land!

Did you laugh when you saw the cartoon above? If so, the cartoonist
was successful. Cartoonists are the people who make cartoons. They
want to catch your interest, and usually, make you laugh with simple
language and creative drawings.

People have made cartoons for hundreds of years. There are many
types of cartoons, and they play different roles. One form of cartoon is
a picture with a few words. It is sometimes called a "gag cartoon." The
cartoonist makes a funny character, and the character makes you laugh
by doing or saying silly things.

Another type of cartoon is called a caricature. In a caricature, some
parts of a character are different or bigger than usual. Look at the
picture on the right. Which parts of the man's face jump out at you?
Artists have used this type of cartoon to make fun of well-known
people.

cartoonist: 만화가

successful: 성공한, 성공적인

catch one's interest: ~의 관심을 끌다

creative: 창의적인, 독창적인

type: 방내

play a role: 역할을 하다

silly: 어리석은

caricature: 캐리커처

usual: 평소의, 보통의

jump out at: ~에게 금방 눈에 띄다, ~에게 분명히 보이다

make fun of: ~을 놀리다

well-known: 잘 알려진, 유명한

확인문제

● 다음 문장이 본문의 내용과 일치하면 T, 일치하지 않으면 F를 쓰시오.

1   We can say that a cartoonist was successful when he made us think about something
    seriously. ☐

2   A few words are used in a gag cartoon. ☐

3   A funny character in a gag cartoon makes you laugh by doing or saying silly
    things. ☐

4   A gag cartoon is used to make fun of famous people. ☐

5   A caricature describes people as they are. ☐

When several cartoon pictures come together and tell a story, we
몇몇의(셀 수 있는 명사 수식)
have a comic strip. Comic strips have been in newspapers for many
현재완료(계속)
years. They are often just amusing stories. People have also used comic
strips for education. Comics can make information clearer and easier
5형식 동사(make+목적어+목적격보어)
to learn. You have probably seen comic history or science books.
to부정사의 부사적 용법 (형용사 수식)   현재완료(경험)

You have surely seen many cartoon movies, or animated movies,
too. These are very popular among people of all ages. Movement and
sounds are added to pictures, so they come alive. Artists and writers
수동태   서술적 용법으로 쓰이는 형용사
can develop fascinating characters and tell interesting stories through
└ 매력을 유발하고 흥미를 유발하는 것이므로 현재분사 ┘
animation.

In the 1990s, a new type of cartoon was developed. It is called
개발되는 것이므로 수동태
a webtoon. Webtoons are published online, so you can read them
webtoons 지칭
anytime, anywhere on your phone or computer. They are very popular,
and some of them are even made into TV dramas or movies.
～으로 만들어지다

New forms of cartoons may appear in the future. They could be
new forms of cartoons 지칭
different and even more exciting than now, but one thing will remain
the same: they will help us laugh, relax, and learn.
준사역동사(help+목적어+(to) V)

come together: 합쳐지다

comic strip: 신문의 연재만화

amusing: 재미있는, 즐거운

education: 교육

probably: 아마도

surely: 분명히, 확실히

among: ～ 중에

of all ages: 모든 연령의

movement: 움직임

develop: 개발하다, 만들다

fascinating: 매력적인

animation: 만화영화 제작

publish: 출판하다

be made into: ～로 만들어지다

appear: 나타나다, 등장하다

remain: 계속 ～이다

📎 확인문제

● 다음 문장이 본문의 내용과 일치하면 T, 일치하지 않으면 F를 쓰시오.

1 A comic strip doesn't tell a story. ☐

2 We can't see comic strips in newspapers. ☐

3 Newspapers can make information clearer. ☐

4 There are comic history books. ☐

5 Webtoons were developed in the 1990s. ☐

6 All of the webtoons were made into TV dramas or movies. ☐

● 우리말을 참고하여 빈칸에 알맞은 말을 쓰시오.

1 Boat! _____!

2 Did you _____ when you _____ the cartoon _____?

0 If _____, the cartoonist was _____.

4 Cartoonists are the people _____ _____ _____.

5 They want _____ _____ your interest, and usually, _____ _____ _____ with simple language and _____ _____.

6 People _____ _____ cartoons _____ hundreds of years.

7 There are _____ _____ _____ _____, and they play different roles.

8 One form of cartoon _____ a picture with _____ _____ _____.

9 It _____ sometimes _____ a "gag cartoon."

10 The cartoonist _____ _____ _____ _____, and the character makes you _____ by _____ or _____ silly things.

11 _____ type of cartoon _____ _____ a caricature.

12 In a caricature, _____ _____ of a character _____ _____ or _____ _____ _____.

13 Look at the picture _____ the right.

14 _____ _____ of the man's face _____ out at you?

15 Artists _____ _____ this type of cartoon _____ _____ _____ _____ well-known people.

16 When _____ cartoon pictures _____ _____ and tell a story, we have _____ _____ _____.

1 배다! 육지다!

2 위의 만화를 보고 웃었는가?

3 그랬다면 그 만화가는 성공했다.

4 만화가들은 만화를 만드는 사람들이다.

5 그들은 여러분의 관심을 끌고, 대개는 간단한 말과 독창적인 그림으로 여러분을 웃게 하고 싶어 한다.

6 사람들은 수백 년 동안 만화를 만들어 왔다.

7 만화에는 많은 종류가 있으며, 그것들은 다양한 역할을 한다.

8 만화의 한 형태로 몇 마디 말을 쓴 그림이 있다.

9 간혹 그것은 '개그 만화'라고 불린다.

10 만화가는 웃긴 캐릭터를 만들고, 그 캐릭터는 우스꽝스러운 행동이나 말을 함으로써 여러분을 웃게 만든다.

11 다른 종류의 만화는 캐리커처라고 불린다.

12 캐리커처에서 캐릭터의 어떤 부분은 평소와 다르거나 더 크다.

13 오른쪽의 그림을 보아라.

14 남자 얼굴의 어떤 부분이 여러분에게 분명히 보이는가?

15 미술가들은 유명한 사람들을 풍자하기 위해 이런 종류의 만화를 그려 왔다.

16 몇 가지 만화 그림이 모여서 이야기를 들려주게 되면, 그것이 연재만화가 된다.

17 Comic strips _____ _____ in newspapers _____ many years.

18 They are often _____ _____ _____.

19 People _____ _____ _____ comic strips _____ _____.

20 Comics can _____ information _____ and _____ _____ _____.

21 You _____ _____ _____ comic history or science books.

22 You _____ _____ _____ many cartoon movies, or _____ _____, too.

23 These are very _____ _____ _____ _____ _____ _____.

24 Movement and sounds _____ _____ _____ pictures, so they _____ _____.

25 Artists and writers can _____ _____ characters and tell _____ stories _____ animation.

26 In the 1990s, a new type of cartoon _____ _____.

27 It _____ _____ a webtoon.

28 Webtoons _____ _____ online, so you can _____ _____ anytime, anywhere _____ your phone or computer.

29 They are very _____, and some of _____ _____ even made _____ TV dramas or movies.

30 New forms of cartoons _____ _____ in the future.

31 They could be _____ and even more _____ _____ now, but one thing will _____ the same: they will help us _____, _____, and _____.

---

17 연재만화는 여러 해 동안 신문에 실려 왔다.

18 그것들은 종종 그저 재미있는 이야기이다.

19 사람들은 연재만화를 교육용으로 사용해 오기도 했다.

20 만화는 정보를 더 명료하고 더 배우기 쉽게 만들 수 있다.

21 여러분은 아마 만화 역사책이나 과학책을 본 적이 있을 것이다.

22 여러분은 많은 만화영화도 당연히 봤을 것이다.

23 이것들은 모든 연령대의 사람들에게 매우 인기가 많다.

24 동작이나 소리가 그림에 더해져서 그림들이 생생하게 살아난다.

25 미술가들과 작가들은 매력적인 캐릭터를 개발하고 만화영화 제작을 통해 재미있는 이야기를 들려준다.

26 1990년대에 새로운 형식의 만화가 개발되었다.

27 그건 웹툰이라고 불린다.

28 웹툰은 온라인으로 출판되기 때문에 여러분이 휴대 전화나 컴퓨터로 언제 어디서나 볼 수 있다.

29 그것은 매우 인기가 있고, 그들 가운데 일부는 심지어 텔레비전 드라마나 영화로 만들어지기도 한다.

30 미래에는 새로운 형태의 만화가 나타날지도 모른다.

31 그것은 지금과는 다르고 한층 더 재미있겠지만, 한 가지는 같을 것이다. 그것은 우리가 웃고, 쉬고, 배우도록 도와줄 것이다.

● 우리말을 참고하여 본문을 영작하시오.

1 배다! 육지다!

➡ _____

2 위의 만화를 보고 웃었는가?

➡ _____

3 그랬다면 그 만화가는 성공했다.

➡ _____

4 만화가들은 만화를 만드는 사람들이다.

➡ _____

5 그들은 여러분의 관심을 끌고, 대개는 간단한 말과 독창적인 그림으로 여러분을 웃게 하고 싶어 한다.

➡ _____

6 사람들은 수백 년 동안 만화를 만들어 왔다.

➡ _____

7 만화에는 많은 종류가 있으며, 그것들은 다양한 역할을 한다.

➡ _____

8 만화의 한 형태로 몇 마디 말을 쓴 그림이 있다.

➡ _____

9 간혹 그것은 '개그 만화'라고 불린다.

➡ _____

10 만화가는 웃긴 캐릭터를 만들고, 그 캐릭터는 우스꽝스러운 행동이나 말을 함으로써 여러분을 웃게 만든다.

➡ _____

11 다른 종류의 만화는 캐리커처라고 불린다.

➡ _____

12 캐리커처에서 캐릭터의 어떤 부분은 평소와 다르거나 더 크다.

➡ _____

13 오른쪽의 그림을 보아라.

➡ _____

14 남자 얼굴의 어떤 부분이 여러분에게 분명히 보이는가?

➡ _____

15 미술가들은 유명한 사람들을 풍자하기 위해 이런 종류의 만화를 그려 왔다.

➡ _____

16 몇 가지 만화 그림이 모여서 이야기를 들려주게 되면, 그것이 연재만화가 된다.

➡ _____

17 연재만화는 여러 해 동안 신문에 실려 왔다.

➡ _____

18 그것들은 종종 그저 재미있는 이야기이다.

➡ _____

19 사람들은 연재만화를 교육용으로 사용해 오기도 했다.

➡ _____

20 만화는 정보를 더 명료하고 더 배우기 쉽게 만들 수 있다.

➡ _____

21 여러분은 아마 만화 역사책이나 과학책을 본 적이 있을 것이다.

➡ _____

22 여러분은 많은 만화영화도 당연히 봤을 것이다.

➡ _____

23 이것들은 모든 연령대의 사람들에게 매우 인기가 많다.

➡ _____

24 동작이나 소리가 그림에 더해져서 그림들이 생생하게 살아난다.

➡ _____

25 미술가들과 작가들은 매력적인 캐릭터를 개발하고 만화영화 제작을 통해 재미있는 이야기를 들려준다.

➡ _____

26 1990년대에 새로운 형식의 만화가 개발되었다.

➡ _____

27 그건 웹툰이라고 불린다.

➡ _____

28 웹툰은 온라인으로 출판되기 때문에 여러분이 휴대 전화나 컴퓨터로 언제 어디서나 볼 수 있다.

➡ _____

29 그것은 매우 인기가 있고, 그들 가운데 일부는 심지어 텔레비전 드라마나 영화로 만들어지기도 한다.

➡ _____

30 미래에는 새로운 형태의 만화가 나타날지도 모른다.

➡ _____

31 그것은 지금과는 다르고 한층 더 재미있겠지만, 한 가지는 같을 것이다. 그것은 우리가 웃고, 쉬고,

배우도록 도와줄 것이다.

➡ _____

_____

[01~07] 다음 글을 읽고 물음에 답하시오.

Boat!

Land!

Did you ①laugh when you saw the cartoon above? If so, the cartoonist was ②successful. Cartoonists are the people who make cartoons. They want to catch your interest, and usually, make you laugh with simple language and creative drawings.

People have made cartoons for hundreds of years. There are many types of cartoons, and they play ③the same roles. One form of cartoon is a picture with a few words. It is sometimes called a "gag cartoon." The cartoonist makes a funny character, and the character makes you laugh ___(A)___ doing or saying ④silly things.

Another type of cartoon is called a caricature. In a caricature, some parts of a character are different or bigger than ⑤usual. Look at the picture on the right. Which parts of the man's face jump out at you? Artists have used this type of cartoon to make fun of well-known people.

01 ①~⑤ 중 글의 흐름상 어색한 것은?

①   ②   ③   ④   ⑤

02 다음 중 빈칸 (A)에 들어갈 말과 같은 말이 들어가는 것은?

① Are you interested _____ the movie?

② Don't give _____ your dream.

③ Please turn _____ the light when you go out.

④ I feel very proud _____ you.

⑤ Let's check them one _____ one.

03 What is the second type of cartoon called? Answer in five words.

➡ _____

04 What does a cartoonist make in a gag cartoon? Answer in English with a full sentence.

➡ _____

05 Which is TRUE about a caricature?

① There are many types of caricatures.

② It makes fun of famous people.

③ Cartoonists don't have an interest in it.

④ It doesn't make people laugh.

⑤ It describes people as they are.

06 다음 중 위 글을 읽고 답할 수 없는 것은?

① What do cartoonists want to do?

② What do cartoonists use to make people laugh?

③ How long have people made cartoons?

④ What is the third type of cartoon?

⑤ What is a gag cartoon?

07 What do cartoonists do? Answer in English with a full sentence.

➡ _____

[08~10] 다음 글을 읽고 물음에 답하시오.

When several cartoon pictures come together and tell a story, we have a comic strip. Comic strips have been in newspapers __(A)__ many years.

[A] You have probably seen comic history or science books. You have surely seen many cartoon movies, or animated movies, too.

[B] They are often just amusing stories. People have also used comic strips for education. Comics can make information clearer and easier to learn.

[C] These are very popular among people of all ages. Movement and sounds are added to pictures, so they come alive.

Artists and writers can develop fascinating characters and tell interesting stories through animation.

08 다음 중 빈칸 (A)에 들어갈 말과 다른 말이 들어가는 것은?

① I haven't seen her _____ a while.

② Carrie has met him _____ a long time.

③ They have lived here _____ last year.

④ She has known him _____ ten years.

⑤ Jina has danced _____ an hour.

09 자연스러운 글이 되도록 [A]~[C]를 바르게 배열한 것은?

① [A] – [C] – [B]

② [B] – [A] – [C]

③ [B] – [C] – [A]

④ [C] – [B] – [A]

⑤ [C] – [A] – [B]

10 Which is NOT true about comic strips?

① It has a story.

② It is also used as an educational purpose.

③ It has one picture.

④ We can see it in newspapers.

⑤ Its stories are amusing.

[11~13] 다음 글을 읽고 물음에 답하시오.

In the 1990s, a new type of cartoon was developed. It is (A)[calling / called] a webtoon. Webtoons are published online, so you can read (B)[it / them] anytime, anywhere on your phone or computer. They are very popular, and some of them are even made into TV dramas or movies.

New forms of cartoons may (C)[appear / be appeared] in the future. They could be different and even more exciting than now, but one thing will remain the same: they will help us laugh, relax, and learn.

11 (A)~(C)에서 어법상 옳은 것을 바르게 짝지은 것은?

① calling – it – appear

② calling – it – be appeared

③ calling – them – be appeared

④ called – them – appear

⑤ called – it – appear

서답형

12 Write the reason why we can read webtoons anytime, anywhere on our phone or computer. Use the phrase 'It's because'.

➡ _____

13 다음 중 위 글을 읽고 답할 수 없는 것은?

① When was a new type of cartoon developed?
② Where are webtoons published?
③ What do we call a new type of cartoon?
④ Who usually sees webtoons?
⑤ What do cartoons help us to do?

[14~16] 다음 글을 읽고 물음에 답하시오.

> Boat!
> Land!
> Did you laugh when you saw the cartoon above? If so, the cartoonist was successful. Cartoonists are the people ___(A)___ make cartoons. They want to catch your interest, and usually, make you laugh with simple language and creative drawings.
> People have made cartoons for hundreds of years. There are many types of cartoons, and they play different roles.

14 빈칸 (A)에 들어갈 말로 적절한 것을 모두 고르시오.

① which   ② that   ③ whom
④ who   ⑤ what

15 다음 중 위 글에 이어질 내용으로 가장 적절한 것은?

① the reason why people see cartoons
② the number of cartoonists
③ various types of cartoons
④ how cartoons have survived for hundreds of years
⑤ what cartoonists want to draw

서답형
16 다음과 같이 풀이되는 말을 위 글에서 찾아 쓰시오.

achieving results you wanted or hoped for

➡ _____

[17~20] 다음 글을 읽고 물음에 답하시오.

> One form of cartoon is a picture with a few words. It is sometimes called a "gag cartoon." The cartoonist makes a funny character, and the character makes you laugh by doing or saying silly things.
> Another type of cartoon is called a caricature. In a caricature, some parts of a character are different or bigger than usual. Look at the picture on the right. Which parts of the man's face jump out at you? Artists have used this type of cartoon to make fun of well-known people.

서답형
17 How do the characters in a gag cartoon make people laugh? Answer in English with a full sentence.

➡ _____
_____

18 다음 중 위 글을 바르게 이해한 사람은?

① 은지: Cartoonists don't want to draw gag cartoons.
② 준석: There are more than two types of cartoons.
③ 지민: It is unnatural to laugh when we see a character in a gag cartoon.
④ 태형: Cartoonists who draw caricatures aren't interested in famous people.
⑤ 정국: Artists draw a caricature to make someone feel good.

19 다음 중 개그 만화에서 볼 수 있는 것은?

① A man's eyes jumping out at readers
② Two characters talking too much
③ A picture with no words
④ A character saying stupid things
⑤ A character's arms bigger than usual

서답형

20 What do we call a picture with a few words? Answer in English with six words.

➡ _____

[21~26] 다음 글을 읽고 물음에 답하시오.

When several cartoon pictures come together and tell a story, we have a comic strip. Comic strips have been in newspapers for many years. They are often just (A) [amusing / amused] stories. People have also used comic strips for education. Comics can make information clearer and easier to learn. You have probably seen comic history or science books.

You have surely seen many cartoon movies, or animated movies, (B)[too / either]. These are very popular among people of all ages. Movement and sounds are added to pictures, so they come (C)[live / alive]. Artists and writers can develop fascinating characters and tell interesting stories through animation.

① In the 1990s, a new type of cartoon was developed. ② Webtoons are published online, so you can read them anytime, anywhere on your phone or computer. ③ They are very popular, and some of them are even made into TV dramas or movies. ④

New forms of cartoons may appear in the future. ⑤ They could be different and even more exciting than now, but (D)<u>one thing</u> will remain the same: they will help us laugh, relax, and learn.

21 다음 중 주어진 문장이 들어가기에 가장 적절한 곳은?

It is called a webtoon.

① ② ③ ④ ⑤

22 (A)~(C)에서 어법상 옳은 것을 바르게 짝지은 것은?

① amused – either – alive
② amused – too – live
③ amusing – too – alive
④ amusing – too – live
⑤ amusing – either – alive

서답형

23 다음 물음에 완전한 문장의 영어로 답하시오.

Q: What is a comic strip made of and what does it tell?

➡ _____

_____

서답형

24 Write the reason why people have used comic strips for education. Use the phrase 'It's because'.

➡ _____

_____

중요

25 다음 중 위 글을 읽고 답할 수 있는 것은?

① How many cartoon pictures do we need to make a comic strip?
② Who makes the animated movies?
③ Where can we read webtoons?
④ How many webtoons were made into TV dramas or movies?
⑤ How do cartoons make people laugh?

서답형

26 밑줄 친 (D)가 의미하는 것을 위 글에서 찾아 우리말로 쓰시오.

➡ _____

[01~07] 다음 글을 읽고 물음에 답하시오.

Boat!

Land!

Did you laugh when you saw the cartoon above? (A)If so, the cartoonist was successful. Cartoonists are the people who make cartoons. They want to catch your interest, and usually, make you laugh with simple language and creative drawings.

(a)

There are many types of cartoons, and (B) they play different roles. One form of cartoon is a picture with a few words. It is sometimes called a "gag cartoon." The cartoonist makes a funny character, and the character makes you laugh by doing or saying silly things.

Another type of cartoon is called a caricature. In a caricature, some parts of a character are different or bigger than usual. Look at the picture on the right. Which parts of the man's face jump out at you? Artists have used this type of cartoon to make fun of well-known people.

중요

01 다음 두 문장을 하나의 문장으로 빈칸 (a)에 쓰시오. 주어진 단어를 활용하시오.

> People started to make cartoons hundreds of years ago. They still make cartoons now. (for)

➡ _____

02 What do cartoonists use to make people laugh? Answer in English with a full sentence.

➡ _____

중요

03 밑줄 친 (A)가 의미하는 것을 구체적으로 쓰시오.

➡ _____

04 밑줄 친 (B)가 가리키는 것을 위 글에서 찾아 쓰시오.

➡ _____

05 According to the passage, what does a gag cartoon make us do? Answer in English with a full sentence.

➡ _____

06 Which type of cartoon is this picture? Answer in English with a full sentence.

Take a look. We are famous.

➡ _____

고난이도

07 다음 중 위 글의 내용과 일치하지 않는 것을 두 군데 찾아 바르게 고치시오.

> Cartoonists make cartoons. They make you laugh with simple language and creative drawings. There are various types of cartoons. One form of cartoon is a picture with many words. There is a funny character which makes you laugh by doing wise things. Caricature is another type of cartoon. In a caricature, some parts of a character are bigger than usual.

_____ ➡ _____

_____ ➡ _____

[08~13] 다음 글을 읽고 물음에 답하시오.

When several cartoon pictures come together and tell a story, we have a comic strip. Comic strips have been in newspapers for many years. They are often just amusing stories. People have also used comic strips for education. Comics can make information clearer and easier to learn. You have probably seen comic history or science books.

You have surely seen many cartoon movies, or animated movies, too. These are very popular among people of all ages. Movement and sounds are added to pictures, so they come alive. Artists and writers can develop fascinating characters and tell interesting stories through animation.

In the 1990s, a new type of cartoon was developed. It is called a webtoon. Webtoons are published online, so you can read them anytime, anywhere on your phone or computer. They are very popular, and some of them are even made into TV dramas or movies.

New forms of cartoons may appear in the future. They could be different and even more exciting than now, but one thing will remain the same: they will help us laugh, relax, and learn.

08 If you want to deliver information more clearly, what type of cartoon can you use?

➡ _____

중요

09 위 글의 내용에 맞게 빈칸에 알맞은 말을 쓰시오.

| In the way that _____, pictures come alive. |

➡ _____

10 What can artists and writers do through animation? Answer in English with eleven words.

➡ _____

_____

11 When were webtoons developed? Answer in English with a full sentence.

➡ _____

고난이도

12 위 글의 내용에 맞게 대화의 빈칸을 채우시오.

| A: Look! There are some cartoon pictures and they tell a story. What is it?
B: It is called _____.
A: How is the story?
B: It is usually _____. It is also used for _____. |

13 위 글의 내용에 맞게 빈칸에 알맞은 말을 쓰시오.

| Although new forms of cartoons may appear in the future, they _____ just like now. |

➡ _____

My Speaking Portfolio – Step 3

Here is a useful tip for you. I've washed my sneakers this way many times.
= 현재완료 (경험)

First, put the sneakers, warm water, and washing powder in a plastic bag.
동명사

Then close the bag and leave it for seven minutes. Lastly, take the sneakers
= Next. And that

out of the bag and wash them. They'll look like new sneakers.
= the sneakers   look like+명사: ~처럼 보이다

구문해설 • useful: 유용한 • sneakers: 운동화 • washing powder: 세제 • plastic bag: 비닐봉지

여기 당신을 위한 유용한 조언이 있어요. 나는 내 운동화를 여러 번 이런 방식으로 세탁했어요. 첫째, 운동화, 온수, 그리고 세제를 비닐봉지에 넣으세요. 그리고 비닐봉지를 묶어 7분 동안 두세요. 마지막으로 운동화를 비닐봉지에서 꺼내 씻으세요. 그들은 새 운동화처럼 보일 거예요.

My Writing Portfolio

Giyeong, My Favorite Cartoon Character

My favorite cartoon character is Giyeong of *Black Rubber Shoes*. He is an

elementary school student. He is humorous and kind. However, he is not very
그러나

smart and sometimes causes trouble. I like him because he looks on the bright
주어 he에 수의 일치   이유를 이끄는 접속사

side of everything and always tries to help others.
다른 사람들

구문해설 • favorite: 가장 좋아하는 • elementary school: 초등학교 • cause: 유발하다
• look on: ~을 바라보다

기영, 내가 가장 좋아하는 만화 캐릭터

내가 가장 좋아하는 만화 캐릭터는 〈검정 고무신〉의 기영이다. 그는 초등학교 학생이다. 그는 재미있고 친절하다. 하지만, 그는 별로 똑똑하지 않고, 때때로 말썽을 피운다. 그는 모든 것의 긍정적인 면을 보고 항상 다른 이들을 도우려 하기 때문에 나는 그를 좋아한다.

Words in Action B

The Best Animated Movie for Children's Education

Animals welcome the city's plan to build an amusement park in the forest.
to부정사의 형용사적 용법(the city's plan 수식)

However, they soon suffer from serious pollution. An old elephant makes a
곧

suggestion. The animals and the city reach an agreement to create a better

world for everyone.

구문해설 • amusement park: 놀이공원 • suffer from: ~으로 고통 받다 • suggestion: 제안
• reach an agreement: 합의점에 도달하다

아이들의 교육을 위한 최고의 만화영화

동물들은 숲속에 놀이공원을 지으려는 도시의 계획을 환영한다. 하지만, 그들은 곧 심각한 오염에 시달린다. 나이 든 코끼리가 한 가지 제안을 한다. 동물들과 도시는 모든 이들을 위한 더 좋은 세상을 만들기 위한 합의에 이른다.

영역별 핵심문제

01 다음 영영풀이가 가리키는 것을 고르시오.

> a type of lotion that you put on your skin to protect it from being damaged by the sun

① sunscreen ② raincoat
③ sauce ④ sneaker
⑤ plate

02 다음 중 밑줄 친 부분의 뜻풀이가 바르지 <u>않은</u> 것은?

① He made a <u>silly</u> mistake. 어리석은
② Why don't you <u>boil</u> water first? 끓이다
③ <u>Spread</u> butter on the bread with the knife. 번지다
④ <u>Cartoons</u> are often fun for people of all ages. 만화
⑤ It's hard to <u>choose</u> just one flavor of ice cream. 고르다

03 다음 우리말을 주어진 단어를 이용하여 영작하시오.

(1) Emma는 오렌지 주스를 유리잔에 부어 그것을 마셨다. (glass, drank)

➡ _____

(2) 우리는 설거지해야 할 많은 접시가 있다. (wash, of)

➡ _____

(3) 나는 달걀과 많은 채소를 볶는 것을 좋아한다. (eggs, lots)

➡ _____

04 다음 문장의 빈칸에 들어갈 말을 〈보기〉에서 골라 쓰시오. (필요한 경우 형태를 바꿀 것.)

> ┤ 보기 ├
> of all ages / watch out / comic strip / jump out at me / come together

(1) When technology and imagination _____, amazing inventions can be created.
(2) His first _____ was published in 1972.
(3) _____ for cars when you ride a bike.
(4) The singer is loved by people _____.
(5) The red balloon really _____.

05 다음 주어진 문장의 밑줄 친 down과 같은 의미로 쓰인 것은?

> You look <u>down</u>. What's wrong with you?

① He bent <u>down</u> to pick up the paper.
② She jumped <u>down</u> off the table.
③ Today, I feel a little <u>down</u>.
④ The stone rolled <u>down</u> the hill.
⑤ Listening to the music, tears ran <u>down</u> on my face.

06 다음 대화가 자연스럽게 이어지도록 순서대로 배열하시오.

> (A) Yes, I've climbed to the top of the mountain twice.
> (B) Have you ever been to Sokcho?
> (C) Really? Then, you've climbed Mt. Seorak, haven't you?
> (D) Yes, I have. Actually my uncle lives there, so I visit him every year.

➡ _____

[07~08] 다음 대화를 읽고 물음에 답하시오.

Emily: Oh, look at the long line at the box office.

Tony: Yeah, there's a ticket machine over there.
_____(A)_____

Emily: All right. Do you know how to use the machine?

Tony: Sure. It's easy. First, select a movie and a showtime.

Emily: Okay. We can watch the seven o'clock show. Then what?

Tony: Well, select the number of tickets and choose our seats.

Emily: Okay. Two tickets, and I want to sit in the back.

Tony: No problem. Lastly, pay for the tickets.

Emily: It's very simple.

07 위 대화의 빈칸 (A)에 들어갈 말로 어색한 것은?

① Let's buy the tickets from the machine.

② How about buying the tickets from the machine?

③ Why don't we buy the tickets from the machine?

④ I think we can buy the tickets from the machine.

⑤ Have you bought the tickets from the machine?

08 위 대화의 내용과 일치하도록 표를 완성하시오.

<How to Use a Ticket Machine>

Step	What to do
1	select (A)_____ and (B)_____
2	select the number of tickets and (C)_____
3	(D)_____

[09~11] 다음 대화를 읽고 물음에 답하시오.

Suji: Good morning, Chef Garcia!

Garcia: Hello, Suji. (A)나초 피자를 만들어 본 적 있나요?

Suji: Nacho pizza? No, I haven't.

Garcia: Kids will love it, and I'll tell you how to make ⓐit.

Suji: Sounds good!

Garcia: It's easy to make. First, put nacho chips on a plate and spread pizza sauce on ⓑthem.

Suji: Okay. Let me help you with the pizza sauce.

Garcia: Thanks. Next, put some ham, onions, and peppers on top.

Suji: Okay. Then?

Garcia: Add cheese and bake for about 12 minutes in the oven.

Suji: I can't wait to taste it!

09 위 대화의 밑줄 친 (A)의 우리말을 6단어로 영작하시오.

➡ _____

10 위 대화의 밑줄 친 ⓐ와 ⓑ가 가리키는 것을 각각 찾아 쓰시오.

➡ ⓐ _____ ⓑ _____

11 위 대화의 내용과 일치하지 않는 것은?

① 수지는 나초 피자를 만들어 본 적이 없다.

② 나초 피자를 만들기는 쉽다.

③ 나초 피자를 만들기 위해 접시 위에 나초 칩을 올려놓고 그 위에 피자 소스를 바른다.

④ 햄, 양파, 피망으로 피자 소스를 만든다.

⑤ 치즈를 올리고 약 12분 동안 오븐에서 굽는다.

12 다음 대화의 내용과 일치하지 <u>않는</u> 것은?

> Anna: Do you know how to make fried rice?
>
> Jinsu: Sure. It's easy. First, cut the vegetables into small pieces.
>
> Anna: Okay. What do you do next?
>
> Jinsu: Put some oil in the pan. Then, fry the vegetables with rice.
>
> Anna: Wow, it's really simple.

① Jinsu knows how to make fried rice.

② To make fried rice, Anna and Jinsu need vegetables, oil, and rice.

③ Before putting some oil in the pan, Anna needs to cut the vegetables into small pieces.

④ Anna needs to fry the small pieces of vegetables with rice after putting some oil in the pan.

⑤ Anna helps Jinsu cut the vegetables into small pieces.

13 다음 대화의 빈칸 (A)~(C)에 들어갈 알맞은 말을 고르시오

> Jane: Kevin, you look (A)[up / down].
>
> Kevin: Nothing (B)[seriously / serious]. Sometimes my feelings change a lot.
>
> Jane: I understand. Many teens have ups and downs in their feelings.
>
> Kevin: Oh, really?
>
> Jane: Have you watched the animated movie "Shining Days"?
>
> Kevin: No, I haven't. Why do you ask?
>
> Jane: It is about a teenager's feelings. It will help you (C)[understand / understanding] your feelings better.
>
> Kevin: That sounds good! I'll watch it.

➡ (A) _____ (B) _____ (C) _____

14 다음 중 동사의 과거분사형으로 바르지 <u>않은</u> 것은?

① put – put 　② read – read

③ do – done 　④ cut – cut

⑤ drive – droven

15 다음 우리말을 영어로 바르게 옮긴 것은?

> 나의 아버지는 전에 미국에 가 본 적이 없다.

① My father didn't go to America.

② My father doesn't have been to America before.

③ My father has gone to America now.

④ My father has not visited America once.

⑤ My father hasn't been to America before.

16 다음 빈칸에 들어갈 말이 바르게 짝지어진 것은?

> • Kevin has been in U.K. _____ .
>
> • Kevin has been in U.K. _____ this Monday.
>
> • Kevin has been in U.K. _____ a week.

① for – since – yet

② once – since – for

③ yet – for – since

④ yet – since – for

⑤ ago – for – since

17 주어진 어구를 바르게 배열하여 다음 우리말을 영어로 쓰시오. 필요하다면 어형을 바꾸시오.

> 무대 위에서 뛰고 있는 소년을 아니?
> (know / jump / you / on / the boy / the stage / do)

➡ _____

18 다음 중 어법상 올바른 문장은?

① When have you seen the singer?
② I have called him two hours ago.
③ I didn't have talked with her for a while.
④ Ryan has been to Spain with his family.
⑤ She has lived in New York when she was young.

19 다음 두 문장을 하나의 문장으로 바르게 쓴 것은?

> I forgot her address. I still can't remember it.

① I have remembered her address.
② I want to remember her address.
③ I forgot her address.
④ I have forgotten her address.
⑤ I haven't forgotten her address.

20 다음 중 빈칸에 들어갈 동사 bake의 형태가 다른 하나는?

① I know the girl _____ some bread.
② They ate _____ potatoes for lunch.
③ What is she _____?
④ We saw her _____ many cookies.
⑤ She needed _____ soda.

21 주어진 단어를 활용하여 다음 우리말을 영어로 쓰시오.

> 나는 작년부터 이 문제를 가지고 있었어.
> (have / problem)

➡ _____

22 주어진 문장의 밑줄 친 부분과 쓰임이 같은 것은?

> I have never seen an elephant.

① Paul has lost his laptop computer.
② Julian has gone to his home.
③ They have been married for 15 years.
④ How long have you stayed here?
⑤ She has used the chair once.

23 다음 중 밑줄 친 부분을 바르게 고치지 않은 것은?

> ⓐ Korea has been in a war in 1952.
> ⓑ Cynthia played tennis since 2011.
> ⓒ I saw my favorite singer once until now.
> ⓓ My cousin has lost his cellphone a week ago.
> ⓔ Who has put this paper on the table the other day?

① ⓐ: was
② ⓑ: has played
③ ⓒ: have seen
④ ⓓ: lost
⑤ ⓔ: putted

24 다음 빈칸에 알맞은 말을 쓰시오.

> 그 도난당한 차는 옆 블록에서 발견되었어.
> The _____ car was _____ on the next block.

25 다음 두 문장을 하나의 문장으로 표현하시오.

> They went to the library at noon. They are still in the library.

➡ _____

Reading

[26~28] 다음 글을 읽고 물음에 답하시오.

Boat!

Land!

Did you laugh when you saw the cartoon above? ① If so, the cartoonist was successful. ② They want to catch your interest, and usually, make you laugh with simple language and creative drawings. ③ People (A)have made cartoons for hundreds of years. ④ There are many types of cartoons, and they play different roles. ⑤ One form of cartoon is a picture with a few words. It is sometimes called a "gag cartoon." The cartoonist makes a funny character, and the character makes you laugh by doing or saying silly things.

26 다음 중 주어진 문장이 들어가기에 가장 적절한 곳은?

> Cartoonists are the people who make cartoons.

①   ②   ③   ④   ⑤

27 다음 중 밑줄 친 (A)와 쓰임이 같은 것은?

① I have been to Paris twice.
② They have gone out.
③ He has read the book for an hour.
④ We haven't met each other before.
⑤ She has lost her key.

28 다음 중 위 글의 내용과 일치하는 것은?

① A cartoonist is successful when he or she makes us sad.
② Cartoonists use language which is not simple.
③ Cartoons were made recently.
④ Cartoonists make us laugh with creative drawings.
⑤ We can find lots of words in a gag cartoon.

[29~30] 다음 글을 읽고 물음에 답하시오.

Another type of cartoon is called a caricature. In a caricature, some parts of a character are different or bigger than _____(A)_____. Look at the picture on the right. Which parts of the man's face jump out at you? Artists have used this type of cartoon to make fun of well-known people.

When several cartoon pictures come together and tell a story, we have a comic strip. Comic strips have been in newspapers for many years. They are often just amusing stories. People have also used comic strips for education. Comics can make information clearer and easier to learn. You have probably seen comic history or science books.

29 다음과 같이 풀이되는 말을 빈칸 (A)에 쓰시오.

> normal; happening most often

➡ _____

30 다음 중 위 글의 앞에 나올 내용으로 가장 적절한 것은?

① lives of many cartoonists
② a type of cartoon made into movies
③ types of cartoon
④ how to make cartoons
⑤ reasons why cartoons are popular

[01~02] 다음 대화를 읽고 물음에 답하시오.

Jane: Kevin, you look down.
Kevin: Nothing ⓐserious. Sometimes my feelings change a lot.
Jane: I understand. Many teens have ⓑups and downs in their feelings.
Kevin: Oh, really?
Jane: Have you ⓒwatching the animated movie "Shining Days"?
Kevin: No, I ⓓhaven't. Why do you ask?
Jane: It is about a teenager's feelings. It will help you ⓔunderstand your feelings better.
Kevin: That sounds good! I'll watch it.

🖉 출제율 90%

01 위 대화의 밑줄 친 ⓐ~ⓔ 중 어법상 어색한 것을 찾아 바르게 고치시오.

➡ _____ ➡ _____

🖉 출제율 100%

02 위 대화를 읽고 대답할 수 없는 것은?

① What does Kevin look like?
② According to Jane, what do teenagers have in their feelings?
③ What does Jane suggest to Kevin?
④ What kind of movie is "Shining Days"?
⑤ How can watching "Shining Days" help Kevin?

[03~05] 다음 대화를 읽고 물음에 답하시오.

Emily: Oh, look at the long line at the box office.
Tony: Yeah, there's a ticket machine over there. Let's buy the tickets from the machine.
Emily: All right. Do you know how to use the machine?

Tony: Sure. It's easy. First, select a movie and a showtime.
Emily: Okay. We can watch the seven o'clock show. Then what?
Tony: Well, select the number of tickets and choose our seats.
Emily: Okay. Two tickets, and I want to sit in the back.
Tony: No problem. Lastly, pay for the tickets.
Emily: It's very simple.

🖉 출제율 90%

03 From what do Tony and Emily want to buy the tickets?

➡ _____

🖉 출제율 95%

04 When will Tony and Emily watch the movie?

➡ _____

🖉 출제율 85%

05 Where does Emily want to sit?

➡ _____

🖉 출제율 95%

06 다음 대화에서 (A)~(E)가 자연스럽게 이어지도록 순서대로 배열하시오.

Suji: Good morning, Chef Garcia!
Garcia: Hello, Suji. Have you ever made nacho pizza?
Suji: Nacho pizza? No, I haven't.
Garcia: Kids will love it, and I'll tell you how to make it.
Suji: Sounds good!
(A) Okay. Let me help you with the pizza sauce.
(B) Lastly, add cheese and bake for about 12 minutes in the oven.

(C) It's easy to make. First, put nacho chips on a plate and spread pizza sauce on them.

(D) Okay. Then?

(E) Thanks. Next, put some ham, onions, and peppers on top.

➡ _____

[07~09] 다음 대화를 읽고 물음에 답하시오.

Anna: Do you know how to make fried rice?

Jinsu: Sure. It's easy. First, (A)[cut / put] the vegetables into small pieces.

Anna: Okay. What do you do next?

Jinsu: (B)[Bake / Put] some oil in the pan. Then, (C)[fry / spread] the vegetables with rice.

Anna: Wow, it's really simple.

출제율 95%

07 위 대화의 빈칸 (A)~(C)에 들어갈 말로 바르게 짝지어진 것은?

	(A)	(B)	(C)
①	cut	Bake	fry
②	cut	Put	spread
③	cut	Put	fry
④	put	Put	spread
⑤	put	Bake	fry

출제율 90%

08 What should Anna and Jinsu do after putting some oil in the pan?

➡ _____

출제율 90%

09 What ingredients should Anna and Jinsu prepare to make fried rice?

➡ _____

출제율 100%

10 다음 짝지어진 대화가 <u>어색한</u> 것은?

① A: Have you ever cooked fried rice?
   B: Yes, I have cooked it many times.

② A: I have never been to Beijing. How about you?
   B: I went there last summer.

③ A: Have you ever touched a snake?
   B: Yes, I did. I was so scared.

④ A: You have been to Canada. Haven't you?
   B: No, I haven't.

⑤ A: Have you been to Busan?
   B: Busan? No, I've never been there.

출제율 95%

11 다음 문장에서 쓰인 현재완료의 용법이 나머지와 <u>다른</u> 하나는?

① We have just eaten dinner.

② Has the concert already started?

③ They haven't met each other yet.

④ I have had a headache for an hour.

⑤ She has just found the ticket.

출제율 90%

12 다음 중 어법상 올바른 것은?

① The man has made a big mistake at work yesterday.

② Mr. Jones is practicing the flute for three years.

③ I don't want to eat freezing food.

④ The walking boy with his friends is my brother.

⑤ Cindy has been interested in painting for many years.

13 출제율 95%

다음 빈칸에 들어갈 말이 바르게 짝지어진 것은?

- The _____ chicken will be served.
- Do you know the _____ boy?

① cook – shout
② cooking – shouted
③ cooking – shouting
④ cooked – shouted
⑤ cooked – shouting

14 출제율 100%

다음 빈칸에 들어갈 시제가 다른 하나는?

① Kelly _____ her laptop computer yesterday. She was relieved.
② Tom _____ the book ten times until now. He really likes reading it.
③ Brad wants to know when Angela _____ home last night.
④ Molly _____ some pictures of Zach when they traveled together.
⑤ When I was young, I _____ a lamb.

15 출제율 95%

주어진 동사를 어법에 맞게 빈칸에 쓰시오.

(1) I met a boy _____ Chris last week. (name)

(2) When are you going to fix the _____ refrigerator? (break)

(3) The _____ news made her say nothing. (surprise)

16 출제율 90%

주어진 단어를 활용하여 다음 우리말을 영어로 쓰시오. 필요하다면 어형을 바꾸시오.

나는 추천된 책을 살 거야.
(the / I / book / will / recommend / buy)

➡ _____

17 출제율 95%

현재완료 시제를 이용하여 다음 우리말을 영어로 쓰시오.

Smith씨는 작년부터 내게 영어를 가르쳐 주고 있다.

➡ _____

[18~24] 다음 글을 읽고 물음에 답하시오.

When several cartoon pictures come together and tell a story, we have a comic strip. Comic strips have been in newspapers for many years. They are often just amusing stories. People have also used comic strips for education. Comics can make information clearer and easier ⓐto learn. You have probably seen comic history or science books.

You have surely seen many cartoon movies, or animated movies, too. These are very popular among people of all ages. Movement and sounds are added to pictures, so they come alive. Artists and writers can develop fascinating characters and tell ___(A)___ stories through animation.

In the 1990s, a new type of cartoon was developed. It is called a webtoon. Webtoons are published online, so you can read them anytime, anywhere on your phone or computer. They are very popular, and some of them are even made into TV dramas or movies.

New forms of cartoons may appear in the future. (B)They could be different and even more exciting than now, but one thing will remain the same: they will help us laugh, relax, and learn.

18 출제율 90%

주어진 단어를 어법에 맞게 빈칸 (A)에 쓰시오.

interest

➡ _____

19 출제율 90%

밑줄 친 (B)가 가리키는 것을 위 글에서 찾아 쓰시오.

➡ _____

20 출제율 90%

다음 중 밑줄 친 ⓐ와 쓰임이 같은 것은?

① We want you to visit your uncle.
② It is difficult to learn a foreign language.
③ He went to the market to buy milk.
④ The problem is easy to solve.
⑤ You need something warm to wear.

21 출제율 90%

Choose one that is NOT true about a comic strip.

① There are history books using it.
② It has been used for education.
③ The stories are amusing.
④ It is published online.
⑤ It is made of several cartoon pictures.

22 출제율 90%

According to the passage, what makes pictures come alive? Answer in English with a full sentence.

➡ _____
_____

23 출제율 100%

다음 중 위 글의 내용을 잘못 이해한 사람은?

① Sam: In order to make a comic strip, I need some cartoon pictures and a story.
② Tom: I will look into newspapers to find a comic strip.
③ Jim: There are many science books using comic strips.
④ June: Only children like animated movies.
⑤ Paul: Sometimes comics are used to teach history easily.

24 출제율 95%

다음 중 위 글을 읽고 답할 수 없는 것은?

① What does a comic strip have?
② How do pictures come alive?
③ What do writers tell through animation?
④ How long does it take to make a comic strip?
⑤ What is very popular among people of all ages?

[25~26] 다음 글을 읽고 물음에 답하시오.

My favorite cartoon character is Giyeong of *Black Rubber Shoes*. He is an elementary school student. He is humorous and kind. ___(A)___, he is not very smart and sometimes causes trouble. I like him because he looks on the bright side of everything and always tries to help others.

25 출제율 95%

다음 중 빈칸 (A)에 들어갈 말로 가장 적절한 것은?

① In addition   ② However
③ For example   ④ Moreover
⑤ Fortunately

26 출제율 90%

Write the reason why the writer likes the cartoon character. Answer in English with a full sentence.

➡ _____
_____

서술형 실전문제

[01~03] 다음 대화를 읽고 물음에 답하시오.

> Jane: Kevin, you look down.
> Kevin: Nothing serious. Sometimes my feelings change a lot.
> Jane: I understand. Many teens have ups and downs in their feelings.
> Kevin: Oh, really?
> Jane: Have you watched the animated movie "Shining Days"?
> Kevin: No, I haven't. Why do you ask?
> Jane: It is about a teenager's feelings. It will help you understand your feelings better.
> Kevin: That sounds good! I'll watch it.

01 Has Kevin seen "Shining Days"?

➡ _____

02 What kind of Movie is "Shining Days"?

➡ _____

03 How can watching "Shining Days" help Kevin?

➡ _____

04 중요 다음 두 문장의 차이를 서술하시오.

> (1) Amelia has been to Canada.
> (2) Amelia has gone to Canada.

➡ _____
_____
_____

05 다음 두 문장을 하나의 문장으로 쓰시오.

> I lost my favorite book. I don't have it now.

➡ _____

06 중요 주어진 단어를 활용하여 다음 우리말을 영어로 쓰시오.

> 그 울고 있는 소년은 삶은 달걀을 다섯 개 먹었어요. (cry / boil)

➡ _____

07 다음은 한국을 방문한 Steve의 일기 중 일부이다. Steve의 경험을 말하는 문장을 완성하시오.

> I _____ a lot of Korean food, but _____ *sannakji* yet. I want to eat it someday.

08 다음 빈칸에 알맞은 말을 쓰시오.

> 그녀는 떨리는 목소리로 "부끄러운 줄 아세요."라고 그에게 말했다.
> She told in _____, "Shame on you."

[09~10] 다음 글을 읽고 물음에 답하시오.

> My favorite cartoon character is Giyeong of *Black Rubber Shoes*. He is an elementary school student. He is humorous and kind.

However, he is not very smart and sometimes causes trouble. I like him because he looks on the bright side of everything and always tries to help others.

09 What cartoon is the writer's favorite character from? Answer in English with a full sentence.

➡ _____

10 What's the character like? Answer in English with a full sentence.

➡ _____

_____

[11~13] 다음 글을 읽고 물음에 답하시오.

People have made cartoons for hundreds of years. There are many types of cartoons, and they play different roles. One form of cartoon is a picture with a few words. It is sometimes called a "gag cartoon." The cartoonist makes a funny character, and the character makes you laugh by doing or saying silly things.

Another type of cartoon is called a caricature. In a caricature, some parts of a character are different or bigger than usual. Look at the picture on the right. Which parts of the man's face jump out at you?

_____(A)_____

When several cartoon pictures come together and tell a story, we have a comic strip. Comic strips have been in newspapers for many years. They are often just amusing stories. People have also used comic strips for education.

11 주어진 글을 하나의 문장으로 빈칸 (A)에 쓰시오.

Artists used this type of cartoon to make fun of well-known people. They still use it.

➡ _____

_____

12 주어진 단어를 바르게 배열하여 위 글의 제목을 쓰시오.

(roles / types / their / various / of / and / cartoons)

➡ _____

13 위 글의 내용에 맞게 빈칸에 알맞은 말을 쓰시오.

There are three types of cartoons in the passage. One is _____. A funny character in the cartoon _____ by doing and saying silly things. Another is _____. It is used to make fun of famous people. The other is _____. They have _____ stories.

14 Read the following paragraph and write the reason why artists have drawn a caricature. Answer in English with a full sentence.

Another type of cartoon is called a caricature. In a caricature, some parts of a character are different or bigger than usual. Look at the picture on the right. Which parts of the man's face jump out at you? Artists have used this type of cartoon to make fun of well-known people.

➡ _____

_____

01 다음 대화의 내용과 일치하도록 Kevin의 일기를 완성하시오.

> Jane: Kevin, you look down.
>
> Kevin: Nothing serious. Sometimes my feelings change a lot.
>
> Jane: I understand. Many teens have ups and downs in their feelings.
>
> Kevin: Oh, really?
>
> Jane: Have you watched the animated movie "Shining Days"?
>
> Kevin: No, I haven't. Why do you ask?
>
> Jane: It is about a teenager's feelings. It will help you understand your feelings better.
>
> Kevin: That sounds good! I'll watch it.

> Mon, Nov 4th, 2019
>
> Today, I was (A)_____ with nothing serious. These days, my feelings changed a lot. At that time, Jane came to me and understood my feeling, saying that many teens have (B)_____ in their feelings. To understand my feelings better, she suggested (C)_____ _____. She explained that it is about (D)_____. It sounded good, so I decided to see this movie soon.

02 다음 만화 캐릭터에 관한 정보를 보며 글을 완성하시오.

• 캐릭터: Iron Man
  - from Tales of Suspense
  - a genius scientist
• 특징: - owns a weapon company
  - invented a suit of armor to save his life
	• 좋아하는 이유:
	 - is very rich
	 - is the leader of the superhero team, the Avengers

> My favorite cartoon character is _____ of _____. He is _____.
> He _____ and _____. I like _____
> because _____.

단원별 모의고사

01 다음 영영풀이가 가리키는 것을 고르시오.

> a process of teaching and learning

① teacher   ② learner
③ classroom   ④ education
⑤ educator

02 다음 우리말에 맞게 주어진 어휘를 사용하여 영작하시오.

(1) Jake는 연극에서 산타 클로스 역할을 했다. (Santa Clause, role)

➡ _____

(2) 사람들이 나를 놀릴 때 화가 난다. (fun, angry)

➡ _____

(3) 채소를 작은 조각으로 자르세요. (cut, pieces)

➡ _____

03 다음 우리말을 주어진 단어를 이용하여 영작하시오.

(1) 축구 팀원들은 공통의 목표를 갖고 있다. (goal)

➡ _____

(2) 만화영화로 영어를 배우는 것은 재미있다. (it, animated)

➡ _____

(3) 삶에는 기복이 있다. (there, ups)

➡ _____

04 다음 문장의 빈칸에 들어갈 말을 〈보기〉에서 골라 쓰시오.

> ┤ 보기 ├
> movement / amusing / publish / probably

(1) I like to listen to _____ stories on the radio.

(2) The old lady _____ knows more about the building than anyone.

(3) The cat made a sudden _____ and caught a mouse.

(4) They agreed to _____ the new novel next year.

[05~07] 다음 대화를 읽고 물음에 답하시오.

Suji: Good morning, Chef Garcia!

Garcia: Hello, Suji. Have you ever made nacho pizza?

Suji: Nacho pizza? No, I haven't.

Garcia: Kids will love it, and I'll tell you how to make it.

Suji: Sounds good!

Garcia: It's easy to make. First, put nacho chips on a plate and spread pizza sauce on them.

Suji: Okay. (A)Let me help you with the pizza sauce.

Garcia: Thanks. Next, put some ham, onions, and peppers on top.

Suji: Okay. Then?

Garcia: Add cheese and bake for about 12 minutes in the oven.

Suji: (B)I can't wait to taste it!

05 위 대화의 밑줄 친 (A)와 바꾸어 쓸 수 있는 것은?

① I'll give you a hand with the pizza sauce.

② I want you to help me with the pizza sauce.

③ Would you help me with the pizza sauce?

④ I need your help with the pizza sauce.

⑤ Can you give me your hand with the pizza sauce?

06 위 대화의 밑줄 친 (B)와 바꾸어 쓸 수 있는 것은?

① I don't want to wait to taste it.
② I don't like to taste it.
③ I'm not good at tasting it.
④ I'm looking forward to tasting it.
⑤ I haven't tasted it.

07 위 대화의 내용과 일치하도록 빈칸을 완성하시오.

<How to make nacho pizza>

Step	Procedure
1	put _____ on a plate
2	_____ pizza sauce on the nacho chips
3	put _____ on top
4	add _____ and bake for _____ in the oven

[08~10] 다음 대화를 읽고 물음에 답하시오.

Jane: Kevin, you look down.
Kevin: Nothing serious. Sometimes my feelings change a lot.
Jane: ⓐ I understand. Many teens have _____ (A) _____ in their feelings.
Kevin: ⓑ Oh, really?
Jane: ⓒ Have you watched the animated movie "Shining Days"?
Kevin: ⓓ No, I haven't. Why do you ask?
Jane: ⓔ It will help you understand your feelings better.
Kevin: That sounds good! I'll watch it.

08 위 대화의 빈칸 (A)에 '기복'을 나타내는 표현을 3단어로 완성하시오.

➡ _____

09 위 대화의 ⓐ~ⓔ 중 주어진 문장이 들어가기에 적절한 곳은?

It is about a teenager's feelings.

① ⓐ ② ⓑ ③ ⓒ ④ ⓓ ⑤ ⓔ

10 위 대화의 내용과 일치하지 않는 것은?

① Kevin은 기분이 안 좋아 보인다.
② Kevin은 때때로 감정이 많이 바뀌는 심각한 문제를 갖고 있다.
③ 많은 십대들이 감정의 기복이 있다.
④ Shining Days라는 만화영화는 십 대의 감정에 관한 것이다.
⑤ Jane은 Shining Days라는 영화가 Kevin의 감정을 더 잘 이해하도록 도와줄 것이라고 생각한다.

[11~12] 다음 대화를 읽고 물음에 답하시오.

Emily: Oh, look at the long line at the box office.
Tony: Yeah, there's a ticket machine over there. Let's buy the tickets from the machine.
Emily: All right. (A)그 기계를 어떻게 쓰는지 아니?
Tony: Sure. It's easy. First, select a movie and a showtime.
Emily: Okay. We can watch the seven o'clock show. Then what?
Tony: Well, select the number of tickets and choose our seats.
Emily: Okay. Two tickets, and I want to sit in the back.
Tony: No problem. Lastly, pay for the tickets.
Emily: It's very simple.

11 위 대화의 밑줄 친 (A)의 우리말을 <보기>에 주어진 단어를 모두 사용하여 영작하시오.

┌─ 보기 ┐
know / to / you / machine / the / do / how / use
└──────┘

➡ _____

12 위 대화의 내용과 일치하는 것은?

① Emily and Tony are going to buy their tickets at the ticket counter.

② Emily and Tony are going to sit in the middle.

③ Emily and Tony have to choose seats before they select the showtime.

④ Emily already knows how to buy tickets using the ticket machine.

⑤ Emily and Tony have to pay for the tickets after choosing their seats.

13 다음 빈칸에 들어갈 말로 가장 적절한 것은?

> Linda hasn't found her car key _____.

① just   ② already   ③ ago
④ yet   ⑤ before

14 다음 중 주어진 문장의 밑줄 친 부분과 쓰임이 같은 것은?

> Where can I find a recycling bin?

① Can you see the crying baby?

② I heard someone calling my name.

③ Who shot the flying bird?

④ There are boys flying kites.

⑤ Diana couldn't find her sleeping bag.

15 다음 중 어법상 바르지 않은 것은?

① Look at the man playing the violin.

② Patrick has just finished the project.

③ Someone called you when you went out.

④ There was an unexpecting danger around us.

⑤ Susan has used this coffee machine for ten years.

16 주어진 단어를 활용하여 다음 우리말을 여덟 단어로 이루어진 한 문장으로 쓰시오.

> 이러한 표현들은 종종 구어체 영어에서 사용된다. (expression / use / speak)

➡ _____

[17~20] 다음 글을 읽고 물음에 답하시오.

Boat! Land!

Did you laugh when you saw the cartoon above? If so, the cartoonist was successful. Cartoonists are the people who make cartoons. They want to catch ①your interest, and usually, make you (A)[laugh / to laugh] with simple language and creative drawings.

People have made cartoons for hundreds of years. There are ②many types of cartoons, and they play different roles. One form of cartoon is a picture with a few words. It is sometimes called a "gag cartoon." The cartoonist makes a funny character, and the character makes you laugh by doing or (B)[say / saying] silly things.

Another type of cartoon is called a caricature. In a caricature, some parts of a character (C)[is / are] different or bigger than usual. Look at the picture on the right. Which parts of the man's face jump out at you? Artists have used this type of cartoon to make fun of well-known people.

When several cartoon pictures ③come together and tell a story, we have a comic strip. Comic strips have been in newspapers for many years. They are often just amusing stories. People ④have also used comic strips for education. Comics can make information clearer and ⑤more difficult to learn. You have probably seen comic history or science books.

17 ①~⑤ 중 글의 흐름상 어색한 것은?

①   ②   ③   ④   ⑤

18 (A)~(C)에서 어법상 알맞은 것을 쓰시오.

➡ (A) _____ (B) _____ (C) _____

19 How long have people made cartoons? Answer in English with a full sentence.

➡ _____

20 다음 중 위 글의 내용과 일치하는 것은?

① Cartoonists aren't interested in drawing creative things.
② People who draw a gag cartoon use as many words as possible.
③ There is only one picture in a comic strip.
④ We can't find a comic strip in newspapers now.
⑤ Comics help us understand history or science clearly.

[21~22] 다음 글을 읽고 물음에 답하시오.

You have surely seen many cartoon movies, or animated movies, too. These are very popular among people of all ages. Movement and sounds are added to pictures, so they come alive. Artists and writers can develop fascinating characters and tell interesting stories through animation.

In the 1990s, a new type of cartoon was developed. It is called a webtoon. Webtoons are published online, so you can read them anytime, anywhere on your phone or computer. They are very popular, and some of them are even made into TV dramas or movies.

New forms of cartoons may appear in the future. They could be different and even more exciting than now, but one thing will remain the same: they will help us laugh, relax, and learn.

21 위 글의 내용과 일치하지 <u>않는</u> 것은?

① Many cartoon movies are loved by people of all ages.
② Artists develop fascinating characters through animation.
③ Webtoons are read online.
④ Some TV dramas are based on webtoons.
⑤ The writer doesn't think a new type of cartoon will appear.

22 웹툰의 강점으로 가장 적절한 것은?

① They have funny characters.
② They are easy to read whenever you want.
③ They have the latest information.
④ They are loved by people of all ages.
⑤ They have sounds and movement.

INSIGHT
on the textbook

교과서 파헤치기

※ 다음 영어를 우리말로 쓰시오.

01	attitude		22	freedom
02	accuse		23	confident
03	throw		24	president
04	behind		25	receive
05	promise		26	right
06	protect		27	allowance
07	avoid		28	truth
08	bullying		29	arrest
09	difficulty		30	victim
10	free		31	ordinary
11	appearance		32	friendly
12	character		33	whisper
13	guilty		34	popular
14	worried		35	care for ~
15	judge		36	be afraid of ~
16	shy		37	calm down
17	prison		38	set+목적어+free
18	beard		39	accuse A of B
19	missing		40	thanks to ~
20	attack		41	be for ~
21	neighbor		42	fight off ~
			43	vote for ~

※ 다음 우리말을 영어로 쓰시오.

01	등	
02	통과하다, 지나가다	
03	활동	
04	휴대하다, 지니다	
05	소리치다, 외치다	
06	희생자	
07	투표하다	
08	선택	
09	들어가다, 참개[출전]하다	
10	숨기다	
11	속삭이다	
12	다정한, 친절한	
13	외모	
14	체포하다	
15	운이 좋은	
16	직면하다, (힘든 상황에) 처하다	
17	신경 쓰다, 꺼리다	
18	유죄의	
19	선택하다, 고르다	
20	곱슬곱슬한	
21	평범한	

22	인기 있는, 대중적인	
23	언제든지, 언제나	
24	공약, 약속	
25	매월의, 한 달에 한 번의	
26	득점하다	
27	자유	
28	보호하다	
29	자신감 있는	
30	용돈	
31	이웃	
32	고발하다, 비난하다	
33	실종된, 행방불명된	
34	감옥	
35	지금까지	
36	~을 두려워하다	
37	B 때문에 A를 고발하다	
38	~을 자르다	
39	~을 잘하다	
40	~ 덕분에	
41	~을 뽑다, ~에게 투표하다	
42	~에게 동의하다	
43	~을 돌보다	

※ 다음 영영풀이에 알맞은 단어를 <보기>에서 골라 쓴 후, 우리말 뜻을 쓰시오.

1 _____ : to make something happen: _____

2 _____ : someone who lives near you: _____

3 _____ : to stay away from a person or place: _____

4 _____ : to get points, goals, runs, etc., in a game or contest: _____

5 _____ : how you think or feel about something: _____

6 _____ : the belief that you are able to do things well or be successful: _____

7 _____ : a person who appears in a story, book, play, movie, or television show: _____

8 _____ : to speak very quietly so that other people cannot hear: _____

9 _____ : to use violence to hurt or damage someone: _____

10 _____ : an action to try to frighten someone who is smaller or weaker: _____

11 _____ : to decide which thing you want: _____

12 _____ : to keep someone or something safe from something dangerous or bad: _____

13 _____ : the money you get back when you pay more money than something costs: _____

14 _____ : someone who has been hurt or killed: _____

15 _____ : an amount of money that parents give to a child each week: _____

16 _____ : to take the person away to ask them about a crime that they might have committed: _____

보기			
attack	allowance	cause	score
neighbor	victim	bullying	attitude
choose	avoid	protect	confidence
whisper	change	character	arrest

※ 다음 우리말과 일치하도록 빈칸에 알맞은 말을 쓰시오.

Communicate: Listen - Listen and Answer. Talk

G: Hi, I'm Gacha. I'm _____ Mongolia. When I first came to Songji Middle School two months _____, I was so _____. I was a little _____, and I wasn't _____ at Korean. However, I'm a _____ girl. All my classmates are nice and _____. I enjoy _____ handball with them in P.E. class. I'm a good player. They _____ me "Golden Hand." There _____ _____ a sports day next week. _____ _____ my class _____ _____ in the handball event.

Communicate: Listen - Listen and Answer. Dialog

B: Hi, Minsol. _____ your class _____?
G: Of _____. We have a _____ _____ _____.
B: You _____ _____ _____ _____ Mongolia?
G: Yes, _____ _____ is Gacha.
B: I've heard a lot about her. But _____ does she _____ _____?
G: She's _____ _____ and _____ a _____.
B: Oh, is she the girl _____ the goal _____ _____?
G: Yes, that's _____ _____ _____.
B: Wow, she's _____ _____.

Communicate: Listen - Listen More

M: _____ _____ _____ _____ _____ for you?
G: I _____ my _____ _____.
M: Okay, _____ _____. What's your _____ name?
G: His name is Wally Brown. He's _____ _____ _____.
M: _____ does he _____ _____?
G: He _____ brown hair and brown eyes.
M: What _____ he _____?
G: He is _____ a _____ _____ and black pants.
M: Can you _____ _____ _____?
G: Oh, he is _____ _____ _____ _____.
M: All right. We'll go out and _____ _____ him. Also, we'll _____ _____ about a _____ child.
G: Thank you so much. _____ _____ I'll _____ him soon.

Communicate: Speak 2 - Talk in pairs

A: I _____ _____ _____ _____ tomorrow!
B: _____ you'll _____ _____ _____ the exam.
A: I _____ _____, _____. Thanks.

여: 안녕, 나는 Gacha라고 해. 나는 몽골에서 왔어. 두 달 전에 내가 처음 송지 중학교에 왔을 때, 나는 무척 걱정이 되었어. 나는 좀 수줍음을 탔고 한국어를 잘 못했어. 하지만 난 운이 좋은 아이야. 내 학급 친구들은 모두 멋지고 다정해. 나는 체육 시간에 친구들과 핸드볼 하는 것을 즐겨. 난 실력이 좋은 선수야. 친구들은 나를 '황금 손'이라고 불러. 다음 주에 운동회가 있을 거야. 난 우리 반이 핸드볼 대회에서 이기길 바라.

남: 안녕, 민솔아. 너희 반이 이기고 있니?
여: 물론이지. 우리는 훌륭한 핸드볼 선수가 있거든.
남: 몽골에서 온 여자아이 말하니?
여: 응, 그녀의 이름은 Gacha야.
남: 그녀에 대해 많이 들었어. 그런데 그녀는 어떻게 생겼어?
여: 그녀는 키가 크고 말총머리를 하고 있어.
남: 아, 지금 막 골을 넣은 여자아이가 그녀니?
여: 맞아, 저건 그녀의 일곱 번째 골이야.
남: 와, 그녀는 정말 잘하는구나.

남: 무엇을 도와드릴까요?
여: 남동생을 잃어버렸어요.
남: 알겠어요, 진정하세요. 남동생 이름이 뭐죠?
여: 그의 이름은 Wally Brown이에요. 다섯 살이고요.
남: 어떻게 생겼나요?
여: 그는 갈색 머리이고 갈색 눈을 지녔어요.
남: 그는 무엇을 입고 있나요?
여: 그는 초록색 셔츠와 검은 바지를 입고 있어요.
남: 더 말해 줄 수 있나요?
여: 아, 그는 빨간 배낭을 메고 있어요.
남: 알겠어요. 우리가 나가서 그를 찾아볼게요. 또, 우리가 미아 방송을 할 겁니다.
여: 정말 감사합니다. 동생을 빨리 찾길 바라요.

A: 나는 내일 중요한 시험이 있어!
B: 네가 시험을 잘 보길 바라.
A: 나도 그러길 바라. 고마워.

Communicate: Speak 2 - Talk in groups

A: _____ is _____ _____ _____?
B: _____ _____ is Buster.
A: _____ _____ he _____ _____?
B: He _____ _____ _____.
A: Does he _____ _____ _____?
B: Yes, he _____.

Communicate: Speak - Rap Time

(1) A: I _____ my puppy _____ _____.
  B: _____ _____ you'll _____ him soon.
(2) A: I hope you'll _____ _____ _____ in the final game.
  B: Thanks. _____ _____ you _____ _____.
(3) A: _____ _____ your sister _____ _____, Claire?
  B: She's tall and _____ _____ _____ _____.
(4) A: _____ your father _____ a blue cap?
  B: Yeah. Now, he's _____ _____ _____.

My Speaking Portfolio

G: _____ _____ the _____ _____. There _____ posters for the next _____.
B: Yeah, I've _____ _____ my _____. I'll _____ _____ Jang Jimin.
G: You _____ the boy _____ _____? He _____ _____, but I don't like his _____.
B: Then _____ _____ you _____?
G: Well, I am for number 1, Han Siwon. She _____ _____ our school _____ _____ _____.
B: She _____ _____ a ponytail, _____?
G: Yes, and Hong Jiho _____ _____.
B: She _____ _____, but I don't like _____ _____.

Wrap Up

1. B: I hear _____ _____ a new student in your class.
  G: Yes. She's _____ Jejudo. Oh, she's _____ _____!
  B: _____ one? _____ _____ she _____ like?
  G: She has _____ hair and is _____ _____.
2. G: You _____ _____. What's _____, Jongmin?
  B: My sister _____ _____ _____ this morning.
  G: What _____?
  B: She _____ her bike.
  G: _____ _____. _____ she'll _____ _____ soon.

A: 네 캐릭터의 이름은 뭐니?
B: 그의 이름은 Buster야.
A: 그는 어떻게 생겼니?
B: 그는 머리카락이 없어.
A: 그는 눈이 크니?
B: 응, 맞아.

(1) A: 나는 오늘 오후에 내 강아지를 잃어버렸어.
  B: 네가 그를 곧 찾기를 바랄게.
(2) A: 나는 네가 결선에서 최선을 다하길 바라.
  B: 고마워. 나도 네가 그러길 바라.
(3) A: 네 언니는 어떻게 생겼니, Claire?
  B: 그녀는 키가 크고 긴 생머리야.
(4) A: 네 아버지는 파란 모자를 쓰고 계시니?
  B: 응. 지금 지도를 보고 계셔.

여: 이 게시판을 봐. 다음 학생회장의 포스터가 있어.
남: 응, 나는 이미 결정을 내렸어. 나는 장지민에게 투표할 거야.
여: 안경을 쓴 남자아이 얘기하는 거야? 그는 똑똑해 보이지만 나는 그의 공약이 마음에 들지 않아.
남: 그럼 넌 누굴 선택할 거야?
여: 음, 나는 1번 한시원을 지지해. 그녀는 우리 학교를 안전한 장소로 만들고 싶어 해.
남: 그녀는 항상 말총머리를 해, 그렇지?
여: 맞아, 그리고 홍지호도 괜찮아 보여.
남: 그녀는 친절해 보이지만, 나는 장기자랑이 싫어.

1. 남: 너희 반에 새로 온 학생이 있다고 들었어.
  여: 응. 그녀는 제주도에서 왔어. 어, 그녀가 저기에 있어!
  남: 어느 아이? 어떻게 생겼어?
  여: 그녀는 곱슬머리이고 안경을 끼고 있어.
2. 여: 너 슬퍼 보여. 무슨 일이니, 종민아?
  남: 여동생이 오늘 아침에 팔이 부러졌어.
  여: 무슨 일이 있었는데?
  남: 자전거에서 떨어졌어.
  여: 안됐구나. 그녀가 곧 회복되기를 바라.

※ 다음 우리말에 맞도록 대화를 영어로 쓰시오.

Communicate: Listen - Listen and Answer. Talk

G: _____
_____
_____
_____
_____

Communicate: Listen - Listen and Answer. Dialog

B: _____
G: _____
B: _____
G: _____
B: _____
G: _____
B: _____
G: _____
B: _____

Communicate: Listen - Listen More

M: _____
G: _____
M: _____
G: _____
M: _____
G: _____
M: _____
G: _____
M: _____
G: _____
M: _____
G: _____

Communicate: Speak 2 - Talk in pairs

A: _____
B: _____
A: _____

해석

여: 안녕, 나는 Gacha라고 해. 나는 몽골에서 왔어. 두 달 전에 내가 처음 송지 중학교에 왔을 때, 나는 무척 걱정이 되었어. 나는 좀 수줍음을 탔고 한국어를 잘 못했어. 하지만 난 운이 좋은 아이야. 내 학급 친구들은 모두 멋지고 다정해. 나는 체육 시간에 친구들과 핸드볼 하는 것을 즐겨. 난 실력이 좋은 선수야. 친구들은 나를 '황금손'이라고 불러. 다음 주에 운동회가 있을 거야. 난 우리 반이 핸드볼 대회에서 이기길 바라.

남: 안녕, 민솔아. 너희 반이 이기고 있니?
여: 물론이지. 우리는 훌륭한 핸드볼 선수가 있거든.
남: 몽골에서 온 여자아이 말하니?
여: 응, 그녀의 이름은 Gacha야.
남: 그녀에 대해 많이 들었어. 그런데 그녀는 어떻게 생겼어?
여: 그녀는 키가 크고 말총머리를 하고 있어.
남: 아, 지금 막 골을 넣은 여자아이가 그녀니?
여: 맞아, 저건 그녀의 일곱 번째 골이야.
남: 와, 그녀는 정말 잘하는구나.

남: 무엇을 도와드릴까요?
여: 남동생을 잃어버렸어요.
남: 알겠어요, 진정하세요. 남동생 이름이 뭐죠?
여: 그의 이름은 Wally Brown이에요. 다섯 살이고요.
남: 어떻게 생겼나요?
여: 그는 갈색 머리이고 갈색 눈을 지녔어요.
남: 그는 무엇을 입고 있나요?
여: 그는 초록색 셔츠와 검은 바지를 입고 있어요.
남: 더 말해 줄 수 있나요?
여: 아, 그는 빨간 배낭을 메고 있어요.
남: 알겠어요. 우리가 나가서 그를 찾아볼게요. 또, 우리가 미아 방송을 할 겁니다.
여: 정말 감사합니다. 동생을 빨리 찾길 바라요.

A: 나는 내일 중요한 시험이 있어!
B: 네가 시험을 잘 보길 바라.
A: 나도 그러길 바라. 고마워.

Communicate: Speak 2 - Talk in groups

A: _____

B: _____

A: _____

B: _____

A: _____

B: _____

Communicate: Speak - Rap Time

(1) A: _____

B: _____

(2) A: _____

B: _____

(3) A: _____

B: _____

(4) A: _____

B: _____

My Speaking Portfolio

G: _____

B: _____

G: _____

B: _____

G: _____

B: _____

G: _____

B: _____

Wrap Up

1. B: _____

G: _____

B: _____

G: _____

2. G: _____

B: _____

G: _____

B: _____

G: _____

A: 네 캐릭터의 이름은 뭐니?
B: 그의 이름은 Buster야.
A: 그는 어떻게 생겼니?
B: 그는 머리카락이 없어.
A: 그는 눈이 크니?
B: 응, 맞아.

(1) A: 나는 오늘 오후에 내 강아지를 잃어버렸어.
　　B: 네가 그를 곧 찾기를 바랄게.
(2) A: 나는 네가 결선에서 최선을 다하길 바라.
　　B: 고마워. 나도 네가 그러길 바라.
(3) A: 네 언니는 어떻게 생겼니, Claire?
　　B: 그녀는 키가 크고 긴 생머리야.
(4) A: 네 아버지는 파란 모자를 쓰고 계시니?
　　B: 응. 지금 지도를 보고 계셔.

여: 이 게시판을 봐. 다음 학생회장의 포스터가 있어.
남: 응, 나는 이미 결정을 내렸어. 나는 장지민에게 투표할 거야.
여: 안경을 쓴 남자아이 얘기하는 거야? 그는 똑똑해 보이지만 나는 그의 공약이 마음에 들지 않아.
남: 그럼 넌 누굴 선택할 거야?
여: 음, 나는 1번 한시원을 지지해. 그녀는 우리 학교를 안전한 장소로 만들고 싶어 해.
남: 그녀는 항상 말총머리를 해, 그렇지?
여: 맞아, 그리고 홍지호도 괜찮아 보여.
남: 그녀는 친절해 보이지만, 나는 장기 자랑이 싫어.

1. 남: 너희 반에 새로 온 학생이 있다고 들었어.
　　여: 응. 그녀는 제주도에서 왔어. 어, 그녀가 저기에 있어!
　　남: 어느 아이? 어떻게 생겼어?
　　여: 그녀는 곱슬머리이고 안경을 끼고 있어.
2. 여: 너 슬퍼 보여. 무슨 일이니, 종민아?
　　남: 여동생이 오늘 아침에 팔이 부러졌어.
　　여: 무슨 일이 있었는데?
　　남: 자전거에서 떨어졌어.
　　여: 안됐구나. 그녀가 곧 회복되기를 바라.

※ 다음 우리말과 일치하도록 빈칸에 알맞은 것을 골라 쓰시오.

1 The _____ To Be _____
   A. Different   B. Right

2 In many _____, 42-year-old Joseph Palmer was an _____ _____.
   A. ordinary   B. ways   C. person

3 He _____ a job and _____ _____ his family.
   A. for   B. cared   C. had

4 But in 1830, _____ he _____ to a small town in Massachusetts, he began to _____ _____.
   A. face   B. moved   C. difficulties   D. after

5 Joseph _____ _____ from _____ people: he had a long beard.
   A. different   B. other   C. looked

6 People _____ not _____ it very much.
   A. like   B. did

7 The town's people _____ the man _____ a _____.
   A. with   B. avoided   C. beard

8 They _____ not want to _____ next _____ him.
   A. to   B. did   C. sit

9 They even _____ _____ his back, "What is he _____ to hide?"
   A. behind   B. trying   C. whispered

10 _____ neighbors _____ his windows.
   A. broke   B. some

11 Others _____ stones _____ him when he walked _____ the street.
   A. threw   B. down   C. at

12 They _____ him to _____ _____ a beard.
   A. stop   B. told   C. growing

13 Joseph _____ not _____.
   A. mind   B. did

14 He _____ wanted the freedom _____ _____ his beard.
   A. have   B. just   C. to

15 _____ day, four men _____ Joseph and _____ him on the ground.
   A. attacked   B. one   C. threw

1 다를 권리

2 여러 면에서 42살의 Joseph Palmer는 평범한 사람이었다.

3 그는 직업이 있었고 가족을 돌보았다.

4 하지만 1830년에 매사추세츠에 있는 작은 도시로 이사를 한 후에 그는 어려움에 직면하기 시작했다.

5 Joseph은 다른 사람들과 달라 보였다. 그는 기다란 턱수염을 기르고 있었다.

6 사람들은 그것을 별로 좋아하지 않았다.

7 마을 사람들은 턱수염을 가진 그 남자를 피했다.

8 그들은 그의 곁에 앉고 싶어 하지 않았다.

9 그들은 심지어 그의 등 뒤에서 "그가 무엇을 숨기려는 거지?"라고 속삭였다.

10 어떤 이웃들은 그의 창문을 깼다.

11 다른 사람들은 그가 길을 걸어 내려갈 때 그에게 돌을 던졌다.

12 그들은 그에게 턱수염을 그만 기르라고 말했다.

13 Joseph은 신경 쓰지 않았다.

14 그는 그저 자신의 턱수염을 기를 자유를 원했다.

15 어느 날, 네 명의 남자가 Joseph을 공격했고 그를 바닥에 던졌다.

16 "We're going to _____ _____ your beard!" they _____.

A. cut   B. shouted   C. off

17 Joseph was a big man, and he was _____ to _____ them _____.

A. fight   B. able   C. off

18 But the men _____ the police and _____ him _____ attacking them.

A. accused   B. called   C. of

19 Poor Joseph _____ _____.

A. arrested   B. was

20 He said to the _____, "I'm the _____ here."

A. victim   B. judge

21 Sadly, no one _____ a man _____ a beard, and he went to _____ for _____ a year.

A. with   B. over   C. believed   D. prison

22 Joseph's son, Thomas, _____ people to _____ the _____ .

A. know   B. wanted   C. truth

23 He _____ letters _____ newspapers _____ the country.

A. sent   B. across   C. to

24 People learned that Joseph was _____ _____ just for _____ _____ and his beard.

A. prison   B. himself   C. protecting   D. in

25 Many people _____ _____ about this, so the judge finally decided to _____ Joseph _____.

A. angry   B. free   C. set   D. became

26 After he was _____, Joseph _____ and told his story to _____ of people.

A. freed   B. lots   C. traveled

27 Slowly, people's _____ _____ beards _____ .

A. toward   B. changed   C. attitudes

28 _____ Joseph _____, a man with a _____ became the President of the United States.

A. died   B. before   C. beard

29 _____ _____ was Abraham Lincoln.

A. name   B. his

30 He _____ beards _____, but Joseph Palmer _____ for the _____ to have them.

A. fought   B. right   C. popular   D. made

---

16 "우리가 당신의 턱수염을 잘라 버리겠어!"라고 그들은 소리쳤다.

17 Joseph은 덩치가 큰 사람이었고, 그는 그들을 싸워 물리칠 수 있었다.

18 하지만 그 남자들은 경찰을 불렀고, 자신들을 공격한 것으로 그를 고발했다.

19 불쌍한 Joseph은 체포되었다.

20 그는 "저는 여기서 희생자입니다."라고 판사에게 말했다.

21 슬프게도, 아무도 턱수염을 가진 남자를 믿지 않았고, 그는 일 년이 넘는 기간 동안 감옥에 갔다.

22 Joseph의 아들인 Thomas는 사람들이 진실을 알기를 원했다.

23 그는 전국에 있는 신문사에 편지를 보냈다.

24 사람들은 Joseph이 단지 자신과 자신의 턱수염을 지키려다 감옥에 갔다는 것을 알게 되었다.

25 많은 사람들은 이에 대해 분개했고, 그래서 판사는 결국 Joseph을 석방하기로 결정했다.

26 Joseph은 석방된 뒤에 순회를 하며 많은 사람들에게 자신의 이야기를 전했다.

27 사람들의 턱수염에 대한 태도는 서서히 변해갔다.

28 Joseph이 죽기 전에, 턱수염을 가진 남자가 미국의 대통령이 되었다.

29 그의 이름은 Abraham Lincoln(에이브러햄 링컨)이었다.

30 그는 턱수염을 대중적으로 만들었지만, Joseph Palmer는 그것을 기를 권리를 위하여 싸웠다.

※ 다음 우리말과 일치하도록 빈칸에 알맞은 말을 쓰시오.

1 The ＿＿＿＿ ＿＿＿＿ ＿＿＿＿ ＿＿＿＿

2 ＿＿＿＿ ＿＿＿＿ ＿＿＿＿, 42-year-old Joseph Palmer was ＿＿＿＿ ＿＿＿＿ ＿＿＿＿.

3 He ＿＿＿＿ ＿＿＿＿ and ＿＿＿＿ ＿＿＿＿ his family.

4 But in 1830, ＿＿＿＿ he ＿＿＿＿ ＿＿＿＿ a small town in Massachusetts, he began ＿＿＿＿ ＿＿＿＿ ＿＿＿＿.

5 Joseph ＿＿＿＿ ＿＿＿＿ ＿＿＿＿ other people: he had a long beard.

6 People ＿＿＿＿ ＿＿＿＿ ＿＿＿＿ ＿＿＿＿ very much.

7 The town's people ＿＿＿＿ ＿＿＿＿ ＿＿＿＿ ＿＿＿＿ ＿＿＿＿.

8 They did not want ＿＿＿＿ ＿＿＿＿ ＿＿＿＿ ＿＿＿＿ ＿＿＿＿.

9 They even whispered ＿＿＿＿ ＿＿＿＿ ＿＿＿＿, "What is he ＿＿＿＿ ＿＿＿＿ ＿＿＿＿?"

10 ＿＿＿＿ neighbors ＿＿＿＿ ＿＿＿＿ ＿＿＿＿.

11 ＿＿＿＿ ＿＿＿＿ ＿＿＿＿ him when he ＿＿＿＿ ＿＿＿＿ the street.

12 They ＿＿＿＿ him ＿＿＿＿ ＿＿＿＿ a beard.

13 Joseph ＿＿＿＿ ＿＿＿＿ ＿＿＿＿.

14 He just wanted the ＿＿＿＿ ＿＿＿＿ ＿＿＿＿ his beard.

15 One day, four men ＿＿＿＿ Joseph and ＿＿＿＿ ＿＿＿＿ ＿＿＿＿.

1 다를 권리

2 여러 면에서 42살의 Joseph Palmer는 평범한 사람이었다.

3 그는 직업이 있었고 가족을 돌보았다.

4 하지만 1830년에 매사추세츠에 있는 작은 도시로 이사를 한 후에 그는 어려움에 직면하기 시작했다.

5 Joseph은 다른 사람들과 달라 보였다. 그는 기다란 턱수염을 기르고 있었다.

6 사람들은 그것을 별로 좋아하지 않았다.

7 마을 사람들은 턱수염을 가진 그 남자를 피했다.

8 그들은 그의 곁에 앉고 싶어 하지 않았다.

9 그들은 심지어 그의 등 뒤에서 "그가 무엇을 숨기려는 거지?"라고 속삭였다.

10 어떤 이웃들은 그의 창문을 깼다.

11 다른 사람들은 그가 길을 걸어 내려갈 때 그에게 돌을 던졌다.

12 그들은 그에게 턱수염을 그만 기르라고 말했다.

13 Joseph은 신경 쓰지 않았다.

14 그는 그저 자신의 턱수염을 기를 자유를 원했다.

15 어느 날, 네 명의 남자가 Joseph을 공격했고 그를 바닥에 던졌다.

16 "We're going to _____ _____ your beard!" they _____.

17 Joseph was a big man, and he _____ _____ _____
_____ _____ _____.

18 But the men called the police and _____ _____
_____ them.

19 Poor Joseph _____ _____.

20 He said to _____ _____, "I'm _____ _____ here."

21 Sadly, no one believed _____ _____ _____ _____
_____, and he _____ _____ _____ for over a year.

22 Joseph's son, Thomas, _____ people _____ _____ the
truth.

23 He _____ letters _____ newspapers _____ _____
_____.

24 People learned that Joseph _____ _____ _____ just for
_____ _____ and his beard.

25 Many people _____ _____ about this, so the judge finally
_____ _____ _____ Joseph _____.

26 After he _____ _____, Joseph traveled and told his story to
_____ _____ people.

27 Slowly, people's _____ _____ _____ _____ _____.

28 _____ Joseph _____, a man _____ _____ _____
became the President of the United States.

29 _____ _____ was Abraham Lincoln.

30 He _____ _____ _____, but Joseph Palmer _____
_____ the _____ _____ _____ them.

16 "우리가 당신의 턱수염을 잘라 버리겠어!"라고 그들은 소리쳤다.

17 Joseph은 덩치가 큰 사람이었고, 그는 그들을 싸워 물리칠 수 있었다.

18 하지만 그 남자들은 경찰을 불렀고, 자신들을 공격한 것으로 그를 고발했다.

19 불쌍한 Joseph은 체포되었다.

20 그는 "저는 여기서 희생자입니다."라고 판사에게 말했다.

21 슬프게도, 아무도 턱수염을 가진 남자를 믿지 않았고, 그는 일 년이 넘는 기간 동안 감옥에 갔다.

22 Joseph의 아들인 Thomas는 사람들이 진실을 알기를 원했다.

23 그는 전국에 있는 신문사에 편지를 보냈다.

24 사람들은 Joseph이 단지 자신과 자신의 턱수염을 지키려다 감옥에 갇혔다는 것을 알게 되었다.

25 많은 사람들은 이에 대해 분개했고, 그래서 판사는 결국 Joseph을 석방하기로 결정했다.

26 Joseph은 석방된 뒤에 순회를 하며 많은 사람들에게 자신의 이야기를 전했다.

27 사람들의 턱수염에 대한 태도는 서서히 변해갔다.

28 Joseph이 죽기 전에, 턱수염을 가진 남자가 미국의 대통령이 되었다.

29 그의 이름은 Abraham Lincoln (에이브러햄 링컨)이었다.

30 그는 턱수염을 대중적으로 만들었지만, Joseph Palmer는 그것을 기를 권리를 위하여 싸웠다.

※ 다음 문장을 우리말로 쓰시오.

1 The Right To Be Different

➡ _____

2 In many ways, 42-year-old Joseph Palmer was an ordinary person.

➡ _____

3 He had a job and cared for his family.

➡ _____

4 But in 1830, after he moved to a small town in Massachusetts, he began to face difficulties.

➡ _____

5 Joseph looked different from other people: he had a long beard.

➡ _____

6 People did not like it very much.

➡ _____

7 The town's people avoided the man with a beard.

➡ _____

8 They did not want to sit next to him.

➡ _____

9 They even whispered behind his back, "What is he trying to hide?"

➡ _____

10 Some neighbors broke his windows.

➡ _____

11 Others threw stones at him when he walked down the street.

➡ _____

12 They told him to stop growing a beard.

➡ _____

13 Joseph did not mind.

➡ _____

14 He just wanted the freedom to have his beard.

➡ _____

15 One day, four men attacked Joseph and threw him on the ground.

➡ _____

16 "We're going to cut off your beard!" they shouted.

➡ _____

17 Joseph was a big man, and he was able to fight them off.

➡ _____

18 But the men called the police and accused him of attacking them.

➡ _____

19 Poor Joseph was arrested.

➡ _____

20 He said to the judge, "I'm the victim here."

➡ _____

21 Sadly, no one believed a man with a beard, and he went to prison for over a year.

➡ _____

22 Joseph's son, Thomas, wanted people to know the truth.

➡ _____

23 He sent letters to newspapers across the country.

➡ _____

24 People learned that Joseph was in prison just for protecting himself and his beard.

➡ _____

25 Many people became angry about this, so the judge finally decided to set Joseph free.

➡ _____

26 After he was freed, Joseph traveled and told his story to lots of people.

➡ _____

27 Slowly, people's attitudes toward beards changed.

➡ _____

28 Before Joseph died, a man with a beard became the President of the United States.

➡ _____

29 His name was Abraham Lincoln.

➡ _____

30 He made beards popular, but Joseph Palmer fought for the right to have them.

➡ _____

Step4

※ 다음 괄호 안의 단어들을 우리말에 맞도록 바르게 배열하시오.

1 (Right / The / Different / Be / To)
➡ _____

2 (many / in / ways, / Joseph / 42-year-old / Palmer / an / was / person. / ordinary)
➡ _____

3 (had / he / job / a / and / for / cared / family. / his)
➡ _____

4 (in / but / 1830, / he / after / to / moved / small / a / town / Massachusetts, / in / began / he / difficulties. / face / to)
➡ _____

5 (looked / Joseph / from / different / people: / other / had / he / beard. / long / a)
➡ _____

6 (did / people / like / not / much. / it / very)
➡ _____

7 (town's / the / people / avoided / man / the / beard. / a / with)
➡ _____

8 (did / they / want / not / sit / to / him. / to / next)
➡ _____

9 (even / they / behind / whispered / back, / his / "what / he / is / hide?" / to / trying)
➡ _____

10 (neighbors / some / windows. / his / broke)
➡ _____

11 (threw / others / at / stones / him / when / walked / he / street. / the / down)
➡ _____

12 (told / they / to / him / growing / stop / beard. / a)
➡ _____

13 (did / Joseph / mind. / not)
➡ _____

14 (just / he / wanted / freedom / the / have / to / beard. / his)
➡ _____

15 (day, / one / men / four / Joseph / attacked / and / him / threw / ground. / the / on)
➡ _____

1 다를 권리

2 여러 면에서 42살의 Joseph Palmer는 평범한 사람이었다.

3 그는 직업이 있었고 가족을 돌보았다.

4 하지만 1830년에 매사추세츠에 있는 작은 도시로 이사를 한 후에 그는 어려움에 직면하기 시작했다.

5 Joseph은 다른 사람들과 달라 보였다. 그는 기다란 턱수염을 기르고 있었다.

6 사람들은 그것을 별로 좋아하지 않았다.

7 마을 사람들은 턱수염을 가진 그 남자를 피했다.

8 그들은 그의 곁에 앉고 싶어 하지 않았다.

9 그들은 심지어 그의 등 뒤에서 "그가 무엇을 숨기려는 거지?" 라고 속삭였다.

10 어떤 이웃들은 그의 창문을 깼다.

11 다른 사람들은 그가 길을 걸어 내려갈 때 그에게 돌을 던졌다.

12 그들은 그에게 턱수염을 그만 기르라고 말했다.

13 Joseph은 신경 쓰지 않았다.

14 그는 그저 자신의 턱수염을 기를 자유를 원했다.

15 어느 날, 네 명의 남자가 Joseph을 공격했고 그를 바닥에 던졌다.

16 (going / "we're / cut / to / your / off / beard!" / shouted. / they)

➡ _____

17 (was / Joseph / big / a / man, / and / was / he / to / able / off. / them / fight)

➡ _____

18 (the / but / called / men / police / the / and / him / accused / of / them / attacking)

➡ _____

19 (Joseph / poor / arrested. / was)

➡ _____

20 (said / he / the / to / judge, / "I'm / the / here." / victim)

➡ _____

21 (no / sadly, / one / a / believed / man / with / beard, / a / and / went / he / prison / to / for / year. / a / over)

➡ _____

➡ _____

22 (son, / Joseph's / Thomas, / people / wanted / know / to / truth. / the)

➡ _____

23 (sent / he / letters / newspapers / to / country. / the / across)

➡ _____

24 (learned / people / Joseph / that / in / was / prison / just / protecting / for / himself / beard. / his / and)

➡ _____

25 (people / many / angry / became / this, / about / so / judge / the / decided / finally / set / to / free. / Joseph)

➡ _____

26 (he / after / freed, / was / Joseph / and / traveled / told / story / his / people. / of / lots / to)

➡ _____

27 (people's / slowly, / attitudes / beards / changed. / toward)

➡ _____

28 (Joseph / before / died, / man / a / with / beard / a / became / President / the / of / States. / United / the)

➡ _____

29 (name / his / Lincoln. / Abraham)

➡ _____

30 (made / he / popular, / beards / but / Palmer / Joseph / for / fought / right / the / them. / have / to)

➡ _____

➡ _____

16 "우리가 당신의 턱수염을 잘라 버리겠어!"라고 그들은 소리쳤다.

17 Joseph은 덩치가 큰 사람이었고, 그는 그들을 싸워 물리칠 수 있었다.

18 하지만 그 남자들은 경찰을 불렀고, 자신들을 공격한 것으로 그를 고발했다.

19 불쌍한 Joseph은 체포되었다.

20 그는 "저는 여기서 희생자입니다."라고 판사에게 말했다.

21 슬프게도, 아무도 턱수염을 가진 남자를 믿지 않았고, 그는 일 년이 넘는 기간 동안 감옥에 갔다.

22 Joseph의 아들인 Thomas는 사람들이 진실을 알기를 원했다.

23 그는 전국에 있는 신문사에 편지를 보냈다.

24 사람들은 Joseph이 단지 자신과 자신의 턱수염을 지키려다 감옥에 갇혔다는 것을 알게 되었다.

25 많은 사람들은 이에 대해 분개했고, 그래서 판사는 결국 Joseph을 석방하기로 결정했다.

26 Joseph은 석방된 뒤에 순회를 하며 많은 사람들에게 자신의 이야기를 전했다.

27 사람들의 턱수염에 대한 태도는 서서히 변해갔다.

28 Joseph이 죽기 전에, 턱수염을 가진 남자가 미국의 대통령이 되었다.

29 그의 이름은 Abraham Lincoln (에이브러햄 링컨)이었다.

30 그는 턱수염을 대중적으로 만들었지만, Joseph Palmer는 그것을 기를 권리를 위하여 싸웠다.

※ 다음 우리말을 영어로 쓰시오.

1 다를 권리

➡ _____

2 여러 면에서 42살의 Joseph Palmer는 평범한 사람이었다.

➡ _____

3 그는 직업이 있었고 가족을 돌보았다.

➡ _____

4 하지만 1830년에 매사추세츠에 있는 작은 도시로 이사를 한 후에 그는 어려움에 직면하기 시작했다.

➡ _____

5 Joseph은 다른 사람들과 달라 보였다. 그는 기다란 턱수염을 기르고 있었다.

➡ _____

6 사람들은 그것을 별로 좋아하지 않았다.

➡ _____

7 마을 사람들은 턱수염을 가진 그 남자를 피했다.

➡ _____

8 그들은 그의 곁에 앉고 싶어 하지 않았다.

➡ _____

9 그들은 심지어 그의 등 뒤에서 "그가 무엇을 숨기려는 거지?"라고 속삭였다.

➡ _____

10 어떤 이웃들은 그의 창문을 깼다.

➡ _____

11 다른 사람들은 그가 길을 걸어 내려갈 때 그에게 돌을 던졌다.

➡ _____

12 그들은 그에게 턱수염을 그만 기르라고 말했다.

➡ _____

13 Joseph은 신경 쓰지 않았다.

➡ _____

14 그는 그저 자신의 턱수염을 기를 자유를 원했다.

➡ _____

15 어느 날, 네 명의 남자가 Joseph을 공격했고 그를 바닥에 던졌다.

➡ _____

16 "우리가 당신의 턱수염을 잘라 버리겠어!"라고 그들은 소리쳤다.

➡ _____

17 Joseph은 덩치가 큰 사람이었고, 그는 그들을 싸워 물리칠 수 있었다.

➡ _____

18 하지만 그 남자들은 경찰을 불렀고, 자신들을 공격한 것으로 그를 고발했다.

➡ _____

19 불쌍한 Joseph은 체포되었다.

➡ _____

20 그는 "저는 여기서 희생자입니다."라고 판사에게 말했다.

➡ _____

21 슬프게도, 아무도 턱수염을 가진 남자를 믿지 않았고, 그는 일 년이 넘는 기간 동안 감옥에 갔다.

➡ _____

22 Joseph의 아들인 Thomas는 사람들이 진실을 알기를 원했다.

➡ _____

23 그는 전국에 있는 신문사에 편지를 보냈다.

➡ _____

24 사람들은 Joseph이 단지 자신과 자신의 턱수염을 지키려다 감옥에 갇혔다는 것을 알게 되었다.

➡ _____

25 많은 사람들은 이에 대해 분개했고, 그래서 판사는 결국 Joseph을 석방하기로 결정했다.

➡ _____

26 Joseph은 석방된 뒤에 순회를 하며 많은 사람들에게 자신의 이야기를 전했다.

➡ _____

27 사람들의 턱수염에 대한 태도는 서서히 변해갔다.

➡ _____

28 Joseph이 죽기 전에, 턱수염을 가진 남자가 미국의 대통령이 되었다.

➡ _____

29 그의 이름은 Abraham Lincoln(에이브러햄 링컨)이었다.

➡ _____

30 그는 턱수염을 대중적으로 만들었지만, Joseph Palmer는 그것을 기를 권리를 위하여 싸웠다.

➡ _____

※ 다음 우리말과 일치하도록 빈칸에 알맞은 말을 쓰시오.

My Speaking Portfolio

1. I _____ _____ for Han Siwon.

2. She _____ _____ and _____.

3. She _____ school _____ _____ a safe place.

4. I _____ _____ her.

5. I like her promises _____ _____ no more _____.

6. I _____ Han Siwon _____ the next school president.

7. I really want my school _____ _____ _____ _____ _____.

My Writing Portfolio: My Book Report

1. The _____ _____ _____ Different

2. A Story _____ Joseph Palmer

3. I read the story _____ Joseph Palmer _____ _____.

4. I _____ _____ it.

5. I _____ _____ the story _____ we should not judge people by their _____.

6. Students _____ _____ about other people's appearance _____ read the story.

7. _____, I _____ _____ _____ about it.

8. _____ did Joseph Palmer want _____ _____ _____ _____?

Words in Action

1. _____ _____ the travel fair. _____ is _____.

2. What countries do you _____ _____ _____?

3. _____ you want _____ _____ South America, you can _____ the booths on the left.

4. If you _____ _____, you can have drinks and _____ _____ _____.

---

1. 나는 한시원을 뽑을 겁니다.
2. 그녀는 자신감 있고 똑똑해 보입니다.
3. 그녀는 학교가 안전한 장소가 되어야 한다고 생각합니다.
4. 저는 그녀에게 동의합니다.
5. 나는 집단 괴롭힘 없애기 같은 공약들이 좋습니다.
6. 나는 한시원이 다음 학생회장이 되길 바랍니다.
7. 나는 우리 학교가 더 안전한 장소가 되길 정말 바랍니다.

---

1. 다를 권리
2. Joseph Palmer에 관한 이야기
3. 나는 지난주에 Joseph Palmer에 관한 이야기를 읽었다.
4. 나는 그게 정말 재미있었다.
5. 나는 그 이야기로부터 우리는 사람들을 외모로 판단해서는 안 된다는 것을 배웠다.
6. 다른 사람들의 외모에 관해 이야기하는 학생들은 이 이야기를 꼭 읽어야 한다.
7. 하지만, 나는 그것에 관한 질문이 하나 있다.
8. Joseph Palmer는 왜 턱수염을 기르고 싶었을까?

---

1. 여행 박람회에 오신 것을 환영합니다. 입장료는 무료입니다.
2. 여러분은 어떤 나라들을 마음에 두고 있나요?
3. 여러분이 남아메리카를 방문하고 싶다면, 왼쪽에 있는 부스들을 살펴볼 수 있습니다.
4. 배가 고파진다면, 음료와 간단한 간식을 드실 수 있습니다.

※ 다음 우리말을 영어로 쓰시오.

My Speaking Portfolio

1. 나는 한시원을 뽑을 겁니다.
➡ _____

2. 그녀는 자신감 있고 똑똑해 보입니다.
➡ _____

3. 그녀는 학교가 안전한 장소가 되어야 한다고 생각합니다.
➡ _____

4. 저는 그녀에게 동의합니다.
➡ _____

5. 나는 집단 괴롭힘 없애기 같은 공약들이 좋습니다.
➡ _____

6. 나는 한시원이 다음 학생회장이 되길 바랍니다.
➡ _____

7. 나는 우리 학교가 더 안전한 장소가 되길 정말 바랍니다.
➡ _____

My Writing Portfolio: My Book Report

1. 다를 권리
➡ _____

2. Joseph Palmer에 관한 이야기
➡ _____

3. 나는 지난주에 Joseph Palmer에 관한 이야기를 읽었다.
➡ _____

4. 나는 그게 정말 재미있었다.
➡ _____

5. 나는 그 이야기로부터 우리는 사람들을 외모로 판단해서는 안 된다는 것을 배웠다.
➡ _____

6. 다른 사람들의 외모에 관해 이야기하는 학생들은 이 이야기를 꼭 읽어야 한다.
➡ _____

7. 하지만, 나는 그것에 관한 질문이 하나 있다.
➡ _____

8. Joseph Palmer는 왜 턱수염을 기르고 싶었을까?
➡ _____

Words in Action

1. 여행 박람회에 오신 것을 환영합니다. 입장료는 무료입니다.
➡ _____

2. 여러분은 어떤 나라들을 마음에 두고 있나요?
➡ _____

3. 여러분이 남아메리카를 방문하고 싶다면, 왼쪽에 있는 부스들을 살펴볼 수 있습니다.
➡ _____
_____

4. 배가 고파진다면, 음료와 간단한 간식을 드실 수 있습니다.
➡ _____

※ 다음 영어를 우리말로 쓰시오.

01	trash	
02	common	
03	pour	
04	traditional	
05	discussion	
06	share	
07	experience	
08	feed	
09	truth	
10	wrong	
11	guest	
12	scared	
13	refund	
14	training	
15	salty	
16	exchange	
17	stuff	
18	upset	
19	work	
20	without	
21	message	
22	teenage	

23	repair	
24	suggestion	
25	receipt	
26	sadness	
27	tear	
28	understand	
29	secret	
30	bowl	
31	promise	
32	listener	
33	text	
34	either	
35	take care of	
36	tell a lie	
37	drop by	
38	be in trouble	
39	give it a try	
40	break down	
41	on one's own	
42	not ~ anymore	
43	be sure to	
44	find out	

※ 다음 우리말을 영어로 쓰시오.

01 강아지

02 제안, 의견

03 훈련, 훈육

04 약속하다

05 잘못된

06 비밀

07 쓰레기

08 교환; 교환하다

09 사발, 그릇

10 물건

11 ~ 없이

12 전통적인

13 경험

14 고치다

15 겁먹은

16 흔한

17 먹이다

18 손님

19 영수증

20 화난

21 진실, 사실

22 (기계가) 작동하다

23 쏟다, 붓다

24 짠

25 거짓말

26 토론

27 (부정문에서) ~도 역시

28 십 대의

29 공유하다

30 청취자

31 한불, 한불금

32 전갈, 메시지

33 슬픔

34 찢다

35 더 이상 ~ 아니다

36 부수다

37 ~에 들르다

38 ~으로 시작하다

39 반드시 ~하다

40 혼자 힘으로

41 곤경에 처하다

42 ~을 돌보다, ~을 처리하다

43 거짓말하다

44 발견하다, 알아내다

※ 다음 영영풀이에 알맞은 단어를 <보기>에서 골라 쓴 후, 우리말 뜻을 쓰시오.

1 _____ : between 13 and 19 years old: _____

2 _____ : a person who listens: _____

3 _____ : a young dog: _____

4 _____ : to send somebody a written message using a mobile/cell phone:
    _____

5 _____ : an idea or a plan that you mention for somebody else to think about:
    _____

6 _____ : to restore something that is broken, damaged or torn to good condition:
    _____

7 _____ : something that is known about by only a few people and not told to
    others: _____

8 _____ : a small machine used for drying your hair by blowing hot air over it:
    _____

9 _____ : a piece of paper that shows that goods or services have been paid for:
    _____

10 _____ : to give food to a person or an animal: _____

11 _____ : a sum of money that is paid back to you, especially because you paid too
    much or because you returned goods to a shop/store: _____

12 _____ : a long vertical solid structure, made of stone, brick or concrete, that
    surrounds, divides or protects an area of land: _____

13 _____ : the knowledge and skill that you have gained through doing something for
    a period of time: _____

14 _____ : to give something to somebody and at the same time receive the same
    type of thing from them: _____

15 _____ : a person that you have invited to your house or to a particular event that
    you are paying for: _____

16 _____ : to tell somebody that you will definitely do or not do something, or that
    something will definitely happen: _____

보기			
wall	suggestion	refund	exchange
repair	listener	hairdryer	feed
promise	text	secret	teenage
puppy	guest	receipt	experience

※ 다음 우리말과 일치하도록 빈칸에 알맞은 말을 쓰시오.

Communication: Listen – Dialog 1

Minsol: I'm not _____ _____ Buster.

Dad: What's _____?

Minsol: He _____ my homework _____ _____ again.

Dad: Puppies _____ do _____.

Minsol: This is not the first time. _____ I find my _____ in the dog house.

Dad: Please be _____ to him. He's just _____ _____ old.

Minsol: You're _____ nice _____ him! He needs some _____.

Dad: Okay. Let's _____ _____ in _____ _____ weeks.

Minsol: 저는 Buster가 마음에 들지 않아요.
Dad: 무엇이 문제니?
Minsol: Buster가 또 제 숙제를 찢어 놓았어요.
Dad: 강아지들은 종종 그런 일을 저지르지.
Minsol: 이번이 처음이 아니에요. 가끔 저는 제 양말을 개집에서 찾기도 해요.
Dad: Buster에게 잘해 주렴. 태어난 지 다섯 달 밖에 안 되었잖니.
Minsol: 아빠는 그를 너무 다정하게 대해 주세요! 그에게는 훈련이 좀 필요해요.
Dad: 좋아. 몇 주 뒤에 훈련을 시작해 보자꾸나.

Communication: Listen – Dialog 2

Mom: Minsu, I'm _____ _____ _____ your dad for a movie.

Minsu: When will you _____ _____, Mom?

Mom: _____ 8 o'clock. Don't forget _____ _____ Buster.

Minsu: Okay.

Mom: _____ _____ to give him some water, _____.

Minsu: No _____.

Mom: One _____ _____. Can you _____ Minsol _____ her science homework? Buster _____ her homework into pieces.

Minsu: Hmm .... Okay. I'll do that.

Mom: 민수야, 엄마는 아빠랑 영화 보러 나간다.
Minsu: 언제 돌아오실 거예요, 엄마?
Mom: 8시쯤. Buster에게 밥 주는 것 잊지 말렴.
Minsu: 네.
Mom: 물도 꼭 주려무나.
Minsu: 그럴게요.
Mom: 한 가지 더. 민솔이 과학 숙제를 도와줄 수 있겠니? Buster가 민솔이의 숙제를 찢어 놓았거든.
Minsu: 음 …. 알겠어요. 그렇게 할게요.

Communication: Listen – Listen More

(The phone rings.)

Mike: Customer Service. _____ can I _____ _____?

Sora: I _____ a _____ at your _____ last week. I'm not _____ _____ it.

Mike: What is _____ _____?

Sora: It doesn't _____ well. I mean the air isn't hot _____.

Mike: I'm sorry. Do you _____ _____ _____ it?

Sora: Well, can I _____ _____ _____?

Mike: Sure. Will you please _____ our _____ with the dryer?

Sora: Yes, I'll _____ _____ tomorrow afternoon.

Mike: _____ _____ to bring the _____.

Sora: Okay. Thanks.

(전화벨이 울린다.)
Mike: 고객 센터입니다. 어떻게 도와 드릴까요?
Sora: 제가 지난주에 가게에서 헤어드라이어를 샀는데요. 마음에 들지 않네요.
Mike: 무엇이 문제인가요?
Sora: 작동이 잘되지 않아요. 제 말은 충분히 뜨거운 바람이 나오질 않는다는 거예요.
Mike: 죄송합니다. 교환을 원하시나요?
Sora: 음. 환불받을 수 있을까요?
Mike: 물론이죠. 드라이어를 가지고 저희 가게를 방문해 주시겠어요?
Sora: 네. 내일 오후에 들를게요.
Mike: 영수증 가지고 오시는 걸 잊지 마세요.
Sora: 네. 고맙습니다.

My Speaking Portfolio – Step 3

A: I'm _____ _____ _____ _____ my brother.

B: What's _____ _____?

A: He uses the _____ _____ _____ _____ in the morning.

B: I know _____ you _____.

A: What _____ I do?

B: Well, you can _____ _____ _____ and _____ the bathroom first.

A: Okay, I'll _____ it _____ _____.

A: 나는 내 남동생이 별로 마음에 들지 않아.
B: 뭐가 문제니?
A: 그는 아침에 너무 오랫동안 욕실을 사용해.
B: 네 기분이 어떤지 알아.
A: 내가 무엇을 할 수 있을까?
B: 음, 너는 더 일찍 일어나서 욕실을 먼저 사용할 수 있어.
A: 알겠어, 내가 한번 해 볼게.

Wrap Up – Listening ❺

G: You _____ _____, Tommy.

B: I'm _____ _____ _____ Sojin.

G: What's _____ _____ her?

B: She isn't _____ _____ _____ of the group project.

G: I _____ you _____ _____ _____ her.

여: Tommy야, 기분이 안 좋아 보이는구나.
남: 나는 소진이 때문에 속상해.
여: 그 애에게 무슨 문제가 있니?
남: 그 애가 모둠 과제에서 맡은 일을 안 해.
여: 내 생각에 너는 그 애랑 이야기를 해 봐야 할 것 같아.

Wrap Up – Listening ❻

M: _____ you _____ _____ your _____, Suji?

G: Yes, I am, Dad. I'm _____ _____ _____.

M: Do you have _____ _____ _____ you?

G: Yeah, I have it _____ _____ _____.

M: Good. _____ _____ _____ _____ me when you _____ _____ the train station.

G: _____.

남: 여행 갈 준비 되었니, 수지야?
여: 네, 아빠. 저는 떠날 준비가 되었어요.
남: 표는 네가 가지고 있고?
여: 네, 제 전화기에 저장해 놓았어요.
남: 잘했구나. 기차역에 도착하면 내게 전화하는 걸 잊지 말렴.
여: 물론이죠.

※ 다음 우리말에 맞도록 대화를 영어로 쓰시오.

Communication: Listen – Dialog 1

Minsol: _____

Dad: _____

Minsol: _____

Dad: _____

Minsol: _____

Dad: _____

Minsol: _____

Dad: _____

Communication: Listen – Dialog 2

Mom: _____

Minsu: _____

Mom: _____

Minsu: _____

Mom: _____

Minsu: _____

Mom: _____

Minsu: _____

Communication: Listen – Listen More

(The phone rings.)

Mike: _____

Sora: _____

Mike: _____

Sora: _____

Mike: _____

Sora: _____

Mike: _____

Sora: _____

Mike: _____

Sora: _____

해석

Minsol: 저는 Buster가 마음에 들지 않아요.

Dad: 무엇이 문제니?

Minsol: Buster가 또 제 숙제를 찢어 놓았어요.

Dad: 강아지들은 종종 그런 일을 저지르지.

Minsol: 이번이 처음이 아니에요. 가끔 저는 제 양말을 개집에서 찾기도 해요.

Dad: Buster에게 잘해 주렴. 태어난 지 다섯 달 밖에 안 되었잖니.

Minsol: 아빠는 그를 너무 다정하게 대해 주세요! 그에게는 훈련이 좀 필요해요.

Dad: 좋아. 몇 주 뒤에 훈련을 시작해 보자꾸나.

Mom: 민수야, 엄마는 아빠랑 영화 보러 나간다.

Minsu: 언제 돌아오실 거예요, 엄마?

Mom: 8시쯤. Buster에게 밥 주는 것 잊지 말렴.

Minsu: 네.

Mom: 물도 꼭 주려무나.

Minsu: 그럴게요.

Mom: 한 가지 더. 민솔이 과학 숙제를 도와줄 수 있겠니? Buster가 민솔이의 숙제를 찢어 놓았거든.

Minsu: 음 …. 알겠어요. 그렇게 할게요.

(전화벨이 울린다.)

Mike: 고객 센터입니다. 어떻게 도와 드릴까요?

Sora: 제가 지난주에 가게에서 헤어 드라이어를 샀는데요. 마음에 들지 않네요.

Mike: 무엇이 문제인가요?

Sora: 작동이 잘되지 않아요. 제 말은 충분히 뜨거운 바람이 나오질 않는다는 거예요.

Mike: 죄송합니다. 교환을 원하시나요?

Sora: 음. 환불받을 수 있을까요?

Mike: 물론이죠. 드라이어를 가지고 저희 가게를 방문해 주시겠어요?

Sora: 네. 내일 오후에 들를게요.

Mike: 영수증 가지고 오시는 걸 잊지 마세요.

Sora: 네. 고맙습니다.

My Speaking Portfolio – Step 3

A: _____

B: _____

A: _____

B: _____

A: _____

B: _____

A: _____

A: 나는 내 남동생이 별로 마음에 들지 않아.
B: 뭐가 문제니?
A: 그는 아침에 너무 오랫동안 욕실을 사용해.
B: 네 기분이 어떤지 알아.
A: 내가 무엇을 할 수 있을까?
B: 음, 너는 더 일찍 일어나서 욕실을 먼저 사용할 수 있어.
A: 알겠어, 내가 한번 해 볼게.

Wrap Up – Listening ❺

G: _____

B: _____

G: _____

B: _____

G: _____

여: Tommy야, 기분이 안 좋아 보이는구나.
남: 나는 소진이 때문에 속상해.
여: 그 애에게 무슨 문제가 있니?
남: 그 애가 모둠 과제에서 맡은 일을 안 해.
여: 내 생각에 너는 그 애랑 이야기를 해 봐야 할 것 같아.

Wrap Up – Listening ❻

M: _____

G: _____

M: _____

G: _____

M: _____

G: _____

남: 여행 갈 준비 되었니, 수지야?
여: 네, 아빠. 저는 떠날 준비가 되었어요.
남: 표는 네가 가지고 있고?
여: 네, 제 전화기에 저장해 놓았어요.
남: 잘했구나. 기차역에 도착하면 내게 전화하는 걸 잊지 말렴.
여: 물론이죠.

※ 다음 우리말과 일치하도록 빈칸에 알맞은 것을 골라 쓰시오.

1 Breeze: Good evening, _____. _____ is _____ DJ, Breeze.

    A. your   B. this   C. listeners

2 Today we have _____ _____ _____, Andy Kim.

    A. special   B. guest   C. a

3 He's a _____ _____. _____, Andy.

    A. welcome   B. artist   C. hip-hop

4 Andy: Nice _____ meet you and thank you _____ _____ me.

    A. having   B. to   C. for

5 Breeze: Okay. What do our _____ want to _____ their _____?

    A. tell   B. listeners   C. family

6 This evening we will find _____ _____ _____ some _____ from them.

    A. out   B. letters   C. reading   D. by

7 Andy, will you _____ _____ _____ the letter _____ a teenage girl?

    A. with   B. start   C. from   D. off

8 _____: _____.

    A. sure   B. Andy

9 Andy: Hello. I'm _____ 15-year-old _____ _____ Wonju.

    A. from   B. a   C. girl

10 I want _____ _____ you _____ my mom.

    A. about   B. tell   C. to

11 My mom _____ _____ _____ everything for me.

    A. tries   B. do   C. to

12 She cleans my room _____ _____ me, so it's sometimes _____ _____ find my stuff.

    A. asking   B. to   C. without   D. hard

13 She also _____ books and makes _____ _____ _____.

    A. study   B. buys   C. them   D. me

14 I want to _____ to my mom, "I know you love me, but I'm not a baby _____. Please _____ me _____ care of things myself."

    A. take   B. let   C. anymore   D. say

---

1 Breeze: 안녕하세요, 청취자 여러분. 저는 여러분의 디제이, Breeze입니다.

2 오늘은 특별한 손님, Andy Kim 씨를 모셨습니다.

3 그는 힙합 아티스트이시죠. 환영합니다, Andy.

4 Andy: 반갑습니다, 그리고 초대해 주셔서 고맙습니다.

5 Breeze: 네. 우리 청취자분들은 가족에게 무슨 말을 하고 싶어 하실까요?

6 오늘 저녁에 우리는 청취자분들로부터 온 몇몇 편지들을 읽으며 알아보려 합니다

7 Andy, 십 대 소녀에게서 온 편지로 시작해 주시겠어요?

8 Andy: 알겠습니다.

9 Andy: 안녕하세요. 저는 원주에 사는 15세 소녀입니다.

10 저는 저의 엄마에 관해 이야기하고 싶습니다.

11 엄마는 저를 위해 모든 것을 해 주려고 하십니다.

12 엄마는 제게 물어보지도 않고 방을 청소해 주시고, 그래서 가끔은 제 물건을 찾기가 힘들 때도 있습니다.

13 또 엄마는 책을 사 와서는 저에게 그것들을 공부하라고 시키세요.

14 저는 엄마께 "엄마가 저를 사랑하는 것은 알지만 전 더 이상 아기가 아니에요. 제 일을 스스로 할 수 있게 해 주세요."라고 말씀드리고 싶습니다.

15 Breeze: I _____ the _____ _____ when I was in middle school.

    A. way   B. felt   C. same

16 Andy: Many moms think their kids are _____ young _____ do _____ on their _____.

    A. to   B. too   C. own   D. things

17 I _____ the girl's mom will _____ the _____.

    A. get   B. hope   C. message

18 Breeze: _____ _____ I. Andy, will you please _____ the next letter?

    A. do   B. read   C. so

19 Andy: Hi. I'm a _____ _____ two _____.

    A. of   B. father   C. children

20 _____ is a high school girl, and _____ _____ is a middle school boy.

    A. other   B. one   C. the

21 They're _____ _____ _____ _____ with me.

    A. busy   B. talk   C. to   D. too

22 When I _____ home from _____, they just say hi and _____ _____ to their rooms.

    A. back   B. get   C. go   D. work

23 Sometimes I _____ them about their school _____, but they only _____ short _____.

    A. answers   B. life   C. give   D. ask

24 We _____ _____ _____ at the table, _____.

    A. either   B. much   C. don't   D. talk

25 I want to _____ to my kids, "I love you so much, and I want to _____ _____ _____ with you."

    A. time   B. spend   C. say   D. more

26 Breeze: Andy, did you talk _____ your parents _____ when you were _____?

    A. with   B. often   C. younger

27 Andy: Not really. I loved them very much, but I thought they were _____ _____ _____ _____ me.

    A. to   B. old   C. too   D. understand

28 Breeze: I see. Does anyone have _____ for the "sad" dad? _____ your _____ to us.

    A. suggestions   B. idea   C. text

---

15 Breeze: 저도 중학교 때 똑같은 기분을 느꼈습니다.

16 Andy: 많은 어머님들이 자녀들이 혼자 힘으로 무언가를 하기에는 너무 어리다고 생각합니다.

17 소녀의 어머님께서 메시지를 들으시길 바랍니다.

18 Breeze: 동감입니다. Andy, 다음 편지를 읽어 주시겠어요?

19 Andy: 안녕하세요. 저는 두 아이의 아버지입니다.

20 한 명은 고등학생인 여자아이이고, 나머지 한 명은 중학생인 남자아이입니다.

21 아이들은 저와 대화를 하기 에는 너무 바쁩니다.

22 제가 일을 하고 집에 돌아오면, 아이들은 그저 인사만 하고 자신의 방으로 돌아갑니다.

23 가끔씩 저는 아이들에게 학교생활에 관해 묻기도 하지만, 아이들은 그냥 짤막한 대답만 합니다.

24 우리는 식사 자리에서조차 대화를 많이 하지 않습니다.

25 저는 아이들에게 "너희들을 무척 사랑한단다, 그리고 너희들과 더 많은 시간을 보내고 싶단다."라고 말하고 싶습니다.

26 Breeze: Andy, 어렸을 때 부모님과 자주 대화를 했나요?

27 Andy: 사실 그렇지는 않습니다. 저는 부모님을 무척 사랑하지만, 부모님이 저를 이해해 주시기에는 너무 나이가 들었다고 생각했습니다.

28 Breeze: 그렇군요. '슬픈' 아빠에게 해 드릴 제안이 있으신 분 계신가요? 여러분의 생각을 저희에게 문자로 보내 주세요.

※ 다음 우리말과 일치하도록 빈칸에 알맞은 말을 쓰시오.

1 Breeze: _____ _____, listeners. _____ _____ your DJ, Breeze.

2 Today we have _____ _____ _____, Andy Kim.

3 He's a _____ _____. _____, Andy.

4 Andy: Nice _____ _____ _____ and _____ _____ _____ _____ _____.

5 Breeze: Okay. What do our listeners _____ _____ _____ their family?

6 This evening we will _____ _____ _____ _____ _____ _____ from them.

7 Andy, will you _____ _____ _____ the letter _____ a _____ _____?

8 Andy: _____.

9 Andy: Hello. I'm a _____ girl _____ Wonju.

10 I want _____ _____ _____ about my mom.

11 My mom _____ _____ _____ everything for me.

12 She cleans my room _____ _____ me, so it's sometimes _____ _____ _____ _____ _____ _____.

13 She also _____ books and makes _____ _____ _____.

14 I want _____ _____ to my mom, "I know you love me, but I'm not a baby _____. Please _____ _____ _____ _____ _____ things _____."

1	Breeze: 안녕하세요, 청취자 여러분. 저는 여러분의 디제이, Breeze입니다.
2	오늘은 특별한 손님, Andy Kim 씨를 모셨습니다.
3	그는 힙합 아티스트이시죠. 환영합니다, Andy.
4	Andy: 반갑습니다. 그리고 초대해 주셔서 고맙습니다.
5	Breeze: 네. 우리 청취자분들은 가족에게 무슨 말을 하고 싶어 하실까요?
6	오늘 저녁에 우리는 청취자분들로부터 온 몇몇 편지들을 읽으며 알아보려 합니다.
7	Andy, 십 대 소녀에게서 온 편지로 시작해 주시겠어요?
8	Andy: 알겠습니다.
9	Andy: 안녕하세요. 저는 원주에 사는 15세 소녀입니다.
10	저는 저의 엄마에 관해 이야기하고 싶습니다.
11	엄마는 저를 위해 모든 것을 해 주려고 하십니다.
12	엄마는 제게 물어보지도 않고 방을 청소해 주시고, 그래서 가끔은 제 물건을 찾기가 힘들 때도 있습니다.
13	또 엄마는 책을 사 와서는 저에게 그것들을 공부하라고 시키세요.
14	저는 엄마께 "엄마가 저를 사랑하는 것은 알지만 전 더 이상 아기가 아니에요. 제 일을 스스로 할 수 있게 해 주세요."라고 말씀드리고 싶습니다.

15 Breeze: I felt _____ _____ _____ I was in middle school.

16 Andy: Many moms think their kids are _____ _____ _____ _____ things _____ _____ _____.

17 I hope the girl's mom will _____ _____ _____.

18 Breeze: So _____ _____. Andy, will you please read the next letter?

19 Andy: Hi. I'm a father _____ _____ _____.

20 _____ is a high school girl, and _____ _____ is a middle school boy.

21 They're _____ _____ _____ _____ with me.

22 When I _____ home _____ _____, they just say hi and _____ _____ _____ their rooms.

23 Sometimes I ask _____ about their _____ _____, but they only _____ _____ _____.

24 We _____ _____ _____ at the table, _____.

25 I want to say to my kids, "I love you so much, and I want _____ _____ _____ _____ with you."

26 Breeze: Andy, did you talk with your parents _____ _____ _____ _____ _____?

27 Andy: Not really. I loved _____ very much, but I _____ they were _____ _____ _____ _____ _____ me.

28 Breeze: I see. Does anyone have _____ for the "sad" dad? _____ _____ _____ _____ to us.

15 Breeze: 저도 중학교 때 똑같은 기분을 느꼈습니다.

16 Andy: 많은 어머님들이 자녀들이 혼자 힘으로 무언가를 하기에는 너무 어리다고 생각합니다.

17 소녀의 어머님께서 메시지를 들으시길 바랍니다.

18 Breeze: 동감입니다. Andy, 다음 편지를 읽어 주시겠어요?

19 Andy: 안녕하세요. 저는 두 아이의 아버지입니다.

20 한 명은 고등학생인 여자아이이고, 나머지 한 명은 중학생인 남자아이입니다.

21 아이들은 저와 대화를 하기에는 너무 바쁩니다.

22 제가 일을 하고 집에 돌아오면, 아이들은 그저 인사만 하고 자신의 방으로 돌아갑니다.

23 가끔씩 저는 아이들에게 학교생활에 관해 묻기도 하지만, 아이들은 그냥 짤막한 대답만 합니다.

24 우리는 식사 자리에서조차 대화를 많이 하지 않습니다.

25 저는 아이들에게 "너희들을 무척 사랑한단다, 그리고 너희들과 더 많은 시간을 보내고 싶단다."라고 말하고 싶습니다.

26 Breeze: Andy, 어렸을 때 부모님과 자주 대화를 했나요?

27 Andy: 사실 그렇지는 않습니다. 저는 부모님을 무척 사랑하지만, 부모님이 저를 이해해 주시기에는 너무 나이가 들었다고 생각했습니다.

28 Breeze: 그렇군요. '슬픈' 아빠에게 해 드릴 제안이 있으신 분 계신가요? 여러분의 생각을 저희에게 문자로 보내 주세요.

※ 다음 문장을 우리말로 쓰시오.

1 Breeze: Good evening, listeners. This is your DJ, Breeze.

➡ _____

2 Today we have a special guest, Andy Kim.

➡ _____

3 He's a hip-hop artist. Welcome, Andy.

➡ _____

4 Andy: Nice to meet you and thank you for having me.

➡ _____

5 Breeze: Okay. What do our listeners want to tell their family?

➡ _____

6 This evening we will find out by reading some letters from them.

➡ _____

7 Andy, will you start off with the letter from a teenage girl?

➡ _____

8 Andy: Sure.

➡ _____

9 Andy: Hello. I'm a 15-year-old girl from Wonju.

➡ _____

10 I want to tell you about my mom.

➡ _____

11 My mom tries to do everything for me.

➡ _____

12 She cleans my room without asking me, so it's sometimes hard to find my stuff.

➡ _____

13 She also buys books and makes me study them.

➡ _____

14 I want to say to my mom, "I know you love me, but I'm not a baby anymore. Please let me take care of things myself."

➡ _____

_____

15 Breeze: I felt the same way when I was in middle school.

⇒ _____

16 Andy: Many moms think their kids are too young to do things on their own.

⇒ _____

17 I hope the girl's mom will get the message.

⇒ _____

18 Breeze: So do I. Andy, will you please read the next letter?

⇒ _____

19 Andy: Hi. I'm a father of two children.

⇒ _____

20 One is a high school girl, and the other is a middle school boy.

⇒ _____

21 They're too busy to talk with me.

⇒ _____

22 When I get home from work, they just say hi and go back to their rooms.

⇒ _____

23 Sometimes I ask them about their school life, but they only give short answers.

⇒ _____

24 We don't talk much at the table, either.

⇒ _____

25 I want to say to my kids, "I love you so much, and I want to spend more time with you."

⇒ _____

26 Breeze: Andy, did you talk with your parents often when you were younger?

⇒ _____

27 Andy: Not really. I loved them very much, but I thought they were too old to understand me.

⇒ _____

⇒ _____

28 Breeze: I see. Does anyone have suggestions for the "sad" dad? Text your idea to us.

⇒ _____

※ 다음 괄호 안의 단어들을 우리말에 맞도록 바르게 배열하시오.

1 (Breeze: / evening, / good / listeners. // is / this / DJ, / your / Breeze.)
➡ _____

2 (we / today / have / a / guest, / special / Kim. / Andy)
➡ _____

3 (a / he's / artist. / hip-hop // Andy. / welcome)
➡ _____

4 (Andy: / to / nice / you / meet / and / you / thank / for / me. / having)
➡ _____

5 (Breeze: / okay. // do / what / listeners / our / to / want / tell / family? / their)
➡ _____

6 (evening / this / will / we / find / by / out / some / reading / from / them. / letters)
➡ _____

7 (Andy, / you / will / off / start / with / letter / the / a / from / girl? / teenage)
➡ _____

8 (Andy: / sure.)
➡ _____

9 (Andy: / hello. // I'm / a / girl / 15-year-old / Wonju. / from)
➡ _____

10 (want / I / tell / to / you / about / mom. / my)
➡ _____

11 (mom / my / to / tries / do / for / me. / everything)
➡ _____

12 (she / my / cleans / room / asking / without / me, / it's / so / sometimes / to / hard / my / stuff. / find)
➡ _____
_____

13 (also / she / books / buys / and / me / makes / them. / study)
➡ _____

14 (I / say / to / want / to / mom, / my / "I / love / you / know / me, / but / not / I'm / anymore. // a / baby // let / please / me / care / of / take / myself." / things)
➡ _____
_____

---

1 Breeze: 안녕하세요, 청취자 여러분. 저는 여러분의 디제이, Breeze입니다.

2 오늘은 특별한 손님, Andy Kim 씨를 모셨습니다.

3 그는 힙합 아티스트이시죠. 환영합니다, Andy.

4 Andy: 반갑습니다. 그리고 초대해 주셔서 고맙습니다.

5 Breeze: 네. 우리 청취자분들은 가족에게 무슨 말을 하고 싶어 하실까요?

6 오늘 저녁에 우리는 청취자분들로부터 온 몇몇 편지들을 읽으며 알아보려 합니다.

7 Andy, 십 대 소녀에게서 온 편지로 시작해 주시겠어요?

8 Andy: 알겠습니다.

9 Andy: 안녕하세요. 저는 원주에 사는 15세 소녀입니다.

10 저는 저의 엄마에 관해 이야기하고 싶습니다.

11 엄마는 저를 위해 모든 것을 해 주려고 하십니다.

12 엄마는 제게 물어보지도 않고 방을 청소해 주시고, 그래서 가끔은 제 물건을 찾기가 힘들 때도 있습니다.

13 또 엄마는 책을 사 와서는 저에게 그것들을 공부하라고 시키세요.

14 저는 엄마께 "엄마가 저를 사랑하는 것은 알지만 전 더 이상 아기가 아니에요. 제 일을 스스로 할 수 있게 해 주세요."라고 말씀드리고 싶습니다.

15 (Breeze: / felt / I / the / way / same / I / when / was / in / school. / middle)

➡ _____

16 (Andy: / moms / many / their / think / kids / too / are / young / do / to / on / things / own. / their)

➡ _____

17 (hope / I / girl's / the / mom / will / the / get / message.)

➡ _____

18 (Breeze: / do / I. / so // Andy, / you / will / read / please / the / letter? / next)

➡ _____

19 (Andy: / hi. // I'm / father / a / two / of / children.)

➡ _____

20 (is / one / high / a / girl, / school / and / other / the / is / school / middle / a / boy.)

➡ _____

21 (too / they're / busy / talk / to / me. / with)

➡ _____

22 (when / get / I / home / work, / from / just / they / hi / say / go / and / to / back / rooms. / their)

➡ _____

23 (I / sometimes / them / ask / their / about / life, / school / they / but / give / only / answers. / short)

➡ _____

24 (don't / we / much / talk / the / at / either. / table,)

➡ _____

25 (want / I / say / to / my / to / kids, / "I / you / love / much, / so / and / want / I / spend / to / time / more / you." / with)

➡ _____

26 (Breeze: / did / Andy, / talk / you / your / with / parents / when / often / were / you / younger?)

➡ _____

27 (Andy: / really. / not // loved / I / very / them / much, / I / but / they / thought / too / were / old / understand / to / me.)

➡ _____

28 (Breeze: / see. / I // anyone / does / suggestions / have / the / for / day? / "sad" // your / text / to / idea / us.)

➡ _____

15 Breeze: 저도 중학교 때 똑같은 기분을 느꼈습니다.

16 Andy: 많은 어머님들이 자녀들이 혼자 힘으로 무언가를 하기에는 너무 어리다고 생각합니다.

17 소녀의 어머님께서 메시지를 들으시길 바랍니다.

18 Breeze: 동감입니다. Andy, 다음 편지를 읽어 주시겠어요?

19 Andy: 안녕하세요. 저는 두 아이의 아버지입니다.

20 한 명은 고등학생인 여자아이이고, 나머지 한 명은 중학생인 남자아이입니다.

21 아이들은 저와 대화를 하기에는 너무 바쁩니다.

22 제가 일을 하고 집에 돌아오면, 아이들은 그저 인사만 하고 자신의 방으로 돌아갑니다.

23 가끔씩 저는 아이들에게 학교생활에 관해 묻기도 하지만, 아이들은 그냥 짧막한 대답만 합니다.

24 우리는 식사 자리에서조차 대화를 많이 하지 않습니다.

25 저는 아이들에게 "너희들을 무척 사랑한단다. 그리고 너희들과 더 많은 시간을 보내고 싶단다."라고 말하고 싶습니다.

26 Breeze: Andy, 어렸을 때 부모님과 자주 대화를 했나요?

27 Andy: 사실 그렇지는 않습니다. 저는 부모님을 무척 사랑하지만, 부모님이 저를 이해해 주시기에는 너무 나이가 들었다고 생각했습니다.

28 Breeze: 그렇군요. '슬픈' 아빠에게 해 드릴 제안이 있으신 분 계신가요? 여러분의 생각을 저희에게 문자로 보내 주세요.

※ 다음 우리말을 영어로 쓰시오.

1 Breeze: 안녕하세요, 청취자 여러분. 저는 여러분의 디제이, Breeze입니다.

➡ _____

2 오늘은 특별한 손님, Andy Kim 씨를 모셨습니다.

➡ _____

3 그는 힙합 아티스트이시죠. 환영합니다, Andy.

➡ _____

4 Andy: 반갑습니다, 그리고 초대해 주셔서 고맙습니다.

➡ _____

5 Breeze: 네. 우리 청취자분들은 가족에게 무슨 말을 하고 싶어 하실까요?

➡ _____

6 오늘 저녁에 우리는 청취자분들로부터 온 몇몇 편지들을 읽으며 알아보려 합니다.

➡ _____

7 Andy, 십 대 소녀에게서 온 편지로 시작해 주시겠이요?

➡ _____

8 Andy: 알겠습니다.

➡ _____

9 Andy: 안녕하세요. 저는 원주에 사는 15세 소녀입니다.

➡ _____

10 저는 저의 엄마에 관해 이야기하고 싶습니다.

➡ _____

11 엄마는 저를 위해 모든 것을 해 주려고 하십니다.

➡ _____

12 엄마는 제게 물어보지도 않고 방을 청소해 주시고, 그래서 가끔은 제 물건을 찾기가 힘들 때도 있습니다.

➡ _____

13 또 엄마는 책을 사 와서는 저에게 그것들을 공부하라고 시키세요.

➡ _____

14 저는 엄마께 "엄마가 저를 사랑하는 것은 알지만 전 더 이상 아기가 아니에요. 제 일을 스스로 할 수 있게 해 주세요."라고 말씀드리고 싶습니다.

➡ _____

_____

15 Breeze: 저도 중학교 때 똑같은 기분을 느꼈습니다.

➡ _____

16 Andy: 많은 어머님들이 자녀들이 혼자 힘으로 무언가를 하기 에는 너무 어리다고 생각합니다.

➡ _____

17 소녀의 어머님께서 메시지를 들으시길 바랍니다.

➡ _____

18 Breeze: 동감입니다. Andy, 다음 편지를 읽어 주시겠어요?

➡ _____

19 Andy: 안녕하세요. 저는 두 아이의 아버지입니다.

➡ _____

20 한 명은 고등학생인 여자아이이고, 나머지 한 명은 중학생인 남자아이입니다.

➡ _____

21 아이들은 저와 대화를 하기에는 너무 바쁩니다.

➡ _____

22 제가 일을 하고 집에 돌아오면, 아이들은 그저 인사만 하고 자신의 방으로 돌아갑니다.

➡ _____

23 가끔씩 저는 아이들에게 학교생활에 관해 묻기도 하지만, 아이들은 그냥 짤막한 대답만 합니다.

➡ _____

24 우리는 식사 자리에서조차 대화를 많이 하지 않습니다.

➡ _____

25 저는 아이들에게 "너희들을 무척 사랑한단다, 그리고 너희들과 더 많은 시간을 보내고 싶단다."
라고 말하고 싶습니다.

➡ _____

26 Breeze: Andy, 어렸을 때 부모님과 자주 대화를 했나요?

➡ _____

27 Andy: 사실 그렇지는 않습니다. 저는 부모님을 무척 사랑하지만, 부모님이 저를 이해해
주시기에는 너무 나이가 들었다고 생각했습니다.

➡ _____

28 Breeze: 그렇군요. '슬픈' 아빠에게 해 드릴 제안이 있으신 분 계신가요? 여러분의 생각을
저희에게 문자로 보내 주세요.

➡ _____

※ 다음 우리말과 일치하도록 빈칸에 알맞은 말을 쓰시오.

My Writing Portfolio

1. Hello, I am a _____ _____ _____ Busan.

2. I _____ _____ _____ to my brother Jaeho, "Sorry."

3. I _____ Mom _____ _____ last Friday.

4. Mom _____ so _____, so he _____ _____ _____.

5. I was _____ scared _____ say sorry to him _____ _____ _____.

6. I _____ I will _____ _____ his _____ again.

1. 안녕하세요. 저는 부산에 살고 있는 15살 소녀예요.
2. 저는 저의 오빠 재호에게 "미안해."라고 말하고 싶어요.
3. 저는 지난주에 오빠의 비밀을 엄마께 말씀드렸어요.
4. 엄마는 정말 화가 나셨고, 오빠는 곤경에 처했죠.
5. 그 당시에 저는 오빠에게 미안하다고 말하기엔 너무 무서웠어요.
6. 오빠의 비밀을 다시는 이야기하지 않겠다고 약속할게요.

Have Fun Together

1. I have _____ _____ _____. I have no friends.

2. Everything _____ too small. I don't like this _____ very much.

3. Heungbu is _____ _____ me now. I'm _____ _____ _____ it.

4. Mom _____ _____ _____ home. We're not happy with it.

5. This soup _____ _____, but I can't eat it.

1. 나는 할 일이 없어. 나는 친구가 없어.
2. 모든 것이 너무 작아. 나는 이곳이 별로 마음에 안 들어.
3. 이제 흥부가 나보다 더 부자야. 나는 그것이 마음에 안 들어.
4. 엄마는 우리가 집을 떠나게 하셨어. 우리는 그것이 마음이 안 들어.
5. 이 수프는 냄새가 좋은데, 나는 그것을 먹을 수 없어.

Wrap Up – Reading Read and answer 3

1. This is a letter _____ a father _____ wants _____ _____ his experience _____ the "sad" father.

2. My kids and I _____ _____ _____ much.

3. There was a wall _____ us. I wanted to _____ it _____.

4. I _____ _____ _____ more time with my children _____ _____.

5. We played computer games, _____ _____, and _____ _____ together.

6. In this way, I had more _____ _____ _____ _____ them.

7. I _____ _____ _____ more about them.

1. 이것은 '슬픈' 아버지와 경험을 공유하고 싶은 한 아버지로부터 온 편지입니다.
2. 제 아이들과 저는 대화를 많이 하지 않았습니다.
3. 우리 사이에는 벽이 있었어요. 저는 그것을 허물고 싶었습니다.
4. 저는 주말마다 아이들과 더 많은 시간을 보내려고 노력했어요.
5. 우리는 함께 컴퓨터 게임을 했고, 자전거를 탔고, 쇼핑을 갔습니다.
6. 이 방법으로 저는 아이들과 이야기할 기회를 더 많이 가졌습니다.
7. 저는 그들을 더 잘 알게 되었죠.

※ 다음 우리말을 영어로 쓰시오.

My Writing Portfolio

1. 안녕하세요. 저는 부산에 살고 있는 15살 소녀예요.
   ➡ _____

2. 저는 저의 오빠 재호에게 "미안해."라고 말하고 싶어요.
   ➡ _____

3. 저는 지난주에 오빠의 비밀을 엄마께 말씀드렸어요.
   ➡ _____

4. 엄마는 정말 화가 나셨고, 오빠는 곤경에 처했죠.
   ➡ _____

5. 그 당시에 저는 오빠에게 미안하다고 말하기엔 너무 무서웠어요.
   ➡ _____

6. 오빠의 비밀을 다시는 이야기하지 않겠다고 약속할게요..
   ➡ _____

Have Fun Together

1. 나는 할 일이 없어. 나는 친구가 없어.
   ➡ _____

2. 모든 것이 너무 작아. 나는 이곳이 별로 마음에 안 들어.
   ➡ _____

3. 이제 흥부가 나보다 더 부자야. 나는 그것이 마음에 안 들어.
   ➡ _____

4. 엄마는 우리가 집을 떠나게 하셨어. 우리는 그것이 마음이 안 들어.
   ➡ _____

5. 이 수프는 냄새가 좋은데, 나는 그것을 먹을 수 없어.
   ➡ _____

Wrap Up – Reading Read and answer 3

1. 이것은 '슬픈' 아버지와 경험을 공유하고 싶은 한 아버지로부터 온 편지입니다.
   ➡ _____

2. 제 아이들과 저는 대화를 많이 하지 않았습니다.
   ➡ _____

3. 우리 사이에는 벽이 있었어요. 저는 그것을 허물고 싶었습니다.
   ➡ _____

4. 저는 주말마다 아이들과 더 많은 시간을 보내려고 노력했어요.
   ➡ _____

5. 우리는 함께 컴퓨터 게임을 했고, 자전거를 탔고, 쇼핑을 갔습니다.
   ➡ _____

6. 이 방법으로 저는 아이들과 이야기할 기회를 더 많이 가졌습니다.
   ➡ _____

7. 저는 그들을 더 잘 알게 되었죠.
   ➡ _____

※ 다음 영어를 우리말로 쓰시오.

01 diary _____

02 matter _____

03 state _____

04 assembly _____

05 way _____

06 traditional _____

07 vote _____

08 Athens _____

09 character _____

10 male _____

11 outdoor _____

12 person _____

13 develop _____

14 final _____

15 hold _____

16 count _____

17 gather _____

18 impossible _____

19 discussion _____

20 meaning _____

21 stay _____

22 about _____

23 almost _____

24 citizen _____

25 Athenian _____

26 question _____

27 sadness _____

28 talent _____

29 gathering place _____

30 take part in _____

31 thousands of _____

32 a lot of _____

33 be busy -ing _____

34 by -ing _____

35 so far _____

36 between A and B _____

37 too ~ to … _____

38 over the age of 20 _____

39 in addition to _____

※ 다음 우리말을 영어로 쓰시오.

01 의미

02 아테네

03 전통적인

04 수를 세다

05 남자의, 수컷의

06 모이다, 집결하다

07 체류, 방문

08 재능

09 토론

10 일기

11 일, 문제, 안건

12 마지막의, 최종의

13 담다, 수용하다

14 집회, 국회, 민회

15 불가능한

16 거의

17 질문하다

18 시민

19 야외의, 실외의

20 약, 대략

21 사람, 인간, 인물

22 투표하다

23 방식

24 개발하다, 발달시키다

25 슬픔

26 아테네 사람

27 등장인물

28 국가

29 모이는 장소

30 지금까지

31 많은

32 수천의

33 ~함으로써

34 ~에 참여하다

35 ~하느라 바쁘다

36 A와 B 사이에

37 20살 이상의

38 너무 ~해서 …하다

39 ~에 더하여, ~일뿐 아니라

※ 다음 영영풀이에 알맞은 단어를 <보기>에서 골라 쓴 후, 우리말 뜻을 쓰시오.

1 _____ : to say numbers: _____

2 _____ : not able to happen: _____

3 _____ : the government of a country: _____

4 _____ : to contain something: _____

5 _____ : a natural ability to do something: _____

6 _____ : to ask someone questions: _____

7 _____ : a period of time that you spend in a place: _____

8 _____ : to choose someone in an election: _____

9 _____ : happening or used outside; not in a building: _____

10 _____ : someone who lives in a particular town or city: _____

11 _____ : typical of or relating to men or boys: _____

12 _____ : a meeting of a large group of people, especially one that happens regularly for a particular purpose: _____

보기			
state	outdoor	stay	vote
assembly	impossible	hold	count
male	citizen	question	talent

Step1

※ 다음 우리말과 일치하도록 빈칸에 알맞은 것을 골라 쓰시오.

1 A _____ from _____

　A. Athens　　　B. Diary

2 **1st Day** _ I am _____ my _____ and _____ in _____ .

　A. uncle　　　B. visiting　　　C. Athens　　　D. aunt

3 Today I _____ to the Agora in the _____ of the _____ .

　A. center　　　B. went　　　C. city

4 It is a _____ _____ for _____ .

　A. Athenians　　　B. place　　　C. gathering

5 There were a _____ of stores, and people were _____ _____ and _____ .

　A. talking　　　B. lot　　　C. shopping　　　D. busy

6 **2nd Day** _ My uncle _____ _____ the _____ .

　A. Assembly　　　B. to　　　C. went

7 Any _____ citizens over the age of 20 can take _____ in the Assembly and _____ on important _____ .

　A. vote　　　B. matters　　　C. part　　　D. male

8 After they _____ speak _____ about the _____ , they vote by _____ their hands.

　A. matters　　　B. each　　　C. showing　　　D. freely

9 My uncle said, "_____ _____ of hands is _____ impossible."

　A. almost　　　B. thousands　　　C. counting

10 **3rd Day** _ I _____ to the Agora _____ .

　A. again　　　B. went

11 I _____ a very interesting discussion _____ a teacher _____ Socrates _____ his students.

　A. named　　　B. and　　　C. heard　　　D. between

1 아테네에서 쓴 일기

2 첫째 날: 나는 아테네에 있는 숙부와 숙모 댁을 방문 중이다.

3 오늘은 도시 중심에 있는 아고라에 갔다.

4 아고라는 아테네 사람들이 모이는 장소이다.

5 많은 상점들이 있었고, 사람들은 이야기하고 쇼핑하느라 분주했다.

6 둘째 날: 숙부는 민회로 가셨다.

7 20살 이상의 모든 남자 시민은 민회에 참여하여 중요한 안건에 관해 투표할 수 있다.

8 그들은 각자 안건에 관해 자유롭게 의견을 말한 후, 손을 들어 투표한다.

9 숙부는 "수천 명의 손을 세는 것은 거의 불가능해."라고 말씀하셨다.

10 셋째 날: 나는 또 아고라에 갔다.

11 소크라테스라고 불리는 선생님과 그의 제자들이 나누고 있는 매우 재미있는 토론을 경청했다.

12 Socrates _____ his students _____ the _____ of life.

A. on   B. questioned   C. meaning

13 I was _____ young _____ understand it, but I liked their _____ of _____ matters.

A. way   B. to   C. discussing   D. too

14 **4th Day** _ Today was the _____ day _____ _____.

A. far   B. best   C. so

15 I _____ _____ the Theater _____ Dionysus.

A. to   B. went   C. of

16 At the _____ theater which can _____ about 17,000 people, we _____ *Antigone*, a _____ by Sophocles.

A. watched   B. play   C. outdoor   D. hold

17 In _____ to _____ songs and dances, the _____ had an _____ story.

A. interesting   B. traditional   C. play   D. addition

18 I sat _____ from the _____, but I could feel the _____ _____.

A. characters'   B. stage   C. sadness   D. far

19 **5th Day** _ Today is the _____ day of my _____ _____ Athens.

A. stay   B. final   C. in

20 My aunt and uncle said to me, "You must _____ your _____. You can help _____ Athens a great _____."

A. make   B. develop   C. state   D. talent

21 Now I _____ to _____ to school and _____ a _____ person.

A. better   B. go   C. want   D. become

12 소크라테스는 제자들에게 인생의 의미에 관해 질문하였다.

13 나는 그것을 이해하기에 너무 어렸지만, 나는 그들의 토론 방식이 마음에 들었다.

14 넷째 날: 오늘은 지금까지의 날 중 최고의 날이었다.

15 나는 디오니소스 극장에 갔다.

16 약 17,000 명을 수용할 수 있는 야외 극장에서 소포클레스의 연극 '안티고네'를 관람하였다.

17 전통적으로 있던 노래와 춤에 더하여, '안티고네'에는 흥미로운 이야기가 있었다.

18 나는 무대에서 먼 곳에 앉아 있었지만, 등장인물들의 슬픔을 느낄 수 있었다.

19 다섯째 날: 오늘은 아테네에서 머무는 마지막 날이다.

20 숙부와 숙모는 "네 재능을 개발해야 된다. 너는 아테네를 위대한 국가로 만드는 데에 기여할 수 있어."라고 말씀하셨다.

21 이제 나는 학교에 다니며 더 나은 사람이 되고 싶다.

※ 다음 우리말과 일치하도록 빈칸에 알맞은 말을 쓰시오.

1 A _____ from _____

2 **1st Day** _ I am _____ my _____ and _____ in _____ .

3 Today I _____ _____ the Agora in the _____ of the city.

4 It is a _____ _____ for Athenians.

5 There _____ _____ _____ _____ stores, and people were _____ _____ and _____ .

6 **2nd Day** _ My uncle _____ _____ the _____ .

7 _____ _____ _____ over the age of 20 can _____ _____ _____ the Assembly and _____ on important _____ .

8 After they _____ speak _____ about the _____ , they _____ _____ _____ their hands.

9 My uncle said, "_____ _____ _____ hands is _____ _____ ."

10 **3rd Day** _ I _____ _____ the Agora _____ .

11 I _____ a very _____ _____ _____ a teacher _____ Socrates _____ his students.

1 아테네에서 쓴 일기

2 첫째 날: 나는 아테네에 있는 숙부와 숙모 댁을 방문 중이다.

3 오늘은 도시 중심에 있는 아고라에 갔다.

4 아고라는 아테네 사람들이 모이는 장소이다.

5 많은 상점들이 있었고, 사람들은 이야기하고 쇼핑하느라 분주했다.

6 둘째 날: 숙부는 민회로 가셨다.

7 20살 이상의 모든 남자 시민은 민회에 참여하여 중요한 안건에 관해 투표할 수 있다.

8 그들은 각자 안건에 관해 자유롭게 의견을 말한 후, 손을 들어 투표한다.

9 숙부는 "수천 명의 손을 세는 것은 거의 불가능해."라고 말씀하셨다.

10 셋째 날: 나는 또 아고라에 갔다.

11 소크라테스라고 불리는 선생님과 그의 제자들이 나누고 있는 매우 재미있는 토론을 경청했다.

12 Socrates _____ his students _____ the _____ _____ _____ .

13 I was _____ young _____ understand it, but I liked their _____ _____ _____ _____ .

14 **4th Day** _ Today was the _____ day _____ _____ .

15 I _____ _____ the Theater of Dionysus.

16 At the _____ theater _____ can _____ _____ 17,000 people, we _____ *Antigone*, a _____ by Sophocles.

17 _____ _____ _____ _____ songs and dances, the _____ had an _____ story.

18 I _____ _____ from the _____ , but I _____ _____ the _____ _____ .

19 **5th Day** _ Today is the _____ _____ of my _____ _____ Athens.

20 My aunt and uncle said to me, "You _____ _____ your _____ . You can _____ _____ Athens a great _____ ."

21 Now I _____ _____ _____ to school and _____ _____ _____ person.

---

12 소크라테스는 제자들에게 인생의 의미에 관해 질문하였다.

13 나는 그것을 이해하기에 너무 어렸지만, 나는 그들의 토론 방식이 마음에 들었다.

14 넷째 날: 오늘은 지금까지의 날 중 최고의 날이었다.

15 나는 디오니소스 극장에 갔다.

16 약 17,000 명을 수용할 수 있는 야외 극장에서 소포클레스의 연극 '안티고네'를 관람하였다.

17 전통적으로 있던 노래와 춤에 더하여, '안티고네'에는 흥미로운 이야기가 있었다.

18 나는 무대에서 먼 곳에 앉아 있었지만, 등장인물들의 슬픔을 느낄 수 있었다.

19 다섯째 날: 오늘은 아테네에서 머무는 마지막 날이다.

20 숙부와 숙모는 "네 재능을 개발해야 된다. 너는 아테네를 위대한 국가로 만드는 데에 기여할 수 있어."라고 말씀하셨다.

21 이제 나는 학교에 다니며 더 나은 사람이 되고 싶다.

※ 다음 문장을 우리말로 쓰시오.

1   A Diary from Athens

➡ _____

2   **1st Day** _ I am visiting my aunt and uncle in Athens.

➡ _____

3   Today I went to the Agora in the center of the city

➡ _____

4   It is a gathering place for Athenians.

➡ _____

5   There were a lot of stores, and people were busy talking and shopping.

➡ _____

6   **2nd Day** _ My uncle went to the Assembly.

➡ _____

7   Any male citizens over the age of 20 can take part in the Assembly and vote on important matters.

➡ _____

8   After they each speak freely about the matters, they vote by showing their hands.

➡ _____

9   My uncle said, "Counting thousands of hands is almost impossible."

➡ _____

10   **3rd Day** _ I went to the Agora again.

➡ _____

11   I heard a very interesting discussion between a teacher named Socrates and his students.

➡ _____

12 ⇨ Socrates questioned his students on the meaning of life.

⇨ _____

13 ⇨ I was too young to understand it, but I liked their way of discussing matters.

⇨ _____

14 ⇨ **4st Day** _ Today was the best day so far.

⇨ _____

15 ⇨ I went to the Theater of Dionysus.

⇨ _____

16 ⇨ At the outdoor theater which can hold about 17,000 people, we watched *Antigone*, a play by Sophocles.

⇨ _____

17 ⇨ In addition to traditional songs and dances, the play had an interesting story.

⇨ _____

18 ⇨ I sat far from the stage, but I could feel the characters' sadness.

⇨ _____

19 ⇨ **5th Day** _ Today is the final day of my stay in Athens.

⇨ _____

20 ⇨ My aunt and uncle said to me, "You must develop your talent. You can help make Athens a great state."

⇨ _____

_____

21 ⇨ Now I want to go to school and become a better person.

⇨ _____

※ 다음 괄호 안의 단어들을 우리말에 맞도록 바르게 배열하시오.

1 (Diary / A / Athens / from)

➡ _____

2 (Day / 1st / _ / I / visiting / am / aunt / my / and / in / uncle / Athens.)

➡ _____

3 (I / today / to / went / Agora / the / the / in / of / center / city. / the)

➡ _____

4 (is / it / gathering / a / place / Athenians. / for)

➡ _____

5 (were / there / lot / a / of / stores, / and / were / people / talking / busy / shopping. / and)

➡ _____

6 (Day / 2nd / _ / uncle / my / to / went / Assembly. / the)

➡ _____

7 (male / any / over / citizens / the / of / age / can / 20 / part / take / in / Assembly / the / and / on / vote / matters. / important)

➡ _____
_____

8 (they / after / speak / each / about / freely / matters, / the / vote / they / showing / by / hands. / their)

➡ _____
_____

9 (uncle / my / said, / thousands / "counting / hands / of / is / impossible." / almost)

➡ _____

10 (Day / 3rd / _ / went / I / to / again. / Agora / the)

➡ _____

11 (heard / I / very / a / discussion / interesting / a / between / teacher / named / and / Socrates / his / students.)

➡ _____
_____

1 아테네에서 쓴 일기

2 첫째 날: 나는 아테네에 있는 숙부와 숙모 댁을 방문 중이다.

3 오늘은 도시 중심에 있는 아고라에 갔다.

4 아고라는 아테네 사람들이 모이는 장소이다.

5 많은 상점들이 있었고, 사람들은 이야기하고 쇼핑하느라 분주했다.

6 둘째 날: 숙부는 민회로 가셨다.

7 20살 이상의 모든 남자 시민은 민회에 참여하여 중요한 안건에 관해 투표할 수 있다.

8 그들은 각자 안건에 관해 자유롭게 의견을 말한 후, 손을 들어 투표한다.

9 숙부는 "수천 명의 손을 세는 것은 거의 불가능해."라고 말씀하셨다.

10 셋째 날: 나는 또 아고라에 갔다.

11 소크라테스라고 불리는 선생님과 그의 제자들이 나누고 있는 매우 재미있는 토론을 경청했다.

12 (questioned / Socrates / students / his / the / on / of / life. / meaning)

➡ _____

13 (was / I / to / young / too / understand / it, / I / but / liked / way / their / discussing / of / matters.)

➡ _____

_____

14 (Day / 4th / _ / was / today / best / the / day / far. / so)

➡ _____

15 (went / I / the / to / Dionysus. / of / Theater)

➡ _____

16 (the / at / theater / outdoor / can / which / about / hold / people, / 17,000 / watched / we / *Antigone*, / play / a / Sophocles. / by)

➡ _____

_____

17 (addition / in / traditional / to / dances, / and / songs / play / the / an / had / story. / interesting)

➡ _____

_____

18 (I / far / sat / the / from / stage, / I / but / could / the / feel / sadness. / characters')

➡ _____

19 (Day / 5th / _ / is / today / final / the / of / day / stay / my / Athens. / in)

➡ _____

20 (aunt / my / and / said / uncle / me, / to / "you / develop / must / talent. / your // can / you / make / help / a / Athens / state." / great)

➡ _____

21 (I / now / to / want / to / go / school / and / become / better / a / person.)

➡ _____

12 소크라테스는 제자들에게 인생의 의미에 관해 질문하였다.

13 나는 그것을 이해하기에 너무 어려웠지만, 나는 그들의 토론 방식이 마음에 들었다.

14 넷째 날: 오늘은 지금까지의 날 중 최고의 날이었다.

15 나는 디오니소스 극장에 갔다.

16 약 17,000 명을 수용할 수 있는 야외 극장에서 소포클레스의 연극 '안티고네'를 관람하였다.

17 전통적으로 있던 노래와 춤에 더하여, '안티고네'에는 흥미로운 이야기가 있었다.

18 나는 무대에서 먼 곳에 앉아 있었지만, 등장인물들의 슬픔을 느낄 수 있었다.

19 다섯째 날: 오늘은 아테네에서 머무는 마지막 날이다.

20 숙부와 숙모는 "네 재능을 개발해야 된다. 너는 아테네를 위대한 국가로 만드는 데에 기여할 수 있어."라고 말씀하셨다.

21 이제 나는 학교에 다니며 더 나은 사람이 되고 싶다.

※ 다음 우리말을 영어로 쓰시오.

1 아테네에서 쓴 일기

➡ _____

2 첫째 날: 나는 아테네에 있는 숙부와 숙모 댁을 방문 중이다.

➡ _____

3 오늘은 도시 중심에 있는 아고라에 갔다.

➡ _____

4 아고라는 아테네 사람들이 모이는 장소이다.

➡ _____

5 많은 상점들이 있었고, 사람들은 이야기하고 쇼핑하느라 분주했다.

➡ _____

6 둘째 날: 숙부는 민회로 가셨다.

➡ _____

7 20살 이상의 모든 남자 시민은 민회에 참여하여 중요한 안건에 관해 투표할 수 있다.

➡ _____

8 그들은 각자 안건에 관해 자유롭게 의견을 말한 후, 손을 들어 투표한다.

➡ _____

9 숙부는 "수천 명의 손을 세는 것은 거의 불가능해."라고 말씀하셨다.

➡ _____

10 셋째 날: 나는 또 아고라에 갔다.

➡ _____

11 소크라테스라고 불리는 선생님과 그의 제자들이 나누고 있는 매우 재미있는 토론을 경청했다.

➡ _____

12 소크라테스는 제자들에게 인생의 의미에 관해 질문하였다.

➡ _____

13 나는 그것을 이해하기에 너무 어렸지만, 나는 그들의 토론 방식이 마음에 들었다.

➡ _____

14 넷째 날: 오늘은 지금까지의 날 중 최고의 날이었다.

➡ _____

15 나는 디오니소스 극장에 갔다.

➡ _____

16 약 17,000명을 수용할 수 있는 야외 극장에서 소포클레스의 연극 '안티고네'를 관람하였다.

➡ _____

17 전통적으로 있던 노래와 춤에 더하여, '안티고네'에는 흥미로운 이야기가 있었다.

➡ _____

18 나는 무대에서 먼 곳에 앉아 있었지만, 등장인물들의 슬픔을 느낄 수 있었다.

➡ _____

19 다섯째 날: 오늘은 아테네에서 머무는 마지막 날이다.

➡ _____

20 숙부와 숙모는 "네 재능을 개발해야 된다. 너는 아테네를 위대한 국가로 만드는 데에 기여할 수 있어." 라고 말씀하셨다.

➡ _____

_____

21 이제 나는 학교에 다니며 더 나은 사람이 되고 싶다.

➡ _____

※ 다음 영어를 우리말로 쓰시오.

01 chef

02 pollute

03 boil

04 showtime

05 probably

06 fascinating

07 appear

08 machine

09 education

10 pour

11 select

12 lastly

13 creative

14 movement

15 common

16 alive

17 amusing

18 plate

19 taste

20 develop

21 simple

22 publish

23 usual

24 recipe

25 among

26 remain

27 silly

28 well-known

29 sunscreen

30 translate

31 choose

32 caricature

33 animated movie

34 cartoonist

35 pay for

36 jump out at

37 make fun of

38 can't wait to

39 ups and downs

40 watch out

41 cut A into pieces

42 play a role

43 come together

※ 다음 우리말을 영어로 쓰시오.

01	나타나다, 등장하다		22	간단한, 단순한
02	요리사		23	극장 매표소
03	오염시키다		24	공통의
04	번역하다		25	만화영화
05	창의적인, 독창적인		26	선택하다
06	개발하다, 만들다		27	조리법, 비법
07	만화가		28	고추
08	더러운		29	접시
09	살아 있는		30	맛보다, 먹다
10	교육		31	유명한, 잘 알려진
11	출판하다		32	아마도
12	볶다, 튀기다		33	매력적인
13	마지막으로		34	움직임
14	평소의, 보통의		35	조심하다
15	붓다		36	역할을 하다
16	~ 중에		37	~로 만들어지다
17	자외선 차단제		38	살펴보다
18	기계		39	~가 기대되다
19	상영 시간		40	기복
20	어리석은		41	~을 놀리다
21	끓이다		42	~에 대한 돈을 내다
			43	모든 연령의

※ 다음 영영풀이에 알맞은 단어를 <보기>에서 골라 쓴 후, 우리말 뜻을 쓰시오.

1 _____ : the act of moving: _____

2 _____ : normal, happening most often: _____

3 _____ : the time when a play, movie, etc., begins: _____

4 _____ : causing laughter: _____

5 _____ : a process of teaching and learning: _____

6 _____ : to start to be seen: _____

7 _____ : showing little thought; foolish: _____

8 _____ : to invent something new: _____

9 _____ : extremely interesting: _____

10 _____ : to be changed from one language to another: _____

11 _____ : to cook something in hot fat or oil: _____

12 _____ : to stay in the same place or in the same condition: _____

13 _____ : a funny drawing of somebody that exaggerates some of their features:
_____

14 _____ : to make information available to people in a book, magazine, or newspaper:
_____

15 _____ : a type of lotion that you put on your skin to protect it from being damaged
by the sun: _____

16 _____ : a professional cook who usually is in charge of a kitchen in a restaurant:
_____

보기			
remain	silly	education	caricature
fascinating	appear	publish	amusing
movement	chef	translate	usual
fry	develop	sunscreen	showtime

※ 다음 우리말과 일치하도록 빈칸에 알맞은 말을 쓰시오.

Communication: Listen – Dialog 1

Jane: Kevin, you _____ _____.

Kevin: Nothing _____. _____ my feelings change _____ _____.

Jane: I understand. Many _____ have _____ _____ _____ in their feelings.

Kevin: Oh, _____?

Jane: _____ _____ _____ the _____ _____ "Shining Days"?

Kevin: No, _____ _____. _____ do you _____?

Jane: It is about a _____ _____. It _____ _____ you _____ your feelings _____.

Kevin: That _____ good! I'll _____ it.

Jane: Kevin, 너 기분이 안 좋아 보이는구나.
Kevin: 별거 아니에요. 때때로 제 감정이 많이 바뀌어요.
Jane: 이해한단다. 많은 십 대가 감정의 기복이 있지.
Kevin: 아, 정말요?
Jane: 'Shining Days'라는 만화영화를 본 적이 있니?
Kevin: 아니요, 본 적이 없어요. 왜 물으세요?
Jane: 그건 십 대의 감정에 관한 거야. 그건 네가 네 감정을 더 잘 이해하도록 도와줄 거야.
Kevin: 괜찮은 거 같네요! 그걸 볼게요.

Communication: Listen – Dialog 2

Emily: Oh, _____ _____ the long _____ at the box office.

Tony: Yeah, there's a _____ _____ over there. _____ _____ the tickets _____ the _____.

Emily: All right. Do you know _____ _____ _____ _____ _____?

Tony: Sure. It's easy. First, _____ a movie and a _____.

Emily: Okay. We can _____ the seven o'clock show. Then _____?

Tony: Well, _____ the number of tickets and _____ our _____.

Emily: Okay. Two tickets, and I want to _____ _____ _____ _____.

Tony: No _____. _____, _____ _____ the tickets.

Emily: It's very _____.

Emily: 아, 극장 매표소에 길게 늘어선 줄을 좀 봐.
Tony: 네, 저쪽에 발매기가 하나 있어요. 저 기계에서 표를 사요.
Emily: 좋아. 그 기계를 어떻게 쓰는지 아니?
Tony: 그럼요. 쉬워요. 먼저, 영화와 상영 시간을 골라요.
Emily: 알았어. 우리는 7시 영화를 볼 수 있겠네. 그리고 뭘 하니?
Tony: 음, 표 매수를 선택하고 우리의 좌석을 골라요.
Emily: 좋아. 표 두 장, 그리고 나는 뒤에 앉고 싶어.
Tony: 좋아요. 마지막으로 표 값을 내요.
Emily: 정말 간단하구나.

Communication: Listen More

Suji: Good morning, Chef Garcia!

Garcia: Hello, Suji. _____ _____ _____ _____ nacho pizza?

Suji: Nacho pizza? _____, _____ _____.

Garcia: Kids will love it, and I'll tell you _____ _____ _____ it.

Suji: _____ good!

Garcia: It's easy to make. _____, _____ nacho chips _____ a _____ and _____ pizza sauce on them.

Suji: Okay. Let me _____ you _____ the pizza sauce.

Garcia: Thanks. _____, put some ham, onions, and _____ on top.

Suji: Okay. Then?

Garcia: _____ cheese and _____ _____ _____ 12 minutes in the _____.

Suji: I _____ _____ _____ _____ it!

Communicate: Speak

Anna: Do you know _____ _____ make _____ _____?

Jinsu: Sure. It's easy. First, _____ the vegetables _____ small pieces.

Anna: Okay. What do you do _____?

Jinsu: _____ some oil in the pan. Then, _____ the vegetables _____ _____.

Anna: Wow, it's really _____.

Wrap Up – Listening ❺

Judy: _____ you ever _____ _____ Sokcho?

Minsu: Yes, I _____. _____ my uncle lives there, so I visit him _____ _____.

Judy: Really? Then, _____ _____ Mt. Seorak, _____ _____?

Minsu: Yes, I've climbed to the top of the mountain _____.

Wrap Up – Listening ❻

Mike: Today, I'll tell you _____ _____ _____ a bear's face. _____, draw a big _____ for the face. _____, make two circles on top of the face. After that, _____ two circles for its eyes and _____ them black. Then, _____ a small _____ for the nose. _____, _____ a mouth.

Suji: 안녕하세요, Garcia 셰프님!

Garcia: 안녕하세요, 수지 씨. 나초 피자를 만들어 본 적 있나요?

Suji: 나초 피자요? 아뇨, 만들어 본 적 없어요.

Garcia: 아이들이 그걸 매우 좋아할 거예요. 그럼 제가 어떻게 만드는지 알려 드리죠.

Suji: 좋아요!

Garcia: 만들기 쉬워요. 첫째로 접시 위에 나초 칩을 올려놓고 그것들 위에 피자 소스를 바르세요.

Suji: 네, 피자 소스를 제가 도와드릴게요.

Garcia: 고맙습니다. 다음으로 햄, 양파, 피망을 위에 올리세요.

Suji: 네. 그다음에는요?

Garcia: 치즈를 올리고 오븐에서 약 12분 동안 구우세요.

Suji: 빨리 맛보고 싶군요!

Anna: 너는 볶음밥을 만드는 법을 아니?

Jinsu: 물론이야. 그건 쉬워. 먼저 채소를 작은 조각으로 잘라.

Anna: 알았어. 다음엔 뭘 하니?

Jinsu: 팬에 기름을 둘러. 그러고는 채소를 밥과 함께 볶아.

Anna: 와, 정말 간단하구나.

Judy: 너는 속초에 가 본 적이 있니?

Minsu: 응, 가 본 적이 있어. 사실은 내 삼촌이 거기 살아서, 나는 매년 그를 방문해.

Judy: 정말? 그러면, 너는 설악산을 올라 본 적이 있지, 그렇지 않니?

Judy: 응, 그 산의 정상에 올라간 적이 두 번 있어.

Mike: 오늘 나는 곰의 얼굴을 그리는 방법을 네게 말해 줄게. 첫 번째로, 얼굴에 해당하는 큰 원을 그려. 다음에, 얼굴 위에 두 개의 원을 그려. 그 후에 눈에 해당하는 두 개의 원을 그리고 그것들을 검게 색칠해. 그리고 코에 해당하는 작은 원을 그려. 마지막으로 입을 만들어.

대화문 Test

※ 다음 우리말에 맞도록 대화를 영어로 쓰시오.

Communication: Listen – Dialog 1

Jane: _____

Kevin: _____

Jane: _____

Kevin: _____

Jane: _____

Kevin: _____

Jane: _____

_____

Kevin: _____

Jane: Kevin, 너 기분이 안 좋아 보이는구나.
Kevin: 별거 아니에요. 때때로 제 감정이 많이 바뀌어요.
Jane: 이해한단다. 많은 십 대가 감정의 기복이 있지.
Kevin: 아, 정말요?
Jane: 'Shining Days'라는 만화영화를 본 적이 있니?
Kevin: 아니요, 본 적이 없어요. 왜 물으세요?
Jane: 그건 십 대의 감정에 관한 거야. 그건 네가 네 감정을 더 잘 이해하도록 도와줄 거야.
Kevin: 괜찮은 거 같네요! 그걸 볼게요.

Communication: Listen – Dialog 2

Emily: _____

Tony: _____

_____

Emily: _____

Tony: _____

Emily: _____

Tony: _____

Emily: _____

Tony: _____

Emily: _____

Emily: 아, 극장 매표소에 길게 늘어선 줄을 좀 봐.
Tony: 네, 저쪽에 발매기가 하나 있어요. 저 기계에서 표를 사요.
Emily: 좋아. 그 기계를 어떻게 쓰는지 아니?
Tony: 그럼요. 쉬워요. 먼저, 영화와 상영 시간을 골라요.
Emily: 알았어. 우리는 7시 영화를 볼 수 있겠네. 그리고 뭘 하니?
Tony: 음, 표 매수를 선택하고 우리의 좌석을 골라요.
Emily: 좋아. 표 두 장, 그리고 나는 뒤에 앉고 싶어.
Tony: 좋아요. 마지막으로 표 값을 내요.
Emily: 정말 간단하구나.

Communication: Listen More

Suji: _____

Garcia: _____

Suji: _____

Garcia: _____

Suji: _____

Garcia: _____

_____

Suji: _____

Garcia: _____

Suji: _____

Garcia: _____

Suji: _____

Communicate: Speak

Anna: _____

Jinsu: _____

Anna: _____

Jinsu: _____

Anna: _____

Wrap Up – Listening ❺

Judy: _____

Minsu: _____

Judy: _____

Minsu: _____

Wrap Up – Listening ❻

Mike: _____

_____

_____

Suji: 안녕하세요, Garcia 셰프님!
Garcia: 안녕하세요, 수지 씨. 나초 피자를 만들어 본 적 있나요?
Suji: 나초 피자요? 아뇨, 만들어 본 적 없어요.
Garcia: 아이들이 그걸 매우 좋아할 거예요, 그럼 제가 어떻게 만드는지 알려 드리죠.
Suji: 좋아요!
Garcia: 만들기 쉬워요. 첫째로 접시 위에 나초 칩을 올려놓고 그것들 위에 피자 소스를 바르세요.
Suji: 네, 피자 소스를 제가 도와드릴게요.
Garcia: 고맙습니다. 다음으로 햄, 양파, 피망을 위에 올리세요.
Suji: 네. 그다음에는요?
Garcia: 치즈를 올리고 오븐에서 약 12분 동안 구우세요.
Suji: 빨리 맛보고 싶군요!

Anna: 너는 볶음밥을 만드는 법을 아니?
Jinsu: 물론이야. 그건 쉬워. 먼저 채소를 작은 조각으로 잘라.
Anna: 알았어. 다음엔 뭘 하니?
Jinsu: 팬에 기름을 둘러. 그러고는 채소를 밥과 함께 볶아.
Anna: 와, 정말 간단하구나.

Judy: 너는 속초에 가 본 적이 있니?
Minsu: 응, 가 본 적이 있어. 사실은 내 삼촌이 거기 살아서, 나는 매년 그를 방문해.
Judy: 정말? 그러면, 너는 설악산을 올라 본 적이 있지, 그렇지 않니?
Judy: 응, 그 산의 정상에 올라간 적이 두 번 있어.

Mike: 오늘 나는 곰의 얼굴을 그리는 방법을 네게 말해 줄게. 첫 번째로, 얼굴에 해당하는 큰 원을 그려. 다음에, 얼굴 위에 두 개의 원을 그려. 그 후에 눈에 해당하는 두 개의 원을 그리고 그것들을 검게 색칠해. 그리고 코에 해당하는 작은 원을 그려. 마지막으로 입을 만들어.

※ 다음 우리말과 일치하도록 빈칸에 알맞은 것을 골라 쓰시오.

1 _____! _____!
A. Land   B. Boat

2 Did you _____ when you _____ the cartoon _____?
A. above   B. saw   C. laugh

3 If _____, the cartoonist was _____.
A. successful   B. so

4 Cartoonists are the people _____ _____ _____.
A. cartoons   B. make   C. who

5 They want to _____ your interest, and usually, _____ you _____ with simple language and _____ drawings.
A. catch   B. laugh   C. creative   D. make

6 People _____ _____ cartoons _____ _____ of years.
A. hundreds   B. made   C. have   D. for

7 There are many _____ of _____, and they play _____ _____.
A. roles   B. types   C. different   D. cartoons

8 _____ form of cartoon _____ a picture with _____ _____ words.
A. few   B. one   C. is   D. a

9 It _____ sometimes _____ a "gag cartoon."
A. called   B. is

10 The cartoonist _____ a funny _____, and the character makes you _____ by doing or _____ silly things.
A. laugh   B. saying   C. character   D. makes

11 _____ type of cartoon _____ _____ a caricature.
A. is   B. another   C. called

12 In a caricature, some _____ of a character are _____ or _____ than _____.
A. bigger   B. parts   C. different   D. usual

13 Look _____ the picture _____ the _____.
A. on   B. at   C. right

14 _____ _____ of the man's face _____ _____ at you?
A. out   B. parts   C. which   D. jump

15 Artists _____ _____ this type of cartoon to _____ _____ of well-known people.
A. used   B. fun   C. have   D. make

16 When _____ cartoon pictures _____ _____ and tell a story, we have a comic _____.
A. together   B. come   C. strip   D. several

1 배다! 육지다!

2 위의 만화를 보고 웃었는가?

3 그랬다면 그 만화가는 성공했다.

4 만화가들은 만화를 만드는 사람들이다.

5 그들은 여러분의 관심을 끌고, 대개는 간단한 말과 독창적인 그림으로 여러분을 웃게 하고 싶어 한다.

6 사람들은 수백 년 동안 만화를 만들어 왔다.

7 만화에는 많은 종류가 있으며, 그것들은 다양한 역할을 한다.

8 만화의 한 형태로 몇 마디 말을 쓴 그림이 있다.

9 간혹 그것은 '개그 만화'라고 불린다.

10 만화가는 웃긴 캐릭터를 만들고, 그 캐릭터는 우스꽝스러운 행동이나 말을 함으로써 여러분을 웃게 만든다.

11 다른 종류의 만화는 캐리커처라고 불린다.

12 캐리커처에서 캐릭터의 어떤 부분은 평소와 다르거나 더 크다.

13 오른쪽의 그림을 보아라.

14 남자 얼굴의 어떤 부분이 여러분에게 분명히 보이는가?

15 미술가들은 유명한 사람들을 풍자하기 위해 이런 종류의 만화를 그려 왔다.

16 몇 가지 만화 그림이 모여서 이야기를 들려주게 되면, 그것이 연재만화가 된다.

17 Comic strips _____ _____ in newspapers _____ many _____.

    A. for   B. been   C. years   D. have

18 They are often _____ _____ _____.

    A. just   B. stories   C. amusing

19 People _____ _____ _____ comic strips for _____.

    A. education   B. have   C. used   D. also

20 Comics can _____ information _____ and _____ to _____.

    A. learn   B. easier   C. make   D. clearer

21 You _____ _____ _____ comic history or science books.

    A. seen   B. probably   C. have

22 You _____ _____ _____ many cartoon movies, or _____ movies, too.

    A. animated   B. surely   C. seen   D. have

23 These are very _____ people of _____ _____.

    A. among   B. ages   C. popular   D. all

24 Movement and sounds are _____ _____ pictures, so they _____ _____.

    A. come   B. added   C. to   D. alive

25 Artists and writers can _____ _____ characters and tell _____ stories _____ animation.

    A. interesting   B. develop   C. through   D. fascinating

26 In the 1990s, a new _____ of cartoon _____ _____.

    A. was   B. type   C. developed

27 It _____ _____ a webtoon.

    A. called   B. is

28 Webtoons _____ _____ online, so you can _____ them anytime, anywhere _____ your phone or computer.

    A. read   B. on   C. published   D. are

29 They are very _____, and some of _____ are _____ made _____ TV dramas or movies.

    A. them   B. into   C. popular   D. even

30 New _____ of cartoons _____ _____ in the future.

    A. appear   B. forms   C. may

31 They could be _____ and even more _____ than now, but one thing will _____ the same: they will help us laugh, _____, and learn.

    A. relax   B. different   C. remain   D. exciting

---

17 연재만화는 여러 해 동안 신문에 실려 왔다.

18 그것들은 종종 그저 재미있는 이야기이다.

19 사람들은 연재만화를 교육용으로 사용해 오기도 했다.

20 만화는 정보를 더 명료하고 더 배우기 쉽게 만들 수 있다.

21 여러분은 아마 만화 역사책이나 과학책을 본 적이 있을 것이다.

22 여러분은 많은 만화영화도 당연히 봤을 것이다.

23 이것들은 모든 연령대의 사람들에게 매우 인기가 많다.

24 동작이나 소리가 그림에 더해져서 그림들이 생생하게 살아난다.

25 미술가들과 작가들은 매력적인 캐릭터를 개발하고 만화영화 제작을 통해 재미있는 이야기를 들려준다.

26 1990년대에 새로운 형식의 만화가 개발되었다.

27 그건 웹툰이라고 불린다.

28 웹툰은 온라인으로 출판되기 때문에 여러분이 휴대 전화나 컴퓨터로 언제 어디서나 볼 수 있다.

29 그것은 매우 인기가 있고, 그들 가운데 일부는 심지어 텔레비전 드라마나 영화로 만들어지기도 한다.

30 미래에는 새로운 형태의 만화가 나타날지도 모른다.

31 그것은 지금과는 다르고 한층 더 재미있겠지만, 한 가지는 같을 것이다. 그것은 우리가 웃고, 쉬고, 배우도록 도와줄 것이다.

※ 다음 우리말과 일치하도록 빈칸에 알맞은 말을 쓰시오.

1 Boat! _____!

2 Did you _____ _____ you _____ the cartoon _____?

3 If _____, the _____ was _____.

4 Cartoonists are the people _____ _____ _____.

5 They want _____ _____ your interest, and usually, _____ _____ _____ with simple language and _____ _____.

6 People _____ _____ cartoons _____ _____ _____.

7 There are _____ _____ _____ _____, and they play _____ _____.

8 _____ _____ of cartoon _____ a picture with _____ _____ _____.

9 It _____ _____ _____ a "gag cartoon."

10 The cartoonist _____ _____ _____ _____, and the character _____ you _____ by _____ or _____ silly things.

11 _____ type of cartoon _____ _____ a caricature.

12 In a caricature, _____ _____ of a character _____ _____ or _____ _____ _____.

13 _____ _____ the picture _____ the right.

14 _____ _____ of the man's face _____ _____ at you?

15 Artists _____ _____ this type of cartoon _____ _____ _____ _____ _____.

16 When _____ cartoon pictures _____ _____ and tell a story, we have _____ _____ _____.

---

1 배다! 육지다!

2 위의 만화를 보고 웃었는가?

3 그랬다면 그 만화가는 성공했다.

4 만화가들은 만화를 만드는 사람들이다.

5 그들은 여러분의 관심을 끌고, 대개는 간단한 말과 독창적인 그림으로 여러분을 웃게 하고 싶어 한다.

6 사람들은 수백 년 동안 만화를 만들어 왔다.

7 만화에는 많은 종류가 있으며, 그것들은 다양한 역할을 한다.

8 만화의 한 형태로 몇 마디 말을 쓴 그림이 있다.

9 간혹 그것은 '개그 만화'라고 불린다.

10 만화가는 웃긴 캐릭터를 만들고, 그 캐릭터는 우스꽝스러운 행동이나 말을 함으로써 여러분을 웃게 만든다.

11 다른 종류의 만화는 캐리커처라고 불린다.

12 캐리커처에서 캐릭터의 어떤 부분은 평소와 다르거나 더 크다.

13 오른쪽의 그림을 보아라.

14 남자 얼굴의 어떤 부분이 여러분에게 분명히 보이는가?

15 미술가들은 유명한 사람들을 풍자하기 위해 이런 종류의 만화를 그려 왔다.

16 몇 가지 만화 그림이 모여서 이야기를 들려주게 되면, 그것이 연재만화가 된다.

17 Comic strips _____ _____ in newspapers _____ _____ _____.

18 They are often _____ _____ _____.

19 People _____ _____ _____ comic strips _____ _____.

20 Comics can _____ information _____ and _____ _____ _____.

21 You _____ _____ _____ comic history or science books.

22 You _____ _____ _____ many cartoon movies, or _____ _____, _____.

23 These are very _____ _____ _____ _____ _____.

24 _____ and sounds _____ _____ _____ pictures, so they _____ _____.

25 Artists and writers can _____ _____ _____ and tell _____ stories _____ animation.

26 In the 1990s, a new _____ _____ cartoon _____ _____.

27 It _____ _____ a webtoon.

28 Webtoons _____ _____ online, so you can _____ _____ anytime, anywhere _____ your phone or computer.

29 They are very _____, and some of _____ _____ even _____ _____ TV dramas or movies.

30 New _____ of cartoons _____ _____ in the future.

31 They could be _____ and even more _____ _____ now, but one thing will _____ the same: they will help us _____, _____, and _____.

17 연재만화는 여러 해 동안 신문에 실려 왔다.

18 그것들은 종종 그저 재미있는 이야기이다.

19 사람들은 연재만화를 교육용으로 사용해 오기도 했다.

20 만화는 정보를 더 명료하고 더 배우기 쉽게 만들 수 있다.

21 여러분은 아마 만화 역사책이나 과학책을 본 적이 있을 것이다.

22 여러분은 많은 만화영화도 당연히 봤을 것이다.

23 이것들은 모든 연령대의 사람들에게 매우 인기가 많다.

24 동작이나 소리가 그림에 더해져서 그림들이 생생하게 살아난다.

25 미술가들과 작가들은 매력적인 캐릭터를 개발하고 만화영화 제작을 통해 재미있는 이야기를 들려준다.

26 1990년대에 새로운 형식의 만화가 개발되었다.

27 그건 웹툰이라고 불린다.

28 웹툰은 온라인으로 출판되기 때문에 여러분이 휴대 전화나 컴퓨터로 언제 어디서나 볼 수 있다.

29 그것은 매우 인기가 있고, 그들 가운데 일부는 심지어 텔레비전 드라마나 영화로 만들어지기도 한다.

30 미래에는 새로운 형태의 만화가 나타날지도 모른다.

31 그것은 지금과는 다르고 한층 더 재미있겠지만, 한 가지는 같을 것이다. 그것은 우리가 웃고, 쉬고, 배우도록 도와줄 것이다.

※ 다음 문장을 우리말로 쓰시오.

1 Boat! Land!

➡ _____

2 Did you laugh when you saw the cartoon above?

➡ _____

3 If so, the cartoonist was successful.

➡ _____

4 Cartoonists are the people who make cartoons.

➡ _____

5 They want to catch your interest, and usually, make you laugh with simple language and creative drawings.

➡ _____

6 People have made cartoons for hundreds of years.

➡ _____

7 There are many types of cartoons, and they play different roles.

➡ _____

8 One form of cartoon is a picture with a few words.

➡ _____

9 It is sometimes called a "gag cartoon."

➡ _____

10 The cartoonist makes a funny character, and the character makes you laugh by doing or saying silly things.

➡ _____

11 Another type of cartoon is called a caricature.

➡ _____

12 In a caricature, some parts of a character are different or bigger than usual.

➡ _____

13 Look at the picture on the right.

➡ _____

14 Which parts of the man's face jump out at you?

➡ _____

15 Artists have used this type of cartoon to make fun of well-known people.

➡ _____

16 When several cartoon pictures come together and tell a story, we have a comic strip.

➡ _____

17 Comic strips have been in newspapers for many years.

➡ _____

18 They are often just amusing stories.

➡ _____

19 People have also used comic strips for education.

➡ _____

20 Comics can make information clearer and easier to learn.

➡ _____

21 You have probably seen comic history or science books.

➡ _____

22 You have surely seen many cartoon movies, or animated movies, too.

➡ _____

23 These are very popular among people of all ages.

➡ _____

24 Movement and sounds are added to pictures, so they come alive.

➡ _____

25 Artists and writers can develop fascinating characters and tell interesting stories through animation.

➡ _____

26 In the 1990s, a new type of cartoon was developed.

➡ _____

27 It is called a webtoon.

➡ _____

28 Webtoons are published online, so you can read them anytime, anywhere on your phone or computer.

➡ _____

29 They are very popular, and some of them are even made into TV dramas or movies.

➡ _____

30 New forms of cartoons may appear in the future.

➡ _____

31 They could be different and even more exciting than now, but one thing will remain the same: they will help us laugh, relax, and learn.

➡ _____

_____

※ 다음 괄호 안의 단어들을 우리말에 맞도록 바르게 배열하시오.

1 (land! / boat!)
➡ _____

2 (you / did / when / laugh / saw / you / cartoon / above? / the)
➡ _____

3 (so, / if / cartoonist / the / successful. / was)
➡ _____

4 (are / cartoonists / people / the / make / who / cartoons.)
➡ _____

5 (want / they / catch / to / interest, / your / usually, / and / you / make / laugh / simple / with / language / and / drawings. / creative)
➡ _____
_____

6 (have / people / cartoons / made / hundreds / for / years. / of)
➡ _____

7 (are / there / many / of / types / cartoons, / and / play / they / roles. / different)
➡ _____

8 (form / one / cartoon / of / is / picture / a / with / words. / few / a)
➡ _____

9 (is / it / sometimes / a / called / cartoon." / "gag)
➡ _____

10 (cartoonist / the / a / makes / character, / funny / and / character / the / you / makes / laugh / doing / by / or / silly / things. / saying)
➡ _____
_____

11 (type / another / cartoon / of / called / is / caricature. / a)
➡ _____

12 (a / in / caricature, / parts / some / a / of / character / different / are / than / or / bigger / usual.)
➡ _____

13 (at / look / picture / the / the / right. / on)
➡ _____

14 (parts / which / the / of / face / man's / out / jump / you? / at)
➡ _____

15 (have / artists / used / type / this / of / cartoon / make / to / fun / make / of / people. / well-known)
➡ _____

16 (several / when / pictures / cartoon / together / come / and / a / tell / story, / have / we / comic / a / strip.)
➡ _____
_____

1 배다! 육지다!

2 위의 만화를 보고 웃었는가?

3 그랬다면 그 만화가는 성공했다.

4 만화가들은 만화를 만드는 사람들이다.

5 그들은 여러분의 관심을 끌고, 대개는 간단한 말과 독창적인 그림으로 여러분을 웃게 하고 싶어 한다.

6 사람들은 수백 년 동안 만화를 만들어 왔다.

7 만화에는 많은 종류가 있으며, 그것들은 다양한 역할을 한다.

8 만화의 한 형태로 몇 마디 말을 쓴 그림이 있다.

9 간혹 그것은 '개그 만화'라고 불린다.

10 만화가는 웃긴 캐릭터를 만들고, 그 캐릭터는 우스꽝스러운 행동이나 말을 함으로써 여러분을 웃게 만든다.

11 다른 종류의 만화는 캐리커처라고 불린다.

12 캐리커처에서 캐릭터의 어떤 부분은 평소와 다르거나 더 크다.

13 오른쪽의 그림을 보아라.

14 남자 얼굴의 어떤 부분이 여러분에게 분명히 보이는가?

15 미술가들은 유명한 사람들을 풍자하기 위해 이런 종류의 만화를 그려 왔다.

16 몇 가지 만화 그림이 모여서 이야기를 들려주게 되면, 그것이 연재만화가 된다.

17 (strips / comic / been / have / newspapers / in / for / years. / many)

➡ _____

18 (are / they / just / often / stories. / amusing)

➡ _____

19 (have / people / also / comic / used / for / strips / education.)

➡ _____

20 (can / comics / make / clearer / information / and / to / learn. / easier)

➡ _____

21 (have / you / seen / probably / history / comic / or / books. / science)

➡ _____

22 (have / you / seen / surely / cartoon / many / movies, / or / movies, / too. / animated)

➡ _____

23 (are / these / popular / very / people / among / all / of / ages.)

➡ _____

24 (sounds / and / movement / added / are / pictures, / to / they / so / alive. / come)

➡ _____

25 (writers / and / artists / develop / can / characters / fascinating / and / interesting / tell / stories / animation. / through)

➡ _____

26 (the / in /. 1990s, / new / a / of / type / was / cartoon / developed.)

➡ _____

27 (is / it / called / webtoon. / a)

➡ _____

28 (are / webtoons / published / online, / you / so / read / can / anytime. / them / anywhere / your / on / computer. / or / phone)

➡ _____

29 (are / they / popular, / very / some / and / them / of / even / are / into / made / dramas / TV / movies. / or)

➡ _____

30 (forms / new / cartoons / of / appear / may / future. / the / in)

➡ _____

31 (could / they / different / be / even / and / exciting / more / now, / than / one / but / will / thing / remain / same: / the / will / they / us / help / laugh, / and / relax, / learn.)

➡ _____

17 연재만화는 여러 해 동안 신문에 실려 왔다.

18 그것들은 종종 그저 재미있는 이야기이다.

19 사람들은 연재만화를 교육용으로 사용해 오기도 했다.

20 만화는 정보를 더 명료하고 더 배우기 쉽게 만들 수 있다.

21 여러분은 아마 만화 역사책이나 과학책을 본 적이 있을 것이다.

22 여러분은 많은 만화영화도 당연히 봤을 것이다.

23 이것들은 모든 연령대의 사람들에게 매우 인기가 많다.

24 동작이나 소리가 그림에 더해져서 그림들이 생생하게 살아난다.

25 미술가들과 작가들은 매력적인 캐릭터를 개발하고 만화영화 제작을 통해 재미있는 이야기를 들려준다.

26 1990년대에 새로운 형식의 만화가 개발되었다.

27 그건 웹툰이라고 불린다.

28 웹툰은 온라인으로 출판되기 때문에 여러분이 휴대 전화나 컴퓨터로 언제 어디서나 볼 수 있다.

29 그것은 매우 인기가 있고, 그들 가운데 일부는 심지어 텔레비전 드라마나 영화로 만들어지기도 한다.

30 미래에는 새로운 형태의 만화가 나타날지도 모른다.

31 그것은 지금과는 다르고 한층 더 재미있겠지만, 한 가지는 같을 것이다. 그것은 우리가 웃고, 쉬고, 배우도록 도와줄 것이다.

※ 다음 우리말을 영어로 쓰시오.

1 배다! 육지다!

➡ _____

2 위의 만화를 보고 웃었는가?

➡ _____

3 그랬다면 그 만화가는 성공했다.

➡ _____

4 만화가들은 만화를 만드는 사람들이다.

➡ _____

5 그들은 여러분의 관심을 끌고, 대개는 간단한 말과 독창적인 그림으로 여러분을 웃게 하고 싶어 한다.

➡ _____

6 사람들은 수백 년 동안 만화를 만들어 왔다.

➡ _____

7 만화에는 많은 종류가 있으며, 그것들은 다양한 역할을 한다.

➡ _____

8 만화의 한 형태로 몇 마디 말을 쓴 그림이 있다.

➡ _____

9 간혹 그것은 '개그 만화'라고 불린다.

➡ _____

10 만화가는 웃긴 캐릭터를 만들고, 그 캐릭터는 우스꽝스러운 행동이나 말을 함으로써 여러분을 웃게 만든다.

➡ _____

11 다른 종류의 만화는 캐리커처라고 불린다.

➡ _____

12 캐리커처에서 캐릭터의 어떤 부분은 평소와 다르거나 더 크다.

➡ _____

13 오른쪽의 그림을 보아라.

➡ _____

14 남자 얼굴의 어떤 부분이 여러분에게 분명히 보이는가?

➡ _____

15 미술들은 유명한 사람들을 풍자하기 위해 이런 종류의 만화를 그려 왔다.

➡ _____

16 몇 가지 만화 그림이 모여서 이야기를 들려주게 되면, 그것이 연재만화가 된다.

➡ _____

17 연재만화는 여러 해 동안 신문에 실려 왔다.

➡ _____

18 그것들은 종종 그저 재미있는 이야기이다.

➡ _____

19 사람들은 연재만화를 교육용으로 사용해 오기도 했다.

➡ _____

20 만화는 정보를 더 명료하고 더 배우기 쉽게 만들 수 있다.

➡ _____

21 여러분은 아마 만화 역사책이나 과학책을 본 적이 있을 것이다.

➡ _____

22 여러분은 많은 만화영화도 당연히 봤을 것이다.

➡ _____

23 이것들은 모든 연령대의 사람들에게 매우 인기가 많다.

➡ _____

24 동작이나 소리가 그림에 더해져서 그림들이 생생하게 살아난다.

➡ _____

25 미술가들과 작가들은 매력적인 캐릭터를 개발하고 만화영화 제작을 통해 재미있는 이야기를 들려준다.

➡ _____

26 1990년대에 새로운 형식의 만화가 개발되었다.

➡ _____

27 그건 웹툰이라고 불린다.

➡ _____

28 웹툰은 온라인으로 출판되기 때문에 여러분이 휴대 전화나 컴퓨터로 언제 어디서나 볼 수 있다.

➡ _____

29 그것은 매우 인기가 있고, 그들 가운데 일부는 심지어 텔레비전 드라마나 영화로 만들어지기도 한다.

➡ _____

30 미래에는 새로운 형태의 만화가 나타날지도 모른다.

➡ _____

31 그것은 지금과는 다르고 한층 더 재미있겠지만, 한 가지는 같을 것이다. 그것은 우리가 웃고, 쉬고, 배우도록 도와줄 것이다.

➡ _____

_____

※ 다음 우리말과 일치하도록 빈칸에 알맞은 말을 쓰시오.

My Speaking Portfolio – Step 3

1. _____ is a _____ _____ for you.
2. I've _____ my sneakers this way _____ _____.
3. First, put the sneakers, _____ water, and _____ _____ in a plastic bag.
4. _____ close the bag and _____ it _____ _____ _____.
5. _____, take the sneakers _____ _____ the bag and wash _____.
6. They'll _____ _____ new sneakers.

1. 여기 당신을 위한 유용한 조언이 있어요.
2. 나는 내 운동화를 여러 번 이런 방식으로 세탁했어요.
3. 첫째, 운동화, 온수, 그리고 세제를 비닐봉지에 넣으세요.
4. 그리고 비닐봉지를 묶어 7분 동안 두세요.
5. 마지막으로 운동화를 비닐봉지에서 꺼내 씻으세요.
6. 그들은 새 운동화처럼 보일 거예요.

My Writing Portfolio

1. Giyeong, My Favorite _____ _____
2. My _____ _____ _____ is Giyeong of *Black Rubber Shoes*.
3. He is an _____ _____ student. He is _____ and _____.
4. _____, he is not very smart and sometimes _____ _____.
5. I like him _____ he looks on the _____ _____ of everything and always _____ _____ help _____.

1. 기영, 내가 가장 좋아하는 만화 캐릭터
2. 내가 가장 좋아하는 만화 캐릭터는 〈검정 고무신〉의 기영이다.
3. 그는 초등학교 학생이다. 그는 재미있고 친절하다.
4. 하지만, 그는 그렇게 똑똑하진 않고, 때때로 말썽을 피운다.
5. 그는 모든 것의 긍정적인 면을 보고 항상 다른 이들을 도우려 하기 때문에 나는 그를 좋아한다.

Words in Action B

1. The Best _____ _____ for Children's Education
2. Animals welcome the city's plan _____ _____ an amusement park _____ _____ _____.
3. However, they _____ _____ _____ serious _____.
4. An old elephant _____ _____ _____.
5. The animals and the city _____ _____ _____ _____ _____ a better world for everyone.

1. 아이들의 교육을 위한 최고의 만화영화
2. 동물들은 숲속에 놀이공원을 지으려는 도시의 계획을 환영한다.
3. 하지만, 그들은 곧 심각한 오염에 시달린다.
4. 나이 든 코끼리가 한 가지 제안을 한다.
5. 동물들과 도시는 모든 이들을 위한 더 좋은 세상을 만들기 위한 합의에 이른다.

※ 다음 우리말을 영어로 쓰시오.

My Speaking Portfolio – Step 3

1. 여기 당신을 위한 유용한 조언이 있어요.
   ➡ _____

2. 나는 내 운동화를 여러 번 이런 방식으로 세탁했어요.
   ➡ _____

3. 첫째, 운동화, 온수, 그리고 세제를 비닐봉지에 넣으세요.
   ➡ _____

4. 그리고 비닐봉지를 묶어 7분 동안 두세요.
   ➡ _____

5. 마지막으로 운동화를 비닐봉지에서 꺼내 씻으세요.
   ➡ _____

6. 그들은 새 운동화처럼 보일 거예요.
   ➡ _____

My Writing Portfolio

1. 기영, 내가 가장 좋아하는 만화 캐릭터
   ➡ _____

2. 내가 가장 좋아하는 만화 캐릭터는 〈검정 고무신〉의 기영이다.
   ➡ _____

3. 그는 초등학교 학생이다. 그는 재미있고 친절하다.
   ➡ _____

4. 하지만, 그는 그렇게 똑똑하진 않고, 때때로 말썽을 피운다.
   ➡ _____

5. 그는 모든 것의 긍정적인 면을 보고 항상 다른 이들을 도우려 하기 때문에 나는 그를 좋아한다.
   ➡ _____

Words in Action B

1. 아이들의 교육을 위한 최고의 만화영화
   ➡ _____

2. 동물들은 숲속에 놀이공원을 지으려는 도시의 계획을 환영한다.
   ➡ _____

3. 하지만, 그들은 곧 심각한 오염에 시달린다.
   ➡ _____

4. 나이 든 코끼리가 한 가지 제안을 한다.
   ➡ _____

5. 동물들과 도시는 모든 이들을 위한 더 좋은 세상을 만들기 위한 합의에 이른다.
   ➡ _____

MEMO

영어 기출 문제집

적중100

2학기

정답 및 해설

천재 | 이재영

중 2

적중100

영어 기출 문제집

적중100

2학기

정답 및 해설

천재 | 이재영

중 2

Understanding Others

시험대비 실력평가   p.08

01 (o)rdinary   02 announcement   03 ⑤

04 ②   05 ⑤   06 mind   07 ③

08 ④

01 둘은 반의어 관계다. 친절한 : 불친절한 – 비범한 : 평범한

02 무언가에 대한 새로운 정보를 주며 누군가가 공식적으로 말하는 것

03 whisper는 '속삭이다'는 뜻이다.

04 위험하거나 나쁜 것으로부터 사람이나 사물을 지키다

05 부모가 매주 아이에게 주는 돈: 용돈

06 mind는 동사로 '신경을 쓰다, 언짢아하다'는 뜻이다.

07 사람들은 긴 턱수염을 매우 싫어했다. 그래서 턱수염을 가진 사람을 피했다.

08 '싸워 물리치다'는 의미로 fight off가 적절하고, 두 번째 빈칸은 그들을 공격한 것 때문에 그를 고소했다(accused)가 적절하다.

서술형 시험대비   p.09

01 (1) appearance   (2) freedom

02 (1) change   (2) train   03 (1) judge   (2) mean

04 (1) do well on   (2) cared for   (3) thanks to

05 (1) face difficulties   (2) looked different from
     (3) in prison, protecting

01 (1) 소유격 their 뒤에는 명사형이 적절하므로 appearance를 쓴다. (2) 정관사 the 뒤에 명사형이 적절하므로 freedom을 써야 한다.

02 (1) '어떤 것을 다르게 만들다'라는 동사의 의미와 '비용보다 더 많은 돈을 지불했을 때 돌려받는 돈(거스름 돈)'이라는 명사의 의미를 가지는 change가 적절하다. (2) '사람이나 동물들에게 어떤 일을 하는 방법을 가르치다(훈련하다)'라는 동사의 의미와 '철도 위에 함께 연결된 많은 차량(기차)'이라는 명사의 의미를 가지는 train이 적절하다.

03 (1) 첫 번째 빈칸은 명사 '판사', 두 번째 빈칸은 동사로 '판단하다'라는 의미이므로 judge가 맞다. (2) 첫 번째 빈칸은 '의미하다'라는 동사이고 두 번째는 be동사 뒤에 형용사 '못된'의 의미인 mean이 적절하다.

04 (1) '네가 시험을 잘 보길 바란다.'는 의미로 do well on이 적절하다. (2) '42살의 Joseph Palmer'는 평범한 사람이었다. 그는

직업이 있었고 가족을 돌보았다.'는 의미로 과거형 cared for가 적절하다. (3) '그는 아들의 편지 덕분에 석방되었다'는 의미로 thanks to가 적절하다.

05 (1) 어려움에 직면하다는 표현은 face difficulties. (2) 'look+형용사'는 '~처럼 보이다'는 의미로 과거형 looked different from이 적절하다 (3) be in prison: 감옥에 갇히다 / 전치사 for 뒤에 동명사 protecting이 적절하다.

교과서

Conversation

핵심 Check   p.10~11

1 ②   2 ①   3 ③, ⑤   4 look like

교과서 대화문 익히기

Check(√) True or False   p.12

1 T   2 F   3 T   4 T

교과서 확인학습   p.14~15

Communicate: Listen-Listen and Answer. Talk

from, ago, worried, shy, good, lucky, friendly, playing, call, I hope

Communicate: Listen-Listen and Answer. Dialog

winning / great / mean / what, look like / has, ponytail / who scored / seventh

Communicate: Listen-Listen More

What / lost / calm down / What, look like / has / wearing / wearing / carrying / look for, announcement, missing / I hope

Communicate: Speak 2-Talk in pairs

have, important / do well on / so

Communicate: Speak 2-Talk in groups

What / What does, like / no / have

Communicate: Speak-Rap Time

I hope, find / do, best / the same / look like / straight / wearing / reading

My Speaking Portfolio

bulletin board, are / made, choice, vote for / mean, promises / choose / seems okay / friendly, talent shows

시험대비 기본평가   p.16

01 What, look like   02 ③   03 ②
04 I wish you the same.

01 사람의 외모를 물어보는 표현으로 'What ~ look like?'를 사용한다.
02 강아지를 잃어버렸다는 말에 이어지는 대답으로 희망이나 바람을 나타내는 'I hope ~.'가 적절하다.
03 내일 중요한 시험이 있으므로 시험을 잘 보길 바란다는 표현이 적절하다.
04 '~이기를 바라'라는 표현은 'I wish ~'를 사용한다.

시험대비 실력평가   p.17~18

01 ③   02 who scored the goal just now
03 ⑤   04 ③   05 ②
06 That's too bad
07 I hope she'll get better soon.
08 (A) What does he look like?   (B) Can you tell me more?   09 ④   10 ②
11 curly, hair, glasses

01 상대방의 말을 확인하기 위한 표현으로 '~을 말하니?'의 의미다.
02 명사 the girl을 수식하는 관계대명사절을 만든다.
03 Ben의 'I've heard a lot about her.'라는 말을 통해 Gacha에 관해 알고 있다는 것을 알 수 있다.
04 대화의 내용으로 보아 차기 학생회장 선거라는 것을 알 수 있다.
05 그녀의 외모를 묻는 표현이 오는 것이 적절하다.
06 상대방의 슬픔을 위로하는 표현으로 That's too bad., 또는 I'm sorry to hear that. 등으로 쓸 수 있다.
07 희망이나 바람을 표현하는 말로 'I hope+주어+동사 ~'를 사용한다.
08 (A)는 남동생의 외모를 묻는 표현이 적절하고, (B)는 추가적으로 남동생에 대해 묻는 표현이 적절하다.
09 여자의 남동생이 어디에 있는지는 대화에 언급되어 있지 않아 답할 수 없다.
10 '자전거에서 떨어졌어'라는 A의 말에 '그 말을 들으니 기뻐'라는 답은 어색하다.
11 주어진 문장은 새로 온 학생에 대한 외모를 묘사하는 글이다.

서술형 시험대비   p.19

01 is[comes] from, same, seven
02 what does she look like   03 vote for
04 (B) glasses   (C) safe place   (D) ponytail
05 make an announcement about a missing child

01 Gacha는 몽골에서 왔고, Minsol과 같은 반이다. Gacha는 7골을 넣었다.
03 공식적인 서류에 표시를 해서 선거에 출마할 사람을 고르다

Grammar

핵심 Check   p.20~21

1 (1) expected, to be   (2) (c)ausedIt, to (j)ump
    (3) (f)orced, to sign
2 (1) Before   (2) comes   (3) after

시험대비 기본평가   p.22

01 ⑤   02 ①   03 ④
04 (1) I want you to clean the windows.
    (2) Before I have dinner, I will clean my room.
    (3) He took my hand and asked me to marry him.
    (4) Tell her to buy a comfortable pair of shoes!
05 Justin had some fruit after he played soccer.

01 ask의 목적격보어는 to부정사이다.
02 잠자리에 들기 전에 손을 씻었다고 하는 것이 자연스럽다.
03 before와 after는 두 개의 절을 연결해 주는 접속사로 어떤 일이 일어나기 전이나 후의 시간 관계를 나타내며 before는 '~하기 전에', after는 '~한 후에'를 뜻한다. ① Before → After ② Before → After ③ after → before ⑤ After → Before
04 (1), (3), (4) want, ask, tell은 to부정사를 목적격보어로 취하는 동사이다. (2) 시간의 부사절에서는 현재시제를 사용하여 미래를 나타낸다.
05 접속사 after(~한 후에)를 이용하여 영작한다.

시험대비 실력평가   p.23~25

01 ⑤   02 ②   03 ③   04 ④
05 (1) to come   (2) to do   (3) expects   (4) to go
    (5) after   (6) before   06 ①   07 ②

08 ②　　　09 ②　　　10 (1) to tell

(2) to study　　(3) (to) push　　11 before　　12 ③

13 (1) After they played tennis, they went shopping.

(2) Before Eunji watched the movie, she bought a hat.

(3) The teacher told us to gather at the gym.

(4) Jiho asked Dohun to clean the window.

14 ⑤　　　15 ③　　16 ①　　17 ④　　18 ②

19 (1) She asked her brother to help her with her homework.

(2) Jim wanted her to go shopping with him.

(3) They advised him to leave the place as soon as possible.

(4) Before he rode his bike, Jason put on his helmet.

(5) She will be a good wife when she gets married.

01 want는 목적격보어로 to부정사가 온다.

02 Before는 접속사로 어떤 일이 일어나기 전의 시간 관계를 나타낸다.

03 tell은 목적격보어로 동사원형이 아니라 to부정사가 온다. to be가 되어야 한다.

04 before: ~하기 전에

05 (1), (2), (4) tell, want, allow는 목적격보어로 to부정사가 온다. (3) hope는 5형식으로 쓰이지 않는다. (5) 문맥상 after가 적절하다. (6) 문맥상 before가 적절하다.

06 빈칸에는 to부정사를 목적격보어로 취할 수 있는 동사가 들어가야 한다.

07 ② 시간의 부사절에서는 현재시제를 사용하여 미래를 나타낸다.

08 ② 해가 떠오른 시점이 다르므로 두 문장의 의미가 다르다.

09 before 부사절은 after를 사용하여 주절과 부사절을 바꿔 쓸 수 있다.

10 ask, encourage, help는 to부정사를 목적격보어로 취하는 동사이다. help는 동사원형을 쓸 수도 있다.

11 after 부사절은 before를 사용하여 주절과 부사절을 바꿔 쓸 수 있다.

12 ask는 목적격보어로 to부정사를 쓴다.

13 (1), (2) before와 after는 접속사로 어떤 일의 시간 관계를 나타내며 before는 '~하기 전에', after는 '~한 후에'를 뜻한다. (3), (4) tell, ask의 목적격보어로 to부정사가 온다.

14 ⑤ make는 사역동사로 동사원형을 목적격보어로 취한다. 나머지는 모두 to부정사를 목적격보어로 취하는 동사들로 to do가 들어가야 한다.

15 ① I read a book before I went to bed last night. ② I brushed my teeth before I went to bed. ④ After he bought the book, he read it. ⑤ Eric will go swimming when Sue arrives.

16 cause, expect, ask, want, tell 모두 목적격보어로 to부정사가 와야 한다. ceremony: 식, 의식 / wake ~ up: ~을 깨우다

17 주절은 미래이지만, 빈칸이 이끄는 절은 현재형이므로 빈칸에는 시간이나 조건의 부사절이 적절하므로 양보절을 이끄는 Even if는 적절하지 않다.

18 ask와 tell은 모두 to부정사를 목적격보어로 취하는 동사이므로 빈칸에는 to부정사가 들어가는 것이 적절하다.

19 (1), (2), (3) ask, want, advise는 모두 목적격보어로 to부정사가 와야 한다. (4) 의미상 After를 Before로 고쳐야 한다. (5) 시간의 부사절에서는 현재시제를 사용하여 미래를 나타낸다.

🦉 서술형 시험대비　　　　　　　　p.26~27

01 (1) Lucy's dad wants her to be a police officer.

(2) My mother asked me to buy milk on my way home.

(3) The teacher told the students to bring some water.

(4) She got her two sons to divide a cake exactly in half.

(5) Her family environment forced her not to continue her studies.

02 (1) I will let you know my mind as soon as I make a decision.

(2) Nancy wanted her brother to cook ramyeon for her.

03 (1) to help　(2) to go　(3) to stay　(4) not to take

(5) comes　(6) have

04 (1) watches, after　(2) Before, did

(3) to call[phone], comes　(4) to feed

05 (1) They took their swimming suit before they went to the beach.

(2) After the students took a bus for one hour, they arrived at their destination.

(3) After they arrived at the museum, they appreciated the works in the museum.

06 (1) before she studies math in her room

(2) after she has lunch with her family 또는 before she goes to the movie with James

(3) after she studies math in her room

07 Laura to study history

08 (1) Before → After　(2) after → before

(3) will come → comes　(4) meeting → to meet

09 (1) My parents always tell me to do my best in school.

(2) Good health enabled him to carry out the plan.

(3) Yuri will put on her uniform after she has breakfast.

01 (1) want, (2) ask, (3) tell, (4) get 등의 동사는 목적격보어로 to부정사가 와야 한다. (5) force의 목적격보어로 쓰인 to부정사의 부정형은 'not to 동사원형'으로 쓴다.

02 (1) 시간의 부사절에서는 현재시제로 미래를 표현한다. make a decision: 결정을 내리다 (2) want는 목적격보 어로 to부정사가 온다.

03 (1), (2), (3), (4) ask, allow, order, warn의 목적격보어로 to부정사가 적절하다. to부정사의 부정형은 'not to 동사원형'으로 쓴다. (5), (6) 시간의 부사절이므로 주절이 미래시제일지라도 현재시제로 써야 한다.

04 (3), (4) 시간의 부사절에서는 현재시제를 사용하여 미래를 나타내며 ask나 tell은 목적격보어로 to부정사가 온다.

05 before와 after는 접속사로 어떤 일이 일어나기 전이나 후의 시간 관계를 나타내며 before와 after가 이끄는 부사절은 보통 주절의 앞이나 뒤에 올 수 있다. destination: 목적지

06 before(~하기 전에)와 after(~한 후에)가 이끄는 부사절은 보통 주절과 부사절을 바꿔 쓸 수 있으며, before와 after를 서로 바꿔 쓸 수 있다.

07 encourage는 목적격보어로 to부정사를 사용한다.

08 (1), (2) before: ~하기 전에, after: ~한 후에 (3) 시간의 부사절에서는 현재시제를 사용하여 미래를 나타낸다. (4) would like는 목적격보어로 to부정사를 취한다. set: (해 따위가) 지다, 저물다 migrate: 이주하다 migrating bird: 철새

09 (1), (2) tell과 enable은 목적격보어로 to부정사가 온다. (3) 시간의 부사절에서는 미래시제 대신에 현재시제를 사용한다.

[교과서] Reading

확인문제   p.28

1 T   2 F   3 T   4 F   5 T   6 F

확인문제   p.29

1 T   2 F   3 T   4 F   5 T   6 F

교과서 확인학습 A   p.30~31

01 Be Different
02 an ordinary person
03 cared for
04 to face difficulties.
05 looked different
06 did not like it
07 the man with a beard
08 sit next to him
09 behind his back
10 broke his windows

11 threw stones at
12 stop growing
13 mind
14 to have
15 attacked, threw
16 cut off
17 fight them off
18 accused him of
19 was arrested
20 the victim
21 a man with a beard, went to prison
22 wanted, to know
23 sent, to
24 was in prison, protecting himself
25 became angry, to set, free
26 was freed
27 attitudes toward beards
28 with a beard
29 His name
30 popular, fought for

교과서 확인학습 B   p.32~33

1 The Right To Be Different

2 In many ways, 42-year-old Joseph Palmer was an ordinary person.

3 He had a job and cared for his family.

4 But in 1830, after he moved to a small town in Massachusetts, he began to face difficulties.

5 Joseph looked different from other people: he had a long beard.

6 People did not like it very much.

7 The town's people avoided the man with a beard.

8 They did not want to sit next to him.

9 They even whispered behind his back, "What is he trying to hide?"

10 Some neighbors broke his windows.

11 Others threw stones at him when he walked down the street.

12 They told him to stop growing a beard.

13 Joseph did not mind.

14 He just wanted the freedom to have his beard.

15 One day, four men attacked Joseph and threw him on the ground.

16 "We're going to cut off your beard!" they shouted.

17 Joseph was a big man, and he was able to fight them off.

18 But the men called the police and accused him of attacking them.

19 Poor Joseph was arrested.

20 He said to the judge, "I'm the victim here."

21 Sadly, no one believed a man with a beard, and he went to prison for over a year.

22 Joseph's son, Thomas, wanted people to know the truth.

23 He sent letters to newspapers across the country.

24 People learned that Joseph was in prison just for protecting himself and his beard.

25 Many people became angry about this, so the judge finally decided to set Joseph free.

26 After he was freed, Joseph traveled and told his story to lots of people.

27 Slowly, people's attitudes toward beards changed.

28 Before Joseph died, a man with a beard became the President of the United States.

29 His name was Abraham Lincoln.

30 He made beards popular, but Joseph Palmer fought for the right to have them.

시험대비 실력평가 p.34~37

01 ②, ⑤   02 ③   03 ⑤   04 to stop
05 (A) them (B) Sadly (C) for   06 ③
07 ②   08 ③   09 ①, ④   10 ②, ③
11 appearance   12 students who talk about other people's appearance   13 ④
14 extraordinary → ordinary 15 behind his back
16 ①, ④   17 ③   18 ⑤   19 ④
20 reading   21 (A) differently (B) hungry
(C) foolish   22 ②   23 ②   24 ⑤
25 ①

01 ⓐ와 ②, ⑤: ~을 돌보다, ① care about: ~에 마음을 쓰다, ~에 관심을 가지다, ③ look for: ~을 찾다, ④ take off: ~을 벗다, 이륙하다

02 ⓑ different from: ~와 다른, ⓒ the man with a beard: 턱수염을 가진 남자

03 ⑤ 마을 사람들은 Joseph Palmer를 피했고 심지어 그의 등 뒤에서 "그가 무엇을 숨기려는 거지?"라고 속삭였다.

04 tell+목적어+to부정사

05 (A) 'four men'을 가리키므로 them이 적절하다. (B) '슬프게도', 아무도 턱수염을 가진 남자를 믿지 않았다고 해야 하므로 Sadly가 적절하다. Luckily: 운 좋게, (문장이나 동사를 수식하여) 다행히도, (C) 'during+특정 기간을 나타내는 명사', 'for+숫자'이므로 for가 적절하다.

06 ③ 부당한, 불공평한, 자신이 희생자인데 체포되었기 때문에 '부당하다'는 심경을 나타낸다고 하는 것이 적절하다. ① 지루한, ② 무서워하는, 겁먹은, ④ 흥분한, ⑤ 부끄러운

07 위 글은 턱수염을 기를 권리를 위하여 싸웠던 Joseph에 관한 글이므로, 제목으로는 '어렵게 얻은 턱수염을 기를 권리'가 적절하다. hard-won: 어렵게 얻은, ① inform A of B: A에게 B를

알리다, ③ 여론의 압력, ④ notice: ~을 알아차리다

08 ⓐ Joseph's son, ⓑ, ⓒ Joseph, ⓓ, ⓔ Abraham Lincoln을 가리킨다.

09 ① 즉시, ④ 정확히, ④와 나머지는 '마침내, 결국'

10 ⑧와 ①, ④, ⑤는 형용사적 용법, ② 명사적 용법, ③ 부사적 용법(원인)

11 소유격 다음에 명사로 쓰는 것이 적절하다. appearance: 외모

12 추천 독자층은 '다른 사람들의 외모에 관해 이야기하는 학생들'이다.

13 ④ 구입 장소는 알 수 없다. ① The Right to Be Different, ② Joseph Palmer, ③ we should not judge people by their appearance. ⑤ Why did Joseph Palmer want to have a beard?

14 직업이 있고 가족을 돌보았던 Joseph Palmer는 여러 면에서 '평범한' 사람이었지만 1830년에 매사추세츠주의 작은 도시로 이사를 한 후에 어려움에 직면하기 시작했던 것이므로, ordinary로 고쳐야 한다. extraordinary: 보기 드문, 비범한; 대단한

15 behind somebody's back: ~의 등 뒤에서, ~가 없는 곳에서

16 ⓒ와 ②, ③, ⑤는 명사적 용법, ① 형용사적 용법, ④ 부사적 용법(목적)

17 some ~, others ...: 어떤 것[사람]들은 ~, 다른 것[사람]들은 ...

18 ⑤ 모난 돌이 정 맞는다(모난 돌이 석공의 정을 만난다.) 남들과 말이나 행동 등이 달라 미움을 받는다는 속담으로 'A cornered stone meets the mason's chisel.'이라고도 한다. ① 불행한 일은 겹치기 마련이다. (엎친 데 덮친다.) ② 쥐구멍에도 볕 들 날이 있다. ③ 제때의 바늘 한 뜸이 아홉 번의 수고를 던다. ④ 떡줄 사람은 꿈도 안 꾸는데 김칫국부터 마신다.

19 Joseph은 덩치가 큰 사람이어서, 그들을 싸워 물리칠 수 있었다.

20 enjoy는 목적어로 동명사를 취한다.

21 (A) 동사 think를 수식하므로 부사 differently가 적절하다. (B), (C) Stay 다음에 보어를 써야 하므로 형용사 hungry와 foolish가 적절하다.

22 위 글은 '독서기록장'이다. ① (신문·잡지의) 글, 기사, ③ 일기, ④ 수필, ⑤ 전기

23 ②번 다음 문장의 this에 주목한다. 주어진 문장의 'Joseph was in prison just for protecting himself and his beard.'를 받고 있으므로 ②번이 적절하다.

24 Joseph은 석방된 뒤에 순회를 하며 많은 사람들에게 자신의 이야기를 전하면서 턱수염을 기를 권리를 위하여 싸웠기 때문에 '의지가 강한' 성격이라고 하는 것이 적절하다. ② 호기심 많은, ③ 관대한, ④ 창의적인, ⑤ 의지가 강한

25 ⓐ와 ①번은 권리(명사), ② 맞는(형용사), ③ 정확히, 바로(부사), ④ 오른쪽의(형용사), ⑤ 바라던 대로(부사)

01 (A) 42-year-old   (B) different   (C) to sit

02 a long beard

03 (1) 마을 사람들은 그의 기다란 턱수염을 별로 좋아하지 않았다.

   (2) 마을 사람들은 그 턱수염을 가진 남자를 피했다.

   (3) 마을 사람들은 그의 곁에 앉고 싶어 하지 않았다.

   (4) 마을 사람들은 심지어 그의 등 뒤에서 "그가 무엇을 숨기려는 거지?"라고 속삭였다.

04 The four men called the police and accused Joseph of attacking them.

05 he had a beard

06 Joseph's son, Thomas, wanted people to know the truth.   **07** ⑤ → for

08 Abraham Lincoln   **09** The others → Others

10 growing   **11** accused him of attacking them

12 victim   **13** (A) over a year   (B) a beard

01 (A) 뒤에 나오는 명사를 꾸며주는 형용사의 역할을 할 때는 42-year-old로 쓰는 것이 적절하다. (B) 감각동사 looked의 보어는 형용사를 써야 하므로 different가 적절하다. (C) want는 목적어로 to부정사를 취하므로 to sit이 적절하다.

02 '기다란 턱수염'을 가리킨다.

03 본문의 difficulties 다음의 내용을 쓰면 된다.

04 네 명의 남자들은 경찰을 불렀고, 자신들을 공격한 것으로 Joseph을 고발했다.

05 아무도 턱수염을 가진 남자를 믿지 않았다고 했으므로, '그가 턱수염을 길렀기' 때문이라고 하는 것이 적절하다.

06 want+목적어+to부정사: 목적어가 ~하기를 원하다, Thomas의 앞과 뒤에 동격을 나타내는 콤마를 찍는 것이 적절하다.

07 Joseph Palmer는 턱수염을 기를 권리를 '위하여' 싸웠다고 해야 하기 때문에, for로 고쳐야 한다. fight for: ~을 위해 싸우다, ~을 얻기 위해 싸우다, fight against: ~에 맞서 싸우다

08 Abraham Lincoln(에이브러햄 링컨)을 가리킨다.

09 '어떤 사람들은 ~, 또 어떤 사람들은 …'의 뜻이 되어야 하므로 The others를 Others로 고쳐야 한다.

10 문맥상 stop 뒤에 동명사가 와야 한다.

11 'of'를 보충한다. accuse A of B: B 때문에 A를 고발하다

12 피해자, 다쳤거나 죽임을 당한 사람

13 Joseph은 그저 자신의 턱수염을 기를 자유를 원했지만 '턱수염'을 가진 남자에 대한 이웃들의 편견 때문에 '일 년이 넘는 기간' 동안 감옥에 갔다.

01 appearance   **02** ⑤   **03** ④

04 ②   **05** like   **06** was arrested

07 ③   **08** ④   **09** ②   **10** ⑤

11 ①   **12** ③   **13** ①, ③, ④

14 (1) she saw a giraffe   (2) before   (3) after she saw a giraffe   **15** ②   **16** ②

17 (1) we ate ice cream, we watched the movie

   (2) I untie my hair, I pass the school gate

18 (1) I will take a photo of myself after I get a haircut tomorrow.

   (2) Fiona wants Andrew not to come to the party.

   (3) The situation required me to have strong belief.

19 ①   **20** Brush your teeth before you go to bed.   **21** ③   **22** beard

23 ②, ③, ⑤   **24** ④   **25** ①

26 Joseph was in prison just for protecting himself and his beard.   **27** it → them   **28** ④

29 ③   **30** ⑤

01 동사 : 명사의 관계이다.

02 네 명의 남자들이 그를 바닥에 던졌다고 했으므로 ⓐ에는 '공격하다'가 적절하다. ⓑ는 '수염을 자르다'는 의미로 cut off가 적절하다.

03 ④번의 judge는 명사로 '판사'다.

04 어떤 일이 일어나도록 하다 / 어떤 일이 발생하는 이유[원인]

05 like는 전치사로 '~와 같은', 동사로 '좋아하다'라는 의미이다.

06 Joseph이 체포가 되었다는 수동의 의미이므로 'be+p.p.' 형태를 사용한다.

07 '그녀는 어떻게 생겼니?'라고 외모를 묻는 표현이므로 She's very tall and has a ponytail. 앞에 오는 것이 적절하다.

08 그는 지도를 보고 있다는 말은 사람의 외모를 묻는 말에 대한 답으로 적절하지 않다.

09 실종된 동생을 빨리 찾기를 바란다는 바람을 나타내는 표현이 적절하다.

10 ⑤번은 대화 속의 남자가 할 일을 묘사한 것이다.

11 빈칸 다음의 대답으로 보아 외모를 물어보는 말이 적절하다.

12 '무슨 일이니?'라는 물음에 (C) 여동생의 팔이 부러졌다는 답이 오고, (A) 무슨 일이 있었는지 묻는다. (B) my sister를 받는 대명사 she로 구체적으로 무슨 일이 있었는지 언급하고, 마지막으로 (D) 빨리 낫기를 바라는 말이 오는 것이 적절하다.

13 빈칸이 이끄는 절은 현재시제이지만 주절은 미래이므로, 빈칸에는 시간이나 조건의 부사절이 들어가야 한다.

14 동물을 본 순서에 맞게 after나 before를 이용하여 쓴다.

15 첫 번째 문장은 5형식이고 두 번째 문장은 3형식이다. 3형식과 5형식에 쓰이면서, to부정사를 목적격보어와 목적어로 받을 수 있는 동사는 want이다.

16 ② persuade는 to부정사를 목적격보어로 취하는 동사이다.

17 Before+주어1+동사1 ~, 주어2+동사2 … = After+주어2+동사2 …, 주어1+동사1 ~

7

18 (1) 시간의 부사절에서는 미래시제 대신에 현재시제를 사용한다. (2) want는 that절을 목적어로 취하지 않으며 to부정사의 부정형은 'not[never]+to 동사원형'이다. (3) require는 목적격보어로 to부정사를 취한다.

19 warn과 ask는 목적격보어로 to부정사가 오며, to부정사의 부정형은 'not[never]+to 동사원형'이다.

20 brush one's teeth: 양치질하다

21 ⓐ와 ③번은 직면하다, ① 얼굴, ② 표면, 겉면, ④ (시계의) 문자반, ⑤ 체면, lose one's face: 체면을 잃다 crisis: 위기

22 beard: (턱)수염, 사람의 턱과 뺨에 나는 털

23 ⓐ와 ②, ③, ⑤는 형용사적 용법, ① 명사적 용법, ④ 부사적 용법

24 이 글은 '턱수염을 가진 남자에 대한 부당한 행동'에 관한 글이다. ① bully: (약자를) 괴롭히다[왕따시키다], 협박하다, ② 희생자를 수감시킨 판사

25 ① 이웃들이 Joseph의 창문을 언제 깼는지는 대답할 수 없다. ② Joseph's neighbors did. ③ He just wanted the freedom to have his beard. ④ He said to the judge, "I'm the victim here." ⑤ For over a year.

26 'Joseph이 단지 자신과 자신의 턱수염을 지키려다 감옥에 갇혔다는 것'을 가리킨다.

27 beards를 받는 것이므로 them이 적절하다.

28 ④ 턱수염을 대중적으로 만든 것은 'Abraham Lincoln'이었다.

29 앞에 나오는 내용과 상반되는 내용이 뒤에 이어지므로 However가 가장 적절하다. ① 게다가, ② 그러므로, ④ 예를 들면 ⑤ 게다가, 더욱이

30 위 독서 기록장의 교훈은 'We should not judge people by their appearance.'이므로, 어울리는 속담은 '표지만 보고 책을 판단하지 말라.(뚝배기보다는 장 맛이다.)'가 적절하다. ① 사공이 많으면 배가 산으로 올라간다. ② 기회를 놓치지 마라. ③ 엎질러진 우유를 놓고 울어봐야 소용없다. ④ 남의 떡이 더 커 보인다.

단원별 예상문제
p.46~49

01 unfriendly 02 (A) attack (B) attitude

03 worried, lost   04 ②   05 ③

06 vote for, short hair, friendly, fun and exciting, promises 07 ⑤ 08 hopes, class will win, handball 09 ④ 10 ①

11 ③, ⑤   12 ③

13 (1) The teacher asked me to close the door.

(2) Dr. Smith advised her to go to bed early.

(3) After the soccer match was over, the players lay on the grass.

14 (1) Judy asked him to make sandwiches.

---

(2) Tom expected Jane to be thin.

(3) My advice caused him to stop smoking.

15 looked like → looked   16 Joseph Palmer

17 (A) growing (B) to have (C) was arrested 18 ②

19 ⑤   20 (A) The judge (B) his beard

21 ③   22 ④

---

01 반의어 관계이다. 유죄의 : 무죄의 = 친절한 : 불친절한

02 (A) 어떤 개가 나를 공격하려고 했을 때, 나의 고양이가 큰 소리로 울었다. (B) 나는 당신의 좋은 태도가 좋아요. 당신은 항상 긍정적으로 생각해요. meow: 야옹하고 울다

04 ⓑ는 남동생의 외모를 물어보는 표현이므로 look for를 look like로 바꾸어야 한다.

05 삼촌과 낚시하러 간다는 말에 네가 꼭 그것을 찾기를 바란다는 말은 어색하다. oval: 달걀 모양의, 타원형의

07 Jiho가 Somin이의 친구인지는 대화에서 언급되어 있지 않다.

08 다음 주 운동회에 대한 Gacha의 바람은 무엇인가?

09 (A) 약간 수줍음을 탔고 한국어를 잘 못했다고 했으므로 무척 걱정이 되었다가 적절하다. (B) 뒤 문장이 '나는 운이 좋은 아이다'로 앞 문장과 대조되므로 '하지만'이 적절하다. (C) 반 친구들이 자신을 '황금 손'이라고 부른다고 했으므로 핸드볼을 잘한다는 것을 알 수 있다.

10 (A)에는 사람의 외모를 묻는 표현이 적절하고, (B)에는 무슨 옷차림을 하고 있는지 묻는 표현이 적절하다.

11 ③ beg는 목적격보어로 to부정사를 취한다. ⑤ 시간의 부사절에서 현재시제로 미래를 나타낸다.

12 ⓑ Would you like me to bring any food to the party? ⓒ Her parents expected her to win the contest. ⓔ She told him to be on time.

13 (1), (2) ask, advise는 목적격보어로 to부정사를 취한다. (3) after: ~한 후에

14 (1) ask (2) expect (3) cause 등의 동사는 목적격보어로 to부정사가 와야 한다.

15 looked+형용사, looked like+명사: ~하게 보이다

16 Joseph Palmer를 가리킨다.

17 (A) '턱수염을 그만 기르라고 말했다'고 해야 하므로 growing이 적절하다. stop+~ing: ~하기를 그만두다, stop+to부정사: ~하기 위해 멈추다, (B) 턱수염을 '기를' 자유라고 해야 하므로 to have가 적절하다. (C) 불쌍한 Joseph은 '체포되었다'고 해야 하므로 수동태인 was arrested가 적절하다.

18 ⓐ와 ②번은 상관하다, 신경 쓰다(동사), ① 기억(력), 마음, 보지 않으면 마음도 멀어진다. ③ 신경, 생각, 관심, ④ (마음을 가진 자로서의) 인간, the greatest mind of the time: 그 시대의 가장 훌륭한 사람, ⑤ 마음, 정신, 건전한 신체에 건전한 정신이 깃든다.

19 ⑤ 판사에게 자기가 '희생자'라고 말했다고 하는 것이 적절하다.

① 공격[폭행]을 한 사람, ② 변호사, ③ 죄수, ④ (약자를) 괴롭히는 사람, ⑤ 피해자[희생자]

20 Joseph이 단지 자신과 '자신의 턱수염'을 지키려 감옥에 갇혔다는 사실에 대해 많은 사람들이 분개했기 때문에, '판사'는 결국 Joseph을 석방하기로 결정했다.

21 이 글은 Joseph이 자신의 턱수염을 지키려 감옥에 갇히기까지 했지만, 석방된 뒤에 순회를 하며 많은 사람들에게 자신의 이야기를 전함으로써 사람들의 턱수염에 대한 태도를 서서히 변화시켰다는 내용의 글이다. 따라서 이에 어울리는 속담은 '뜻이 있는 곳에 길이 있다'가 적절하다. ① 무소식이 희소식이다. ② 남의 떡이 더 커 보인다. ④ 뛰기 전에 살펴봐라.(신중하게 행동하라.) ⑤ 연습이 완벽하게 만들어 준다.

22 ④ 몇 사람이 턱수염에 대한 그들의 태도를 바꿨는지는 알 수 없다. ① Because he wanted people to know the truth. ② They learned that Joseph was in prison just for protecting himself and his beard. ③ He traveled and told his story to lots of people. ⑤ Abraham Lincoln did.

서술형 실전문제
p.50~51

01 what does she look like?

02 school president / vote / confident / our school a safe place

03 (A) I hope you'll do well on the exam.
(B) I hope so, too.

04 (1) My history teacher told us to hand in the project by tomorrow.
(2) The teacher warned the students to be quiet in class.
(3) Amy's best friend wants her to listen to his songs.
(4) Her manager always forces Melanie to throw away the trash.
(5) The doctor encouraged Jack not to give up doing exercise.

05 (1) Mom told me to walk the dog.
(2) Mark will control Maria's customers until she returns.

06 I set my alarm clock, I went to bed

07 freedom

08 Joseph was a big man, and he was able to fight them off.

09 (A) victim (B) beard

10 (A) protecting (B) angry (C) free

11 Joseph's son, Thomas, sent letters to newspapers across the country

---

01 외모를 묻는 표현은 'What ~ look like?'를 사용한다.

03 (A) 바람을 나타내는 표현으로 'I hope+주어+동사 ~' 형태를 이용한다. '시험을 잘 보다'는 표현은 'do well on the exam'이다. (B) '또한'의 의미로 문장 끝에 too를 사용한다.

04 (1) tell (2) warn (3) want (4) force 등의 동사는 목적격보어로 to부정사가 와야 한다. (5) to부정사의 부정형은 'never[not] to 동사원형'으로 쓴다.

05 (1) tell은 목적격보어로 to부정사를 취한다. (2) 시간의 부사절에서는 현재시제를 사용하여 미래를 나타낸다.

06 Before+주어1+동사1 ~, 주어2+동사2 … = After+주어2+동사2 …, 주어1+동사1 ~

07 to부정사로 수식받고 있기 때문에 명사 형태로 쓰는 것이 적절하다.

08 목적어가 인칭대명사이므로 fight off them이 아니라, fight them off가 적절하다.

09 Joseph은 따돌림의 '희생자'였지만, 아무도 '턱수염'을 가진 남자를 믿지 않았기 때문에 일년이 넘는 기간 동안 감옥에 갔다. bully: (약자를) 괴롭히다[왕따시키다], 협박하다

10 (A) 자기 자신과 턱수염을 '지키려고'라고 해야 하므로 protecting이 적절하다. prevent: 막다, 예방하다, (B) become 뒤에 형용사가 보어로 와야 하므로 angry가 적절하다. (C) set free 석방하다

11 'Joseph의 아들인 Thomas가 전국에 있는 신문사에 편지를 보냈기' 때문에 알게 되었다.

창의사고력 서술형문제
p.52

|모범답안|

01 [A] (1) A: What does Minsu look like?
B: He has short hair and is wearing jeans.
(2) A: What does Sumi look like?
B: She is tall and has a ponytail. She is wearing glasses.

[B] (1) A: I lost my puppy this afternoon.
B: I hope you'll find it soon.
(2) A: I have an important exam tomorrow!
B: I hope you'll do well on the exam.
(3) A: I'm going to my favorite singer's concert tonight.
B: I hope you have a good time.

02 (1) Dad wants me to come home early.
(2) My classmates asked me to be quiet in class.
(3) She told him to fix the computer.
(4) She didn't allow us to play the piano.
(5) I advised her to go home early after the concert.
(6) The teacher forced the students to attend the class.

단원별 모의고사

p.53~56

01 ③	02 difficulty	03 ①	04 ④
05 ⑤	06 ②	07 ③	08 ②
09 ⑤	10 ②	11 ⑤	

12 is she the girl who scored the goal just now?

13 ③	14 ②	15 ①

16 (1) not to drive so fast　(2) to play the piano for us

17 after she had dinner / before she studied history

18 he had a long beard　19 ④　20 ①

21 four men　22 ②　23 People learned that Joseph was in prison just for protecting himself and his beard.　24 Abraham Lincoln did.

01 ③번의 attack은 '공격하다'라는 의미로 'to use violence to hurt or damage someone'을 뜻한다. ③의 설명은 bullying(괴롭히기)에 대한 것이다.

02 반의어 관계이다. 유죄의 : 무죄의 = 쉬움 : 어려움

03 동사로 '바닥으로 떨어지다', 명사로 '여름과 겨울 사이에 있는 계절'을 뜻하는 fall이 적절하다.

04 What does he look like?는 외모를 묻는 표현으로 ④번은 사람의 성격이나 성질을 말하는 것이므로 적절하지 않다.

05 (A) 여동생의 팔이 부러졌다고 했으므로 자전거에서 떨어졌다 (fell off)가 적절하다. (B) '곧 회복하기를 바라'라는 바람을 나타내는 말이 적절하다.

06 (B) 너희 반에 새로운 학생이 왔다는 말을 들었다는 말이 먼저 오고 → (D) 긍정의 답을 하고 저기에 있다는 말 다음에 → (C) 어느 아이인지 묻고 외모를 묻는 말이 온다, → (A) 마지막으로 외모를 설명하는 말이 오는 것이 적절하다.

07 결선 경기에서 최선을 다하길 바란다는 말에 '너도 그러길 바라.' 라는 말이 가장 자연스럽다.

08 잃어버린 남동생에 관한 정보를 제공하고 있는 상황에서 추가적인 정보를 묻는 것이 가장 적절하다.

10 여학생이 어디서 동생을 잃어버렸는지는 대화에서 알 수 없다.

11 '우리는 훌륭한 핸드볼 선수가 있어.'라는 말에 그 선수가 누구인지에 대한 정보를 확인하는 말이 오는 것이 적절하다.

12 의문문이므로 be동사로 문장을 시작한다. 그리고 '막 골을 넣은 소녀'는 관계대명사 who를 이용하여 the girl을 수식하는 문장을 만든다.

13 ① Do you want me to clean your house for you? ② He told Perry to put on a penguin shirt. ④ The doctor advised Kathy to stop smoking. ⑤ Ms. Green asked him to carry the boxes.

14 ② 시간의 부사절에서는 미래시제 대신에 현재시제를 사용한다.

15 첫 번째 문장: expect는 to부정사를 목적격보어로 받는다. 두 번째 문장: 시간의 부사절에서는 현재시제를 사용하여 미래를 나타낸다.

16 tell과 ask는 목적격보어로 to부정사를 쓰고 부정사의 부정은 not[never]을 to부정사 앞에 붙인다.

17 before와 after는 접속사로 어떤 일이 일어나기 전이나 후의 시간 관계를 나타낸다.

18 Joseph Palmer는 '기다란 턱수염을 기르고 있었기 때문에' 다른 사람들과 달라 보였다.

19 behind somebody's back: ~의 등 뒤에서

20 ⓐ throw A at B: A를 B에게 던지다, ⓒ accuse A of B: A를 B 때문에 고발하다

21 '네 명의 남자'를 가리킨다.

22 ⓐ와 ②번은 판사, sentence: …에게 판결을 내리다[형을 선고하다], ① 판결하다, guilty: 유죄의, ③ 심판하다, ④ 감정가, 감식가, ⑤ 판단하다, 평가하다

23 'for'를 보충하면 된다.

24 did = made beards popular

Lesson
6

Near and Dear

시험대비 실력평가
p.60

01 listener   **02** ②   **03** ②

04 (1) drop by   (2) take care of   (3) find out

    (4) start off with   (5) break down   **05** ②

06 (1) without   (2) stuff   (3) leave   (4) either

    (5) suggestions

01 주어진 관계는 반의어 관계를 나타낸다. speaker: 화자, listener: 청취자

02 '당신이 너무 많이 지불했거나 또는 당신이 상품을 가게에 돌려주었기 때문에 당신에게 다시 지불되어야 하는 돈의 합계'를 가리키는 말은 refund(환불)이다.

03 exchange: 교환

04 take care of: ~을 처리하다, drop by: ~에 들르다, break down: ~을 부수다, find out: ~을 알아내다, start off with: ~으로 시작하다.

05 주어진 문장에서 text는 '문자 메시지를 보내다'라는 의미로 쓰였으며 이와 같은 의미로 쓰인 것은 ②번이다. 나머지는 모두 '본문, 원문'의 의미로 사용되었다.

06 suggestion: 제안, without: ~ 없이, either; ~도 역시, stuff: 물건, leave: 남기다

서술형 시험대비
p.61

01 remember

02 (1) training   (2) feed   (3) customer service

03 (1) sharing   (2) experience   (3) wall   (4) secret

    (5) text

04 (1) Can you show me the receipt of your order?

    (2) They gave me a full refund of my purchase.

    (3) Jessie promised to keep the news a secret.

05 (1) When you study a new language, you should start off with some vocabulary.

    (2) If you tell a lie to your friends, you can lose them.

    (3) What should I do to break down the wall?

01 주어진 관계는 반의어 관계를 나타낸다. forget: 잊다, remember: 기억하다

02 training: 훈련, feed: 먹이다, customer service: 고객 지원 센터

03 text: 문자 메시지를 보내다, wall: 벽, secret: 비밀, share: 공유하다, experience: 경험

04 receipt: 영수증, refund: 환불, secret: 비밀, promise: 약속하다

교과서
Conversation

핵심 Check
p.62~63

1 (1) happy / wrong   (2) complain / problem

2 (1) Don't forget to   (2) Remember to   (3) sure to

교과서 대화문 익히기

Check(✓) True or False
p.64

1 T   2 F   3 T   4 F

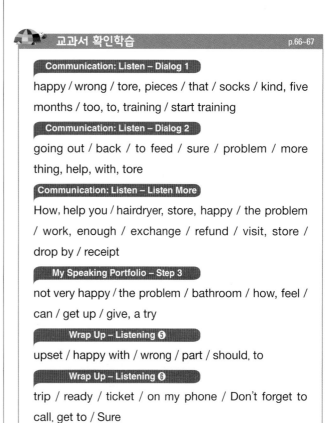

교과서 확인학습
p.66~67

Communication: Listen – Dialog 1

happy / wrong / tore, pieces / that / socks / kind, five months / too, to, training / start training

Communication: Listen – Dialog 2

going out / back / to feed / sure / problem / more thing, help, with, tore

Communication: Listen – Listen More

How, help you / hairdryer, store, happy / the problem / work, enough / exchange / refund / visit, store / drop by / receipt

My Speaking Portfolio – Step 3

not very happy / the problem / bathroom / how, feel / can / get up / give, a try

Wrap Up – Listening ❺

upset / happy with / wrong / part / should, to

Wrap Up – Listening ❻

trip / ready / ticket / on my phone / Don't forget to call, get to / Sure

01 ②　　　　02 ⑤
03 (B) → (D) → (C) → (A) → (E)

01 주어진 문장은 헤어드라이어의 문제점을 구체적으로 설명하고 있으므로 (B)가 적절하다.
02 소라는 그녀의 헤어드라이어를 교환이 아닌 환불을 받을 예정이다.
03 (B) 불만 원인 질문 → (D) 불만 설명 → (C) 공감 표현 → (A) 조언 요청 → (E) 해결책 제시

01 ②　　　02 ④　　　03 ④　　　04 ①
05 ①, ④　　06 (A) Feed　(B) water　(C) her science homework　　07 how　　08 ⑤
09 (D) → (B) → (A) → (E) → (C)
10 I'm ready to leave.　　11 ⑤　　12 ⑤

02 Minsol은 Buster 때문에 기분이 좋지 않음을 알 수 있다. unpleased: 불쾌한, satisfied: 만족스러운
03 Buster는 태어난 지 5개월 되었다.
04 One more thing: 한 가지 더, Conversely: 반대로
05 (a)는 무언가를 상기시키기 위한 표현으로 ①, ④번으로 바꾸어 쓸 수 있다.
07 how you feel: 네가 어떤 기분인지
08 밑줄 친 (B)와 바꾸어 쓸 수 있는 표현은 제안하는 표현이다. ⑤번은 궁금증을 나타낸다.
09 (D) 화나 보인다고 언급 → (B) 불만 표현 → (A) 문제 질문 → (E) 불만의 이유 설명 → (C) 제안
11 수지는 이미 기차표를 전화기에 저장해 놓았다.
12 개를 산책시키러 간다는 A의 말에 숙제를 가져오는 것을 잊지 마라는 대답은 어색하다.

01 He asks her to call him at the train station.
02 She keeps it on her phone.
03 She will come back around 8 o'clock.
04 He should feed and give some water to him.
05 Because Buster tore her homework into pieces.
06 (A) Hairdryer　(B) The air is not hot enough.
　　(C) Refund
07 I'm not happy with the school lunch menu.

01 아빠는 수지에게 기차역에 도착하면 그에게 전화할 것을 요청하였다.
02 수지는 표를 전화기에 저장해 놓았다.
03 민수의 엄마는 8시쯤 돌아올 것이다.
04 민수는 Buster를 위해 먹이를 주고 물을 주어야 한다.
05 민수의 엄마는 Buster가 민솔의 숙제를 찢었기 때문에 민수에게 민솔의 숙제를 도와줄 것을 요청하였다.
07 I'm not happy with ~: ~가 마음에 들지 않다

1 (1) do our best　(2) us find his dog
　(3) helped, (to) stand
2 (1) too tired to talk / so tired that he can't talk
　(2) well enough to pick / so well that I can pick

01 (1) to buy → buy　(2) fixed → fix
　(3) to missing → to miss　(4) that → to
02 (1) me go out and play　(2) made me clean
　(3) let me go　(4) too tired to drive
　(5) so busy that
03 (1) She has me do the job instead of her.
　(2) Ms. Jones let Mike drive her car.
　(3) It is too dark to go outside.
　(4) He was so sick that he couldn't go to school.

01 (1), (2) 사역동사의 목적어와 목적격 보어의 관계가 능동인 경우 목적격 보어로 동사원형을 쓰는 것이 적절하다. (3) '너무 ~해서 V할 수 없는'이라는 의미로 쓰이는 'too ~ to V'에는 to부정사를 쓴다. (4) 'too ~ to V'는 'so ~ that 주어 can't 동사원형'과 같다.
02 (1), (2), (3) 사역동사의 목적격 보어는 목적어와 목적격 보어의 관계가 능동인 경우 동사원형 형태를 쓴다. (4), (5) '너무 ~해서 V할 수 없는'이라는 의미로 쓰이는 'too ~ to V'는 'so ~ that 주어 can't 동사원형'과 같다.
03 (1), (2) 사역동사로 쓰인 have와 let은 목적격 보어로 동사원형 형태를 쓴다. (3), (4) '너무 ~해서 V할 수 없는'이라는 의미로 쓰이는 'too ~ to V'는 'so ~ that 주어 can't 동사원형'과 같다.

01 ③　　　　02 ④　　　　03 ⑤

04 You are too young to drive a car.

05 ⑤　　　　06 ②, ④　　　07 ③

08 This coffee is too hot to drink.

09 ③　　　　10 ④　　　　11 ③

12 Ron got up too late to catch the train.

13 ④　　　　14 ④　　　　15 ②

16 Judy was so fast that she couldn't stop at the finish line.

17 ④　　　　18 ②　　　　19 ①

20 The boy is too young to solve the puzzle.

21 ②, ④　　　22 ③　　　　23 ⑤

01 have는 사역동사로 쓰여 목적격 보어로 동사원형을 취한다.

02 '너무 초조해서 시험을 잘 볼 수 없었다'는 말이 들어가는 것이 적절하다. '너무 ~해서 …할 수 없는'은 'too ~ to V' 혹은 'so ~ that 주어 can't 동사원형'을 쓰며 시제 일치에 유의한다.

03 모두 목적격 보어로 동사원형을 취할 수 있는 동사이므로 'go'를 쓸 수 있지만 want는 목적격 보어로 to부정사를 받는 동사이므로 'to go'를 쓴다.

04 '너무 ~해서 V할 수 없는'은 'too ~ to V'를 이용하여 나타낼 수 있다.

05 지각동사와 사역동사는 목적격 보어로 동사원형을 쓸 수 있지만, encourage는 to부정사를 목적격 보어로 취하는 동사이다.

06 '너무 약해서 그것을 들 수 없다'고 하였으므로 'too weak to lift it' 혹은 'so weak that he can't lift it'이라고 쓸 수 있다.

07 사역동사의 목적어와 목적격 보어가 능동 관계에 있는 경우 목적격 보어로 동사원형을 쓸 수 있다. '너무 많이 자서 제 때에 그곳에 갈 수 없었다.'는 의미로 too much to go there를 쓰는 것이 적절하다.

08 '이 커피는 너무 뜨거워서 마실 수 없다'는 문장을 쓸 수 있다. 'so ~ that 주어 can't 동사원형'은 'too ~ to V'와 같다.

09 사역동사로 쓰인 make는 목적격 보어로 동사원형을 쓰는 것이 적절하다.

10 'too ~ to V'는 'so ~ that 주어 can't 동사원형'과 같으며, 이때 주절의 시제에 유의하여 couldn't를 쓰는 것이 적절하다.

11 사역동사로 쓰인 have는 목적격 보어로 동사원형 형태를 취한다. 따라서 watch가 적절하다.

12 'too ~ to V'를 활용하여 'Ron은 너무 늦게 일어나서 기차를 탈 수 없었다.'는 문장으로 쓸 수 있다.

13 사역동사 let은 목적격 보어로 동사원형을 쓴다. 따라서 go out으로 쓰는 것이 적절하다.

14 주어진 우리말을 영어로 옮기면 'I was too sleepy to finish my homework.'이다.

15 목적어와 목적격 보어의 관계가 수동이므로 cleaned라고 쓰는

것이 적절하다.

16 '너무 ~해서 V할 수 없는'은 'so ~ that 주어 can't'로 표현할 수 있으며 주절의 시제에 맞게 종속절의 시제를 일치시켜 주는 것에 유의한다.

17 '너무 ~해서 V할 수 없는'이라는 의미로 쓰이는 'too ~ to V'는 'so ~ that 주어 can't 동사원형'과 같다.

18 목적격 보어로 동사원형이 쓰이고 있으므로 사역동사 have를 쓰는 것이 적절하다.

19 이어지는 문장으로 보아 '너무 목이 말라서 더 이상 걸을 수 없었다'는 의미가 적절하다.

20 '너무 ~해서 V할 수 없는'이라는 의미로 쓰이는 'too ~ to V'는 'so ~ that 주어 can't 동사원형'과 같다.

21 내용상 'Amelia는 우리에게 조언을 해 줄 만큼 충분히 현명하다'는 의미가 적절하다. '~할 만큼 충분히 …한'은 '~ enough to V' 혹은 'so ~ that 주어 can 동사원형'을 쓴다.

22 사역동사 let의 목적격 보어로 동사원형을 쓸 수 있으며 '너무 ~해서 V할 수 없는'은 'too ~ to V'이다.

23 '너무 ~해서 V할 수 없는'은 'too ~ to V'로 표현한다.

01 (1) Kevin is too tired to go out.
　　(2) Kevin is so tired that he can't go out.

02 blow up the balloon / set by Hippo / eat the nuts / dance

03 Some students were too late to catch the bus.

04 The doctor had me take the medicine every six hours.

05 live alone / to live alone

06 (1) Patrick is tall enough to play the basketball well.
　　(2) Patrick is so tall that he can play the basketball well.

07 cry

08 (1) What made you think so?
　　(2) Mom let me buy a bike.
　　(3) You slept too much to get there on time.

09 old to ride

10 (1) I was too shy to make friends easily.
　　(2) I was so shy that I couldn't make friends easily.

11 (1) to watch → watch　(2) left → leave

12 My uncle let me have a piece of cake.

13 A: Did he make you solve this problem?
　　B: Yes. But this problem is too difficult to solve.

14 She is kind enough to accept your apology.

01 '너무 ~해서 V할 수 없는'이라는 의미로 쓰인 'too ~ to V'를 활용하여 문장을 쓸 수 있다.

02 사역동사 have는 목적어와 목적격 보어의 관계가 능동인 경우 목적격 보어로 동사원형을 쓰고 수동인 경우 과거분사를 쓴다.

03 '너무 ~해서 V할 수 없는'은 'too ~ to V'로 표현할 수 있다.

04 사역동사로 쓰인 have는 목적격 보어로 동사원형을 쓴다. every six hours: 여섯 시간마다

05 혼자서 살기에 너무 어려서 혼자 살게 하지 않겠다는 의미이다. 사역동사 let의 목적격 보어로 동사원형을 쓰며, 'too ~ to V'를 써서 '너무 ~ 해서 V할 수 없는'이라는 의미를 완성한다.

06 'V하기에 충분히 ~한'은 'enough to V' 혹은 'so ~ that 주어 동사 can'으로 쓸 수 있다.

07 make가 사역동사로 쓰이고 있으므로 목적격 보어로 동사원형을 쓴다.

08 사역동사의 목적어와 목적격 보어가 능동 관계에 있으면 목적격 보어로 동사원형을 쓴다. '네가 그렇게 생각하게 만들었다'고 하였으므로 사역동사 make를 써서 make you think so라고 쓰는 것이 적절하다.

09 파파 스머프는 너무 나이가 들어서 롤러코스터를 탈 수 없어서 슬프다.

10 나는 매우 수줍어서 쉽게 친구를 사귈 수 없었다는 의미이다. 따라서 '너무 ~해서 …할 수 없는'이라는 의미로 쓰이는 'too ~ to V' 혹은 'so ~ that 주어 can't 동사원형'을 활용하여 문장을 만든다.

11 사역동사로 쓰인 let과 have는 목적어와 목적격 보어의 관계가 능동인 경우 목적격 보어로 동사원형을 쓴다.

12 사역동사 let은 목적격 보어로 동사원형을 취할 수 있으며 have는 '~을 먹다'는 의미로 쓸 수 있다.

13 사역동사 make를 사용하여 '그가 너에게 이 문제를 풀게 하다'라는 문장을 쓸 수 있으며, '너무 ~해서 V할 수 없는'은 'too ~ to V'를 이용하여 쓸 수 있다.

14 accept one's apology: ~의 사과를 받아들이다

교과서
Reading

확인문제   p.80

1 T 2 F 3 F 4 T 5 T

확인문제   p.81

1 F 2 T 3 F 4 F 5 F 6 T

01 Good evening, This is
02 a special guest   03 Welcome
04 to meet you, for having me
05 want to tell   06 by reading some letters
07 start off with, from   08 Sure
09 from   10 to tell you
11 tries to do
12 without asking, hard to find
13 buys, me study them
14 to say, anymore, let me take care of
15 the same way   16 too young to do
17 get the message   18 do I
19 of two children   20 One, the other
21 too busy to talk   22 get, go back to
23 them, give short answers
24 don't talk much, either   25 to spend more time
26 often, younger
27 them, too old to understand
28 suggestions, Text your idea

1 Breeze: Good evening, listeners. This is your DJ, Breeze.

2 Today we have a special guest, Andy Kim.

3 He's a hip-hop artist. Welcome, Andy.

4 Andy: Nice to meet you and thank you for having me.

5 Breeze: Okay. What do our listeners want to tell their family?

6 This evening we will find out by reading some letters from them.

7 Andy, will you start off with the letter from a teenage girl?

8 Andy: Sure.

9 Andy: Hello. I'm a 15-year-old girl from Wonju.

10 I want to tell you about my mom.

11 My mom tries to do everything for me.

12 She cleans my room without asking me, so it's sometimes hard to find my stuff.

13 She also buys books and makes me study them.

14 I want to say to my mom, "I know you love me, but I'm not a baby anymore. Please let me take care of things myself."

15 Breeze: I felt the same way when I was in middle school.

16 Andy: Many moms think their kids are too young to do things on their own.

17 I hope the girl's mom will get the message.

18 Breeze: So do I. Andy, will you please read the next letter?

19 Andy: Hi. I'm a father of two children.

20 One is a high school girl, and the other is a middle school boy.

21 They're too busy to talk with me.

22 When I get home from work, they just say hi and go back to their rooms.

23 Sometimes I ask them about their school life, but they only give short answers.

24 We don't talk much at the table, either.

25 I want to say to my kids, "I love you so much, and I want to spend more time with you."

26 Breeze: Andy, did you talk with your parents often when you were younger?

27 Andy: Not really. I loved them very much, but I thought they were too old to understand me.

28 Breeze: I see. Does anyone have suggestions for the "sad" dad? Text your idea to us.

시험대비 실력평가
p.86~89

01 ④　　02 ②　　03 guest　　04 ③

05 ④　　06 She tries to do everything for her.

07 ②　　08 ④　　09 ②

10 Because they are too busy.　　11 ③

12 ③　　13 ③　　14 our listeners

15 She tries to talk about her mom.　　16 ⑤

17 ④　　18 ④　　19 ⑤

20 He has two children.　　21 ③　　22 ④

23 ④　　24 ②

25 He played computer games, rode bikes, and went shopping with his children on weekends.

01 사연을 읽어 주는 사람은 특별 손님인 Andy이다.

02 Andy가 어느 십 대 소녀로부터 온 편지를 읽을 것이다.

03 어떠한 행사에 초대된 사람은 '손님'이다.

04 사연 신청자의 엄마가 방 청소를 얼마나 자주 하는지는 사연을 읽고 답할 수 없다.

05 사연을 신청한 소녀는 자신의 엄마가 자신을 위해 모든 것을 다 해 주려 하는 것이 고민이라고 말하며, 자신이 더 이상 아기가 아니므로 자기 일을 스스로 할 수 있게 해 달라는 말을 하고 있다. 따라서 ④번이 가장 적절하다.

---

06 소녀의 어머니는 소녀를 위해 모든 것을 다 해 주려고 한다.

07 on one's own은 '혼자 힘으로'라는 의미이다. by oneself와 같다.

08 둘 중 남은 하나를 가리키는 말은 the other이다.

09 빈칸 (B)에는 전치사 from이 들어간다. ① take care of: ~을 돌보다 ② graduate from: ~을 졸업하다 ③ get out of: ~에서 나가다 ④ be full of: ~으로 가득 차다 ⑤ look forward to: ~을 기대하다

10 아이들이 너무 바빠서 아버지와 대화를 하지 않는다고 하였다.

11 'I see'는 '그렇군요.'라는 의미로 상대방의 말을 이해했을 때 쓰는 말이다. 따라서 understand를 대신 쓸 수 있다.

12 Andy는 부모님과 많은 대화를 나누지 않았다고 말했다.

13 초대해 주어서 고맙다는 의미의 ②번이 가장 적절하다..

14 청취자들을 가리키는 말이다.

15 편지에서 소녀는 그녀의 엄마에 관하여 말하려고 한다.

16 편지를 보낸 청취자의 이름은 알 수 없다.

17 밑줄 친 (C)와 ④는 강조용법으로 쓰인 재귀대명사이다. ①, ③, ⑤는 주어와 목적어가 같을 경우 목적어로 재귀대명사를 쓰는 재귀적 용법으로 사용되고 있다. ②는 재귀대명사가 관용어구로 쓰이는 경우이다.

18 청취자들이 라디오 프로그램에 사연을 보내는 것이다.

19 Andy의 말처럼, 소녀의 어머니가 메시지를 듣기를 바란다는 말에 동감을 표현하고 있다.

20 아버지에게는 두 명의 자녀가 있다고 하였다.

21 바쁜 자녀들과 대화가 없고, 아이들과 더 많은 시간을 보내고 싶다는 사연이므로 ③번이 가장 적절하다.

22 사연을 신청한 아버지는 편지에서 아이들에게 자신의 사랑과 바람을 전하고 있다.

23 글의 흐름상 don't talk라고 하는 것이 적절하다.

24 (A)에는 '~을 무너뜨리다'는 의미의 break down이 들어간다. break into: ~에 침입하다, break up: 부서지다, 헤어지다, break away: ~에서 달아나다, break off: 분리되다

25 아이들과 대화할 기회를 갖기 위하여 주말마다 함께 시간을 보냈다고 하였다.

서술형 시험대비
p.90~91

01 He is a hip-hop artist.

02 She will find out what listeners want to tell their family by reading some letters from them.

03 special guest , Andy Kim, to read, start off, teenage girl

04 Please let me take care of things myself.

05 It is hard to find her stuff.

06 She tries to do everything for her daughter.

07 They are so busy that they can't talk with me.

08 two kids[children], talk with him, spend more time

09 Many of them think that their kids are too young to do things on their own.

10 It's because he thought they were too old to understand him.

11 a wall between us

12 I had more chances to talk with them.

---

01 Andy Kim은 힙합 아티스트이다.

02 Breeze는 청취자들이 보낸 사연을 읽음으로써 그들이 자신의 가족에게 말하고 싶은 것을 알아보려고 하고 있다..

03 라디오 쇼에서, Breeze는 특별 손님인 Andy Kim을 소개한다. 그녀는 그가 한 십 대 소녀가 보낸 편지를 읽기를 원한다.

04 사역동사 let은 동사원형을 목적격 보어로 취하는 동사이다. 따라서 'let+목적어+동사원형' 형식으로 답을 작성하는 것이 적절하다.

05 어머니가 방을 치우면 자신의 물건을 찾는 것이 힘들다고 하였다.

06 편지에 따르면, 소녀의 어머니는 자신의 딸을 위해 모든 것을 해주려고 애쓴다고 하였다. try to V: V하려고 애쓰다

07 '너무 ~해서 …할 수 없는'이라는 의미의 'too ~ to V'는 'so ~ that 주어 can't V'와 같다.

08 사연을 보낸 사람은 두 아이의 아버지로, 아이들과 함께 대화할 시간이 없는 것이 고민이다. 그는 자신의 아이들과 함께 더 많은 시간을 보내기를 원한다.

09 많은 엄마들은 자신의 자녀들이 혼자서 무언가를 하기에는 너무 어리다고 생각한다.A

10 Andy는 부모님이 자신을 이해해 주시기에는 너무 나이가 들었다고 생각해서 어렸을 때 부모님과 자주 대화하지 않았다고 말했다.

11 자녀들과 자신 사이에 있는 벽을 가리키는 말이다.

12 '아이들과 이야기할 더 많은 기회'라고 하였으므로 'to talk with them'이 'more chances'를 수식하도록 문장을 만든다.

영역별 핵심문제

p.93~97

01 false   02 ⑤

03 (1) sure   (2) exchange   (3) receipt
   (4) near and dear   (5) wrong   (6) torn

04 ⑤   05 ③

06 (1) She never tells a lie.
   (2) Tom was in trouble because he broke the rule.

---

(3) Jimmy was not a member of the team anymore.

07 ⑤   08 ⓑ → tore   09 ③

10 (E) → (C) → (A) → (D) → (B)

11 ⓒ → to feed   12 feed   13 ②

14 Her brother uses the bathroom for too long in the morning.

15 His suggestion is that Amy can get up earlier and use the bathroom first.

16 ④   17 ③   18 ④   19 ④

20 ③   21 ③   22 ⑤   23 ③

24 too tired to catch

25 The bus driver made me get off the bus.

26 The nurse teacher let me rest in the nurse's office.

27 ③   28 ②   29 ⑤   30 study

31 ②   32 ④   33 ④

34 [B]-[A]-[C]

---

01 주어진 관계는 반의어 관계를 나타낸다. true: 사실의, false: 거짓의

02 without: ~ 없이

03 be sure to: 반드시 ~하다, exchange: 교환, receipt: 영수증, near and dear: 소중한, wrong: 잘못된, tear: 찢다

04 '누군가에게 무언가를 주고 동시에 그들로부터 같은 유형의 것을 받다'를 가리키는 말은 exchange(교환하다)이다.

05 be in trouble: 곤경에 처하다, trouble: 문제

06 tell a lie: 거짓말하다, be in trouble: 곤경에 처하다, not ~ anymore: 더 이상 ~ 아니다

07 ⑤번은 직업을 묻는 질문이다.

08 tear(찢다)의 과거형은 tore, 과거분사형은 torn이다.

09 위 대화를 통해 Buster가 Minsol의 숙제를 몇 번 찢었는지는 알 수 없다.

10 (E) 헤어드라이어의 문제점 설명 → (C) 사과 및 질문 → (A) 대답 및 환불 요청 → (D) 대답 및 방문 요청 → (B) 대답

11 forget ~ing: ~한 것을 잊다, forget to ~: ~할 것을 잊다

12 '사람이나 동물에게 음식을 주다'를 뜻하는 것은 feed(먹이를 주다)이다.

13 엄마와 아빠는 8시쯤 돌아올 것이다.

14 Amy의 남동생이 아침에 욕실을 너무 오랫동안 사용한다.

15 Brian의 제안은 Amy가 아침에 일찍 일어나서 먼저 욕실을 사용할 수 있다는 것이다.

16 '너무 ~해서 V할 수 없는'은 'too ~ to V'으로 표현한다.

17 make가 사역동사로 쓰이고 있으므로 목적격 보어로 동사원형을 쓰는 것이 적절하다.

18 allow는 to부정사를 목적격 보어로 취하며 '목적어가 V하게 허

락하다'는 의미이다. 따라서 사역동사 'let+목적어+동사원형'과 그 의미가 같다.

19 사역동사로 쓰인 make는 동사원형을 목적격 보어로 취할 수 있으며 'too ~ to V'는 '너무 ~해서 V할 수 없는'이라는 의미이다.

20 '우리가 일기를 쓰게 하다'이므로 '사역동사 have+us+keep a diary'라고 쓰는 것이 적절하다.

21 주어진 우리말을 영어로 쓰면 'The dog was so weak that he couldn't run to the park.'이다.

22 목적격 보어로 to부정사가 쓰이고 있으므로, 사역동사 make는 쓸 수 없다.

23 'too ~ to V'는 'so ~ that 주어 can't 동사원형'과 같다. 따라서 too를 so로 쓰는 것이 적절하다.

24 Azrael은 너무 피곤해서 스머프들을 잡을 수 없다는 말이 들어가는 것이 적절하다.

25 '목적어가 V하게 하다'는 '사역동사+목적어+동사원형'으로 표현할 수 있다.

26 '~가 V하도록 허락하다'는 사역동사 'let+목적어+동사원형'으로 표현할 수 있다.

27 편지를 읽음으로써 청취자들이 자신의 가족들에게 무슨 이야기를 하고자 하는지 알아보자는 의미이다. by Ving: V함으로써

28 자신을 초대해 주어서 고맙다는 의미이다.

29 이 라디오 방송에는 Andy와 Breeze 두 사람이 있다.

30 사역동사 make의 목적격 보어 자리이며 목적어와의 관계가 능동이므로 동사원형을 쓰는 것이 적절하다.

31 엄마가 자신에게 묻지 않고 방을 청소하기 때문에 물건을 찾기가 힘들 때가 있다고 보는 것이 적절하다. with → without

32 밑줄 친 (A)는 진주어로 쓰인 to부정사이다. ①, ② 부사적 용법 중 목적 ③ 형용사적 용법 ④ 진주어 ⑤ 부사적 용법 중 이유

33 소녀는 자신을 아기 취급 하는 엄마 때문에 불행하다.

34 자신과 아이들 사이에 벽이 있음 - [B] 그 벽(it)을 무너뜨리고 싶어서 아이들과 함께 많은 시간을 보내려고 애씀 - [A] 함께 시간을 보내기 위해 한 일들 - [C] 이렇게 해서(in this way) 아이들과 함께 대화할 기회를 더 많이 가짐

단원별 예상문제
p.98~101

01 ④   02 (C) → (A) → (E) → (D) → (B)   03 ⑤
04 ⑤   05 The air isn't hot enough.
06 She should bring the hairdryer and the receipt.
07 She is going to drop by tomorrow afternoon.
08 I think you should talk to her.   09 ①
10 (1) Kelly is going to drop by her uncle's house this weekend.

(2) She solved the math problem on her own.
(3) Mike wanted to find out the secret of Steve's success

11 ②, ⑤   12 ⑤   13 ④   14 ③
15 that I couldn't play soccer yesterday
16 The painter was too angry to focus on his painting.
17 let us use the science room
18 ④   19 ④   20 ③
21 so old that they couldn't
22 They only give him short answers.
23 ③   24 ④
25 She promises that she will never tell his secrets again.

01 '뜨거운 공기를 머리 위로 불어서 당신의 머리를 건조시키기 위해 사용되는 작은 기계'를 가리키는 말은 hairdryer(헤어드라이어)이다.

02 (C) Minsol의 불만에 대한 반응 → (A) 또 다른 불만 제기 → (E) Buster에게 친절할 것을 부탁 → (D) 불만 및 훈련의 필요성 제기 → (B) 수용 및 훈련을 시작할 것을 제안

03 (A) 잊지 말 것을 상기시키고 있으므로 forget, (B) Be sure to ~: ~을 명심하라, (C) piece: 조각, peace: 평화

04 민수가 집에 약 8시쯤 돌아올 것이라는 설명은 대화의 내용과 일치하지 않는다.

05 소라의 헤어드라이어는 뜨거운 바람이 충분히 나오지 않는다.

06 소라는 환불을 받기 위해 헤어드라이어와 영수증을 가져가야 한다.

07 소라는 내일 오후에 가게를 들를 것이다.

09 annoyed: 화난, lonely: 외로운, excited: 신이 난, satisfied: 만족한, nervous: 긴장한

10 drop by: ~에 들르다, on one's own: 혼자 힘으로, find out: 알아내다

11 '너무 ~해서 V 할 수 없는'은 'too ~ to V'으로 표현한다. 이는 'so ~ that 주어 can't 동사원형'과 같다.

12 advise는 to부정사를 목적격 보어로 취하는 동사이다. 주어진 문장의 목적격 보어는 동사원형이므로 advised는 답이 될 수 없다.

13 사역동사의 목적격 보어로 동사원형을 쓰는 것이 적절하며, '너무 어려서 생계를 위해 일할 수 없다'는 의미이므로 too ~ to V을 쓰는 것이 좋다.

14 사역동사로 쓰인 have는 목적어와 목적격 보어의 관계가 능동인 경우 목적격 보어로 동사원형을 쓴다.정

15 '너무 아파서 축구를 할 수 없었다'는 말이 들어가는 것이 적절하다. 주절의 시제가 과거이므로 couldn't를 쓰는 것에 유의한다.

16 '너무 ~해서 V할 수 없는'은 'too ~ to V'으로 표현할 수 있다.

17 '목적어가 V하게 하다'는 의미로 쓰이는 사역동사 중 let은 허락의 의미가 강하다.

18 직장에서 집으로 오는 것이고, 자신들의 방으로 들어간다는 의미이다. '~에서'라고 해석되는 from, '~로'라는 의미의 전치사 to를 쓰는 것이 적절하다.

19 부정에 대한 동의는 either를 쓴다.

20 식사 자리에서조차 대화를 많이 하지 않는다고 하였다.

21 '너무 ~해서 …할 수 없는'이라는 의미의 'too ~ to V'는 'so ~ that 주어 can't V'와 같다. 주절의 시제가 과거이므로 couldn't를 쓰는 것에 유의한다.

22 아버지에게 짤막한 대답만을 한다고 하였다.

23 지원이의 이야기로 미루어 보아 sorry가 들어가는 것이 가장 적절하다.

24 지원이 오빠의 비밀이 무엇인지는 위 글을 읽고 알 수 없다.

25 그녀는 다시는 오빠의 비밀을 말하지 않겠다고 약속한다.

적절하다.

06 'too ~ to V'는 'so ~ that 주어 can't 동사원형'과 같다.

07 '목적어가 V하게 하다' 이므로 '사역동사+목적어+동사원형'을 써서 나타낼 수 있다.

08 강당이 너무 작아서 모든 학생들을 수용할 수 없다는 의미이다.

09 사역동사 make, have, let은 목적격 보어로 동사원형을 취할 수 있는 동사이다.

10 한 십 대 소녀에게서 온 편지를 먼저 읽을 것이라고 하였다.

11 엄마가 묻지도 않고 소녀의 방을 청소하기 때문이다.

12 소녀의 어머니는 소녀의 방을 청소할 뿐만 아니라 자신이 구매한 책을 소녀가 공부하게 한다고 하였다. 사역동사 make의 목적격 보어로 동사원형을 쓴다.

13 아이들과 함께 할 기회를 더 가지면서 아이들에 관하여 더 많이 알게 되었다는 의미가 자연스럽다.

14 편지를 보냄으로써 자신의 경험을 공유하기를 원한다.

서술형 실전문제
p.102~103

01 I'm not happy with Buster.

02 He is five months old.

03 She suggests that Buster (should) need some training.

04 Yesterday they were too busy to start their meeting on time.

05 sleepy to pick

06 My dog is so big that it can't go into the dog house.

07 The man made me push his car.

08 too small to hold

09 (1) She had me play her piano.
   (2) I let them take a walk.
   (3) Did he make you climb the mountain?

10 He will read the letter from a teenage girl first.

11 It's because her mom cleans her room without asking her.

12 study books   13 less → more

14 He wants to share his experience with the "sad" father.

02 Buster는 5개월 되었다.

03 Minsol은 Buster가 훈련이 좀 필요하다고 제안한다.

04 '너무 ~해서 V할 수 없다'는 의미로 쓰이는 것은 'so ~ that 주어 can't 동사원형'이며, 'too ~ to V'과 같다.

05 Lazy는 너무 졸려서 사과를 딸 수 없다는 말이 들어가는 것이

창의사고력 서술형 문제
p.104

|모범답안|

01 (A) the air wasn't hot enough   (B) get a refund
   (C) with the dryer and the receipt

02 my mother, I talked back to her in a very rude way, we haven't talked to each other for several days, I will never talk back to you in such a rude way again

01 나는 지난주 가게에서 헤어드라이어를 샀지만 만족스럽지 않았다. 그것은 바람이 충분히 뜨겁지 않은 문제가 있었다. 나는 고객 센터에 전화를 하였고 이 문제를 설명하였다. 나는 헤어드라이어를 교환하기보다 환불을 받고 싶었다. 환불 받기 위해 나는 가게에 드라이어와 영수증을 갖고 방문할 필요가 있다. 그래서 나는 상점에 내일 오후에 들릴 것이다.

단원별 모의고사
p.105~108

01 ②   02 ①

03 (1) There is not enough food to feed all students.
   (2) Would you pour milk into this bowl?
   (3) Salty food is not good for your health.

04 ②, ④

05 Because Sojin isn't doing her part of the group project.

06 you can get up earlier and use the bathroom first.

07 ⑤　　　　　08 ⑤　　　　　09 receipt　　　10 ④

11 He tore my homework into pieces again.

12 ③　　　　13 ④　　　　14 ③, ⑤　　　15 ②

16 I made Jamie open the window.

17 far away from you to hear　　　18 ③

19 her mother treated her like a baby.　　20 ②

21 She wants her mom to let her take care of things herself.

22 ④　　　　　23 ⑤

24 She asks them to give some suggestions to the "sad" father by texting them.

이 너무 나이가 들어서 자신을 이해하지 못할 것이라고 생각했기 때문이다.

24 Breeze는 슬픈 아빠에게 해줄 제안이 있다면 문자로 그 생각을 보내 줄 것을 요청한다.

01 주어진 문장에서 work는 '작동하다'라는 의미로 사용되었으며 이와 같은 의미로 쓰인 것은 ②번이다. 나머지는 모두 '일하다'를 의미한다.

02 tell a lie: 거짓말하다, lie: 거짓말하다, 눕다

04 이어지는 대화에서 문제점을 묻고 있으므로 빈칸에 불만을 나타내는 표현이 적절하다.

05 Tommy는 Sojin이 모둠 과제에서 맡은 일을 하지 않아 화가 났다.

08 ⑤번을 제외한 나머지 표현은 모두 불만을 나타낸다.

09 '상품이나 서비스가 지불되었다는 것을 보여주는 종이 조각'을 나타내는 말은 receipt(영수증)이다.

10 소라는 헤어드라이어를 환불 받기를 원한다.

12 (A)는 이어지는 대화에서 Minsol의 불만이 이어지므로 happy가 적절하다, (B)는 앞선 아빠의 대화에서 Buster에 대해 친절한 태도를 볼 수 있으므로 nice, (C)는 '몇 주 후에'라는 의미가 이어져야 하므로 a few가 적절하다

13 teach는 목적격 보어로 to부정사를 취하는 동사이다.

14 ③ Wendy woke up too late to hear the news.라고 쓰는 것이 적절하다. ⑤ 목적어 her는 목적격 보어의 행위 주체가 될 수 있으므로 go라고 쓰는 것이 적절하다.

15 'too ~ to V'는 'so ~ that 주어 can't 동사원형'과 같다.

16 '목적어가 V하게 하다'는 의미로 쓰이고 있으므로 사역동사 'make+목적어+동사원형'으로 나타낼 수 있다.

17 나는 너로부터 너무 멀리 떨어져 있어서 네가 하고 있는 말을 듣지 못했다는 문장을 쓸 수 있다.

18 on one's own: 스스로

19 Breeze는 중학교 때 엄마가 자신을 아기처럼 대한다고 느꼈다.

20 소녀는 엄마가 자신에게 묻지 않고 방을 청소하는 것에 불만을 표시하고 있다.

21 소녀는 엄마가 자신의 일을 스스로 할 수 있게 해 주기를 원한다.

22 Andy의 마지막 말에서 소녀의 문제가 흔하다고 생각함을 알 수 있다.

23 Andy가 부모님과 함께 많은 대화를 나누지 않은 이유는 그들

A Diary from Athens

Reading

확인문제
p.112

1 T 2 F 3 F 4 T

확인문제
p.113

1 T 2 T 3 F 4 T 5 F

교과서 확인학습 A
p.114~115

01 Diary, Athens
02 visiting, aunt, uncle, Athens
03 center   04 gathering
05 were a lot of, busy talking, shopping
06 Assembly
07 Any male citizens, take part in, vote, matters
08 each, freely, matters, vote by showing
09 Counting thousands of, almost
10 again
11 heard, interesting discussion between, named, and
12 questioned, on, meaning
13 too, to, way, discussing
14 best, so far   15 went
16 outdoor, which, hold about, watched, play
17 In addition to traditional, play, interesting
18 far, stage, characters' sadness
19 final, stay
20 must develop, talent, help make, state
21 want to go, a better

교과서 확인학습 B
p.116~117

1 A Diary from Athens
2 1st Day _ I am visiting my aunt and uncle in Athens.

3 Today I went to the Agora in the center of the city
4 It is a gathering place for Athenians.
5 There were a lot of stores, and people were busy talking and shopping.
6 2nd Day _ My uncle went to the Assembly.
7 Any male citizens over the age of 20 can take part in the Assembly and vote on important matters.
8 After they each speak freely about the matters, they vote by showing their hands.
9 My uncle said, "Counting thousands of hands is almost impossible."
10 3rd Day _ I went to the Agora again.
11 I heard a very interesting discussion between a teacher named Socrates and his students.
12 Socrates questioned his students on the meaning of life.
13 I was too young to understand it, but I liked their way of discussing matters.
14 4th Day _ Today was the best day so far.
15 I went to the Theater of Dionysus.
16 At the outdoor theater which can hold about 17,000 people, we watched Antigone, a play by Sophocles.
17 In addition to traditional songs and dances, the play had an interesting story.
18 I sat far from the stage, but I could feel the characters' sadness.
19 5th Day _ Today is the final day of my stay in Athens.
20 My aunt and uncle said to me, "You must develop your talent. You can help make Athens a great state."
21 Now I want to go to school and become a better person.

서술형 실전문제
p.118~120

01 (1) take part in (2) talent (3) assembly
   (4) So far (5) hold (6) question (7) discussion
02 (1) citizen (2) hold (3) stay (4) vote
   (5) impossible
03 (1) In addition to (2) took part in
   (3) was busy enjoying (4) over the age of
   (5) by doing (6) between, and
04 (1) They were busy preparing for class.
   (2) A lot of preparation was needed.
   (3) I liked their way of discussing matters.

05 (1) Charlotte is so sick that she can't go to school today.

(2) The box is so heavy that I can't carry it.

(3) The math problems were so easy that we could solve them.

(4) The ribbon was so short that I couldn't tie with it.

06 (1) He spoke too fast for me to understand.

(2) He is so young that he can't drive a car.

(3) Remembering people is important.

07 people were busy talking and shopping

08 assembly

09 voted, important matters by showing

10 I was so young that I couldn't understand it.

11 At the outdoor theater which can hold about 17,000 people

12 The writer went to the Theater of Dionysus.

13 My aunt and uncle told me to develop my talent.

14 (G)oal

15 ②, ④

(1) ② Any male citizens over the age of 20 can take part in the Assembly and vote on important matters.

(2) ④ I was too young to understand the meaning of life.

01 assembly: 집회, 국회, 민회, hold: 담다, 수용하다, so far: 지금까지, discussion: 토론, take part in: ~에 참여하다, talent: 재능, question: 질문하다

02 vote: 투표하다, stay: 체류, 방문, citizen: 시민, hold: 담다, 수용하다, impossible: 불가능한

03 (1) in addition to: ~에 더하여, ~일뿐 아니라 (2) take part in: ~에 참여하다 (3) be busy -ing: ~하느라 바쁘다 (4) over the age of: ~살 이상의 (5) by -ing: ~함으로써 (6) between A and B: A와 B 사이에

04 (1) be busy -ing: ~하느라 바쁘다 (2) a lot of 다음에 단수 명사가 나오므로 단수 동사가 적절하다. (3) 뒤에 목적어가 나오므로 명사가 아니라 동명사가 나와야 한다.

05 too + 형용사[부사] + to + 동사원형 = so + 형용사[부사] + that + 주어 + can't[couldn't] + 동사원형, 형용사[부사] + enough+to부정사 = so + 형용사[부사] + that + 주어 + can[could] + 동사원형, to부정사의 의미상의 주어와 문장의 주어가 다를 경우 의미상의 주어를 써 주어야 한다. to부정사의 목적어가 문장의 주어일 경우 to부정사의 목적어를 쓰지 않았지만 that절로 바뀔 때 주어가 다른 경우 목적어를 써 주어야 함에 주의한다.

06 (1), (2) too + 형용사/부사 + to + 동사원형: 너무 ~해

서 …할 수 없다 = so + 형용사/부사 + that + 주어 + can't[couldn't] + 동사원형 (3) 동명사 주어는 단수 취급한다.

07 '~하느라 바쁘다'는 의미로 'be busy –ing'를 이용한다.

08 assembly: 집회, 민회 / 특히 특정한 목적을 위해 정기적으로 일어나는 많은 사람들의 모임

09 민회에 참석한 남자 시민들은 그들의 손을 들어 중요한 안건에 관해 투표했다.

10 'too+형용사+to부정사'는 'so+형용사+that+주어+can't+동사원형'으로 바꾸어 쓸 수 있다.

11 부사구 'At the outdoor theater(야외 극장에서)'로 문장을 시작하고, 주격 관계대명사 which절이 theater를 수식하는 구조로 배열한다.

12 네 번째 날에 필자는 어디에 갔는가?

13 밑줄 (A)는 직접화법으로 tell을 이용한 간접화법으로 문장을 전환한다. said to는 told로, 인용문의 2인칭 'you'는 문장의 목적어인 1인칭으로 바꾸고, 동사는 to부정사로 바꾸어 준다.

14 숙부와 숙모가 재능을 개발하고 아테네를 위대한 국가로 만드는 데 기여할 수 있다는 말에 학교에 다니고 더 나은 사람이 되고 싶다고 말하고 있으므로 '내 삶의 새로운 목표'가 일기의 제목으로 자연스럽다.

15 ② 모든 시민들이 민회에 참여하는 것이 아니라 20세 이상의 남자 시민들이 참여한다. ④ 소크라테스의 학생들이 너무 어려서 삶의 의미를 이해하지 못한 것이 아니라 필자가 너무 어려서 이해하지 못했다.

단원별 예상문제   p.121~124

01 ④   02 ⑤   03 ②   04 ①

05 ③   06 (1) by   (2) take, part   (3) far

(4) between   07 ②   08 ③

09 (1) The soup is so hot that we can't eat it.

(2) I was so tired that I can't visit you.

(3) Anne is so wise that she can lead them.

10 (1) I saw something called a walking bus.

(2) I was busy taking notes and listening to the teacher.

(3) Consumers are smart enough to know that.

(4) His family was too poor to educate him further.

(5) The bag was so big that it could hold almost 1,000 presents.

(6) But he became so heavy that he couldn't move at all.

(7) This problem is so hard that I can't solve it.

(8) This computer is small enough for me to carry.

11 ⑤   12 they vote by showing their hands

13 ④   14 ⑤

15 You can help (to) make Athens a great state.

16 (A) interesting   (B) named   (C) questioned

17 I liked their way of discussing matters

18 the meaning of life   19 ④   20 ②

21 ④   22 talking, shopping, discussion

23 Counting thousands of hands is almost
   impossible.

---

01 ① wide: 넓은, narrow: 좁은 ② male: 남자의, 수컷의,
   female: 여자의, 암컷의 ③ sad: 슬픈, glad: 기쁜 ④ stay: 체
   류, 방문, visit: 방문 ⑤ impossible: 불가능한, possible: 가
   능한

02 '밖에서 일어나거나 사용되는; 건물 안에서가 아닌'을 의미하는
   것은 outdoor(야외의, 실외의)이다.

03 in addition to ~에 더하여, ~일뿐 아니라, too ~ to ... 너무 ~
   해서 …하다

04 so far: 지금까지, over the age of ~: ~살 이상의

05 '남자들이나 소년들에게 전형적인 또는 관련된'을 뜻하는 것은
   'male(남자의, 수컷의)'이 적절하다.

06 (1) by -ing: ~함으로써, make fun of: ~을 놀리다 (2) take
   part in: ~에 참여하다 (3) so far: 지금까지 (4) between A
   and B: A와 B 사이에

07 There are a lot of guys selling things.

08 ① She is too tired to walk. ② My aunt told me that
   I must develop my talent. ④ The writer decided to
   go to school. ⑤ I heard a very interesting discussion
   between a teacher named Socrates and his students.

09 too+형용사[부사]+to+동사원형 = so+형용사[부사]+
   that+주어+can't[couldn't]+동사원형, 형용사/부사+
   enough+to부정사 = so+형용사[부사]+that+주어+
   can[could]+동사원형. to부정사의 목적어가 문장의 주어일
   경우 to부정사의 목적어를 쓰지 않지만 that절로 바뀔 때는 써
   주어야 함에 주의한다.

10 (1) 부르는 것이 아니라 불리는 것이므로 '수동'의 의미를 갖는
   called가 되어야 한다. (2) be busy -ing ~하느라 바쁘다 (3),
   (5) 형용사[부사]+enough+to부정사 = so+형용사[부사]+
   that+주어+can[could]+동사원형 (4), (6) too+형용사
   [부사]+to+동사원형 = so+형용사[부사]+that+주어+
   can't[couldn't]+동사원형 (7) to부정사의 목적어가 문장의
   주어일 경우 to부정사의 목적어를 쓰지 않았지만 that절로 바뀔
   때는 써 주어야 한다. (8) to부정사의 의미상의 주어와 문장의
   주어가 다를 경우 의미상의 주어로 'for+목적격'을 써 주어야 한
   다.

11 ⓔ는 동명사 Counting이 주어이므로 단수 동사 is가 맞다.

12 민회에 참석한 남자 시민들은 그들의 손을 들어 중요한 문제에
   관해 투표를 한다. 동사 'vote'를 첨가하고, 전치사 by 다음에 동

명사 'showing'을 사용한다.

13 필자가 민회에 참석하여 투표를 했다는 내용은 없다.

14 더 나은 사람이 되고 싶다는 말로 미루어 보아 '단단히 결심한'이
   적절하다.

15 'help+동사원형/to부정사', 'make+목적어(Athens)+목적보
   어(a great state)' 형태를 사용한다.

16 (A)는 명사 discussion을 수식하는 형용사 'interesting'이 적
   절하고, (B)는 Socrates라고 불리는 선생이란 뜻으로 과거분사
   'named', (C)는 과거 동사 'questioned'가 적절하다.

17 'way'는 '방식'이라는 뜻이고, 전치사 of 뒤에 동명사
   'discussing'이 적절하다.

18 대명사 it은 앞 문장의 '삶의 의미'를 가리키는 말이다.

19 연극 Antigone에 관한 설명으로 전통적인 노래와 춤에 더하여
   흥미로운 이야기가 있었다는 의미이므로 첨가의 의미를 가지는
   in addition to가 적절하다.

20 ⓐ는 '지금까지'의 의미로 'so far', ⓑ는 '무대에서 먼 곳에'란
   의미로 'far'가 적절하다.

21 이 글은 필자가 숙부, 숙모가 계신 아테네를 방문한 내용을 하루
   하루 기록한 일기 형식의 글이므로 ④가 적절하다.

22 Agora는 아테네 사람들이 모이고 이야기 나누고, 쇼핑하고 토
   론을 위한 장소이다.

23 동사 'count'를 동명사 'counting'으로 바꾸고 '수천 명의'를 나
   타내는 'thousands of'를 쓴다.

A Life Full of Fun

01 ⑤   02 ⑤   03 ①   04 ④

05 (1) Lastly   (2) spread   (3) plate   (4) is made into
    (5) caught my interest   (6) take a look

06 ①

01 pour: 붓다, bake: 굽다, fry: 볶다, cook: 요리하다, publish: 출판하다

02 agree의 명사형은 agreement이다.

03 하나의 언어에서 다른 언어로 바뀌는 것을 가리키는 말은 translate(번역하다)이다.

04 fascinating: 매력적인

05 lastly: 마지막으로, spread: 바르다. plate: 접시 be made into ~로 만들어지다, catch one's interest ~의 관심을 끌다, take a look 살펴보다

06 주어진 문장에서 spread는 '바르다'는 뜻으로 쓰였으며 이와 같은 의미로 쓰인 것은 ①번이다. ②, ③번은 '펼치다', ④, ⑤번은 '번지다, 확산시키다'는 뜻으로 쓰였다.

01 dead   02 (1) creative   (2) cartoonist
    (3) silly   (4) usual   (5) well-known

03 (1) box office   (2) showtime   (3) pay for

04 (1) You should not make fun of your friends.
    (2) Lucy is always calm through life's ups and downs.
    (3) I take a look at the webtoons of the day.

05 Education, amusement, pollution, suggestion, agreement

01 주어진 문장은 반의어 관계를 나타낸다. dead: 죽은, alive: 살아 있는

02 creative: 창의적인, cartoonist: 만화가, silly: 어리석은, usual: 보통의, well-known: 유명한, 잘 알려진

03 box office: 매표소, showtime: 상영 시간, pay for: ~에 대한 돈을 내다

04 make fun of: ~을 놀리다, ups and downs: 기복, take a look: 살펴보다

05 동물들은 숲속에 놀이공원을 지으려는 도시의 계획을 환영한다.

하지만, 그들은 곧 심각한 오염에 시달린다. 나이 든 코끼리가 한 가지 제안을 한다. 동물들과 도시는 모든 이들을 위한 더 좋은 세상을 만들기 위해 합의에 이른다.

1 (1) met / haven't, Have / have
    (2) Have you ever been / have been / did

2 (1) how to / First, Second / next / Boil
    (2) fall asleep easily / First of all, Next, Lastly

1 F   2 T   3 T   4 F

Communication: Listen – Dialog 1

down / serious, a lot / ups and downs / Have you watched / I haven't . Why / feelings, understand, better / sounds, watch

Communication: Listen – Dialog 2

line / ticket machine, from, machine / how to use the machine / select / watch, what / select, seats / back / Lastly , pay for / simple

Communication: Listen More

Have you ever made / No, I haven't / how to make / First, put, on, spread / help, with / Next, peppers / Add, bake, oven / wait, taste

Communicate: Speak

fried rice / cut, into / next / Put, fry / simple

Wrap Up – Listening ❺

Have, been / have, Actually / you've climbed, haven't you / twice

Wrap Up – Listening ❻

how to draw / First, circle, Next / draw, color, circle, Lastly

23

01 He needs six circles.　　　　02 ⑤

03 Do you know how to make fried rice?

04 채소를 작은 조각으로 자르고 팬에 기름을 두른 후 채소를 밥과 함께 볶는다.

05 (1) I've never been to Baltimore before.

　　(2) Have you ever been to China?

01 Mike는 곰의 얼굴을 그리기 위해 6개의 원이 필요하다.

02 마지막에 입을 만들어야 한다.

05 Have you ever p.p: ~해 본 적이 있니?

01 ②　　　　02 ①

03 Have you watched the animated movie "Shining Days"?　　　　04 ③　　05 ④

06 ⓐ put　ⓑ help　ⓒ bake　ⓓ wait

07 ⑤　　　　08 (E) → (C) → (A) → (D) → (B)

09 haven't you?

10 Have you ever been to Sokcho?

11 (1) Have you ever been to Dokdo?

　　(2) I have read the Harry Potter series.

01 'Have you ever ~?'의 경험을 묻는 질문에 'Yes, I have.' 또는 'No, I haven't.'로 대답한다.

02 (A)의 'down'은 '우울한'을 의미한다.

04 (A) 기계를 사용하는 방법을 묻고 있으므로 how, (B) select 와 병렬 구조로 동사 choose, (C) Lately: 최근에, Lastly: 마지막으로

05 표 매수와 좌석을 고른 후 표 값을 지불한다.

06 bake: 굽다

07 Garcia와 Suji가 피자 소스를 만들기 위해 무슨 재료를 준비해야 하는지 알 수 없다.

08 (E) 볶음밥 만드는 법 질문 → (C) 대답 및 첫 번째 단계 설명 → (A) 두 번째 단계 질문 → (D) 두 번째 단계 및 세 번째 단계 설명 → (B) 반응

09 선행하는 문장의 시제가 현재완료이므로 'haven't you?'가 적절하다.

11 Have you ever been to ~?: ~에 가 본 적이 있니?

01 (3) → (4) → (2)

02 He will make nacho pizza.

03 He put nacho chips on a plate.

04 He put pizza sauce, ham, onions. peppers, and cheese.

05 (D) → (E) → (C) → (A) → (B)

06 Yes, he has.

07 Because his uncle lives there.

01 나초 칩을 접시 위에 올려놓고 피자 소스를 바른 후 햄, 양파, 피망을 위에 올린다. 그리고 피자를 올린다.

02 요리사는 나초 피자를 만들 것이다.다.

03 요리사는 첫 번째로 나초 칩을 접시 위에 올려놓았다.

04 나초 칩 위에 피자 소스, 햄, 양파, 피망 그리고 치즈를 올려놓았다.

05 (D) 기계를 사용하는 방법으로 첫 번째 단계 설명 → (E) 상영 시간 선택 → (C) 두 번째 단계 설명→ (A) 앉고 싶은 자리 설명 → (B) 마지막 단계 설명

06 민수는 설악산에 올라가 본 적이 있다.

07 민수는 그의 삼촌이 속초에 살고 계시기 때문에 매년 속초를 방문한다.

1 (1) has been　(2) has, left　(3) have called

2 (1) typing　(2) boring　(3) sung

01 (1) hasn't gone → hasn't been

　　(2) saw → have seen　(3) did → have done

　　(4) have work → have worked

02 (1) living　(2) crying　(3) written　(4) made

　　(5) barking

03 (1) I have read 500 books since I was six.

　　(2) The boy has already drunk the milk.

　　(3) Is this a baked potato?

　　(4) Did you find your sleeping bag?

01 (1) 'have gone to ~'는 '~에 가고 없다'는 의미로 결과를 나타내는 현재완료이다. '~에 가 본 적이 없다'는 것은 'have[has] not been to ~'로 표현한다. (2) 지금까지 프로그램을 몇 번 보았다는 의미이므로 현재완료 시제로 표현하는 것이 적절하다. (3) 어제 이래로 아무것도 하지 않았다는 것이므로 과거의 일이 현재까지 이어지는 것이라 볼 수 있다. 따라서 현재완료 시제가 적절하다. (4) 현재완료의 형태는 'have+p.p.'이다.

02 (1) '그 마을에서 살고 있는'이라는 의미이므로 현재분사로 people을 수식한다. (2) 아기가 울고 있는 것이므로 현재분사로 baby를 수식하는 것이 적절하다. (3) 책이 유명한 작가에 의해 '쓰여진' 것이므로 과거분사를 쓴다. (4) '금으로 만들어진 수저'라는 의미이므로 과거분사로 spoon을 수식한다. (5) '짖는 개'라는 의미이므로 현재분사를 쓰는 것이 적절하다.

03 (1) 여섯 살 이후로 계속 책을 읽은 것이므로 현재완료 시제를 써서 나타낸다. (2) 벌써 우유를 마셨다는 완료를 나타내고 있으므로 현재완료 시제를 쓰는 것이 적절하다. (3) 감자는 구워지는 것이므로 과거분사로 potato를 수식한다. (4) 잠자는 용도로 쓰이는 자루를 말하는 것이므로 동명사 sleeping이 적절하다.

시험대비 실력평가
p.143~145

01 ④	02 ③	03 ③	04 ③
05 ⑤	06 ④	07 ④, ⑤	

08 Eunji has lived in Busan since she was five years old.

09 ⑤	10 ③	11 ④

12 I have just had a piece of frozen pizza.

13 ⑤	14 ③	15 ④
16 I bought a used car.	17 ③	18 ⑤
19 ④	20 ⑤	

21 The surprising news is not true.   22 ⑤

23 Cold winds blew into the house through the broken window.

24 exciting / excited

---

01 현재완료 시제와 함께 쓰이면서 특정 시점을 이끌 수 있는 것은 since이다.

02 현재완료의 형태는 'have+p.p.'이다. 따라서 seen이 적절하다.

03 무언가가 '타고 있는' 것이므로 현재분사 burning으로 수식하고, 'Jessica라고 이름 지어진' 것이므로 과거분사로 a girl을 수식하는 것이 적절하다.

04 stop의 과거분사는 stopped이다.

05 주어진 문장은 경험을 나타내는 현재완료이다. 밑줄 친 현재완료의 용법은 각각 ① 결과 ②, ③ 완료 ④ 계속 ⑤ 경험을 나타내고 있다.

06 지금까지 3년 동안 그녀를 만나 왔다는 의미이므로 현재완료 시제를 사용하는 것이 적절하다.

07 목적격 보어로 과거분사를 취할 수 없는 동사는 help와 seem이다.

08 은지는 5살 때부터 부산에서 살기 시작하여 현재도 부산에서 살고 있다고 하였으므로 현재완료 시제를 활용하여 은지는 5살 이래로 부산에서 살고 있다는 문장으로 쓸 수 있다.

09 주어진 문장의 밑줄 친 부분은 현재분사로 쓰인 것이다. '손을 올리고 있는 소녀'라는 의미의 ⑤번이 현재분사로 쓰였으므로

⑤번이 답이다.

10 Has로 묻고 있으므로 has로 답하는 것이 적절하다.

11 ① that smiling girl ② the injured man ③ did you meet ⑤ for three years

12 '막 먹었다'는 완료의 의미는 현재완료 시제를 통하여 나타낼 수 있다.

13 (A) 흥분을 유발하는 게임이라는 의미이므로 현재분사로 game을 수식하는 것이 적절하다. (B) 5살 때부터 기타를 연주해 오고 있다는 의미이므로 현재완료 시제를 쓴다. (C) 과거를 나타내는 어구인 yesterday와 현재완료 시제는 함께 쓸 수 없다.

14 답변으로 미루어 보아 영화를 본 적이 있는지 경험을 묻는 말이 들어가는 것이 적절하다.

15 Paul이 10살 때부터 쭉 Tom이 가르치고 있다는 의미이므로 현재완료 시제가 적절하며, Tom이 Paul을 잘 안다는 것은 현재 상태를 나타내는 것이므로 현재시제를 쓴다.

16 중고차는 used car이다.

17 모두 특정 시점을 이끄는 since가 쓰이지만 ③번에는 기간을 이끄는 전치사 for가 쓰인다.

18 동생이 쇼핑몰에 가고서 현재 이곳에 없다는 의미이므로, 현재완료 시제를 사용하여 '동생은 쇼핑몰에 가고 없어.'라는 문장을 쓸 수 있다. 'have gone to'는 '~에 가고 없다'는 의미를 갖는다.

19 그는 오늘 아침 이래로 불타는 태양 아래에서 하루 종일 일해 왔다는 의미이다. 따라서 현재완료 시제를 쓰는 것이 적절하며, '불타는 태양'이므로 현재분사로 sun을 수식하는 것이 적절하다.

20 내가 즐거움을 느끼는 것이므로 과거분사 amused를 쓰는 것이 적절하다.

21 그 소식이 '놀라움을 주는' 것이므로 현재분사로 news를 수식한다.

22 주어진 문장을 영어로 옮기면 I have fought with my brother before.이다.

23 blow의 과거형 blew를 쓰고, '부서진 창문'이라고 하였으므로 과거분사로 window를 수식하도록 문장을 쓰는 것이 적절하다.

24 콘서트는 흥분을 유발하는 것이므로 현재분사로, 팬들은 흥분을 느낀 것이므로 과거분사로 쓰는 것이 적절하다.

서술형 시험대비
p.146~147

01 (1) rising   (2) baked, sleeping   (3) dancing
   (4) cheering   (5) sliced

02 Jenny has been friends with Christina since 2010.

03 A: Have you ever cooked fried rice?
   B: Yes, I have cooked it many times.

04 Have you been to other countries before?

25

05 (1) drove (2) has been (3) has rained (4) lost
(5) has read

06 Look at the boy wearing a red cap.

07 My brother has been sick since last night.

08 (1) 현재분사   이유: '수영하는 아기'라는 의미로
swimming이 baby를 수식하고 있다.
(2) 동명사   이유: 수영하는 용도로 쓰이는 풀'이라는
의미로 쓰이고 있다.

09 (1) I have been to Jejudo twice until now.
(2) I broke the window yesterday.
(3) We haven't seen the movie yet.

10 has lived, 2011, 2011, has learned, for

11 My grandmother has broken her right arm.

12 She made me bring a boiled egg and chopped
carrot.

13 has worked

14 (1) boring → bored   (2) making → made
(3) excited → exciting   (4) barked → barking

01 분사의 수식을 받는 명사가 행위 주체인 경우에는 현재분사로,
그렇지 않은 경우에는 과거분사로 수식한다.

02 현재완료 시제를 이용하여 Jenny는 Christina와 2010년 이래
도 쭉 친구라고 쓸 수 있다.

03 경험을 묻고 답하는 말이므로 현재완료 시제를 써서 나타낼 수
있다. '볶아진 밥'이라는 말로 '볶음밥'을 표현할 수 있음 에 유의
하자.

04 경험을 묻는 말이므로 현재완료 시제를 이용하여 문장을 만들
수 있다.

05 과거를 나타내는 어구와 현재완료는 함께 쓸 수 없다. 그러나 과
거의 일이 현재까지 영향을 미치는 경우 현재완료 시제를 쓸 수
있다.

06 분사가 목적어나 부사구와 함께 쓰일 때는 명사를 뒤에서 수식한
다.

07 어젯밤부터 아픈 것이 현재까지 이어지고 있으므로 현재완료시
제를 활용하여 표현할 수 있다.

08 현재분사는 명사를 수식하고, 동명사는 '~한 용도로 쓰이는 명
사'라고 해석된다.

09 (1) 지금까지의 경험을 나타내고 있으므로 현재완료 시제를 쓰
는 것이 적절하다. (2) 어제 일어난 일을 말하고 있으므로 과거
시제를 쓴다. (3) 현재완료 시제의 용법 중 '완료'를 사용하여 나
타낼 수 있다.

10 캐나다에서 태어난 Jason은 10살이던 2011년에 한국으로 이
사를 오자마자 태권도를 배우기 시작했다. 그는 현재 18세이므
로 8년간 태권도를 배워 왔다고 말할 수 있다.

11 지난달에 할머니의 오른팔이 부러졌고, 할머니는 여전히 오른팔
을 쓰실 수 없으므로 현재완료 시제를 이용하여 오른팔이 부러
진 상황이 지속됨을 말할 수 있다.

12 '삶은 달걀'은 삶아진 달걀을 뜻하므로 과거분사 boiled로 egg
를 수식해야 하며, '다진 당근' 역시 다져진 당근을 뜻하므로
chopped carrot이라고 쓰는 것이 적절하다.

13 현재도 일을 하고 있고, 5년 동안 이 회사에서 일해 오고 있다는
의미이므로 현재완료 시제를 쓰는 것이 적절하다.

14 (1) 지루한 감정을 느낀 것이므로 과거분사 (2) 중국에서 만들
어진 가방이므로 과거분사 (3) 흥분을 유발하는 모험영화이므로
현재분사를 쓰는 것이 적절하다. (4) 짖는 개라는 의미이므로 현
재분사로 dog를 수식하는 것이 적절하다.

교과서
Reading

확인문제   p.148

1 F   2 T   3 T   4 F   5 F

확인문제   p.149

1 F   2 F   3 F   4 T   5 T   6 F

교과서 확인학습 A   p.150~151

01 Land   02 laugh, saw, above
03 so, successful   04 who make cartoons
05 to catch, make you laugh, creative drawings.
06 have made, for   07 many types of cartoons
08 is, a few words   09 is, called
10 makes a funny character, laugh, doing, saying
11 Another, is called
12 some parts, are different, bigger than usual
13 on   14 Which parts, jump
15 have used, to make fun of
16 several, come together, a comic strip
17 have been, for   18 just amusing stories
19 have also used, for education
20 make, clearer, easier to learn
21 have probably seen
22 have surely seen, animated movies
23 popular among people of all ages
24 are added to, come alive
25 develop fascinating, interesting, through
26 was developed   27 is called
28 are published, read them, on
29 popular, them are, into 30 may appear
31 different, exciting than, remain, laugh, relax, learn

1 Boat! Land!

2 Did you laugh when you saw the cartoon above?

3 If so, the cartoonist was successful.

4 Cartoonists are the people who make cartoons.

5 They want to catch your interest, and usually, make you laugh with simple language and creative drawings.

6 People have made cartoons for hundreds of years.

7 There are many types of cartoons, and they play different roles.

8 One form of cartoon is a picture with a few words.

9 It is sometimes called a "gag cartoon."

10 The cartoonist makes a funny character, and the character makes you laugh by doing or saying silly things.

11 Another type of cartoon is called a caricature.

12 In a caricature, some parts of a character are different or bigger than usual.

13 Look at the picture on the right.

14 Which parts of the man's face jump out at you?

15 Artists have used this type of cartoon to make fun of well-known people.

16 When several cartoon pictures come together and tell a story, we have a comic strip.

17 Comic strips have been in newspapers for many years.

18 They are often just amusing stories.

19 People have also used comic strips for education.

20 Comics can make information clearer and easier to learn.

21 You have probably seen comic history or science books.

22 You have surely seen many cartoon movies, or animated movies, too.

23 These are very popular among people of all ages.

24 Movement and sounds are added to pictures, so they come alive.

25 Artists and writers can develop fascinating characters and tell interesting stories through animation.

26 In the 1990s, a new type of cartoon was developed.

27 It is called a webtoon.

28 Webtoons are published online, so you can read them anytime, anywhere on your phone or computer.

29 They are very popular, and some of them are even made into TV dramas or movies.

30 New forms of cartoons may appear in the future.

31 They could be different and even more exciting than now, but one thing will remain the same: they will help us laugh, relax, and learn.

01 ③   02 ⑤

03 It is called a caricature.

04 A cartoonist makes a funny character in a gag cartoon.

05 ②   06 ④   07 They make cartoons.

08 ③   09 ②   10 ③   11 ④

12 It's because they are published online. 13 ④

14 ②, ④   15 ③   16 successful

17 The characters in a gag cartoon make people laugh by doing or saying silly things.

18 ②   19 ④   20 We call it a gag cartoon.   21 ②   22 ③

23 A comic strip is made of several cartoon pictures and tells a story.

24 It's because comics can make information clearer and easier to learn.

25 ③   26 우리가 웃고, 쉬고, 배우도록 돕는 것

01 이어지는 글의 내용을 보면 다양한 종류의 만화는 서로 다른 역할을 한다. 따라서 different라고 쓰는 것이 적절하다.

02 빈칸 (A)에는 by+Ving로 '~함으로써'라는 의미를 완성하는 전치사 by가 들어간다. be interested in: ~에 흥미를 갖 다, give up: ~을 포기하다, turn off: ~을 끄다, be proud of: ~을 자랑스러워하다, one by one: 하나씩

03 두 번째 종류의 만화는 캐리커처라고 하였다.

04 만화가는 개그 만화에서 웃긴 캐릭터를 만든다고 하였다.

05 캐리커처는 유명한 사람들을 풍자하는 것이다.

06 글에는 두 가지 종류의 만화만 제시되어 있다.

07 만화가들은 만화를 만드는 사람들이다.

08 빈칸 (A)에는 기간을 이끄는 전치사 for가 쓰인다. ③번에는 특정 시점을 이끄는 since가 쓰인다.

09 연재만화는 여러 해 동안 신문에 실려 옴 - [B] 연재만화는 종종 단지 재미있는 이야기이고 교육용으로도 쓰임 - [A] 교육용 만화 역사책이나 과학책이 있음. 또한 만화영화도 있는데 - [C] 이는 모든 연령의 사람들에게 인기가 있고 동작이나 소리가 더해져서 그림들이 생생하게 살아남.

10 몇 가지 만화 그림을 모아 연재만화를 만든다고 하였다.

11 (A) 웹툰이라고 불리는 것이므로 수동태, (B) 지칭하는 것이 복수명사 webtoons이므로 복수 대명사, (C) appear는 자동사

이므로 수동태로 쓰일 수 없다.

12 우리가 휴대 전화나 컴퓨터로 언제 어디서나 웹툰을 읽을 수 있는 이유는 웹툰이 온라인으로 출판되기 때문이다.

13 웹툰을 주로 누가 보는지는 알 수 없다.

14 사람을 선행사로 받아주는 주격 관계대명사 who가 쓰이며, who를 대신하여 that을 쓸 수 있다.

15 다양한 종류의 만화가 있다고 하였으므로 만화의 종류가 이어지는 것이 가장 적절하다.

16 바라던 결과를 성취하는 것은 '성공적인(successful)'이다.

17 개그 만화에 등장하는 캐릭터는 우스꽝스러운 행동이나 말을 함으로써 사람들을 웃게 만든다고 하였다.

18 one과 another로 만화의 종류를 소개하고 있으므로 만화의 종류에는 두 가지 이상이 있음을 알 수 있다. another는 남아 있는 것 중 하나를 가리키는 대명사이다.

19 개그 만화에서는 우스꽝스러운 행동이나 말을 함으로써 독자를 웃게 만드는 캐릭터를 볼 수 있다고 하였다.

20 몇 마디 말을 쓴 그림은 '개그 만화'라고 부른다.

21 주어진 문장의 대명사 It은 a new type of cartoon을 지칭하는 것이다.

22 (A) 즐거움을 유발하는 이야기이므로 현재분사로 stories를 수식, (B) 긍정에 대한 동의이므로 too, (C) come alive: 생생하게 살아나다, 활기를 띠다, come live: 생방송하다

23 연재만화는 몇 가지 만화 그림으로 이루어져 있으며 이야기를 들려준다고 하였다.

24 만화는 정보를 더 명료하고 더 배우기 쉽게 만들 수 있기 때문에 사람들은 연재만화를 교육용으로 사용해 오기도 했다.

25 웹툰은 온라인으로 출판되기 때문에 여러분이 휴대 전화나 컴퓨터로 언제 어디서나 볼 수 있다고 하였다.

26 미래에 새로운 형태의 만화가 나타날지라도 우리가 웃고, 쉬고, 배우도록 돕는 것은 여전히 같을 것이라고 하였다.

서술형 시험대비 p.158~159

01 People have made cartoons for hundreds of years.
02 They use simple language and creative drawings.
03 If you laughed when you saw the cartoon above
04 many types of cartoons 05 It makes us laugh.
06 It is a gag cartoon.
07 many words → a few words wise → silly[foolish]
08 We can use comic strips.
09 movement and sounds are added to pictures
10 They can develop fascinating characters and tell interesting stories through animation.
11 Webtoons were developed in the 1990s.
12 a comic strip / amusing / education
13 will help us laugh, relax, and learn

01 사람들은 수 백 년 전에 만화를 만들었고 현재도 만들고 있다고 하였으므로, 현재완료 시제를 이용하여 '사람들은 수 백 년 동안 만화를 만들어 왔다'는 문장을 쓸 수 있다.

02 만화가들은 사람들을 웃게 하기 위해서 간단한 말과 독창적인 그림을 사용한다고 하였다.

03 If so는 '만약 그렇다면'이라는 뜻으로, '위 만화를 보고 웃었다면'이라는 의미로 쓰였다.

04 많은 종류의 만화를 가리키는 대명사이다.

05 개그 만화는 우리를 웃게 만든다.

06 간단한 말을 쓴 그림이므로 개그 만화이다.

07 만화의 한 형태로 몇 마디 말을 쓴 그림이 있고, 웃긴 캐릭터가 우스꽝스러운 행동을 한다고 하였다.

08 만화는 정보를 더 명료하고 더 배우기 쉽게 만들 수 있다고 하였다. 만약 정보를 좀 더 분명하게 전달하기를 원한다면 연재만화를 사용할 수 있다.

09 동작이나 소리가 그림에 더해져서 그림들이 생생하게 살아난다고 하였다.

10 미술가들과 작가들은 매력적인 캐릭터를 개발하고 만화영화 제작을 통해 재미있는 이야기를 들려준다고 하였다.

11 웹툰이 개발된 시기는 1990년대라고 하였다.

12 만화 그림이 모여 이야기를 들려주면 연재만화가 되고, 연재만화는 재미있는 이야기라고 하였다. 또한 연재만화는 교육용으로 사용된다.

13 해석: 비록 미래에 새로운 형태의 만화가 나타난다 할지라도, 그것은 지금처럼 우리가 웃고, 쉬고, 배우도록 도와줄 것이다.

영역별 핵심문제 p.161~165

01 ① 02 ③
03 (1) Emma poured orange juice into a glass and drank it.
   (2) We have lots of[a lot of] plates to wash.
   (3) I like to fry eggs and lots of vegetables.
04 (1) come together (2) comic strip (3) Watch out
   (4) of all ages (5) jumps out at me
05 ③   06 (B) → (D) → (C) → (A)   07 ⑤
08 (A) a movie (B) a showtime (C) choose seats
   (D) pay for the tickets
09 Have you ever made nacho pizza?
10 ⓐ nacho pizza ⓑ nacho chips
11 ④   12 ⑤
13 (A) down (B) serious (C) understand
14 ⑤   15 ⑤   16 ②
17 Do you know the boy jumping on the stage?
18 ④   19 ④   20 ②
21 I have had this problem since last year.

01 태양에 의해 손상되는 것으로부터 피부를 보호하기 위해 피부에 바르는 로션의 한 유형을 가리키는 말은 sunscreen(자외선 차단제)이다.

02 spread는 '바르다'는 의미로 쓰였다.

03 pour: 붓다, plate: 접시, fry: 볶다

04 of all ages: 모든 연령의, watch out for: ~을 조심하다, comic strip: 신문 연재만화 / jump out at: ~에게 금방 눈에 띄다, come together: 합쳐지다

05 주어진 문장에서 down은 '우울한'을 뜻하며 이와 같은 의미로 쓰인 것은 ③번이다. 나머지는 모두 '아래로, ~ 아래쪽으로'를 뜻한다.

06 (B) 속초 방문한 경험 질문 → (D) 대답 및 이유 설명 → (C) 설악산에 올라가 본 적이 있는지 확인 → (A) 대답 및 올라간 횟수 설명

07 빈칸 (A)에 들어갈 말로 나머지는 모두 제안을 나타내지만 ⑤번은 경험을 묻는 표현이다.

09 'Have you ever ~?' 표현을 사용하여 경험을 물어 볼 수 있다.

11 위 대화에서 피자 소스를 무엇으로 만드는지는 알 수 없다.

12 Anna가 Jinsu가 채소를 작게 자르는 것을 돕는지 대화를 통해 알 수 없다.

13 (A)에서 down은 '우울한'을 가리킨다. (B)에는 대명사를 수식하는 형용사 serious가 적절하다. (C)에는 help 뒤에 원형 부정사 understand가 적절하다.

14 drive의 과거분사형은 driven이다.

15 경험을 나타내는 문장은 현재완료로 표현할 수 있으며, '~에 가 본 적이 있다'는 'have been to'를 쓴다.

16 첫 번째 빈칸에는 경험을 나타내어 once, twice, before 등이 들어갈 수 있다. 특정 시점을 이끄는 것은 since, 기간을 이끄는 것을 for를 쓴다.

17 '무대 위에서 뛰고 있는'이 '소년'을 수식하는 구조이므로 the boy jumping on the stage라고 쓰는 것이 적절하다. 분사가 부사구와 함께 쓰이고 있으므로 명사를 뒤에서 수식하도록 문장을 만든다.

18 명백히 과거를 나타내는 어구인 when, ~ ago 등은 현재완료 시제와 함께 쓰일 수 없다. 현재완료의 과거형은 haven't p.p.이다.

19 주소를 잊었고 여전히 기억할 수 없다고 하였으므로 현재완료 시제를 이용하여 주소를 잊은 상황을 말할 수 있다.

20 모두 baking이 들어가지만 ②번에는 baked가 들어간다. ⑤번에 쓰인 baking은 동명사로 '빵을 굽는 용도로 쓰이는 소다'라는 의미를 완성한다.

21 작년부터 지금까지 이 문제를 가지고 있었다고 하였으므로 현재완료 시제로 나타낼 수 있다.

22 주어진 문장의 밑줄 친 부분은 현재완료의 용법 중 '경험'을 나타낸다. 각각 ① 결과 ② 결과 ③ 계속 ④ 계속 ⑤ 경험 용법으로 쓰였다.

23 과거를 나타내는 어구인 the other day가 있으므로 과거시제를 쓰는 것이 적절하다. put은 과거와 과거완료의 형태가 모두 동일한 put–put–put이다.

24 '도난당한 차'이므로 과거분사 stolen으로 car를 수식하고, '발견되었다'고 하였으므로 수동태를 완성하는 과거분사 found를 쓴다.

25 정오에 도서관을 가서 여전히 도서관에 있다고 하였으므로, 현재완료 시제를 이용하여 그들이 정오 이래로 도서관에 계속 있다는 말을 쓸 수 있다.

26 ②번 문장의 주어인 They가 지칭하는 것은 주어진 문장의 Cartoonists이다. 따라서 ②번에 들어가는 것이 가장 적절하다.

27 밑줄 친 (A)는 현재완료의 '계속' 용법으로 쓰였다. ① 경험 ② 결과 ③ 계속 ④ 경험 ⑤ 결과

28 만화가들은 창의적인 그림으로 우리를 웃게 만든다고 하였다.

29 보통의; 아주 자주 발생하는 usual(평소의, 보통의)

30 글의 서두를 만화의 또 다른 종류(Another type of cartoon)라는 말로 이끌고 있으므로, 앞에서 다른 종류의 만화에 대해 언급했음을 알 수 있다.

단원별 예상문제
p.166~169

01 경험을 묻는 현재완료 시제를 사용하여야 하므로 watched가 적절하다.

02 위 대화를 통해 Kevin이 어떻게 생겼는지는 알 수 없다.

03 Tony와 Emily는 발매기에서 표를 사고 싶어 한다.

04 Tony와 Emily는 영화를 7시에 볼 것이다.

05 Emily는 뒤에 앉고 싶어 한다.

06 (C) 첫 번째 단계 설명 → (A) 도움 제공 → (E) 두 번째 단계 설명 → (D) 다음 단계 질문 → (B) 마지막 단계 설명

07 (A) cut: 자르다, put: 놓다 (B) bake: 굽다, (C) fry: 볶다, spread: 바르다

08 그들은 팬에 기름을 두른 후 채소와 밥을 함께 볶아야 한다.

09 Anna와 Jinsu는 볶음밥을 만들기 위해 채소, 기름, 밥이 필요하다.

10 경험을 묻는 질문에 'Yes, I have.'라고 대답하는 것이 알맞다.

11 모두 '완료'를 나타내지만 ④번은 '계속'을 의미하는 현재완료이다.

12 ① made ② has practiced ③ frozen food ④ The boy walking with his friends가 적절하다.

13 '조리된 닭고기'라는 의미이므로 과거분사로, '소리치는 소년'이라는 의미이므로 현재분사로 명사를 수식하는 것이 적절하다.

14 모두 과거를 나타내는 어구와 함께 쓰여 과거동사가 들어가야하지만, ②번은 현재완료 시제가 쓰인다. ① found ② has read ③ went ④ took ⑤ raised 혹은 had가 쓰일 수 있다.

15 'Chris라고 이름 지어진 소년'이므로 과거분사로, (2) '고장 난 냉장고'이므로 과거분사로, (3) '놀라움을 유발하는 소식'이므로 현재분사로 수식하는 것이 적절하다.

16 '추천된 책'이라고 하였으므로 과거분사로 book을 수식하는 것이 적절하다.

17 Mr. Smith has taught English to me since last   year.라고 써도 좋다..

18 흥미를 유발하는 이야기들이므로 현재분사로 stories를 수식하는 것이 적절하다.

19 새로운 형태의 만화를 가리키는 대명사이다.

20 ⓐ는 형용사를 수식하는 부사로 쓰인 to부정사이다. ① 명사적 용법 중 목적격 보어 ② 명사적 용법 중 진주어 ③ 부사적 용법 중 목적 ④ 부사적 용법 중 형용사 수식 ⑤ 형용사적 용법으로 something을 수식

21 온라인에서 볼 수 있는 것은 웹툰이다.

22 동작이나 소리가 그림들이 생생하게 살아나게 한다.

23 만화영화는 모든 연령대의 사람들에게 매우 인기가 많다고 하였다.

24 만화를 제작하는 데 얼마만큼의 시간이 소요되는지는 위 글을 읽고 알 수 없다.

25 글쓴이가 좋아하는 캐릭터는 유머 있고 친절하지만 똑똑하지 않고 가끔 문제를 일으킨다는 연결이 자연스럽다. 따라서 However가 적절하다.

26 글쓴이가 '기영'을 좋아하는 이유는 모든 것의 긍정적인 측면을 바라보고 항상 남을 도우려 애쓰기 때문이라고 하였다.

01 No, he hasn't.

02 It's an animated movie about a teenager's feelings.

03 It can help him understand his feelings better.

04 (1)번 문장은 Amelia가 캐나다에 가 본 적이 있다는 경험을 나타내고, (2)번 문장은 Amelia가 캐나다로 가고 없다는 결과를 나타낸다.

05 I have lost my favorite book.

06 The crying boy ate five boiled eggs.

07 have had, have not had   08 a shaking voice

09 It is from *Black Rubber Shoes*.

10 He is humorous and kind. However, he is not very smart and sometimes causes trouble.

11 Artists have used this type of cartoon to make fun of well-known people.

12 Various types of cartoons and their roles

13 a gag cartoon, makes you laugh, a caricature, a comic strip, amusing

14 They have drawn a caricature to make fun of well-known people.

01 Kevin은 "Shining Days"를 보지 않았다.

02 "Shining Days"는 십대의 감정에 관한 것이다.

03 "Shining Days"는 Kevin이 자기의 감정들을 더욱 잘 이해할 수 있게 도와줄 수 있다.

04 현재완료 시제에서 '~에 가 본 적이 있다'는 have been to로 나타내고 '~에 가고 없다'는 'have gone to'로 나타내 는 것에 유의한다.

05 내가 가장 좋아하는 책을 잃어버리고 여전히 가지고 있지 않다고 하였으므로 현재완료 시제를 이용하여 책을 잃어버린 상황이 지속되고 있음을 말할 수 있다.

06 '울고 있는 소년'이므로 crying이 boy를 수식하고, 삶은 달걀은 '삶아진 달걀'인 boiled egg로 써서 문장을 만들 수 있다.

07 had를 대신하여 eaten을 써도 좋다.

08 '떨리는 목소리'라고 하였으므로 현재분사로 voice를 수식하는 것이 적절하다.

09 '검정고무신' 만화의 캐릭터이다.

10 캐릭터는 유머 있고 친절하지만 별로 똑똑하지 않고 가끔씩 말썽을 일으킨다고 하였다.

11 미술가들은 과거부터 지금까지 유명한 사람들을 풍자하기 위해 이런 종류의 만화를 그려왔다는 것이므로 현재완료 시제를 이용하여 하나의 문장으로 쓸 수 있다.

12 '다양한 종류의 만화와 그것들의 역할'이 글의 제목이 될 수 있다.

13 위 글에서 만화의 종류는 세 가지가 제시되어 있으며 그 종류는 개그 만화, 캐리커처, 그리고 연재만화이다.

14 미술가들은 유명한 사람들을 풍자하기 위해서 캐리커처를 그려 왔다.

|모범답안|

01 (A) down   (B) ups and downs
    (C) watching the animated movie "Shining Days"
    (D) a teenager's feelings

02 Iron Man, Tales of Suspense, a genius scientist, owns a weapon company, invented a suit of armor to save his life, Iron Man, he is very rich and is the leader of the superhero team, the Avengers

---

01 오늘 나는 별일 없이 우울했다. 요즘, 내 감정이 많이 바뀌었다. 그 때 Jane이 내게 다가왔고 많은 십대들이 기분에 기복을 갖는다고 이야기하며 내 기분을 이해해 주었다. 내 감정을 더욱 잘 이해하기 위해, 그녀는 만화 영화 "Shining Days"를 볼 것을 제안하였다. 그녀는 이 영화가 십대의 기분에 관한 것이라고 설명해 주었다. 이 영화는 괜찮은 것 같았고, 그래서 나는 이 영화를 곧 보기로 결정했다.

---

01 ④

02 (1) Jake played the role of Santa Clause in the play.
    (2) I feel angry when people make fun of me.
    (3) Cut the vegetables into small pieces.

03 (1) The soccer team members have a common goal.
    (2) It is fun to learn English with animated movies.
    (3) There are ups and downs in life.

04 (1) amusing   (2) probably   (3) movement
    (4) publish   **05** ①   **06** ④

07 nacho chips / spread / some ham, onions, and peppers / cheese, about 12 minutes

08 ups and downs   **09** ⑤   **10** ②

11 Do you know how to use the machine?

12 ⑤   **13** ④   **14** ⑤   **15** ④

16 These expressions are often used in spoken English.

17 ⑤   **18** (A) laugh   (B) saying   (C) are

19 They have made them for hundreds of years.

20 ⑤   **21** ⑤   **22** ②

---

01 가르치고 배우는 과정을 가리키는 말은 education(교육)이다.

02 play the role: 역할을 하다, make fun of: ~을 놀리다, cut A into pieces ~A를 조각으로 자르다

03 common: 공통의, animated movie: 만화영화, ups and downs: 기복

04 movement: 움직임, amusing: 재미있는, 즐거운, publish: 출판하다, probably: 아마도

05 (A)는 도와주겠다는 표현으로 이와 바꾸어 쓸 수 있는 표현은 ①번이다. 나머지는 모두 도움을 요청하는 표현이다.

06 can't wait to ~: ~가 기대되다 = look forward to

09 주어진 문장은 "Shining Days"에 관해 설명하는 문장으로 ⓔ번이 적절하다.

10 Kevin의 Nothing serious.라는 말을 통해 심각한 문제가 아니라는 것을 알 수 있다.

12 ⑤ Emily와 Tony는 좌석을 선택한 후 표 값을 지불해야 한다.

13 현재완료 시제에서 부정어와 함께 쓰여 '아직'이라는 의미를 나타내는 것은 yet이다.

14 주어진 문장의 밑줄 친 부분은 '재활용을 위한 쓰레기통'이라는 의미로 쓰이는 동명사이다. 모두 현재분사이지만, ⑤번은 '잠자는 용도로 쓰이는 가방', 즉 '침낭'이라는 의미로 쓰이는 동명사이다.

15 danger는 '예상되지 않는' 것이므로 과거분사 unexpected로 수식하는 것이 적절하다.

16 구어체 언어란 일상 대화에서 쓰이는 말투를 의미한다. 따라서 과거분사 spoken으로 English를 수식하여 문장을 완성하는 것이 적절하다.

17 만화는 정보를 더 분명하고 학습하기 쉽게 만들어 준다는 것이 자연스럽다. more difficult → easier

18 (A) 사역동사의 목적격 보어로 동사원형이 쓰인다. (B) 캐릭터는 우스꽝스러운 행동이나 말을 함으로써 사람들을 웃게 만드는 것이므로 doing과 병렬로 연결되는 것이 자연스럽다. (C) 수의 일치의 대상이 some parts이므로 복수 동사를 쓰는 것이 적절하다.

19 사람들은 수 백 년 동안 만화를 만들어왔다고 하였다.

20 만화는 정보를 더 분명하게 만들어 준다고 하였으므로 ⑤번이 글의 내용과 일치한다.

21 글쓴이는 미래에 새로운 형태의 만화가 나타날지도 모른다고 하였다.

22 온라인에서 출판되는 특성상 언제 어디서든 웹툰을 읽을 수 있다는 강점이 있다.

교과서 파헤치기

Lesson 5

단어 TEST Step 1   p.53

01 태도, 자세   02 고발하다, 비난하다

03 던지다   04 ~ 뒤에   05 공약, 약속

06 보호하다   07 피하다   08 약자 괴롭히기

09 어려움   10 석방하다   11 외모

12 등장인물, 캐릭터   13 유죄의   14 걱정하는

15 판사; 판단하다   16 부끄럼을 많이 타는, 수줍어하는

17 감옥   18 턱수염   19 실종된, 행방불명된

20 공격하다   21 이웃   22 자유

23 자신감 있는   24 회장   25 받다

26 권리   27 용돈   28 진실

29 체포하다   30 희생자   31 평범한

32 다정한, 친절한   33 속삭이다   34 인기 있는, 대중적인

35 ~을 돌보다   36 ~을 두려워하다   37 진정하다

38 ~을 석방하다   39 B 때문에 A를 고발하다

40 ~ 덕분에   41 ~을 지지하다, ~을 찬성하다

42 ~을 싸워 물리치다

43 ~을 뽑다, ~에게 투표하다

단어 TEST Step 2   p.54

01 back   02 pass   03 activity

04 carry   05 shout   06 victim

07 vote   08 choice   09 enter

10 hide   11 whisper   12 friendly

13 appearance   14 arrest   15 lucky

16 face   17 mind   18 guilty

19 choose   20 curly   21 ordinary

22 popular   23 anytime   24 promise

25 monthly   26 score   27 freedom

28 protect   29 confident   30 allowance

31 neighbor   32 accuse   33 missing

34 prison   35 so far   36 be afraid of

37 accuse A of B   38 cut off ~   39 be good at ~

40 thanks to ~   41 vote for ~

42 agree with+사람   43 care for ~

단어 TEST Step 3   p.55

1 cause, 야기하다   2 neighbor, 이웃   3 avoid, 피하다

4 score, 득점하다   5 attitude, 태도   6 confidence, 자신감

7 character, 등장인물   8 whisper, 속삭이다

9 attack, 공격하다   10 bullying, 괴롭히기

---

11 choose, 선택하다, 고르다   12 protect, 보호하다

13 change, 잔돈   14 victim, 피해자, 희생자

15 allowance, 용돈   16 arrest, 체포하다

대화문 TEST Step 1   p.56~57

Communicate: Listen-Listen and Answer. Talk

from, ago, worried, shy, good, lucky, friendly, playing, call, will be, I hope, will win

Communicate: Listen-Listen and Answer. Dialog

Is, winning / course, great handball player / mean the girl from / her name / what, look like / very tall, has, ponytail / who scored, just now / her seventh goal / really great

Communicate: Listen-Listen More

What can I do / lost, younger brother / calm down, brother's / five years old / What, look like / has / is, wearing / wearing, green shirt / tell me more / carrying a red backpack / look for, make an announcement, missing / I hope, find

Communicate: Speak 2-Talk in pairs

have an important exam / I hope, do well on / hope so, too

Communicate: Speak 2-Talk in groups

What, your character's name / His name / What does, look like / has no hair / have big eyes / does

Communicate: Speak-Rap Time

(1) lost, this afternoon / I hope, find

(2) do your best / I wish, the same

(3) What does, look like / has long straight hair

(4) Is, wearing / reading a map

My Speaking Portfolio

Look at, bulletin board, are, school president / already made, already made, choice, vote for / mean, with glasses, looks smart, promises / who will, choose / wants to make, a sate place / always has, right / seems okay / looks friendly, talent shows

Wrap Up

1 there is / from, over there / Which, What does, look / curly, wearing glasses

2 look sad, wrong / broke her arm / happened / fell off / That's too bad, I hope, get better

대화문 TEST Step 2   p.58~59

Communicate: Listen-Listen and Answer. Talk

G: Hi, I'm Gacha. I'm from Mongolia. When I first came to Songji Middle School two months ago, I was so worried. I was a little shy, and I wasn't good at Korean. However, I'm a lucky girl. All my classmates are nice and friendly. I enjoy playing handball with them in P.E. class. I'm a good player. They call me "Golden Hand." There will be a sports day next week. I hope my class will win in the handball event.

Communicate: Listen-Listen and Answer. Dialog

B: Hi, Minsol. Is your class winning?

G: Of course. We have a great handball player.

B: You mean the girl from Mongolia?

G: Yes, her name is Gacha.

B: I've heard a lot about her. But what does she look like?

G: She's very tall and has a ponytail.

B: Oh, is she the girl who scored the goal just now?

G: Yes, that's her seventh goal.

B: Wow, she's really great.

Communicate: Listen-Listen More

M: What can I do for you?

G: I lost my younger brother.

M: Okay, calm down. What's your brother's name?

G: His name is Wally Brown. He's five years old.

M: What does he look like?

G: He has brown hair and brown eyes.

M: What is he wearing?

G: He is wearing a green shirt and black pants.

M: Can you tell me more?

G: Oh, he is carrying a red backpack.

M: All right. We'll go out and look for him. Also, we'll make an announcement about a missing child.

G: Thank you so much. I hope I'll find him soon.

Communicate: Speak 2-Talk in pairs

A: I have an important exam tomorrow!

B: I hope you'll do well on the exam.

A: I hope so, too. Thanks.

Communicate: Speak 2-Talk in groups

A: What is your character's name?

B: His name is Buster.

A: What does he look like?

B: He has no hair.

A: Does he have big eyes?

B: Yes, he does.

Communicate: Speak-Rap Time

(1) A: I lost my puppy this afternoon.

B: I hope you'll find him soon.

(2) A: I hope you'll do your best in the final game.

B: Thanks. I wish you the same.

(3) A: What does your sister look like, Claire?

B: She's tall and has long straight hair.

(4) A: Is your father wearing a blue cap?

B: Yeah. Now, he's reading a map.

My Speaking Portfolio

G: Look at the bulletin board. There are posters for the next school president.

B: Yeah, I've already made my choice. I'll vote for Jang Jimin.

G: You mean the boy with glasses? He looks smart, but I don't like his promises.

B: Then who will you choose?

G: Well, I am for number 1, Han Siwon. She wants to make our school a safe place.

B: She always has a ponytail, right?

G: Yes, and Hong Jiho seems okay.

B: She looks friendly, but I don't like talent shows.

Wrap Up

1 B: I hear there is a new student in your class.

G: Yes. She's from Jejudo. Oh, she's over there!

B: Which one? What does she look like?

G: She has curly hair and is wearing glasses.

2 G: You look sad. What's wrong, Jongmin?

B: My sister broke her arm this morning.

G: What happened?

B: She fell off her bike.

G: That's too bad. I hope she'll get better soon.

본문 TEST Step 1   p.60~61

01 Right, Different

02 ways, ordinary person

03 had, cared for

04 after, moved, face difficulties

05 looked different, other   06 did, like

07 avoided, with, beard   08 did, sit, to,

09 whispered, behind, trying   10 some, broke

11 threw, at, down   12 told, stop growing

13 did, mind   14 just, to have

15 One, attacked, threw   16 cut off, shouted

17 able, fight, off   18 called, accused, of

19 was arrested   20 judge, victim

21 believed, with, prison, over

22 wanted, know, truth   23 sent, to, across

24 in prison, protecting himself

25 became angry, set, free   26 freed, traveled, lots

27 attitudes toward, changed   28 Before, died, beard

29 His name

30 made, popular, fought, right

33

01 Right To Be Different
02 In many ways, an ordinary person
03 had a job, cared for
04 after, moved to, to face difficulties
05 looked different from   06 did not like it
07 avoided the man with a beard
08 to sit next to him
09 behind his back, trying to hide
10 Some, broke his windows
11 Others threw stones at, walked down
12 told, to stop growing
13 did not mind   14 freedom to have
15 attacked, threw him on the ground
16 cut off, shouted
17 was able to fight them off
18 accused him of attacking   19 was arrested
20 the judge, the victim
21 a man with a beard, went to prison
22 wanted, to know
23 sent, to, across the country
24 was in prison, protecting himself
25 became angry, decided to set, free
26 was freed, lots of
27 attitudes toward beards changed
28 Before, died, with a beard   29 His name
30 made beards popular, fought for, right to have

15 어느 날, 네 명의 남자가 Joseph을 공격했고 그를 바닥에 던졌다.
16 "우리가 당신의 턱수염을 잘라 버리겠어!"라고 그들은 소리쳤다.
17 Joseph은 덩치가 큰 사람이었고, 그는 그들을 싸워 물리칠 수 있었다.
18 하지만 그 남자들은 경찰을 불렀고, 자신들을 공격한 것으로 그를 고발했다.
19 불쌍한 Joseph은 체포되었다.
20 그는 "저는 여기서 희생자입니다."라고 판사에게 말했다.
21 슬프게도, 아무도 턱수염을 가진 남자를 믿지 않았고, 그는 일 년이 넘는 기간 동안 감옥에 갔다.
22 Joseph의 아들인 Thomas는 사람들이 진실을 알기를 원했다.
23 그는 전국에 있는 신문사에 편지를 보냈다.
24 사람들은 Joseph이 단지 자신과 자신의 턱수염을 지키려다 감옥에 갇혔다는 것을 알게 되었다.
25 많은 사람들은 이에 대해 분개했고, 그래서 판사는 결국 Joseph을 석방하기로 결정했다.
26 Joseph은 석방된 뒤에 순회를 하며 많은 사람들에게 자신의 이야기를 전했다.
27 사람들의 턱수염에 대한 태도는 서서히 변해갔다.
28 Joseph이 죽기 전에, 턱수염을 가진 남자가 미국의 대통령이 되었다.
29 그의 이름은 Abraham Lincoln(에이브러햄 링컨)이었다.
30 그는 턱수염을 대중적으로 만들었지만, Joseph Palmer는 그것을 기를 권리를 위하여 싸웠다.

1 다를 권리
2 여러 면에서 42살의 Joseph Palmer는 평범한 사람이었다.
3 그는 직업이 있었고 가족을 돌보았다.
4 하지만 1830년에 매사추세츠에 있는 작은 도시로 이사를 한 후에 그는 어려움에 직면하기 시작했다.
5 Joseph은 다른 사람들과 달라 보였다. 그는 기다란 턱수염을 기르고 있었다.
6 사람들은 그것을 별로 좋아하지 않았다.
7 마을 사람들은 턱수염을 가진 그 남자를 피했다.
8 그들은 그의 곁에 앉고 싶어 하지 않았다.
9 그들은 심지어 그의 등 뒤에서 "그가 무엇을 숨기려는 거지?" 라고 속삭였다.
10 어떤 이웃들은 그의 창문을 깼다.
11 다른 사람들은 그가 길을 걸어 내려갈 때 그에게 돌을 던졌다.
12 그들은 그에게 턱수염을 그만 기르라고 말했다.
13 Joseph은 신경 쓰지 않았다.
14 그는 그저 자신의 턱수염을 기를 자유를 원했다.

1 The Right To Be Different
2 In many ways, 42-year-old Joseph Palmer was an ordinary person.
3 He had a job and cared for his family.
4 But in 1830, after he moved to a small town in Massachusetts, he began to face difficulties.
5 Joseph looked different from other people: he had a long beard.
6 People did not like it very much.
7 The town's people avoided the man with a beard.
8 They did not want to sit next to him.
9 They even whispered behind his back, "What is he trying to hide?"
10 Some neighbors broke his windows.
11 Others threw stones at him when he walked down the street.
12 They told him to stop growing a beard.
13 Joseph did not mind.

14 He just wanted the freedom to have his beard.

15 One day, four men attacked Joseph and threw him on the ground.

16 "We're going to cut off your beard!" they shouted.

17 Joseph was a big man, and he was able to fight them off.

18 But the men called the police and accused him of attacking them.

19 Poor Joseph was arrested.

20 He said to the judge, "I'm the victim here."

21 Sadly, no one believed a man with a beard, and he went to prison for over a year.

22 Joseph's son, Thomas, wanted people to know the truth.

23 He sent letters to newspapers across the country.

24 People learned that Joseph was in prison just for protecting himself and his beard.

25 Many people became angry about this, so the judge finally decided to set Joseph free.

26 After he was freed, Joseph traveled and told his story to lots of people.

27 Slowly, people's attitudes toward beards changed.

28 Before Joseph died, a man with a beard became the President of the United States.

29 His name was Abraham Lincoln.

30 He made beards popular, but Joseph Palmer fought for the right to have them.

Words in Action

1. Welcome to, Admission, free
2. have in mind
3. If, to visit, look around
4. get hungry, a light snack

구석구석지문 TEST Step 1   p.70

My Speaking Portfolio

1. will vote
2. looks confident, smart
3. thinks, should be
4. agree with
5. such as, bullying
6. hope, becomes
7. to be a safer place

My Writing Portfolio: My Book Report

1. Right to Be
2. About
3. about, last week
4. really enjoyed
5. learned from, that, appearance
6. who talk, must
7. However, have a question
8. Why, to have a beard

구석구석지문 TEST Step 2   p.71

My Speaking Portfolio

1. I will vote for Han Siwon.
2. She looks confident and smart.
3. She thinks school should be a safe place.
4. I agree with her.
5. I like her promises such as no more bullying.
6. I hope Han Siwon becomes the next school president.
7. I really want my school to be a safer place.

My Writing Portfolio: My Book Report

1. The Right to Be Different
2. A Story About Joseph Palmer
3. I read the story about Joseph Palmer last week.
4. I really enjoyed it.
5. I learned from the story that we should not judge people by their appearance.
6. Students who talk about other people's appearance must read the story.
7. However, I have a question about it.
8. Why did Joseph Palmer want to have a beard?

Words in Action

1. Welcome to the travel fair. Admission is free.
2. What countries do you have in mind?
3. If you want to visit South America, you can look around the booths on the left.
4. If you get hungry, you can have drinks and a light snack.

Lesson 6

10 feed, 먹이를 주다   11 refund, 환불   12 wall, 벽

13 experience, 경험   14 exchange, 교환하다

15 guest, 손님   16 promise, 약속하다

단어 TEST Step 1   p.21

01 쓰레기	02 흔한, 보통의	03 쏟다, 붓다
04 전통적인	05 토론	06 공유하다
07 경험	08 먹이다	09 진실, 사실
10 잘못된	11 손님	12 겁먹은
13 환불, 환불금	14 훈련, 훈육	15 짠
16 교환; 교환하다	17 물건	18 화난
19 (기계가) 작동하다, 일하다		20 ~ 없이
21 전갈, 메시지	22 십 대의	23 고치다
24 제안, 의견	25 영수증	26 슬픔
27 찢다	28 이해하다	29 비밀
30 사발, 그릇	31 약속하다	32 청취자
33 문자 메시지를 보내다		
34 (부정문에서) ~도 역시		
35 ~을 돌보다, ~을 처리하다		36 거짓말하다
37 ~에 들르다	38 곤경에 처하다	39 한번 해 보다
40 부수다	41 혼자 힘으로	42 더 이상 ~ 아니다
43 반드시 ~하다	44 발견하다, 알아내다	

단어 TEST Step 2   p.22

01 puppy	02 suggestion	03 training
04 promise	05 wrong	06 secret
07 trash	08 exchange	09 bowl
10 stuff	11 without	12 traditional
13 experience	14 repair	15 scared
16 common	17 feed	18 guest
19 receipt	20 upset	21 truth
22 work	23 pour	24 salty
25 lie	26 discussion	27 either
28 teenage	29 share	30 listener
31 refund	32 message	33 sadness
34 tear	35 not ~ anymore	36 break down
37 drop by	38 start off with	39 be sure to
40 on one's own	41 be in trouble	42 take care of
43 tell a lie	44 find out	

단어 TEST Step 3   p.23

1 teenage, 십 대의   2 listener, 청취자   3 puppy, 강아지

4 text, 문자 메시지를 보내다   5 suggestion, 제안

6 repair, 고치다   7 secret, 비밀

8 hairdryer, 헤어드라이어   9 receipt, 영수증

대화문 TEST Step 1   p.24~25

Communication: Listen – Dialog 1

happy with / wrong / tore, into pieces / often, that / Sometimes, socks / kind, five months / too, to, training / start training, a few

Communication: Listen – Dialog 2

going out with / be back / Around, to feed / Be sure, too / problem / more thing, help, with, tore

Communication: Listen – Listen More

How, help you / bought, hairdryer, store, happy with / the problem / work, enough / want to exchange / get a refund / visit, store / drop by / Don't forget, receipt

My Speaking Portfolio – Step 3

not very happy with / the problem / bathroom for too long / how, feel / can / get up earlier, use / give, a try

Wrap Up – Listening ❺

look upset / not happy with / wrong with / doing her part / think, should talk to

Wrap Up – Listening ❻

Are, ready for, trip / ready to leave / your ticket with / on my phone / Don't forget to call, get to / Sure

대화문 TEST Step 2   p.26~27

Communication: Listen – Dialog 1

Minsol: I'm not happy with Buster.

Dad: What's wrong?

Minsol: He tore my homework into pieces again.

Dad: Puppies often do that.

Minsol: This is not the first time. Sometimes I find my socks in the dog house.

Dad: Please be kind to him. He's just five months old.

Minsol: You're too nice to him! He needs some training.

Dad: Okay. Let's start training in a few weeks.

Communication: Listen – Dialog 2

Mom: Minsu, I'm going out with your dad for a movie.

Minsu: When will you be back, Mom?

Mom: Around 8 o'clock. Don't forget to feed Buster.

Minsu: Okay.

Mom: Be sure to give him some water, too.

Minsu: No problem.

Mom: One more thing. Can you help Minsol with her
    science homework? Buster tore her homework
    into pieces.
Minsu: Hmm .... Okay. I'll do that.

Communication: Listen – Listen More

Mike: Customer Service. How can I help you?
Sora: I bought a hairdryer at your store last week. I'm
    not happy with it.
Mike: What is the problem?
Sora: It doesn't work well. I mean the air isn't hot
    enough.
Mike: I'm sorry. Do you want to exchange it?
Sora: Well, can I get a refund?
Mike: Sure. Will you please visit our store with the
    dryer?
Sora: Yes, I'll drop by tomorrow afternoon.
Mike: Don't forget to bring the receipt.
Sora: Okay. Thanks.

My Speaking Portfolio – Step 3

A: I'm not very happy with my brother.
B: What's the problem?
A: He uses the bathroom for too long in the morning.
B: I know how you feel.
A: What can I do?
B: Well, you can get up earlier and use the bathroom
    first.
A: Okay, I'll give it a try.

Wrap Up – Listening ❺

G: You look upset, Tommy.
B: I'm not happy with Sojin.
G: What's wrong with her?
B: She isn't doing her part of the group project.
G: I think you should talk to her.

Wrap Up – Listening ❻

M: Are you ready for your trip, Suji?
G: Yes, I am, Dad. I'm ready to leave.
M: Do you have your ticket with you?
G: Yeah, I have it on my phone.
M: Good. Don't forget to call me when you get to
    the train station.
G: Sure.

본문 TEST Step 1   p.28~29

01 listeners, This, your   02 a special guest
03 hip-hop artist, Welcome

04 to, for having   05 listeners, tell, family
06 out by reading, letters 07 start off with, from
08 Andy, Sure   09 a, girl from
10 to tell, about   11 tries to do
12 without asking, hard to
13 buys, me study them
14 say, anymore, let, take 15 felt, same way
16 too, to, things, own   17 hope, get, message
18 So do, read   19 father, of, children
20 One, the other   21 too busy to talk
22 get, work, go back
23 ask, life, give, answers
24 don't talk much, either
25 say, spend more time
26 with, often, younger
27 too old to understand
28 suggestions, Text, idea

본문 TEST Step 2   p.30~31

01 Good evening, This is
02 a special guest
03 hip-hop artist, Welcome
04 to meet you, thank you for having me
05 want to tell
06 find out by reading some letters
07 start off with, from, teenage girl
08 Sure   09 15-year-old, from
10 to tell you   11 tries to do
12 without asking, hard to find my stuff
13 buys, me study them
14 to say, anymore, let me take care of, myself
15 the same way when
16 too young to do, on their own
17 get the message   18 do I
19 of two children   20 One, the other
21 too busy to talk
22 get, from work, go back to
23 them, school life, give short answers
24 don't talk much, either 25 to spend more time
26 often when you were younger
27 them, thought, too old to understand
28 suggestions, Text your idea

1 Breeze: 안녕하세요, 청취자 여러분. 저는 여러분의 디제이, Breeze입니다.

2 오늘은 특별한 손님, Andy Kim 씨를 모셨습니다.

3 그는 힙합 아티스트이시죠. 환영합니다, Andy.

4 Andy: 반갑습니다. 그리고 초대해 주셔서 고맙습니다.

5 Breeze: 네. 우리 청취자분들은 가족에게 무슨 말을 하고 싶어 하실까요?

6 오늘 저녁에 우리는 청취자분들로부터 온 몇몇 편지들을 읽으며 알아보려 합니다.

7 Andy, 십 대 소녀에게서 온 편지로 시작해 주시겠어요?

8 Andy: 알겠습니다.

9 Andy: 안녕하세요. 저는 원주에 사는 15세 소녀입니다.

10 저는 저의 엄마에 관해 이야기하고 싶습니다.

11 엄마는 저를 위해 모든 것을 해 주려고 하십니다.

12 엄마는 제게 물어보지도 않고 방을 청소해 주시고, 그래서 가끔은 제 물건을 찾기가 힘들 때도 있습니다.

13 또 엄마는 책을 사 와서는 저에게 그것들을 공부하라고 시키세요.

14 저는 엄마께 "엄마가 저를 사랑하는 것은 알지만 전 더 이상 아기가 아니에요. 제 일을 스스로 할 수 있게 해 주세요." 라고 말씀드리고 싶습니다.

15 Breeze: 저도 중학교 때 똑같은 기분을 느꼈습니다.

16 Andy: 많은 어머님들이 자녀들이 혼자 힘으로 무언가를 하기에는 너무 어리다고 생각합니다.

17 소녀의 어머님께서 메시지를 들으시길 바랍니다.

18 Breeze: 동감입니다. Andy, 다음 편지를 읽어 주시겠어요?

19 Andy: 안녕하세요. 저는 두 아이의 아버지입니다.

20 한 명은 고등학생인 여자아이이고, 나머지 한 명은 중학생인 남자아이입니다.

21 아이들은 저와 대화를 하기에는 너무 바쁩니다.

22 제가 일을 하고 집에 돌아오면, 아이들은 그저 인사만 하고 자신의 방으로 돌아갑니다.

23 가끔씩 저는 아이들에게 학교생활에 관해 묻기도 하지만, 아이들은 그냥 짤막한 대답만 합니다.

24 우리는 식사 자리에서조차 대화를 많이 하지 않습니다.

25 저는 아이들에게 "너희들을 무척 사랑한단다. 그리고 너희들과 더 많은 시간을 보내고 싶단다."라고 말하고 싶습니다.

26 Breeze: Andy, 어렸을 때 부모님과 자주 대화를 했나요?

27 Andy: 사실 그렇지는 않습니다. 저는 부모님을 무척 사랑하지만, 부모님이 저를 이해해 주시기에는 너무 나이가 들었다고 생각했습니다.

28 Breeze: 그렇군요. '슬픈' 아빠에게 해 드릴 제안이 있으신 분 계신가요? 여러분의 생각을 저희에게 문자로 보내 주세요.

1 Breeze: Good evening, listeners. This is your DJ, Breeze.

2 Today we have a special guest, Andy Kim.

3 He's a hip-hop artist. Welcome, Andy.

4 Andy: Nice to meet you and thank you for having me.

5 Breeze: Okay. What do our listeners want to tell their family?

6 This evening we will find out by reading some letters from them.

7 Andy, will you start off with the letter from a teenage girl?

8 Andy: Sure.

9 Andy: Hello. I'm a 15-year-old girl from Wonju.

10 I want to tell you about my mom.

11 My mom tries to do everything for me.

12 She cleans my room without asking me, so it's sometimes hard to find my stuff.

13 She also buys books and makes me study them.

14 I want to say to my mom, "I know you love me, but I'm not a baby anymore. Please let me take care of things myself."

15 Breeze: I felt the same way when I was in middle school.

16 Andy: Many moms think their kids are too young to do things on their own.

17 I hope the girl's mom will get the message.

18 Breeze: So do I. Andy, will you please read the next letter?

19 Andy: Hi. I'm a father of two children.

20 One is a high school girl, and the other is a middle school boy.

21 They're too busy to talk with me.

22 When I get home from work, they just say hi and go back to their rooms.

23 Sometimes I ask them about their school life, but they only give short answers.

24 We don't talk much at the table, either.

25 I want to say to my kids, "I love you so much, and I want to spend more time with you."

26 Breeze: Andy, did you talk with your parents often when you were younger?

27 Andy: Not really. I loved them very much, but I thought they were too old to understand me.

28 Breeze: I see. Does anyone have suggestions for the "sad" dad? Text your idea to us.

My Writing Portfolio

1. 15-year-old girl from
2. want to say
3. told, his secret
4. got, angry, was in trouble
5. too, to, at that time
6. promise, never tell, secrets

Have Fun Together

1. nothing to do
2. is, place
3. richer than, not happy with
4. made us leave
5. smells good

Wrap Up – Reading Read and answer 3

1. from, who, to share, with
2. did not talk
3. between, break, down
4. tried to spend, on weekends
5. rode bikes, went shopping
6. chances to talk with
7. came to know

My Writing Portfolio

1. Hello, I am a 15-year-old girl from Busan.
2. I want to say to my brother Jaeho, "Sorry."
3. I told Mom his secret last Friday.
4. Mom got so angry, so he was in trouble.
5. I was too scared to say sorry to him at that time.
6. I promise I will never tell his secrets again.

Have Fun Together

1. I have nothing to do. I have no friends.
2. Everything is too small. I don't like this place very much.
3. Heungbu is richer than me now. I'm not happy with it.
4. Mom made us leave home. We're not happy with it.
5. This soup smells good, but I can't eat it.

Wrap Up – Reading Read and answer 3

1. This is a letter from a father who wants to share his experience with the "sad" father.
2. My kids and I did not talk much.
3. There was a wall between us. I wanted to break it down.
4. I tried to spend more time with my children on weekends.
5. We played computer games, rode bikes, and went shopping together.
6. In this way, I had more chances to talk with them.
7. I came to know more about them.

단어 TEST Step 1   p.40

01 일기	02 일, 문제, 안건	03 국가
04 집회, 국회, 민회	05 방식	06 전통적인
07 투표하다	08 아테네	09 등장인물
10 남자의, 수컷의	11 야외의, 실외의	12 사람, 인간, 인물
13 개발하다, 발달시키다		14 마지막의, 최종의
15 담다, 수용하다	16 수를 세다	
17 모으다, 모이다, 집결하다		18 불가능한
19 토론	20 의미	21 체류, 방문
22 약, 대략	23 거의	24 시민
25 아테네 사람	26 질문하다	27 슬픔
28 재능	29 모이는 장소	30 ~에 참여하다
31 수천의	32 많은	33 ~하느라 바쁘다
34 ~함으로써	35 지금까지	36 A와 B 사이에
37 너무 ~해서 …하다		38 20살 이상의
39 ~에 더하여, ~일뿐 아니라		

단어 TEST Step 2   p.41

01 meaning	02 Athens	03 traditional
04 count	05 male	06 gather
07 stay	08 talent	09 discussion
10 diary	11 matter	12 final
13 hold	14 assembly	15 impossible
16 almost	17 question	18 citizen
19 outdoor	20 about	21 person
22 vote	23 way	24 develop
25 sadness	26 Athenian	27 character
28 state	29 gathering place	
30 so far	31 a lot of	32 thousands of
33 by -ing	34 take part in	35 be busy -ing
36 between A and B		
37 over the age of 20		38 too ~ to …
39 in addition to		

단어 TEST Step 3   p.42

1 count, 수를 세다   2 impossible, 불가능한

3 state, 국가   4 hold, 담다, 수용하다   5 talent, 재능

6 question, 질문하다   7 stay, 체류, 방문

8 vote, 투표하다   9 outdoor, 야외의, 실외의

10 citizen, 시민   11 male, 남자의, 수컷의

12 assembly, 집회, 국회, 민회

본문 TEST Step 1   p.43~44

01 Diary, Athens

02 visiting, aunt, uncle, Athens

03 went, center, city

04 gathering place, Athenians

05 lot, busy talking, shopping

06 went to, Assembly

07 male, part, vote, matters

08 each, freely, matters, showing

09 Counting thousands, almost

10 went, again

11 heard, between, named, and

12 questioned, on, meaning

13 too, to, way, discussing

14 best, so far   15 went to, of

16 outdoor, hold, watched, play

17 addition, traditional, play, interesting

18 far, stage, characters' sadness

19 final, stay in

20 develop, talent, make, state

21 want, go, become, better

본문 TEST Step 2   p.45~46

01 Diary, Athens

02 visiting, aunt, uncle, Athens

03 went to, center   04 gathering place

05 were a lot of, busy talking, shopping

06 went to, Assembly

07 Any male citizens, take part in, vote, matters

08 each, freely, matters, vote by showing

09 Counting thousands of, almost, impossible

10 went to, again

11 heard, interesting discussion between, named, and

12 questioned, on, meaning of life

13 too, to, way of discussing matters

14 best, so far   15 went to

16 outdoor, which, hold about, watched, play

17 In addition to traditional, play, interesting

18 sat far, stage, could feel, characters' sadness

19 final day, stay in

20 must develop, talent, help make, state

21 want to go, become a better

1 아테네에서 쓴 일기

2 첫째 날: 나는 아테네에 있는 숙부와 숙모 댁을 방문 중이다.

3 오늘은 도시 중심에 있는 아고라에 갔다.

4 아고라는 아테네 사람들이 모이는 장소이다.

5 많은 상점들이 있었고, 사람은 이야기하고 쇼핑하느라 분주했다.

6 둘째 날: 숙부는 민회로 가셨다.

7 20살 이상의 모든 남자 시민은 민회에 참여하여 중요한 안건에 관해 투표할 수 있다.

8 그들은 각자 안건에 관해 자유롭게 의견을 말한 후, 손을 들어 투표한다.

9 숙부는 "수천 명의 손을 세는 것은 거의 불가능해."라고 말씀하셨다.

10 셋째 날: 나는 또 아고라에 갔다.

11 소크라테스라고 불리는 선생님과 그의 제자들이 나누고 있는 매우 재미있는 토론을 경청했다.

12 소크라테스는 제자들에게 인생의 의미에 관해 질문하였다.

13 나는 그것을 이해하기에 너무 어렸지만, 나는 그들의 토론 방식이 마음에 들었다.

14 넷째 날: 오늘은 지금까지의 날 중 최고의 날이었다.

15 나는 디오니소스 극장에 갔다.

16 약 17,000명을 수용할 수 있는 야외 극장에서 소포클레스의 연극 '안티고네'를 관람하였다.

17 전통적으로 있던 노래와 춤에 더하여, '안티고네'에는 흥미로운 이야기가 있었다.

18 나는 무대에서 먼 곳에 앉아 있었지만, 등장인물들의 슬픔을 느낄 수 있었다.

19 다섯째 날: 오늘은 아테네에서 머무는 마지막 날이다.

20 숙부와 숙모는 "네 재능을 개발해야 된다. 너는 아테네를 위대한 국가로 만드는 데에 기여할 수 있어." 라고 말씀하셨다.

21 이제 나는 학교에 다니며 더 나은 사람이 되고 싶다.

1 A Diary from Athens

2 1st Day _ I am visiting my aunt and uncle in Athens.

3 Today I went to the Agora in the center of the city.

4 It is a gathering place for Athenians.

5 There were a lot of stores, and people were busy talking and shopping.

6 2nd Day _ My uncle went to the Assembly.

7 Any male citizens over the age of 20 can take part in the Assembly and vote on important matters.

8 After they each speak freely about the matters, they vote by showing their hands.

9 My uncle said, "Counting thousands of hands is almost impossible."

10 3rd Day _ I went to the Agora again.

11 I heard a very interesting discussion between a teacher named Socrates and his students.

12 Socrates questioned his students on the meaning of life.

13 I was too young to understand it, but I liked their way of discussing matters.

14 4th Day _ Today was the best day so far.

15 I went to the Theater of Dionysus.

16 At the outdoor theater which can hold about 17,000 people, we watched *Antigone*, a play by Sophocles.

17 In addition to traditional songs and dances, the play had an interesting story.

18 I sat far from the stage, but I could feel the characters' sadness.

19 5th Day _ Today is the final day of my stay in Athens.

20 My aunt and uncle said to me, "You must develop your talent. You can help make Athens a great state."

21 Now I want to go to school and become a better person.

10 translate, 번역하다　11 fry, 볶다, 튀기다

12 remain, 계속 ~이다　13 caricature, 풍자문화

14 publish, 출판하다　15 sunscreen, 자외선 차단제

16 chef, 요리사

단어 TEST Step 1　p.53

01 요리사	02 오염시키다	03 끓이다, 끓다
04 상영 시간	05 아마도	06 매력적인
07 나타나다, 등장하다		08 기계
09 교육	10 붓다	11 선택하다, 고르다
12 마지막으로	13 창의적인, 독창적인	
14 움직임	15 공통의	16 살아 있는
17 재미있는, 즐거운	18 접시	19 맛보다, 먹다
20 개발하다, 만들다	21 간단한, 단순한	22 출판하다
23 평소의, 보통의	24 조리법, 비법	25 ~ 중에
26 계속 ~이다	27 어리석은	28 유명한, 잘 알려진
29 자외선 차단제	30 번역하다	31 고르다, 선택하다
32 캐리커쳐, (풍자) 만화		33 만화영화
34 만화가	35 ~에 대한 돈을 내다	
36 ~에게 금방 눈에 띄다, ~에게 분명히 보이다		
37 ~을 놀리다	38 ~가 기대되다	39 기복
40 조심하다	41 A를 조각으로 자르다	
42 역할을 하다	43 합쳐지다	

단어 TEST Step 2　p.54

01 appear	02 chef	03 pollute
04 translate	05 creative	06 develop
07 cartoonist	08 dirty	09 alive
10 education	11 publish	12 fry
13 lastly	14 usual	15 pour
16 among	17 sunscreen	18 machine
19 showtime	20 silly	21 boil
22 simple	23 box office	24 common
25 animated movie		26 choose
27 recipe	28 pepper	29 plate
30 taste	31 well-known	32 probably
33 fascinating	34 movement	35 watch out
36 play a role	37 be made into	38 take a look
39 can't wait to	40 ups and downs	
41 make fun of	42 pay for	43 of all ages

단어 TEST Step 3　p.55

1 movement, 움직임　2 usual, 평소의, 보통의

3 showtime, 상영 시간　4 amusing, 재미있는, 즐거운

5 education, 교육　6 appear, 나타나다　7 silly, 어리석은

8 develop, 개발하다, 만들다　9 fascinating, 매력적인

대화문 TEST Step 1　p.56~57

Communication: Listen – Dialog 1

look down / serious, Sometimes, a lot / teens, ups and downs / really / Have you watched, animated movie / I haven't, Why, ask / teenager's feelings, will help, understand, better / sounds, watch

Communication: Listen – Dialog 2

look at, line / ticket machine, Let's buy, from, machine / how to use the machine / select, showtime / watch, what / select, choose, seats / sit in the back / problem, Lastly, pay for / simple

Communication: Listen More

Have you ever made / No, I haven't / how to make / Sounds / First, put, on, plate, spread / help, with / Next, peppers / Add, bake for about, oven / can't wait to taste

Communicate: Speak

how to, fried rice / cut, into / next / Put, fry, with rice / simple

Wrap Up – Listening ❺

Have, been to / have, Actually, every year / you've climbed, haven't you / twice

Wrap Up – Listening ❻

how to draw, First, circle, Next, 'draw, color, draw, circle, Lastly, make

대화문 TEST Step 2　p.58~59

Communication: Listen – Dialog 1

Jane: Kevin, you look down.

Kevin: Nothing serious. Sometimes my feelings change a lot.

Jane: I understand. Many teens have ups and downs in their feelings.

Kevin: Oh, really?

Jane: Have you watched the animated movie "Shining Days"?

Kevin: No, I haven't. Why do you ask?

Jane: It is about a teenager's feelings. It will help you understand your feelings better.

Kevin: That sounds good! I'll watch it.

Communication: Listen – Dialog 2

Emily: Oh, look at the long line at the box office.

Tony: Yeah, there's a ticket machine over there. Let's buy the tickets from the machine.

Emily: All right. Do you know how to use the machine?

Tony: Sure. It's easy. First, select a movie and a showtime.

Emily: Okay. We can watch the seven o'clock show. Then what?

Tony: Well, select the number of tickets and choose our seats.

Emily: Okay. Two tickets, and I want to sit in the back.

Tony: No problem. Lastly, pay for the tickets.

Emily: It's very simple.

Communication: Listen More

Suji: Good morning, Chef Garcia!

Garcia: Hello, Suji. Have you ever made nacho pizza?

Suji: Nacho pizza? No, I haven't.

Garcia: Kids will love it, and I'll tell you how to make it.

Suji: Sounds good!

Garcia: It's easy to make. First, put nacho chips on a plate and spread pizza sauce on them.

Suji: Okay. Let me help you with the pizza sauce.

Garcia: Thanks. Next, put some ham, onions, and peppers on top.

Suji: Okay. Then?

Garcia: Add cheese and bake for about 12 minutes in the oven.

Suji: I can't wait to taste it!

Communicate: Speak

Anna: Do you know how to make fried rice?

Jinsu: Sure. It's easy. First, cut the vegetables into small pieces.

Anna: Okay. What do you do next?

Jinsu: Put some oil in the pan. Then, fry the vegetables with rice.

Anna: Wow, it's really simple.

Wrap Up – Listening ❺

Judy: Have you ever been to Sokcho?

Minsu: Yes, I have. Actually my uncle lives there, so I visit him every year.

Judy: Really? Then, you've climbed Mt. Seorak, haven't you?

Minsu: Yes, I've climbed to the top of the mountain twice.

Wrap Up – Listening ❻

Mike: Today, I'll tell you how to draw a bear's face.

First, draw a big circle for the face. Next, make two circles on top of the face. After that, draw two circles for its eyes and color them black. Then, draw a small circle for the nose. Lastly, make a mouth.

본문 TEST Step 1 p.60~61

01 Both, Land
02 laugh, saw, above
03 so, successful
04 who make cartoons
05 catch, make, laugh, creative
06 have made, for hundreds
07 types, cartoons different roles
08 One, is, a few
09 is, called
10 makes, character, laugh, saying
11 Another, is called
12 parts, different, bigger, usual
13 at, on, right
14 Which parts, jump out
15 have used, make fun
16 several, come together, strip
17 have been, for, years
18 just amusing stories
19 have also used, education
20 make, clearer, easier, learn
21 have probably seen
22 have surely seen, animated
23 popular among, all ages
24 added to, come alive
25 develop fascinating, interesting, through
26 type, was developed
27 is called
28 are published, read, on
29 popular, them, even, into
30 forms, may appear
31 different, exciting, remain, relax

본문 TEST Step 2 p.62~63

01 Land
02 laugh when, saw, above
03 so, cartoonist, successful
04 who make cartoons
05 to catch, make you laugh, creative drawings
06 have made, for hundreds of years
07 many types of cartoons, different roles
08 One form, is, a few words
09 is sometimes called
10 makes a funny character, makes, laugh, doing, saying

43

11 Another, is called

12 some parts, are different, bigger than usual

13 Look at, on 14 Which parts, jump out

15 have used, to make fun of well-known people

16 several, come together, a comic strip

17 have been, for many years

18 just amusing stories

19 have also used, for education

20 make, clearer, easier to learn

21 have probably seen

22 have surely seen, animated movies, too

23 popular among people of all ages

24 Movement, are added to, come alive

25 develop fascinating characters, interesting, through

26 type of, was developed

27 is called

28 are published, read them, on

29 popular, them are, made into

30 forms, may appear

31 different, exciting than, remain, laugh, relax, learn

---

20 만화는 정보를 더 명료하고 더 배우기 쉽게 만들 수 있다.

21 여러분은 아마 만화 역사책이나 과학책을 본 적이 있을 것이다.

22 여러분은 많은 만화영화도 당연히 봤을 것이다.

23 이것들은 모든 연령대의 사람들에게 매우 인기가 많다.

24 동작이나 소리가 그림에 더해져서 그림들이 생생하게 살아난다.

25 미술가들과 작가들은 매력적인 캐릭터를 개발하고 만화영화 제작을 통해 재미있는 이야기를 들려준다.

26 1990년대에 새로운 형식의 만화가 개발되었다.

27 그건 웹툰이라고 불린다.

28 웹툰은 온라인으로 출판되기 때문에 여러분이 휴대 전화나 컴퓨터로 언제 어디서나 볼 수 있다.

29 그것은 매우 인기가 있고, 그들 가운데 일부는 심지어 텔레비전 드라마나 영화로 만들어지기도 한다.

30 미래에는 새로운 형태의 만화가 나타날지도 모른다.

31 그것은 지금과는 다르고 한층 더 재미있겠지만, 한 가지는 같을 것이다. 그것은 우리가 웃고, 쉬고, 배우도록 도와줄 것이다.

본문 TEST Step 3 p.64~65

1 배다! 육지다!

2 위의 만화를 보고 웃었는가?

3 그랬다면 그 만화가는 성공했다.

4 만화가들은 만화를 만드는 사람들이다.

5 그들은 여러분의 관심을 끌고, 대개는 간단한 말과 독창적인 그림으로 여러분을 웃게 하고 싶어 한다.

6 사람들은 수백 년 동안 만화를 만들어 왔다.

7 만화에는 많은 종류가 있으며, 그것들은 다양한 역할을 한다.

8 만화의 한 형태로 몇 마디 말을 쓴 그림이 있다.

9 간혹 그것은 '개그 만화'라고 불린다.

10 만화가는 웃긴 캐릭터를 만들고, 그 캐릭터는 우스꽝스러운 행동이나 말을 함으로써 여러분을 웃게 만든다.

11 다른 종류의 만화는 캐리커처라고 불린다.

12 캐리커처에서 캐릭터의 어떤 부분은 평소와 다르거나 더 크다.

13 오른쪽의 그림을 보아라.

14 남자 얼굴의 어떤 부분이 여러분에게 분명히 보이는가?

15 미술가들은 유명한 사람들을 풍자하기 위해 이런 종류의 만화를 그려 왔다.

16 몇 가지 만화 그림이 모여서 이야기를 들려주게 되면, 그것이 연재만화가 된다.

17 연재만화는 여러 해 동안 신문에 실려 왔다.

18 그것들은 종종 그저 재미있는 이야기이다.

19 사람들은 연재만화를 교육용으로 사용해 오기도 했다.

본문 TEST Step 4-Step 5 p.66~69

1 Boat! Land!

2 Did you laugh when you saw the cartoon above?

3 If so, the cartoonist was successful.

4 Cartoonists are the people who make cartoons.

5 They want to catch your interest, and usually, make you laugh with simple language and creative drawings.

6 People have made cartoons for hundreds of years.

7 There are many types of cartoons, and they play different roles.

8 One form of cartoon is a picture with a few words.

9 It is sometimes called a "gag cartoon."

10 The cartoonist makes a funny character, and the character makes you laugh by doing or saying silly things.

11 Another type of cartoon is called a caricature.

12 In a caricature, some parts of a character are different or bigger than usual.

13 Look at the picture on the right.

14 Which parts of the man's face jump out at you?

15 Artists have used this type of cartoon to make fun of well-known people.

16 When several cartoon pictures come together and tell a story, we have a comic strip.

17 Comic strips have been in newspapers for many years.

18 They are often just amusing stories.

19 People have also used comic strips for education.

20 Comics can make information clearer and easier to learn.

21 You have probably seen comic history or science books.

22 You have surely seen many cartoon movies, or animated movies, too.

23 These are very popular among people of all ages.

24 Movement and sounds are added to pictures, so they come alive.

25 Artists and writers can develop fascinating characters and tell interesting stories through animation.

26 In the 1990s, a new type of cartoon was developed.

27 It is called a webtoon.

28 Webtoons are published online, so you can read them anytime, anywhere on your phone or computer.

29 They are very popular, and some of them are even made into TV dramas or movies.

30 New forms of cartoons may appear in the future.

31 They could be different and even more exciting than now, but one thing will remain the same: they will help us laugh, relax, and learn.

My Speaking Portfolio – Step 3

1. Here, useful tip
2. washed, many times
3. warm, washing powder
4. Then, leave, for seven minutes
5. Lastly, out of, them
6. look like

My Writing Portfolio

1. Cartoon Character
2. favorite cartoon character
3. elementary school, humorous, kind
4. However, causes trouble
5. because, bright side, tries to, others

Words in Action B

1. Animated Movie
2. to build, in the forest
3. soon suffer from, pollution
4. makes a suggestion
5. reach an agreement to create

My Speaking Portfolio – Step 3

1. Here is a useful tip for you.
2. I've washed my sneakers this way many times.
3. First, put the sneakers, warm water, and washing powder in a plastic bag.
4. Then close the bag and leave it for seven minutes.
5. Lastly, take the sneakers out of the bag and wash them.
6. They'll look like new sneakers.

My Writing Portfolio

1. Giyeong, My Favorite Cartoon Character
2. My favorite cartoon character is Giyeong of *Black Rubber Shoes*.
3. He is an elementary school student. He is humorous and kind.
4. However, he is not very smart and sometimes causes trouble.
5. I like him because he looks on the bright side of everything and always tries to help others.

Words in Action B

1. The Best Animated Movie for Children's Education
2. Animals welcome the city's plan to build an amusement park in the forest.
3. However, they soon suffer from serious pollution.
4. An old elephant makes a suggestion.
5. The animals and the city reach an agreement to create a better world for everyone.

MEMO

MEMO

적중 100

영어 기출 문제집

정답 및 해설

천재 | 이재영